Demon Hordes and Burning Boats

SUNY Series in Chinese Local Studies

Harry J. Lamley, Editor

Demon Hordes and Burning Boats

THE CULT OF MARSHAL WEN
IN LATE IMPERIAL CHEKIANG

PAUL R. KATZ

STATE UNIVERSITY OF NEW YORK PRESS

Published by
State University of New York Press

© 1995 State University of New York Press

For information, address the State University of New York Press,
State University Plaza, Albany, NY 12246

Production by Bernadine Dawes • Marketing by Fran Keneston

Library of Congress Cataloging-in-Publication Data

Katz, Paul R., 1961–
    Demon hordes and burning boats: the cult of Marshal Wen in late imperial
Chekiang/Paul R. Katz.
        p. cm.—(Suny series in Chinese local studies)
    Includes bibliographical references and index.
    ISBN 0–7914–2661–0 (HC : acid-free). —ISBN 0–7914–2662–9 (PB : acid-free)
    1. Marshal Wen (Chinese Deity) 2. Chekiang Province (China)—Religious life and customs. I. Title. II. Series
BL1812. G63K37 1995
299' .51—dc20

                                                                95–15323
                                                                CIP

To Mom and Dad

CONTENTS

LIST OF MAPS

LIST OF TABLES

LIST OF ILLUSTRATIONS

ACKNOWLEDGMENTS

I would like to express my deepest gratitude to my thesis advisers at Princeton, Professors Stephen F. Teiser, Denis C. Twitchett, and Ying-shih Yü, for the guidance they provided. Two of my teachers who have retired, the late Professor James T.C. Liu (1919–1993) and Professor Frederick W. Mote, also gave generously of their time and energy. I also wish to thank the staffs of the East Asian Studies department office and Gest Library. I am especially grateful to Carol Benedict, Cynthia Brokaw, T.J. Ellermeier, David Jordan, Harry Lamley, Susan Naquin, Donald Sutton, and Yü Chün-fang, whose detailed comments on the drafts were of immense value. All remaining errors in this work are of course my own.

This book is dedicated to the memory of Anna Seidel (1938–1991) and Michel Strickmann (1942–1994), two outstanding scholars whose work inspired my own and whose deaths constitute an immeasurable loss for the field of Chinese religion.

Part of the research for this book was supported by a grant from the Luce Foundation administered by the Taiwan History Field Research Project at Academia Sinica in Nankang, Taiwan, from 1988–1989. In addition, many of the final revisions were completed while I was a visiting fellow at the Institute of History & Philology, Academia Sinica, from 1993–1994. I would like to thank all the people at the Academia Sinica who were so helpful, especially Ting Pang-hsin, Kuan Tung-kuei, Chuang Ying-chang, Hsü Hsüeh-chi, Li Chien-min, Lin Fu-shih, P'an Ying-hai, and Chiang Hui-ying. My colleages and students at National Tsing-hua University and National Chung-cheng University also provided a great deal of support and encouragement, particularly Huang K'uan-ch'ung, Liu Hsiu-ying, Ts'ai P'ei-chen, C.K. Wang, and James Wilkerson. Thanks also to Chao Chen-hsün for his expert help with the maps, as well as H. David Connelly, Sun Zhixin, and Yang Yung-pao for their help with the figures.

The fieldwork I undertook in Taiwan to supplement the historical research for this paper could not have been completed without the warm hospitality and unstinting cooperation of the people of Tung-kang (Pingtung County). I should also thank a number of scholars in Chekiang who showed me around Hangchow and Wenchow and helped me collect valuable archival materials, especially Xu Shuofang, Ma Hua, and Ye Dabing. These men and their colleagues throughout Chekiang have done path-breaking research on numerous aspects of this province's history. My debt to them is apparent in the notes.

Finally, a special note of gratitude to Bernadine Dawes, Hannah J. Hazen, Fran Keneston, Chris Worden, and the wonderful staff at SUNY Press.

Most of all I wish to tell my family, especially my wife Liu Shu-fen and our daughter Emily Louise, and our son Philip Andrew, how grateful I am for their love and support. I love you all.

PERIODS OF CHINESE HISTORY

Chou Dynasty	1122–256 B.C.E.
Ch'in	221–207 B.C.E.
Former Han	206 B.C.E.–8 C.E.
Hsin	9–23 C.E.
Later Han	25–220
Three Kingdoms	220–289
Chin	265–420
Six Dynasties	420–589
Sui	581–618
T'ang	618–907
Five Dynasties	907–960
Northern Sung	960–1127
Chin (Jurchen)	1115–1234
&	
Mongol rule in north	1234–1279
Southern Sung in south	1127–1279
Yüan (Mongols)	1279–1368
Ming	1368–1644
Ch'ing (Manchus)	1644–1911
Republic	1912–
People's Republic	1949–

PRINCIPLES OF CITATION

(a) Many Chinese primary sources, particularly local gazetteers, are listed under title; modern Chinese and Japanese writings, however, are listed under author. Characters for all Chinese and Japanese sources are supplied in the Bibliography.

(b) When Chinese sources are cited in the body of this thesis, numbers divided by a colon indicate the *chüan* (book, part, or chapter) and page for the particular edition of the work which is entered in the Bibliography. Thus, *P'ing-yang hsien-chih* (1571), 4:15a signifies *chüan* 4, page 15a of the 1571 edition of this county gazetteer. In cases where I have used a modern edition of a work, both *chüan* and page number are supplied.

(c) In numbering texts in the *Taoist Canon*, I have followed the system Kristofer Schipper uses in the *Concordance du Tao-tsang* (Paris: Publications de l'École Française d'Extrême Orient, 1975), which uses sequential numbers instead of fascicle numbers. For the reader's convenience, works in the *Canon* are referred to using both systems (*TT* refers to fascicle number; *CT* to sequential number).

(d) The Bibliography includes only items actually mentioned in the body of this thesis. Not included are many standard and essential research tools, unless they were cited in the text.

(e) A Western translation obviates the need for citing a Chinese edition.

ABBREVIATIONS

CCFSCC   *Che-chiang feng-su chien-chih* 浙江風俗簡志.

CCTC   *Che-chiang t'ung-chih* 浙江通志.

CEA   *Cahiers d'Extrême Asie.*

CHFC   *Chia-hsing fu-chih* 嘉興府志.

CKMCCS   *Chung-kuo min-chien chu-shen* 中國民間諸神.

CSWT   *Ch'ing-shih wen-t'i.*

CT   *Concordance du Tao-tsang.*

CTHC   *Ch'ien-t'ang hsien-chih* 錢塘縣志.

DMB   *Dictionary of Ming Biography.*

ECCP   *Eminent Chinese of the Ch'ing Period.*

HCFC   *Hang-chou fu-chih* 杭州府志.

HCLAC   *Hsien-ch'un Lin-an chih* 咸淳臨安志.

HCTHHP   *Hang-chou ta-hsüeh hsüeh-pao* 杭州大學學報.

HJAS   *Harvard Journal of Asiatic Studies.*

HR   *History of Religions.*

ICC   *I-chien chih* 夷堅志.

JAS   *Journal of Asian Studies.*

JHHC   *Jen-ho hsien-chih* 仁和縣志.

KCTSCC   *Ku-chin t'u-shu chi-ch'eng* 古今圖書集成.

LSHC   *Li-shui hsien-chih* 麗水縣志.

MLL   *Meng-liang lu* 夢梁錄.

PYHC	*P'ing-yang hsien-chih* 平陽縣志.	
SHC	*Sheng-hsien chih* 嵊縣志.	
SHFC	*Shao-hsing fu-chih* 紹興府志.	
T	*Taishō shinshū daizōkyō.*	
TCHC	*Te-ch'ing hsien-chih* 德清縣志.	
TFHY	*Tao-fa hui-yüan* 道法會元.	
THHC	*T'ung-hsiang hsien-chih* 桐鄉縣志.	
TT	*Tao-tsang* 道藏.	
WCFC	*Wen-chou fu-chih* 溫州府志.	
WCFSC	*Wen-chou feng-su chih* 溫州風俗志.	
WLCKTP	*Wu-lin chang-ku ts'ung-pien* 武林掌故叢編.	
WLFHC	*Wu-lin fang-hsiang chih* 武林坊巷志.	
WLFSC	*Wu-lin feng-su chi* 武林風俗記.	
YCHC	*Yung-chia hsien-chih* 永嘉縣志.	
YCWCL	*Yung-chia wen-chien lu* 永嘉聞見錄.	

Introduction

Summertime, for most people today, denotes a period of rest and relaxation, but for the people of late imperial Chekiang, the hot and humid summer months were often a time of terror. Higher temperatures allowed insects and microparasites to breed in large numbers, particularly in the food and water, through which they infected the populace in the form of contagious diseases like cholera, dysentery, smallpox, malaria, etc., as well as others which have yet to be identified. Even though these diseases rarely spread on the pandemic scale of the Black Death in the fourteenth century, they could devastate the local populace during times of famine, flood or war. They also remained a persistent threat in their endemic forms, frequently taking the lives of the old, the young, and the infirm.

Faced with this terrifying array of diseases, the people of Chekiang turned to a number of countermeasures, including government and private relief, traditional Chinese medicines, Buddhist and Taoist rituals, prophylactic charms, the advice of spirit mediums, etc. The most elaborate, colorful, and intense response to the ever-present threat of contagious disease involved staging plague expulsion festivals,[1] either before the summer epidemic season had begun or while an epidemic was already in progress. These festivals featured a powerful symbolism, expressing both a strong sense of guilt and a deep-rooted fear of marginal or external forces. Elaborate processions featured large numbers of men, women, and children who dressed up as convicted criminals in order to atone for previous misdeeds. Beggars were hired to impersonate the plague demons afflicting the populace. The last day of such festivals was usually marked by a midnight procession, with young men holding torches

---

[1] I use the term 'plague' in the general sense of the word to refer to all manner of epidemics, not just bubonic plague. I have chosen to label those deities, demons, and festivals associated with epidemics using the term plague simply because terms like 'plague demon' read more smoothly than 'epidemic demon'.

racing through the streets and screaming at the top of their lungs to scare away all demonic forces. Taoist priests were often hired to summon deities capable of capturing these spirits and imprisoning them on a boat, which was then floated out to sea and burned.

Plague festivals featuring boat expulsion rites appear to have originated in Chekiang and other parts of south China during the Sung dynasty, although these rituals were frequently performed for individuals as well. They appear to have derived from plague expulsion rites held during the Dragon Boat Festival, which in turn may have developed out of rituals staged by minority peoples long before the area had been settled by Han Chinese (see chapter 2). Such festivals spread throughout China during subsequent centuries, becoming most popular in the southeastern coastal regions. Those Chinese who migrated from Fukien and Kwangtung to Taiwan during the seventeenth century transmitted this festival tradition to their new island home. Such festivals continue to be immensely popular today, with communities spending hundreds of thousands of U.S. dollars to stage colorful processions and build huge and elaborately decorated plague boats — all this in spite of the fact that the dread diseases of the past have been almost completely eradicated. Now that the days of the Cultural Revolution have passed, plague expulsion festivals are making a modest comeback in parts of south China as well.

Most Chekiang festivals that featured the expulsion of plague demons centered on the cult of a deity known as Marshal Wen (Wen Yüan-shuai 溫元帥).[2] While Wen's cult did not spread throughout all of China like those of deities such as Kuan Kung 關公, the Emperor of the Eastern Peak (Tung-yüeh ta-ti 東嶽大帝), the bodhisattva Avalokiteśvara (Kuan-yin 觀音), etc., it became firmly established in many of Chekiang's major cities and market towns during the late imperial era (sixteenth through nineteenth centuries). Originating in P'ing-yang County of Wenchow Prefecture during the Sung Dynasty, the cult of Marshal Wen soon spread to both Wenchow and Hangchow, from there moving northwards to Chia-hsing, Hu-chou, Shaohsing, Soochow, and even Hopeh; west to Szechwan; and south to Fukien and Taiwan, where it survives to this day. During the late imperial era, Marshal Wen's festival became one of the most important religious events in late imperial Hangchow (the provincial capital) and Wenchow (one of the province's major trading ports), but gradually declined during the tumultuous years of the late nineteenth and early twentieth centuries.

---

[2] His given name was Wen Ch'iung 溫瓊, and he was also known as the Loyal and Defending King (Chung-ching Wang 忠靖王).

The first chapter of this book provides historical information about Chekiang necessary for understanding how and why Marshal Wen's cult arose in that province. Particular emphasis is placed on the province's geographic, linguistic, and cultural features, as well as changes affecting local cults and religious Taoism during the Sung dynasty. Chapter 2 describes the devastating impact epidemics could have on Chekiang, as well as the ways in which people attempted to cope with such calamities. The many different yet interrelated versions of Marshal Wen's hagiography are the focus of chapter 3, while chapter 4 traces the spread of his cult throughout Chekiang. Chapter 5 consists of detailed descriptions of Wen's festival as celebrated in Wenchow and Hangchow.

As the term 'cult' is used frequently in this work, I should explain how I have chosen to define this term. By 'cult', I refer to a body of men and women who worship a deity and give of their time, energy, and wealth in order for the worship of this deity to continue and thrive. Sites for cult worship range in size from a room in a cult member's house to small roadside shrines to more sizable village temples, culminating in mammoth multi-storyed temples built in cities and market towns. A single cult may exist only in one locale, but it can also spread to cover a province, parts of a number of provinces, or even all of China. Cults can also vary by membership: some deities tend to be worshipped by religious specialists and their supporters; some by members of a specific trade/guild; some by members of sectarian organizations; and others by members of clan or native-place associations. In contrast, a popular deity like Marshal Wen was worshipped by people representing the entire spectrum of Chinese society. It is also important to note that popular Chinese cults like Wen's are inclusive; in other words, people can belong to more than one cult.

Who is Marshal Wen? In general, Marshal Wen belongs to a class of deities who specialize in preventing outbreaks of epidemics or expelling pestilential forces if epidemics are in progress, the most well-known of which today are the Lords (*wang-yeh* 王爺) of Taiwan (see below). Such deities, often represented as historical military figures, are invoked to curb or combat calamities like epidemics that, while perceived as undesirable, are nonetheless looked upon as inevitable natural anomalies or a richly-deserved type of divine punishment. As with so many Chinese deities, Marshal Wen developed a range of different histories and functions within Taoism and popular religion. During late imperial times, he came to be worshipped by different groups of people, each having its own representation of him. Anybody who has witnessed a Taoist offering ritual (*chiao* 醮) would recognize Marshal Wen as the guardian of the eastern side of the altar, where his portrait is placed. He is portrayed as a guardian deity not only in Taoist liturgical texts but also in ritual dramas such as the Mu-lien operas and popular novels like the *Journey to the West*. As early as the twelfth century, Taoist priests worshipped him as a staunch defender of their "orthodox" (*cheng* 正) religion against the influence of local cults they viewed as "heterodox" (*hsieh* 邪) or "licentious" (*yin* 淫). The gentry in turn viewed him as a symbol of Confucian ideology, a young scholar who had devoted himself to his studies during his lifetime and defended the interests of the state by expelling noxious demons after his death. Popular representations of Wen present another view of this deity though, portraying him as someone who gave his life so that others might not suffer from an epidemic. The existence of these varying representations of Marshal Wen does not mean that they were mutually exclusive, however, as continuous interaction occurred in a process described in chapter 3 which I have termed 'reverberation'.

Apart from exploring the varying representations of Marshal Wen in late imperial China, I will also examine the different groups of people who held them. The paucity of written sources allowing us to study the representations of Marshal Wen held by specific individuals, as well as the fact that most late imperial Chinese could not compose a written record of their beliefs, necessitate exploring this problem by studying the participation of different social groups in Wen's cult and festival. The evidence to be presented below will show that each group supporting his cult and festival did so for specific social and religious reasons. For example, the gentry and other members of the local elite managed Marshal Wen's temples and organized his festivals in order to maintain or strengthen their leadership positions in the community, actions which may have been linked to their attempts to acquire what Pierre Bourdieu calls "symbolic capital" (see Conclusion).[3] At the other end of the social spectrum, beggars dressed up as the plague demons to be expelled, using Wen's festival to assert their unique ritual powers and also make some money in the process. Taoist priests performed rituals during Wen's festivals not only to

---

[3] I follow scholars such as Philip Kuhn in distinguishing between the gentry (*shen-shih* 紳士; degree-holders who may also have served as officials) and the elite (*ching-ying* 精英; individuals who exterted considerable influence over local affairs). See Philip A. Kuhn, *Rebellion and Its Enemies in Late Imperial China* (Cambridge, Mass.: Harvard University Press, 1970), pp. 3–5. See also Joseph W. Esherick and Mary Backus Rankin, "Introduction," in Esherick and Rankin, eds. *Chinese Local Elites and Patterns of Dominance* (Berkeley: University of California Press, 1990), pp. 1–24. I use the term 'scholar-officials' to refer to members of the gentry who also held office.

make a living but also as one way of attempting to control the ritual aspects of such events. For people with wealth and means, Wen's festival was a time to celebrate good times and flaunt status symbols, while those less fortunate often filed grievances against their neighbors in spiritual tribunals run by Marshal Wen, and others burdened with feelings of guilt and sin dressed as criminals and performed penitential acts of self-mortification. All in all, it seems clear that the festival of Marshal Wen did much more than strengthen community solidarity. It also appears to have provided a safety valve for the release of community tensions by airing specific grievances and even providing a forum to settle them.

In researching the cult of Marshal Wen, one of the most difficult problems I have faced has involved defining the geographic scope of this project. Cults like Wen's clearly transcended the boundaries of the administrative hierarchy, but determining their actual range and the factors which shaped this is very difficult, because of the lack of source materials. Some might question focusing on the province of Chekiang and passing over William Skinner's macroregions as the geographic unit for researching the cult of Marshal Wen, particularly as Wen's cult spread beyond Chekiang to Kiangsu, Fukien, and other provinces. I have decided against using macroregions because of their apparently limited value in the study of cult growth. For example, according to Skinner's theories, Chekiang belongs to the Lower Yangtze macroregion, which also includes parts of Kiangsu and Anhwei. While Marshal Wen's cult did exist in the former province, there is no evidence that it ever spread to the latter. In addition to this, Wenchow does not belong to the Lower Yangtze macroregion but to the Southeast Coast macroregion, which includes most of Fukien and northern Kwangtung. Marshal Wen's cult only appears to have spread as far south as Fukien, never gaining a foothold in Kwangtung.

In general, it seems that macroregions might best be suited to the study of China's economic or urban hierarchy, not cult growth. At the same time, it is important to note that the spread of Marshal Wen's cult beyond Chekiang appears to conform to Skinner's theories in that it frequently occurred along trade routes between regional cores, as was also the case with the cult of Wen-ch'ang 文昌, China's god of learning.[4] Nevertheless, for the purposes of this work, Chekiang has proved to be a more useful geographic framework than the Lower Yangtze or Southeast Coast macroregions, although data from

[4] See Terry Kleeman, "The Expansion of the Wen-ch'ang Cult," in Patricia B. Ebrey and Peter N. Gregory, eds., *Religion and Society in T'ang and Sung China* (Honolulu: University of Hawaii Press, 1993), p. 57.

Chekiang's neighboring provinces has been brought into the discussion where relevant.

The primary goal of this work is to bridge the long-standing gap between Taoist studies and social history. Over the past three decades in particular, scholars researching Taoism have made significant contributions to our knowledge of this religion's specialists, their traditions, and the rituals they perform. At the same time, however, there has been a tendency in the field of Taoist studies to overstate the differences between organized Taoist religion and local cults. In exploring the relationship between the two, many scholars have tended to adopt the attitudes of the Taoists they study, often portraying local cults as separate from and even subordinate to Taoism. Social historians, on the other hand, rarely consult the works of Taoist studies, and what they do read tends to confirm their own preconception that Taoist religion had little influence on local cults, and vice versa. My work, therefore, seeks to present a more comprehensive picture of cults to popular Chinese deities by examining the various roles Taoist priests and lay believers played in the growth of cults like Marshal Wen's. In terms of hagiography, I will show in chapter 3 that both Taoist and non-Taoist representations of Marshal Wen existed at any given time, and that these representations could interact and even influence each other over time. Chapter 4 shows that while Taoist priests played an important role in the early spread of Wen's cult, efforts by lay believers were also critical to his cult's subsequent growth. The description of Wen's festivals in Wenchow and Hangchow presented in chapter 5 reveals that while Taoist priests might have played a prominent role in such events, it appears highly unlikely that these festivals belonged to what scholars such as Kristofer Schipper and Ken Dean call the "Taoist liturgical framework." All in all, my analysis of these problems indicates the need for greater open-mindedness when treating the highly different but not mutually exclusive religious phenomena of Taoist religion and local cults.

In an even broader sense, this work hopes to combine the disciplines of social history and religious studies to achieve a more profound understanding of the cultural significance of Chinese cults and festivals. Such an interdisciplinary approach can be highly beneficial, particularly in terms of showing how the study of these phenomena can help determine whether or not late imperial (or modern) China possessed a "civil society" or a "public sphere." Large amounts of ink have already been spilled over this issue, and it may seem odd for me to raise it here and now, just when the debate appears to be subsiding. I do so because the failure of nearly all scholars debating these issues to consider the important role cults and festivals played in both the Chinese realm of public activity and the relationship between state and society has resulted in the neglect of important evidence, which may be used to analyze these problems in greater depth. It is not the purpose of this book to determine the presence or absence of a civil society or public sphere in China which corresponds to Jürgen Habermas' concepts. At the same time however, I believe that if scholars interested in this issue wish to locate one important Chinese public space in which opinions were formed and manipulated, in which significant elite activism took place, in which merchants attempted to increase their power and prestige, in which conflicts could be resolved in a semi-institutional setting, and in which both state and society attempted to assert their interests while also compromising with each other, they need look no further than local temples and their festivals. These appear to have been a part of what Philip C.C. Huang has described as China's "third realm," an area between state and society featuring the participation of both.[5] Therefore, cults and festivals to popular deities such as Marshal Wen deserve to be studied not simply as religious phenomena but also in terms of how they affected Chinese society as a whole.

---

[5] See Philip C.C. Huang, "'Public Sphere'/'Civil Society' in China? The Third Realm between State and Society," *Modern China* 19.2 (April 1993): 216–240.

ONE

Chekiang

For 1,000 years myriad shrines have stood by the rivers,
Every year prayers and gifts are offered by countless givers;
Clear skies come when needed, as does the rain,
The gods thus grant what the people wish to gain.

Auspicious harvests to the prefecture are borne,
Before the temple, female mediums song and dance perform;
The ringing of their songs; the banging of their drums,
Amidst clouds of incense they speak the gods' tongues.

Cakes the size of plates, succulent offerings,
Bow low, offer to the gods, they refuse not such things;
By evening, the drunken people bear each other home,
Cicadas' music fills the temple in the gathering gloom.

> —Lu Yu 陸游, "Song of the Festival" (*Sai-shen ch'ü* 賽神曲), in *Chien-nan shih-chi, chüan* 16[1]

The Land and Its People

Chekiang lies on the southeast coast of China between the provinces of Kiangsu and Fukien; it also shares borders with Anhwei and Kiangsi (see Map 1). The name Chekiang literally means "winding river," in reference to the Ch'ien-t'ang River, which wends and

---

[1] For more on Lu Yu's poems about rural life (including festivals), see Michael S. Duke, *Lu You* (Boston: G. K. Hall, 1977), pp. 124–131; and, Burton Watson, *The Old Man Who Does as He Pleases* (New York and London: Columbia University Press, 1973), pp. 3, 51, 56–57 and 61. Neither scholar has translated the "Song of the Festival." A punctuated edition of Lu's *Chien-nan shih-chi* may be found in *Lu Yu chi* (Peking: Chung-hua shu-chü, 1976).

Map 1 — Late Imperial China

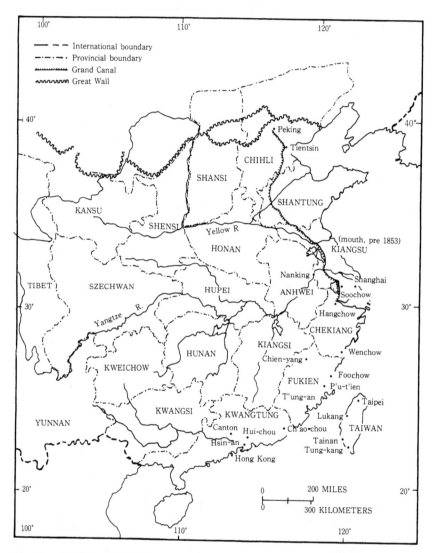

Courtesy of David Johnson, et. al. *Popular Culture in Late Imperial China.*
Copyright © 1985 The Regents of the University of California, p. xii. With
permission of the publisher.

weaves its way 186 miles (310 kilometers) from the mountains bordering on Anhwei to Hangchow Bay (see Map 2). With an area of 39,300 square miles (101,800 square kilometers), Chekiang is China's smallest province in terms of size, but currently ranks tenth in population. Although the Ch'ien-t'ang River had been called the "Che-chiang" (Chekiang) for centuries, this name was not applied to the province until the Ming dynasty.

Located between latitudes 27 and 30 degrees north, Chekiang falls within the subtropical monsoon climate zone. While the winters are not bitterly cold, snow and frost are often seen in the northern plains and mountain regions. The annual rainfall averages between 44 and 76 inches (1,100 and 1,700 millimeters), with more rain falling in the mountains than in the plains. Add to this a frost-free period of between 230–270 days and one can see that Chekiang is a province wellsuited for agricultural cultivation. However, this relatively mild climate also helped spawn the germs which caused epidemics during the summer months, when the average temperature would jump to 82 degrees Fahrenheit (28 degrees Celsius) in Hangchow and 84 degrees Fahrenheit (29 degrees Celsius) in Wenchow. Because epidemics in Chekiang occurred most frequently during the warm summer months, most plague expulsion festivals there were held either just before or during this season.[2]

Chekiang's topography is rugged, with mountains and hills occupying over 70 percent of the land, plains and basins another 22.4 percent, and rivers/lakes 5.2 percent (the rest is tidal flats). The territory of Chekiang also encompasses 36 percent of China's islands, over 18,000 in number. The best (if not most comfortable) way to get a sense of this region's topography is to ride a long-distance bus like the one between Hangchow and Wenchow, which takes the traveler over fertile fields and through craggy mountains down to one of Chekiang's most bustling ports. Even in the age of highway and railroad transportation systems, much of the province's commercial and passenger traffic still flows along a network of rivers and canals extending nearly eight thousand kilometers in length. This network was particularly well-developed in the northern areas of Chekiang (known as the "water country" [*shui-hsiang* 水鄉]), and one need only glance through a Ming or Ch'ing period travelogue to see how frequently travelers, merchants, and religious specialists used these routes. There was also a network of forty ports, the largest being

---

[2] See *Che-chiang ti-li chien-chih* (Hangchow: Che-chiang jen-min ch'u-pan-she, 1985), pp. 93–143. I have yet to determine whether the timing of these festivals corresponded with agricultural slack periods. However, as most of Wen's festivals were held in cities, this may not have been an issue.

Map 2 — Late Imperial Chekiang: Administrative Divisions

Traced with alterations from *Chung-kuo li-shih ti-t'u chi* (Shanghai: Ti-t'u ch'u-pan-she, 1982).

Ningpo and Wenchow, which coastal junks used on their way up and down the China coast.[3] As we shall see in chapter 4, the existence of such highly developed transportation networks proved instrumental in the spread of Marshal Wen's cult.

In attempting to subdivide Chekiang geographically, one might best follow the schema presented by Chang Ch'i-yün (see Map 3). Chang divides Chekiang into the following three sub-regions: 1) The northern plains sub-region, which consists of the Hangchow-Chia-hsing-Hu-chou Plain (hereafter referred to as the Hang-Chia-Hu Plain) and the Ningpo-Shaohsing Plain (hereafter referred to as the Ning-Shao Plain); 2) The coastal sub-region between the Ch'ien-t'ang and Ou river deltas; and, 3) The mountainous sub-region of the west and southwest.[4] The cult of Marshal Wen originated in Wenchow Prefecture of the coastal sub-region of Chekiang, an area which proved highly inhospitable and difficult to cultivate. According to one Ming-dynasty local gazetteer:

> Wenchow is difficult to reach by either mountain or ocean route . . . The people are poor, and exhaust themselves growing crops which can only be harvested once a year.[5] If a flood or drought strikes, people may well starve. This area is not suitable for sericulture, so most women work hard at weaving cloth. Those living near the coast either fish or work at cultivating salt.[6]

Because the city of Wenchow was located near an ideal natural harbor, many of its natives engaged in commercial activities and sought their fortunes throughout southern China and even abroad.[7] From

---

[3] *Che-chiang ti-li chien-chih*, pp. 418–426. See also Lin Cheng-ch'iu, *Che-chiang ching-chi wen-hua shih yen-chiu* (Hangchow: Che-chiang ku-chi ch'u-pan-she, 1989), pp. 46–48, 84–98. For more on Ming-Ch'ing routes, see Timothy Brook, "Guides for Vexed Travellers: Route Books in the Ming and Ch'ing," *CSWT* 4.5 (June 1981): 32–77. See also his "Supplement," *CSWT* 4.6 (Dec. 1981): 130–140; and, "Second Supplement," *CSWT* 4.8 (Dec. 1982): 96–109.

[4] See Chang Ch'i-yün, "Lun Ning-po chien-she sheng-hui chih hsi-wang," *Shih-ti hsüeh-pao* 3.7 (May 1925): 1–17. R. Keith Schoppa divides Chekiang into four zones (inner/outer core and inner/outer periphery) in his *Chinese Elites and Political Change: Zhejiang Province in the Early Twentieth Century* (Cambridge, Mass: Harvard University Press, 1982), pp. 13–26.

[5] People living in the northern plains sub-region generally practiced double- or even triple-cropping.

[6] *WCFC* (1605), 2:47b–48a.

[7] See *Che-chiang ti-li chien-chih*, pp. 460–463. See also Chou Hou-ts'ai, *Wen-chou kang-shih* (Peking: Jen-min chiao-t'ung ch'u-pan-she, 1990); and, Yeh Ta-ping, *Wen-chou shih-hua* (Hangchow: Che-chiang jen-min ch'u-pan-she, 1982).

Map 3 — Chekiang's Sub-regions

Traced with alterations from *Che-chiang sheng ti-t'u tse* (Shanghai: Hsin-hua shu-tien, 1988).

this sub-region, Wen's cult quickly spread along coastal trade routes used by Wenchow merchants to the northern plains sub-region of Chekiang, his first temples in that sub-region being built in Hangchow during the Southern Sung dynasty. Merchants from in and around Hangchow later transmitted Wen's cult to other sites within this sub-region, particularly two important market towns named Ch'ing-chen (in Chia-hsing) and Hsin-shih (in Hu-chou; see Maps 2 and 5). It is not clear why Wen's cult never gained a significant foothold in the mountainous sub-region of western and southwestern Chekiang, his only cult site in the entire sub-region being at Li-shui (see chapter 4). Perhaps this was because the mountains there provided an effective barrier to most forms of transport, or because most Wenchow and Hangchow merchants do not appear to have engaged in a significant amount of trade in this sub-region.

Linguistically, the vast majority of Chekiang's present population of forty million inhabitants speak the Wu 吳 dialect, which is still spoken by eight percent of China's populace.[8] Wu dialect in Chekiang features four different varieties: northern plains, west and southwest, T'ai-chou, and Wenchow (see Map 4).[9] The ability of Marshal Wen's cult to spread throughout much of the province of Chekiang, and even cross provincial boundaries, was in part due to the fact that it arose in and initially spread through areas which possessed similar dialectical characteristics.

Marshal Wen's cult first arose in P'ing-yang County of Wenchow Prefecture, an area which lies on the border of the Wu and Min dialect regions. P'ing-yang is one of China's dialectical melting pots, with five distinct dialects spoken there. One linguist researching the southern part of P'ing-yang[10] has determined that over 54 percent of the million-plus inhabitants speak Min dialect, while a further 16.2

---

[8] Wu dialect is one of three dialects which grew out of the Ancient Yüeh language (Ku Yüeh-yü 古越語), the other two being Cantonese (Yüeh 粤) and Fukienese/Taiwanese (Min 閩).

[9] Chou Chen-ch'üeh and Yu Ju-chieh, *Fang-yen yü Chung-kuo wen-hua* (Shanghai: Shang-hai jen-min ch'u-pan-she, 1986) has an introduction to China's dialect regions, as well as an analysis of Wu dialect variants in Chekiang; see pp. 8–14, 59–68. See also S. Robert Ramsey, *The Languages of China* (Princeton: Princeton University Press, 1987), pp. 88–95, and Y.R. Chao (Chao Yüan-jen), *Hsien-tai Wu-yü yen-chiu* (Peking: K'o-hsüeh ch'u-pan-she, 1958).

[10] Now known as Ts'ang-nan. In 1981, P'ing-yang County was divided into P'ing-yang and Ts'ang-nan counties.

Map 4 — Chekiang's Dialect Sub-regions

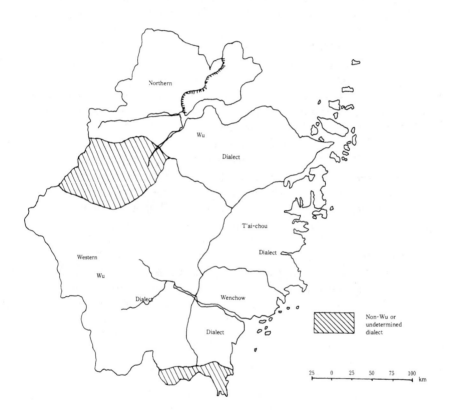

Traced with alterations from Chou Chen-ch'üeh & Yu Ju-chieh, *Fang-yen yü Chung-kuo wen-hua*.

percent speak the Wenchow form of Wu dialect.[11] The spread of Marshal Wen's cult from P'ing-yang north to Wenchow city and south to Fukien (see chapter 4), as well as the spread of the cult of the Five Commissioners of Epidemics north from Fukien to Wenchow (see chapter 2) may have been facilitated by the fact that many residents of P'ing-yang county could communicate with natives of both regions.

Historical linguists have determined that the Wu and Min dialects have profound links and enjoy considerable overlap in terms of vocabulary and pronunciation, making the spread of popular beliefs from one area to the other all the easier. These scholars have convincingly demonstrated that the form of Wu dialect which existed before the Six Dynasties is the ancestor language of modern Min, and that the northern Chinese dialects spoken by those people who migrated south during that era gradually became modern Wu dialect. According to their research, as northerners moved southwards into Kiangsu and northern Chekiang following the fall of the Han dynasty, the dialects they spoke intermingled extensively with ancient Wu dialect, causing great changes in the latter as it existed in these two provinces. However, Wu dialect in southern Chekiang and Fukien during the Six Dynasties was relatively unaffected and retained many of its original features.[12] One can see this from the fact that Japanese readings of Chinese characters termed "Wu Pronunciation" (*Go-on* 吳音) more closely resemble modern Min dialect than modern Wu dialect.[13]

Turning to the spread of Marshal Wen's cult inside the province of Chekiang, one finds that its spread along trade routes may also have been facilitated by linguistic factors. Wen's cult moved northwards from Wenchow to Hangchow during the Southern Sung dynasty, one important reason being that while the Wenchow form of

---

[11] The other inhabitants speak either a local dialect called Man 蠻 (there is considerable debate over whether this derives from Wu or Min dialects), another dialect called Chin-hsiang 金鄉, or the language of the minority She tribes. See Wen Tuan-cheng, *Ts'ang-nan fang-yen chih* (Peking: Yü-wen ch'u-pan-she, 1991), pp. 1–31. See also Lu Chia-mei, "Wen-chou P'ing-yang Min-nan-yü yen-chiu" (M.A. thesis, National Taiwan University, 1983). I would like to thank Ho Ta-an 何大安 and Hung Wei-jen 洪惟仁 of the Institute of History and Philology, Academia Sinica, for referring me to these and other works on historical linguistics mentioned in the notes below.

[12] See Ting Pang-hsin, "Wu-yü chung te Min-yü ch'eng-fen," *Bulletin of the Institute of History and Philology, Academia Sinica* 59 (1988): 13–22; Chang Kuang-yü, "Wu-Min fang-yen kuan-hsi shih-lun," *Chung-kuo yü-wen* 3 (1993): 161–170; and Chou and Yü, *Fang-yen*, pp. 25, 38–39.

[13] See Margaret M.Y. Sung, "Chinese Dialects and Sino–Japanese," in *Chinese Languages and Linguistics*, volume 1, *Chinese Dialects* (Taipei: Nankang: Institute of History and Philology, 1992), pp. 563–585.

Wu dialect is largely unintelligible to other Chekiang natives it does share a number of grammatical and pronunciation features with the Hangchow form of Wu dialect. Hangchow itself proved an important linguistic stepping stone as Wen's cult expanded throughout the northern plains sub-region of Chekiang and even parts of southern Kiangsu and Hopeh. This is because large numbers of northern Chinese speakers migrated to Hangchow at the beginning of the Southern Sung, causing the present-day Hangchow form of Wu dialect to exhibit a strongly northern character even while retaining many of its southern features. It is also certainly no coincidence that Wen's cult spread to sites in Hu-chou, Chia-hsing, and Soochow prefectures, as the forms of Wu dialect spoken there share many common features with Hangchow Wu dialect.[14]

What kind of individuals would have been able to transmit Marshal Wen's cult across dialect boundaries? While the sources do not reveal the names of any such individuals, it does seem likely that people who could communicate in more than one dialect, particularly Taoist priests, merchants, and scholar-officials, played the most important roles in this process.

Geographical, commercial, and linguistic features help to explain the spread of Wen's cult within Chekiang, while the climate and frequent outbreaks of epidemics suggest the need for plague-expulsion festivals in that province. The distinctive cultural history of Chekiang further suggests an explanation for the localist nature of the cult, for this region had developed a culture of its own long before contact with Han Chinese from the Yellow River plain. Indeed, many scholars now agree that it is imperative to discard the assumption that the Han "civilized" the "barbarian tribes" below the Yangtze River as they migrated southwards. Scholars such as Wolfram Eberhard worked to overturn this prejudice, attempting to study China as a world of distinct yet continuously interacting regional cultures.[15] More recent archaeological discoveries have reinforced this hypothesis to the point that more and more historians in China today are beginning to see their cultural origins as multi-dimensional.[16]

---

[14] See Richard Van Ness Simmons, "Northern and Southern Forms in Hangchow Grammar," in *Chinese Languages and Linguistics*, pp. 539–561.

[15] Wolfram Eberhard, *The Local Cultures of South and East China* (Leiden: E. J. Brill, 1968), pp. 1–31.

[16] See Tu Cheng-sheng, "Tao-lun — Chung-kuo shang-ku-shih yen-chiu te yi-hsieh kuan-chien wen-t'i," in Tu Cheng-sheng, ed., *Chung-kuo shang-ku-shih lun-wen hsüan-chi* (Taipei: Hua-shih ch'u-pan-she, 1979), pp. 15–82. See also Ning Chu-ch'en, "Chung-kuo hsin-shih-ch'i shih-tai wen-hua te to-chung-hsin fa-chan ho fa-chan

The first inhabitants of Chekiang named in historical sources were the Yüeh 越,[17] a coastal people who dwelled in the area extending from the Huai River as far south as Kwangtung. While their ethnic identity has yet to be defined, they were probably the descendants of indigenous peoples who intermarried with Han Chinese and other southerners.[18] Their most striking physical features described by Han chroniclers included cutting their hair short and tattooing their bodies.[19] Although the Yüeh and other peoples of south China were eventually subjugated and enslaved by the Han,[20] many of their customs, including snake worship[21] and skill in boating

pu-p'ing-heng lun," *Wen-wu*, 357 (Feb. 1986): 16–30; Yen Wen-ming, Chung-kuo shih-ch'ien wen-hua te t'ung-yi-hsing yü to-yang-hsing," *Wen-wu* 370 (March 1987): 38–50. For a review of the archaeological data pertaining to Chekiang, see Tung Ch'u-p'ing, *Wu-Yüeh wen-hua hsin-t'an* (Hangchow: Che-chiang jen-min ch'u-pan-she, 1988), pp. 1–48.

[17] The character Yüeh is a varient of the older character Yüeh 戉 , a type of stone axe used by the local inhabitants. See Tung, *Wu-Yüeh wen-hua*, pp. 8, 16–48.

[18] Eberhard postulates that the Yüeh are a mixture of Thai and Yao peoples (*Local Cultures*, pp. 24, 432–436), while Edward Schafer stresses the influence of the northern Lung-shan 龍山 culture in *The Vermillion Bird — T'ang Images of the South* (Berkeley: University of California Press, 1967), p. 12. K.C. Chang has uncovered evidence pointing to possible intermingling with Malayo-Polynesian peoples; see his "Chinese Prehistory in Pacific Perspective," *Harvard Journal of Oriental Studies*, 22 (1959), pp. 100–149, and his *Archaeology of Ancient China*, 4th ed. (New Haven and London: Yale University Press, 1983), pp. 410–476. The general consensus is that the Yüeh were a partly sinicized Thai people who intermingled with other southern ethnic groups. See Li Chi, *The Formation of the Chinese People: An Anthropological Inquiry* (Cambridge: Cambridge University Press, 1928), pp. 275–276; and, H.J. Wiens, *Han Chinese Expansion in South China* (Hamden, Conn: Shoe String Press, 1967), pp. 39, 41, 114–115, 124 (this work was originally published in 1954 under the title *China's March Toward the Tropics*).

[19] Tung, *Wu-Yüeh wen-hua*, pp. 171–181; and Hsiao Fan, *Ch'un-ch'iu chih Liang-Han shih ch'i Chung-kuo hsiang nan-fang te fa-chan* (Taipei: Kuo-li T'ai-wan ta-hsüeh wen-shüeh yüan, 1973), esp. pp. 57–58, 68–69. The first chapter of *Chuang Tzu*, entitled "Hsiao-yao yu" ("Free and Easy Wandering"), contains a description of these customs. See Burton Watson's translation (New York: Columbia University Press, 1968), p. 34.

[20] Schafer, *Vermillion Bird*, pp. 13–14; see pp. 59–69 for accounts of slavery, prejudice, and native insurrections. See also Wiens, *Han Chinese Expansion*, pp. 114–115.

[21] See *Sou-shen chi, chüan* 7, 12, 13, 20, (Peking: Chung-hua shu-chü, 1979): 94, 109, 155–158, 164–165, 242–243; and *Po-wu chih chiao-cheng, chüan* 2, 7, 10, (Taipei: Ming-wen shu-chü, 1981): 37–38, 83–92, 111–113. For secondary scholarship on snake cults, see Chiang Pin, "Chiang-nan ti-ch'ü she ch'uan-shuo chung ku-tai t'u-t'eng ch'ung-pai te nei-han," in *Chung-kuo min-chien wen-hua* (Shanghai: Hsüeh-lin ch'u-pan-she, 1992), volume 7, pp. 145–160; Wolfram Eberhard, *Local Cultures*, pp. 378–379, 381–390, 399–400; Miyakawa Hisayuki, "Local Cults Around Mount Lu at the Time of Sun En's Rebellion," in Holmes Welch and Anna Seidel, eds., *Facets of Taoism* (New Haven and London: Yale University Press, 1979), pp. 83–102; Schafer, *The Divine Woman* (San Francisco: North Point Press, 1980), pp. 7–54; and, Katz, "Demons or

survived.[22] The latter two customs appear to lie behind the origins of the Dragon Boat Festival (to be discussed below), held in the heat of summer to expel pestilential vapors by means of serpentine ships.[23]

Snake worship in Chekiang was popular for a number of reasons, one of which was that people believed that snakes were among the natural forces responsible for outbreaks of contagious diseases. The following Sung dynasty story provides a vivid example of such a view:

> In the fifth month of the year 1195, there appeared outside the South Gate of the city of Hu-chou a woman in white wearing black shoes, walking alone. She hired a boat and after climbing aboard lay down to sleep and covered herself with a reed mat. Normally when a boat moves there is a lot of noise, but this time all was quiet. The boatmen were surprised by this, and when people lifted up the mat [to take a closer look at their passenger] they saw thousands of foot-long black snakes intertwined in a tangle. Terrified by what they saw, they broke into a sweat and quickly replaced the mat [After they reached their destination 60 *li* upriver], the woman offered to pay 200 cash, but the boatmen didn't dare accept. When she asked why, they said: "After we'd seen you like that, how could we dare accept [money]?" She laughed and said: "Don't tell anybody [about what you have seen]. I have come from the city to spread the snake plague (*hsing she-wen* 行蛇瘟). I'll leave in a month." . . . From spring to early summer of that year, the prefectures of Hu-chou, Ch'ang-chou, and Hsiu-chou (the latter two are in Kiangsu) suffered greatly from epidemics (*yi-li* 疫癘), with Hu-chou suffering worst of all. The epidemics abated somewhat during the fifth month, but worsened again during the sixth month. That must have been due to the return of the snake woman (*she-fu* 蛇婦).[24]

Deities? — The *Wangye* of Taiwan," *Asian Folklore Studies* 46.2 (1987): 211–212.

[22] See Tung, *Wu-Yüeh wen-hua*, pp. 274–291; Hsiao, *Nan fang te fa-chan*, pp. 69–70; and Eberhard, *Local Cultures*, pp. 397–398, 402–405.

[23] See Chang Hsiang-hua, "Pai-Yüeh min-tsu yü tuan-wu hsi-su," *Tung-nan wen-hua* 5 (1991): 93–94; and, Wu Yung-chang, *Chung-kuo nan-fang min-tsu wen-hua* (Nan-ning: Kuang-hsi chiao-yü ch'u-pan-she, 1991), pp. 66–68, 292–319. Useful works describing the cultural history of Chekiang include *Che-chiang wen-hua shih* (Hangchow: Che-chiang jen-min ch'u-pan-she, 1992); and, *Che-chiang min-su yen-chiu* (Hangchow: Che-chiang jen-min ch'u-pan-she, 1992).

[24] Hung Mai (1123-1201), *I-chien chih (ICC)* (Peking: Chung-hua shu-chü, 1981), p. 892. For a story about frogs spreading epidemics, see *Chu-ting yü-wen* (1899),

This woman in white may very well have been related to the White Snake, one of the favorite subjects of Chekiang popular fiction and drama in the Legend of the White Snake (*Pai-she chuan* 白蛇傳). Although later works portray the White Snake as a benevolent creature trapped by the Buddhist monk Fa-hai 法海, in her earliest form she was a malevolent plague demon who lived in the houses of families she had killed in epidemics. Some versions of the story even state that she infected people with contagious diseases in order to help her husband sell his medicines.[25] Edward Schafer has shown that snake-women were important deities in ancient southern Chinese culture.[26] The Legend of the White Snake reveals that although many of these were benevolent river nymphs, another class consisted of demons who made people ill.

When reading the works of the first Han Chinese who settled the south, including Chekiang, one gets the feeling that they were both overwhelmed and bewildered by their new environment. They had to adjust to a world vastly different from the one they had known: possessing lusher terrain, warmer climate, and more abundant flora and fauna: yet also a region full of hostile peoples and their unfamiliar customs. Much of what these Han Chinese wrote seems an effort to come up with a new vocabulary to describe what they saw, and works as late as the T'ang dynasty abound with stories of things Schafer has described as "either the fantastic creations of fear or the partly true images of incomprehension."[27]

By the Sung dynasty, however, Chekiang had been transformed into China's economic heartland, not to mention the home of many of its top scholars, artists, and bureaucrats. This transformation was in large part brought about by the shift of the national capital to Hangchow following the fall of the Northern Sung

4:32a–33b.

[25] See "Eternal Prisoner Under Thunder Peak Pavilion," in Y.W. Ma and Joseph Lau, eds., *Traditional Chinese Stories* (New York: Columbia University Press, 1981), p. 362; Fu Hsi-hua, ed., *Pai-she chuan chi* (Shanghai: Shang-hai ch'u-pan kung-ssu, 1955), pp. 3, 21, 27; and Ch'en Ch'in-chien, "Pai-she hsing-hsiang chung-hsin chieh-kou te min-su yüan-yüan chi ch'i ch'ien-tsai tung-li," in *Pai-she chuan lun-wen chi* (Hangchow: Ku-chi ch'u-pan-she, 1986), pp. 62–78. Thunder Peak Pavillion (Lei-feng t'a 雷峰塔) was originally located near West Lake in Hangchow, but fell into disrepair and eventually collapsed at the beginning of this century.

[26] Schafer, *Divine Woman*, pp. 7–54.

[27] Schafer, *Vermillion Bird*, p. 114. For more on Chekiang's early history, see Liu Shu-fen, "San chih liu shih-chi Che-tung ti-ch'ü tê ching-chi fa-chan," *Bulletin of the Institute of History and Philology, Academia Sinica* 58 (1987): 485–523. For data on Hangchow, see Lü Yi-ch'un, "Hang-chou li-shih yen-ko k'ao-lüeh," *HCTHHP* 17.4 (Dec. 1987): 11–12; and, *Nan-pei Ch'ao ch'ien-ku Hang-chou* (Hangchow: Che-chiang jen-min ch'u-pan-she, 1992).

dynasty, a political shift which in part also reflected the rapid economic growth Chekiang had experienced during the T'ang and Five Dynasties periods. The changes that occurred in Chekiang and the impact they had on that province's religious life will be discussed in detail below. I should note here however that the economic and political integration of Chekiang into the Chinese state did not by any means totally extirpate this region's local religious and cultural characteristics.

The Development of Chekiang during the Sung

The political, social, and economic changes that occurred in China during the Sung dynasty are by now well-known to most scholars.[28] They included rapid urban growth, intensified local and inter-regional commercialization, the spread of printing, the growth of the size of the gentry class, and the intellectual ferment that gave rise to Neo-Confucianism, Ch'an (Zen) Buddhism and Perfect Realization (Ch'üan-chen 全眞) Taoism, etc.[29] Such changes were particularly striking in a province like Chekiang, which experienced significant growth during this period. While Chekiang had been gradually settled and developed before the Sung, politically and culturally the province had remained largely a backwater, the empire's core being located in the dusty plains of the Yellow River valley. China's center of gravity had been gradually shifting southwards ever since the Han dynasty,[30] but it took the Jurchen invaders who overthrew the Northern Sung and established the Chin dynasty to provide the final impetus which was to bring this long process to its fruition. During the calamitous

---

[28] See for example the numerous essays in James T.C. Liu and Peter J. Golas, eds., *Change in Sung China. Innovation or Renovation?* (Lexington, Mass: D. C. Heath and Co., 1969).

[29] For an overview of these changes, see Robert Hartwell, "Demographic, Political, and Social Transformations of China," *HJAS* 42 (1982): 365–442. A statistical analysis of southern China's economic growth during the Sung may be found in Chang Chia-chü, *Liang Sung ching-chi chung-hsin chih nan-yi* (Taipei: Po-shu ch'u-pan-she, 1985), pp. 8–36, 53–94. Further work on commercial growth during the Sung may be found in Shiba Yoshinobu, *Commerce and Society in Sung China*, trans. Mark Elvin (Ann Arbor: University of Michigan Press, 1970), pp. 4–44; and, Mark Elvin, *The Pattern of the Chinese Past* (Stanford: Stanford University Press, 1973), pp. 131–144.

[30] For a description of this shift, see Denis Twitchett, *Financial Administration Under the T'ang Dynasty* (Cambridge: Cambridge University Press, 1963), esp. pp. 12–14, 49–58, 84–96, 175, 193 and 312–313; Shih Nien-hai, *Chung-kuo shih-ti lun-kao, ho-shan chi* (Taipei: Hung-wen kuan ch'u-pan-she, 1986), pp. 239–253; and Jacques Gernet, *A History of Chinese Civilization* (Cambridge: Cambridge University Press, 1983), pp. 268–273.

years of the 1120s and 1130s, people living in north China fled southwards much as the Han Chinese of the third and fourth centuries had done. Many of these migrants were from the gentry and merchant classes, and they tended to congregate in the cities, especially Hangchow, where the government had established its capital in 1138. This influx of talented individuals, combined with the development of printing and a large increase in the number of schools, transformed Chekiang (especially the northern plains sub-region) into the political and cultural center of the empire.[31] The northern plains sub-region became fertile ground on which Marshal Wen's cult flourished after spreading there during the Sung from its base in Wenchow, with the cult's most important supporters in this sub-region consisting of members of the gentry and merchant classes mentioned above.

The development of cults like Marshal Wen's was also due to the commercial transformation of the province. The countryside of the Hang-Chia-Hu Plain became the heartland of a thriving silk trade, dotted with groves of mulberry trees (on which grew the leaves used to feed silkworms) and scores of newly developed market towns. Porcelain from the Lung-ch'uan region of Li-shui prefecture reigned supreme as China's finest product until the rise of Ching-te chen (in Kiangsi) during the Ming. Shaohsing, Chia-hsing, and Wenchow produced high-quality paper, while the ship-building industry flourished in Hangchow, Ningpo, and Wenchow. Rapid growth in industries such as textiles, mining, tea, and ceramics led to the rise of powerful merchants who later became important supporters of popular cults like Wen's. The province quickly developed a huge network of cities and market towns connected by water transport via canals, rivers, and the sea. Of the forty largest Southern Sung cities, Chekiang boasted twenty-three (58 percent). Many products flowed from the inland regions to the coast, where they were shipped abroad via the ports of Kan-p'u (just east of Hangchow), Ningpo, and Wenchow, with imports flowing back inland in the opposite direction.[32] As I shall explain in detail below, the commercialization of Chekiang appears to have contributed to the rise of new deities who

---

[31] See Ch'ien Mu, *Kuo-shih ta-kang* (Taipei: Kuo-li pien-yi-kuan, 1953), volume 2, pp. 414–449; Ch'en Cheng-hsiang, *Chung-kuo wen-hua ti-li* (Taipei: Mu-to ch'u-pan-she, 1984), pp. 1–22; Jacques Gernet, *Daily Life in China on the Eve of the Mongol Invasion, 1250-1276* (Stanford: Stanford University Press, 1962), pp. 14–16, 22–25; and, Chang, *Liang Sung ching-chi*, pp. 44–51, 126–150.

[32] See Ni Shih-yi and Fang Ju-chin, "Nan-Sung Liang-che she-hui ching-chi te fa-chan," *HCTHHP* 13.2 (June, 1983): 110-119; Lin, *Che-chiang ching-chi wen-hua shih*, pp. 30–49; and, Shiba Yoshinobu, *Sōdai Kōnan keizai kenkyu* (Tōkyo: Toyō bunka kenkūjō 1988), pp. 459–550.

not only protected crops but also merchants and their goods. Data in chapter 4 also reveals that cults like Marshal Wen's gradually spread along the trade routes mentioned above to cover much of the province.

During the Southern Sung, Wenchow became one of the empire's most important ports, while Hangchow grew into the largest metropolis of its era with a population of over one million inside and outside the city walls.[33] In cities like Hangchow, merchants gained great influence in local affairs, both through participating in government monopolies and engaging in internal and foreign trade on their own. At the same time, commercial growth led to the creation of guilds and other commercial organizations, while urban growth attracted thousands of peasants from the countryside.[34] As I will demonstrate in the following chapters, this migration from rural to urban areas may have affected the growth of Marshal Wen's cult, inasmuch as it spread from early sites in less developed parts of southern Chekiang like P'ing-yang to urban centers like Hangchow and Wenchow.

Religious Changes in Sung Dynasty Chekiang

While most scholars today pretty much agree on the nature of the political and socioeconomic changes affecting Sung China, the impact these changes had on that era's religious history is less clear. Fortunately, the stimulating and informative essays in the recent conference volume on T'ang-Sung religion edited by Patricia Ebrey and Peter Gregory go a long way toward solving this problem. As the editors properly point out in their introduction to this work, many aspects of Chinese religious life remained largely unchanged, including ancestor worship, the idea of a reciprocal relationship

---

[33] We know more about this city than any other contemporary urban site, both from Chinese works like the *Tu-ch'eng chi-sheng, Hsi-hu lao-jen fan-sheng lu, Meng-liang lu*, and *Wu-lin chiu-shih*, as well as accounts by Westerners such as Marco Polo and Oderic de Pordenone. Jacques Gernet has utilized all these works and many others to present a lively and colorful picture of Southern Sung Hangchow in his *Daily Life in China*.

[34] Gernet, *Daily Life*, pp. 39–40, 46–48, 59–62, 67–68, 77–78, 81–88. For more on Hangchow's commercial growth, see Shiba, *Sōdai Kōnan*, pp. 312–339; Lin Cheng-ch'iu and Chin Min, *Nan-Sung ku-tu Hang-chou* (Honan: Chung-chou shu-hua she, 1984), pp. 24–40; and, Lin Cheng-ch'iu, *Nan-Sung tu-ch'eng Lin-an* (Shanghai: Hsi-ling yin-she, 1986), pp. 233–279. For information on guilds and other commercial associations in Hangchow, see Ch'üan Han-sheng, *Chung-kuo hang-hui chih-tu shih* (Shanghai: Hsin sheng-ming ch'u-pan-she, 1934), pp. 44–45, 46–49, 58–62 and 92–94.

between people and the deities they worshipped, the lack of a clear distinction between secular and sacred, the use of the "bureaucratic metaphor" to conceive of the structure of the supernatural realm, the doctrine of the mandate of heaven, etc.[35] It is also important to remember that the apparent transformation of local religious life during the Sung may in part reflect the larger quantity and higher quality of the sources available for this period. Nevertheless, the evidence presented below indicates that a number of important changes in local religious life did occur (especially in developing provinces like Chekiang), with greater numbers of local gods, able to answer a wider variety of needs, coming to be worshipped in larger and more ornate temples than ever before.

Perhaps the most significant change in Sung local religion had to do with the nature of those deities worshipped. From ancient times up to Sung dynasty, most people in Chekiang had engaged in ritual activities centering on local earth god cults (formally known as the Gods of Earth and Grain [She-chi shen 社稷神]). While frequently viewed with suspicion and sometimes even contempt by scholar-officials and members of Buddhist and Taoist movements, these ancient cults flourished for many centuries despite attempts at suppression. As early as the Han dynasty, the people of Chekiang had already gained a reputation for being intensely devoted to their local earth gods.[36] Even during the early years of the Sung dynasty, the annual spring and autumn sacrifices to these deities remained the hallmark of ritual life in rural Chekiang.[37] The sources usually refer to these rituals as "sacrificing to the gods of the soil" (*chi-she* 祭社), and indicate that spirit mediums (almost always referred to as *wu* 巫) played a leading role in presiding over them. The Gods of Earth and Grain appear to have had one major function, caring for the crops, and the rural rites to them centered on this power. In the spring, people appealed to the earth gods to grant a bountiful harvest; in the fall they

---

[35] See Ebrey and Gregory, "The Religious and Historical Landscape," in *Religion and Society*, pp. 6–11.

[36] For a description of Yüeh divination and spirit-mediumship, see the *Feng-shan* 封禪 section of Ssu-ma Ch'ien's (ca. 135–93 B.C.E.) *Shih-chi*, in *Records of the Grand Historian of China*, Burton Watson trans., (New York: Columbia University Press, 1961), p. 63.

[37] Rural cults and festivals had been a part of Chinese culture from ancient times. Many of the works preserved in the *Book of Poetry* (*Shi-ching*) and the *Songs of Ch'u* (*Ch'u-tz'u*), particularly the *Nine Songs* (*Chiu-ko*), derived from such ritual events. See Marcel Granet, *Festivals and Songs of Ancient China*, trans. E.D. Edwards, (London: Routledge, 1932), pp. 147–206; as well as his *Danses et legendes de la Chine ancienne* (Paris: Presses Universitaries de France, 1926), 2 vols., esp. volume 1, pp. 229–390.

gave thanks if such had been the case.[38]

By the time the Sung dynasty had reached its maturity, however, numerous cults to new types of deities had begun to flourish in Chekiang and other parts of south China. These newer deities did not merely control matters relating to agriculture (though they could intervene in such affairs when necessary), but also dealt with a wide range of problems such as suppressing bandits, aiding commercial ventures, and exorcising demonic forces. Cults to such deities not only gained immense popularity on the local level, but quickly spread throughout south China along the commercial networks mentioned above.[39] This is not to say that the people of Chekiang and its neighboring provinces only worshipped earth deities before the Sung; other nature spirits, Buddhist and Taoist deities, as well as ancestors and the souls of the unknown or unruly dead also received sacrifices. In addition, cults to new deities like Marshal Wen never completely replaced those to the earth gods; these ancient gods continued to be worshipped, albeit usually in small shrines along a road or in a field. However, the decline of the earth god cults did have a significant impact on Chekiang local religion that was readily apparent to contemporary scholar-officials.

As cults to new deities like Wen began to flourish, the beliefs and practices associated with earth god cults appear to have entered a period of decline. The number of altars/temples to these deities steadily dwindled, and people became less diligent in carrying out the required sacrifices.[40] In the case of Yung-chia County in Wenchow Prefecture, the Southern Sung literatus Yeh Shih (1150–1223) noted in 1218 that: "During the Sui and T'ang dynasties, the number [of altars] to the Gods of Earth and Soil gradually grew to 2,816 . . . but by the Ch'un-hsi reign (1174–1189) over 2,000 had disappeared."[41] In describing the decline of earth deity cults throughout Wenchow prefecture, Yeh explained that:

---

[38] See Ling Ch'un-sheng, "Chung-kuo ku-tai she chih yüan-liu," *Bulletin of the Institute of Ethnology, Academia Sinica* 17 (1964): 1–44. See also Kanai Noriyuki, "Sōdai no sonsha to shajin," *Tōyōshi kenkyū* 38 (1979): 62–65, and Nakamura Jihei, "Sōdai no fū no tokucho," *Chuō daigaku bengakubu kiyō, shigaku ko* 104 (March 1982): 51–75.

[39] See Kanai Noriyuki, "Sōdai Seisai no sonsha to dōshin," in *Sōdai no shakai to shūkyō, Sōdaishi kenkyūkai kenkyū hōkoku* 2 (1985): 81–108; and, Valerie Hansen, *Changing Gods in Medieval China, 1127–1276* (Princeton: Princeton University Press, 1990), pp. 9–10, 75–78, 105–159.

[40] See Kanai, "Sonsha to shajin," pp. 73–74, 77–78, 80.

[41] Yeh Shih, *Shui-hsin chi* (Ssu-pu pei-yao edition), 11:5a. This work has also been reprinted in the *Yeh Shih chi* (Peking: Chung-hua shu-chü, 1961), pp. 190–191. For a study of this scholar's place in Sung history, see Winston Wan Lo, *The Life and Thought of Yeh Shih* (Gainesville: University Presses of Florida, 1974).

The earth gods [govern] the soil, while the grain gods
[govern] the cereals. Without the soil there is no life;
without the cereals there is no nourishment. When
kingdoms were created, they first erected these altars to
offer sacrifices, in order to show the people they had
received the Mandate of Heaven . . . These rites (performed
by officials) were solemn and reverential in the extreme,
and no one dared to neglect them. [Today however] beliefs
that are weird and licentious, false and absurd have arisen
. . . Alas! Are the people so irreverent that they are ignorant
of ritual propriety?[42]

Yeh was not the only Southern Sung literatus to lament the
decline of cults to the earth gods. Wang Po (1197–1274), a native of
Chin-hua in western Chekiang, attributed this to the spread of
Buddhism and Taoism to rural areas, noting with outrage that: "[For
the Gods of Earth and Grain] to fall to their knees in shrines dedicated
to Lao-tzu, Sakyamuni, and evil demons is far indeed [from their
original majesty]."[43] Buddhist monasteries and Taoist temples often
supplanted ancient cult sites, although the specialists of these religions
did allow local deities to remain in these new sites as minor gods, and
even occasionally permitted such sites to be used in staging traditional
local rites.[44]

The rapid growth of cults to new types of local deities was
also marked by the expansion of socio-religious organizations which
had traditionally been associated with the worship of earth gods.[45]
Traditional Chinese sources, including works like the *Book of Rites*
(*Li-chi* 禮記), frequently refer to such organizations as *she-hui* 社會,
literally "earth god associations," the term currently used in modern
Chinese to mean "society." By the Sung dynasty, however, these
organizations had developed into groups supporting the worship of
all manner of local deities, although their primary functions continued

---

[42] Yeh, *Shui-hsin chi*, 11:3a; and *Yeh Shih chi*, pp. 186–188.

[43] See Wang's *Lu-chai chi*, *chüan* 9. See also Miyakawa Hisayuki, "Dōkyōshi
joyori mitaru Godai," *Tōhō shūkyō* 42 (1973): 14–15 and 22–24; and, Fukui Kojun and
Sakai Tadao, eds., *Dōkyō* (Tokyo: Heika Chuppansha, 1983), volume 1, pp. 59–62.

[44] See Kanai, "NanSō saishi shakai no tenkai," in *Shūkyō shakaishi kenkyū* (Tokyo:
Yuzankoku Chuppan Kaisha, 1977), pp. 595–597; and, "Sonsha to shajin," pp. 74–76,
80–81. For an example of the eclectic mix of temples at sacred sites, see Edouard
Chavannes, *Le T'ai Chan* (Paris: Ernest Leroux, 1910), pp. 44–158.

[45] These are referred to by Chinese scholars as "sacrificial organizations" (*chi-ssu
tsu-chih* 祭祀組織) or "sacrificial networks" (*chi-ssu ch'üan* 祭祀圈), and by Japanese
scholars as "sacrificial associations" (*saishi shakai* 祭祀社會).

to involve raising money for the upkeep of the temple and staging annual rites on a local deity's birthday. Such organizations also expanded beyond local boundaries, with worshippers setting up branch temples in areas they migrated to or did business in, retaining links with the main temple through regular (often annual) pilgrimages.[46] The festivals they staged have many characteristics in common with those extant today, including processions featuring armed troupes (whose members did not hesitate to use their weapons during local feuds), people wearing cangues to atone for previous sins; rotating recruitment of leaders known as "association heads" (*she-shou* 社首 or *hui-shou* 會首), huge and vibrant market fairs, the presence of hordes of beggars, etc.[47]

Another important trend in Sung religious life involved the ever-increasing number of official titles (*feng-hao* 封號) awarded to all manner of local deities by the state. Sung dynasty worshippers attempted to ensure the continued existence of popular local deities by applying to the government for a title. The usual procedure involved the cult's leaders submitting a petition to the county magistrate, using the deity's miracles as evidence of its numinous efficacy (*ling* 靈). If, after careful investigation, the magistrate determined that there was cause to award a title, he would report to higher authorities who transmitted the petition to the Board of Rites, Imperial Secretariat, and Court of Imperial Sacrifices, which conducted their own investigations. Only after everything relating to a particular local cult had been meticulously examined could a title be awarded. The process of applying for an official title required great outlays of time, effort, and money, and if it backfired could even result in the suppression of the cult of the local god in question.[48] Many cults of the new deities described above were branded as "illicit cults" (*yin-tz'u* 淫祠) or "illicit sacrifices" (*yin-ssu* 淫祀),[49] and faced the threat of

---

[46] Hansen, *Changing Gods*, pp. 128–159.

[47] For a colorful and detailed description of one such festival, see Huang Chen (1213-1280), *Huang-shih jih-ch'ao*, 74:19a–34a, in *Wen-yüan Ko Ssu-k'u ch'üan-shu* (Taipei: Shang-wu yin-shu-kuan, 1983), volume 708, pp. 746–752.

[48] Hansen, *Changing Gods*, pp. 79–104.

[49] Scholars of Chinese religion disagree on how to translate these terms. Some researching Taoism, including Judith Boltz and Rolf Stein, tend to translate *yin* as "excessive". See for example Boltz, "Not by the Seal of Office Alone: New Weapons in the Battle with the Supernatural," in Ebrey and Gregory, eds., *Religion and Society in T'ang and Sung China*, p. 244. Most scholars researching popular religion however (including Valerie Hansen and Daniel Overmyer) prefer "licentious". See in particular Overmyer, "Attitudes Towards Popular Religion in Ritual Texts of the Chinese State: The Collected Statutes of the Great Ming," *CEA* 5, (1989–1990): 201; and Hansen, *Changing Gods*, pp. 84–86. Richard von Glahn prefers "profane" or "profligate", arguing in his

state persecution unless cult leaders could convince the authorities of the cult's legitimacy.[50]

In the case of Chekiang, a large body of Sung dynasty stele inscriptions documents the growth of local cults and the efforts of local leaders to gain state recognition for them. One excellent example involves the cult of the Six Dynasties official Lu Tsai 陸載 in Hu-chou. Lu had performed a number of miracles after his death, including protecting traveling merchants and sending spirit-soldiers to assist local strongmen in driving off bandits. Out of gratitude for his divine protection, the locals decided in early 1163 to apply for a title for Lu, which was duly awarded in the twelfth lunar month of that year. The inscription for Lu's Temple of Manifest Numinosity (Ling-hsien Miao 靈顯廟) reveals the importance of both gentry and elite support, as this work contains the names of seven *chin-shih* 進士 degree holders, as well as four local elders.[51]

One interesting feature of the titles awarded to local deities is that they often attempted to conceal the original demonic attributes of many such deities. Common titles for male deities included king (*wang* 王) or great king (*ta-wang* 大王), marshal, and general (*chiang-chün* 將軍). Female deities were often called mother (*niang-niang* 娘娘) or madam (*fu-jen* 夫人). Ming dynasty sources preserve an account attributed to the Sung dynasty poet Lu Yu (but not contained in his collected writings) entitled "A Record of Unofficial Temples" (*Yeh-miao chi* 野妙記), which describes such deities as follows:

> In the Ou-Yüeh 甌越 region (covering most of Chekiang province, especially the southeast coast), people devote themselves to worshipping the dead. On mountain tops and along river banks are many temples where illicit sacrifices are performed. Inside these temples [are all manner of deities]. Some are called "generals", with appearances firm and heroic, dark and resolute. Some are

---

review of Hansen's book that the translation of *yin* as licentious "adds an unwarranted moral dimension". See *HJAS* 53.2 (Dec. 1993): p. 624, note 21. I prefer the term "illicit" because most scholar-officials who used the word *yin* in describing local cults were usually less concerned with their moral aspects than the fact that they had not been approved by the government. I would only use "licentious" or "excessive" in translating the remarks of Taoist priests or other people who were clearly offended by what they viewed as immoral practices, particularly the presence of spirit-mediums and offerings of "bloody (=meat) sacrifices" (*hsüeh-shih* 血食).

[50] Kanai, "Sonsha to dōshin," pp. 83-86; Nakamura, "Sōdai no fū," p. 61.

[51] See Juan Yüan (1764–1849), *Liang-che chin-shih chih*, 9:33b-36a, 13:23a–27b, in *Shih-k'o shih-liao ts'ung-shu*, volumes 40–41 (Taipei: Yi-wen yin-shu-kuan, 1966). Hansen describes the growth of Lu's cult in *Changing Gods*, pp. 116–117 and 121–122.

called "masters" (*mou-lang* 某郎); they look warm and kind,
fair and youthful. Those who look like old women and
have a dignified appearance are called "matrons" (*lao* 姥),
while those of beautiful appearance are called "maidens"
(*ku* 姑). [These deities] inhabit humble old buildings,
covered with branches and vines in which owls make their
nests . . . The farmers fear [these deities] greatly: [in
sacrificing], at most they will brain an ox, or failing that
slaughter a pig; at the meanest, [their offerings] will not be
worse than a dog . . . To allow their families to want is
permissible, but to allow the gods to lack is never
permissible. If one day the worshippers become lazy and
neglect the sacrifices, calamities will surely follow. The
young and the old, the animals and the livestock, all live in
dread.[52]

The large numbers of new cults appearing on the scene led to
a divergence in the views of local officials and their clerical
subordinates in terms of how to deal with them, with clerk support
occasionally easing or even preventing official persecution of these
cults.[53] For example, one account preserved in the *I-chien chih* describes
a local official who wanted to imprison and beat a local spirit medium,
only to have his clerk attempt to persuade him to desist. Undaunted,
he had both of them flogged, only to find his face covered with huge
boils a few hours later. He summoned the clerk, and after tricking him
into revealing the location the medium's residence rode out there with
his troops, laying waste to the site and all sacred items within, thereby
overcoming the medium's magic powers. He later had the medium
executed by having him thrown in the river, most likely taking as his
precedent the story of Hsi-men Pao 西門豹 (a Warring States figure)
drowning the mediums who had once ordered maidens sacrificed to
the Earl of the Yellow River.[54] Other officials even attempted to deal

---

[52] See Chiang Chün (a native of Wenchow during the late Ming), *Ch'i-hai
so-t'an chi*, 12:1a. The links between these deities and the cults to various "generals",
"masters", and "ladies", which were frequently attacked by Six Dynasties Taoists, have
yet to be determined. See Rolf Stein, "Religious Taoism and Popular Religion from the
Second to Seventh Centuries," in Welch and Seidel, eds., *Facets of Taoism*, pp. 53–81.

[53] Wu Cheng-han sees this as signifying a restructuring of local authority in
Ming China; however, it appears that such a restructuring may have begun during the
Southern Sung. See Wu Cheng-han, "The Temple Fairs in Late Imperial China" (Ph.D.
thesis, Princeton University, 1988), pp. 93–97; and Brian E. McKnight, *Village and
Bureaucracy in Southern Sung China* (Chicago: University of Chicago Press, 1971), pp.
38–72, esp. pp. 51–66.

[54] See *ICC*, p. 532. The ancient custom was called "the Earl of the River takes a

with troublesome local cults by learning exorcistic techniques from Taoist priests or ritual masters.[55]

The rise and initial spread of Marshal Wen's cult in Chekiang during the Sung dynasty described in chapter 4 should be understood in light of the changes in local religious life described above. However, one important difference between Wen's cult and many of those described above is that it tended to thrive in cities or market towns, apparently failing to gain great popularity in rural parts of Chekiang.[56] Urban cult worship also seems to have undergone significant changes during the Sung, though not necessarily identical to those affecting rural cults. Southern Sung Hangchow became a veritable melting pot of local cults, with numerous new temples dedicated to deities popular among people from other parts of China, particularly the area in and around the former Northern Sung capital of Kaifeng. At the same time, however, other cults to popular deities such as Erh-lang 二郎 and Wen-ch'ang spread to Hangchow from western China (Szechwan), while cults to deities such as Marshal Wen and the Five Commissioners of Epidemics were transmitted to Hangchow from southern Chekiang and Fukien.[57] In the case of Wenchow, its coastal location and exposure to outside influences made it a focal point in the spread of Manichaeism and Tantric Buddhism to south China, the growth of southern drama (*nan-hsi* 南戲), and, of particular importance to this thesis, the development of new ritual movements like the Divine Empyrean (Shen-hsiao 神霄) movement described below.[58]

Contemporary sources also refer to a wide range of urban socio-religious organizations, some more secular in nature but most clearly featuring some form of religious activity. These included

wife" (*ho-po ch'u-fu* 河伯娶婦). For the story of Hsi-men Pao's suppression of this custom, see *Shih-chi*, *chüan* 126 (Peking: Chung-hua shu-chü, 1973), pp. 3211–3212. Burton Watson does not include this story in his translation of the *Shih-chi*.

[55] See Boltz, "Not by the Seal of Office Alone," pp. 254–272.

[56] For information on people worshipping Marshal Wen in rural areas of northern Chekiang, see Clarence Day, *Chinese Peasant Cults: Being a Study of Chinese Paper Gods* (Shanghai: Kelly and Walsh, Ltd., 1940), pp. 22, 24–25, 26–27.

[57] See *Che-chiang wen-hua shih*, p. 193.

[58] See Chou, *Wen-chou kang shih*, pp. 6–22; Lin, *Che-chiang ching-chi wen-hua shih*, pp. 47–48; and Yeh, *Wen-chou shih-hua*, pp. 37–42. On Manichaeism and its spread to Chekiang, see E. Chavannes and P. Pelliot, "Un Traite Manichéen Retrouvé en Chine," *Journal Asiatique* Series 11, Vol. 1 (March-April 1913): 99–391; and, Samuel N.C. Lieu, *Manichaeism in the Later Roman Empire and Medieval China* (Dover, N.H.: Manchester University Press, 1985), pp. 224–264. On southern drama, see Liu Nien-tz'u, *Nan-hsi hsin-cheng* (Peking: Chung-hua shu-chü, 1986), pp. 16-58; and, Colin Mackerras, *Chinese Theatre: From its Origins to the Present Day* (Honolulu: University of Hawaii Press, 1983), pp. 32–35.

poetry societies (*shih-she* 詩社), Buddhist societies for releasing living things (*fang-sheng she* 放生社), associations of gods and ghosts (*shen-kuei she* 神鬼社), associations of the Eight Immortals (*pa-hsien she* 八仙社), etc. Many of these organizations had clear links to local cults, and participated in festivals staged during the birthdays of popular deities. While the leaders of rural socio-religous organizations tended to be elders and landlords, the men in charge of such urban organizations usually included resident merchants, members of the urban elite, or traveling merchants from the cult's home region.[59]

The Divine Empyrean Movement: A Taoist Renaissance?

The religious changes taking place in Chekiang during the Sung dynasty were also marked by the emergence of new ritual movements whose priests performed rites combining elements of Taoism and local ritual traditions. One scholar, referring to the establishment of four such movements in Chekiang and other parts of south China — Divine Empyrean (Shen-hsiao), Ch'ing-wei 清微, T'ien-hsin cheng-fa 天心正法, and T'ung-ch'u 童初 — has even claimed that this period was marked by a "Taoist renaissance."[60] However, as I shall explain below, these new movements were not originally Taoist but represented local ritual traditions which interacted with or were absorbed into Taoism beginning in the Sung. Many of the rites performed by the ritual masters (*fa-shih* 法師) belonging to these movements in fact utilized possession techniques adopted from the practices of local mediums.[61] Such rituals, and the numerous local deities invoked by ritual masters in their exorcisms, seem barely

---

[59] For more on these organizations, see the following works in the *Tung-ching meng-hua lu, wai ssu-chung* (Shanghai: Ku-tien wen-hsüeh ch'u-pan-she, 1956): *Tu-ch'eng chi-sheng*, p. 98; *Hsi-hu lao-jen fan-sheng lu*, pp. 111, 113; *Meng-liang lu, chüan* 19, pp. 299–300; and, *Wu-lin chiu-shih, chüan* 3, pp. 377–378.

[60] See Michel Strickmann, "The Taoist Renaissance of the Twelfth Century." Paper presented at the Third International Conference on Taoist Studies. Unterageri, Switzerland, Sept. 3–9, 1979. For a description of these new Taoist movements, see Judith Boltz, *A Survey of Taoist Literature: Tenth to Seventeenth Centuries* (Berkeley: University of California Press, 1987), pp. 23–53.

[61] The Fukien Taoist Pai Yü-ch'an 白玉蟾 (fl. 1209–1224) clearly stated that some of the contemporary ritual techniques he knew of derived from those performed by spirit mediums; see *Hai-ch'iung Pai chen-jen yü-lu* (TT 1016; CT 1307:8b–9a). For more on Pai's life and career, see Judith Berling, "Channels of Connection in Southern Sung Religion: The Case of Pai Yü-ch'an," in Ebrey and Gregory, eds., *Religion and Society in T'ang and Sung China*, pp. 307-333.

distinguishable from the rites and deities often labeled "heterodox" or "licentious" by Taoist priests and some scholar-officials.[62]

In Chekiang, the most important of these new ritual movements was known as the Divine Empyrean (Shen-hsiao). This movement also played a key role in the initial growth of Marshal Wen's cult in Chekiang and other parts of south China during the Sung and Yüan dynasties. This is because Wen was an important deity in the Divine Empyrean pantheon, and many members of this movement helped transmit his cult throughout the region by performing rituals to him and erecting temples in his name (see chapters 3 and 4).

The most renowned member of the Divine Empyrean movement was Lin Ling-su 林靈素 (1076–1120), a native of Wenchow. Lin gained great influence at the court of the Sung emperor Hui-tsung (r. 1101–1125) by convincing the emperor that he (Hui-tsung) was the terrestrial incarnation of the movement's main deity, the Grand Sovereign of Long Life (Ch'ang-sheng ta-ti 長生大帝). The Hui-tsung emperor's devotion to the Divine Empyrean movement prompted him to issue an imperial decree stating that all Taoist (and many Buddhist) temples and monasteries be placed under the control of Divine Empyrean personnel, although the extent to which this was enforced remains unclear. Lin's influence at court did not last long, however, and he subsequently returned to his home in Wenchow. However, other members of the movement, such as Wang Wen-ch'ing 王文卿 (1093–1153) and Mo Yüeh-ting 莫月鼎 (1223–1291), actively recruited new members and spread its teachings, enabling it to become one of the most influential ritual movements of the Southern Sung dynasty. The Divine Empyrean movement was eventually absorbed into Heavenly Master Taoism, most likely after Khubilai Khan granted the Heavenly Masters control over all "Taoist" movements in south China in 1273, just before his final conquest of the region.[63]

---

[62] See Matsumoto Koichi, "Chō Tenshi to NanSō no Dōkyō," in *Rekishi ni okeru minshū to bunka* [Tadao Sakai Festschrift] (Tokyo: Kokushō Kankokai, 1982), pp. 337–350, esp. pp. 346–348.

[63] The most thorough study of the Divine Empyrean movement remains Michel Strickmann's "Sōdai no raigi: Shinshō undō to Dōka nanshū ni tsuite no ryakusetu," *Tōhō shūkyō* 46 (1975): 15–28. Strickmann describes this movement's rise to prominence at the Sung court in his "The Longest Taoist Scripture," *HR* 17.3/4 (Feb.– May 1978): 331–354. See also Sun K'o-k'uan, *Sung-Yüan Tao-chiao chih fa-chan* (Taichung: Tung-hai University, 1965), pp. 93–122; and Jen Chi-yü, *Chung-kuo Tao-chiao shih* (Shanghai: Shang-hai jen-min ch'u-pan-she, 1990), pp. 434–488. For more on the spread of the Divine Empyrean movement during the Southern Sung and Yüan dynasties, see Ch'en Ping, "Yüan-tai Chiang-nan Tao-chiao," *Shih-chieh tsung-chiao yen-chiu* 2 (1986): 69–70.

New ritual movements like the Divine Empyrean were characterized by their members' skill in performing all manner of exorcistic rituals, often featuring a wide range of "thunder techniques" (*lei-fa* 雷法).[64] Divine Empyrean priests practiced many such techniques, while also invoking a host of martial deities like Marshal Wen to exorcise demons. In particular, Divine Empyrean liturgies that featured Marshal Wen expelling plague demons by means of a boat-burning rite proved influential in stimulating the growth of Wen's cult. Similar rituals continue to be performed today in parts of south China and Taiwan, albeit usually by Heavenly Master priests (see chapter 5).[65]

At the same time however, ritual movements like the Divine Empyrean also drew on the liturgical tradition of religious Taoism. For example, the opening mythic sequence of the Divine Empyrean scripture *Kao-shang shen-hsiao tsung-shih shou-ching shih* 高上神霄 宗師受經詩 (*TT* 1005, *CT* 1282) appears to have been inspired by the medieval rituals of Shang-ch'ing 上清 and Ling-pao 靈寶 Taoism. In addition, the opening text of the *Taoist Canon*, a Divine Emyrean work entitled *Ling-pao wu-liang tu-jen shang-p'in miao-ching* 靈寶無量 度上品妙經, is headed by the venerable Ling-pao scripture known as the *Tu-jen ching* 度人經, followed by an additional sixty *chüan* of ritual recastings of this scripture done by members of the Divine Empyrean movement.[66]

Another striking feature of these new ritual movements was their emphasis on orthodoxy and orthopraxy, something they shared in common with many Taoist movements.[67] The liturgical texts of these new movements, many of which are preserved in the Yüan dynasty ritual compendium *Tao-fa hui-yüan* (*TFHY*) (*TT* 884–941; *CT* 1220),[68] contain numerous exhortations to "support the orthodox and expel the heterodox" (*fu-cheng ch'u-hsieh* 扶正除邪), "eradicate evil and heterodoxy" (*chan-mieh yao-hsieh* 斬滅妖邪), etc. Many texts also

---

[64] For more on these techniques, see Boltz, "Not by the Seal of Office Alone", pp. 272–286.

[65] I discuss the history and spread of Divine Empyrean boat-burning rituals in greater detail in Katz, "Rite of Passage or Rite of Affliction? A Preliminary Analysis of the Pacification of Plagues," *Min-su ch'ü-yi*, 92 (Nov. 1994): 1013–1092.

[66] Boltz, *Survey*, pp. 26–27.

[67] See Stein, "Religious Taoism and Popular Religion". A similar trend was also occuring in contemporary Confucian circles; see James T.C. Liu, *China Turning Inward: Intellectual-Political Changes in the Early Twelfth Century* (Cambridge, Mass.: Harvard University Press, 1988), esp. pp. 55–80 and 131–150.

[68] For more data on this work, see Piet van der Loon, "A Taoist Collection of the Fourteenth Century," in *Studia Sino-Mongolica: Festschrift fur Herbert Franke* (Wiesbaden: Franz Steiner Verlag, GMBH, 1979), pp. 401–405.

feature heavenly codes (*t'ien-lü* 天律) listing punishments to be meted out to religious specialists and deities who defy orthodox principles.[69] As we shall see in chapter 3, the author of Marshal Wen's 1274 hagiography in the *Taoist Canon*, a Divine Empyrean priest named Huang Kung-chin 黃公瑾, ardently advocated orthodoxy and orthopraxy.

Perhaps one can best understand this obsession with orthodoxy and orthopraxy by considering the predicament in which members of these new ritual movements found themselves. On the one hand they were practicing rituals drawn from local cultic traditions, yet at the same time they wanted to avoid being equated with local cults which had been labeled "heterodox" or "illicit," as that would have spelled doom for their movements. In attempting to gain favor with the court, or at least avoid suppression, these men supported the state in attacking suspect local cults, thereby attempting to align themselves alongside the government in its attempts to control them. The state may have accepted such support because doing so gave it a better chance of controlling these new ritual movements, or even of using them to watch over potentially troublesome local cults, no mean concern at a time when the Mandate of Heaven was threatened by foreign armies and internal chaos.[70] Some local officials proved willing to receive training in some of the rituals of these new movements, even becoming ritual masters themselves, in order to maintain their authority over local cults.[71]

Should the Divine Empyrean movement as it existed before its absorption into Heavenly Master Taoism be considered "Taoist" or as a part of a "Taoist renaissance" occurring during the Sung dynasty? Divine Empyrean specialists do not appear to have been ordained as Taoist priests, nor did they worship the First Heavenly Master Chang Tao-ling 張道陵 as their movement's patriarch. In addition, the deities invoked in Divine Empyrean liturgical texts bear little resemblance to those worshipped by the Heavenly Masters, even though such texts are preserved in the *Taoist Canon* and may have undergone some editing by members of the Heavenly Master movement during the

---

[69] For example, earth gods who inflicted calamities in order to extort offerings would have their spiritual forms dismembered (*fen-hsing* 分形; see THFY, *chüan* 251–252 and 267).

[70] See Strickmann, "Sōdai no raigi," pp. 24–25; and, Matsumoto, "Chō Tenshi," pp. 345–347. Terry Kleeman has shown that many religious works composed during the Southern Sung expressed concern with the threat of invasion, as well as what he describes as "Sinocentrism". See *A God's Own Tale. The Book of Transformations of Wenchang, the Divine Lord of Zitong* (Albany: SUNY Press, 1994), pp. 70, 72–73.

[71] Boltz, "Not by the Seal of Office Alone," pp. 244–272.

Ming (see below). It is true that members of this movement were not simply religious innovators but also drew on established Taoist traditions, but this appears to have been an attempt to establish the movement's prestige and legitimacy in the eyes of the state and perhaps other religious movements as well. While some ritual movements such as the Ch'ing-wei and T'ien-hsin cheng-fa quickly accepted the supremacy of the Heavenly Masters, the Divine Empyrean movement appears to have stubbornly retained its own traditions for over a century, worshipping different deities, practicing different rituals, and maintaining a different organizational structure.

Based on the evidence presented above, I prefer to treat the Divine Empyrean movement as a *local* ritual tradition which was later influenced by Taoism and finally absorbed into the Heavenly Master movement during the Yüan dynasty. While the exact dates when all this occurred remain in doubt, I would argue that the Divine Empyrean movement should only be considered to be Taoist after its absorption. By the time Huang Kung-chin composed his hagiography of Marshal Wen (in 1274, just prior to the formed establishment of the Yüan dynasty), the Divine Empyrean movement had clearly become deeply influenced by Heavenly Master Taoism, to the point where Huang showed great reverence towards Sung dynasty Heavenly Masters. For these reasons, I consider Huang's hagiography of Marshal Wen to generally reflect a Taoist viewpoint.

The question of whether one should define as "Taoist" ritual movements which developed out of local traditions has been a constant thorn in the sides of scholars researching Taoism; most have yet to make up their minds on this complicated issue. For example, Kristofer Schipper treats ritual masters on Taiwan as belonging to Taoism, albeit occupying "the lowest rank in the Taoist hierarchy."[72] At the same time however, Schipper clearly states that only Taoist priests (*tao-shih* 道士; which he alternately translates as "Taoist masters" or "Dignitaries of the Tao") may be regarded as "the true Taoist masters."[73] Regarding the Taoist pantheon, he states that it should be viewed as "abstract," and its prayers "impersonal."[74] However, such a generalization will unfortunately not hold if Schipper and other scholars researching Taoism choose to define as "Taoist" members of

---

[72] See Kristofer Schipper, *The Taoist Body*, Karen C. Duval trans. (Berkeley: University of California Press, 1993 [1982]), p. 50. See also his "Vernacular and Classical Ritual in Taiwan," *JAS* 45 (1985), 21–57.

[73] Schipper, *Taoist Body*, p. 55.

[74] See his "Taoist Ritual and Local Cults of the T'ang Dynasty," in Michel Strickmann, ed., *Tantric and Taoist Studies in Honor of Rolf A. Stein* (Brussels: Institut Belge des Hautes Études Chinoises, 1985), volume 3, p. 831.

the ritual movements mentioned above, or Lü-shan 閭山 specialists in Fukien and Taiwan commonly referred to as "red-headed ritual masters" (*hung-t'ou fa-shih* 紅頭法師). This is because the rituals such specialists perform feature numerous deities who are neither abstract nor impersonal, but historical or quasi-historical figures worshipped throughout parts of south China and Taiwan.[75]

Other scholars, such as Ken Dean, also fail to be consistent in terms of whether ritual masters should be defined as Taoists. In his path-breaking new book on Taoist ritual and local cults in Fukien, Dean opens his discussion of Taoist specialists in that province by claiming that: "With the exception of some Ch'üan-chen (Perfect Realization) monastic centers in northern Fukien . . . Taoists in Fukien have always been Cheng-yi 正一 (Orthodox Unity) Taoists, otherwise known as T'ien-shih 天師 (Celestial Master or Heavenly Master) Taoists."[76] However, his account of the distribution of "Taoist traditions" in Fukien also includes the Ch'ing-wei and Lü-shan traditions, and he also refers to one religious practitioner as a "Taoist Ritual Master."[77]

In order to clear up this confusion, it might be best to adhere to the definitions of Taoism proposed by scholars such as Nathan Sivin and Michel Strickmann, who argue that it would be best to define as "Taoist" only those religious movements whose members worship Chang Tao-ling as their patriarch (or one of their patriarchs), or at least view him as one of Taoism's founders.[78] Even this view is somewhat problematic though, as Judith Boltz has shown that in some cases recognition of Chang Tao-ling may have been just an afterthought, or the result of Heavenly Master Taoists tampering with other movements' scriptures before including them in the Ming edition of the *Taoist Canon*.[79] Nevertheless, this tentative definition of Taoism allows us to include not only the Heavenly Master movement

---

[75] For a detailed description of the Lü-shan movement, including its deities and rituals, see Brigitte Baptandier-Berthier, *La Dame du Bord de l'Eau* (Nanterre, Paris: Société d'Ethnologie, 1988); and, "The Kaiguan 開關 Ritual and the Construction of the Child's Identity," in *Proceedings of the International Conference on Popular Beliefs and Chinese Culture* (Taipei: Center for Chinese Studies, 1994), volume II, pp. 523–586.

[76] Ken Dean, *Taoist Ritual and Popular Cults of Southeast China* (Princeton: Princeton University Press, 1993), p. 24. See also my review of this book in *Hsin shih-hsüeh* 新史學 (*New History*) 5.3 (Sept. 1994): 165–176.

[77] *Ibid.*, pp. 42 and 123.

[78] See Nathan Sivin, "On the Word 'Taoist' as a Source of Perplexity. With Special Reference to the Relations of Science and Religion in Traditional China," *HR* 17.3–4 (Feb.–May 1978): 306; and, Michel Strickmann, "On the Alchemy of T'ao Hung-ching," in Welch and Seidel, eds., *Facets of Taosim*, pp. 164–167.

[79] Boltz, *Survey*, p. 17.

itself, but also movements such as the Ch'ing-wei or T'ien-hsin cheng-fa, which subsequently adopted Chang Tao-ling as their patriarch. Such a definition can also encompass movements such as the Divine Empyrean, but only after it became absorbed into Heavenly Master Taoism. The Lü-shan movement, or the above-mentioned movements before their absorption into Heavenly Master Taoism, are best considered not Taoist but systematizations or elaborations of local ritual traditions.

How does the rise of Marshal Wen's cult during the Sung dynasty relate to the data presented above? As we shall see in chapters 3 and 4, he represented a new type of deity whose cult may be seen as one example of the religious changes occurring in Chekiang and other parts of south China during the Sung. In addition to this, the people who promoted his cult, members of the Divine Empyrean movement as well as up-and-coming members of the gentry and elite classes, were all important actors in the religious and socioeconomic events affecting the province. However, before describing the growth of Wen's cult in detail, I must first explore one other important phenomenon which directly and immediately contributed to the rise and continuing popularity of Wen's cult: the epidemics which periodically ravaged the province.

TWO

Epidemics and Responses to Them[1]

Mauve rivers and green mountains mean nothing,
When the famed doctor Hua T'o 華佗 failed to conquer a little
    worm.[2]
Thousand of villages fell in ruin, overgrown with weeds; men were
    lost arrows.
Ghosts howled in the doorways of those empty homes.

—Mao Tse-tung, "Sending off the Plague
Gods" (Sung Wen-shen 送瘟神).[3]

The Historical Impact

It is very difficult to fully ascertain the effects of epidemics on
Chekiang's history because of the limitations of the source materials
available. For one thing, most accounts in dynastic histories or local
gazetteers fail to use precise medical terminology or give a description
of each disease's symptoms.[4] In addition, Chinese historical writings
tend to record epidemics in a manner which emphasizes the role they
play in the dynastic cycle, and when local officials reported

---

[1] For an overview of the history of epidemics in China, see Ch'en Sheng-k'un,
Chung-kuo chi-ping shih (Taipei: Tzu-jan k'o-hsüeh ch'u-pan-she, 1981); and Fan
Hsing-chün, *Chung-kuo ping-shih hsin-yi* (Peking: Chung-yi ku-chi ch'u-pan-she, 1987),
pp. 263–316.

[2] An allusion to the blood fluke (*Schistosoma japonicum*) that causes
schistosomiasis.

[3] My translation is based on Willis Barnstone's and Ko Ching-po's translation
in *The Poems of Mao Tse-tung* (New York: Harper and Row, 1972), pp. 91–93.

[4] For problems associated with identifying epidemics, see Denis Twitchett,
"Population and Pestilence in T'ang China," in *Studia Sino-Mongolica*, p. 40; Helen
Dunstan, "The Late Ming Epidemics: A Preliminary Survey," *CSWT*, 3.3 (Nov. 1975):
18–28; and, Fan Hsing-chün, *Chung-kuo yi-hsüeh shih-lüeh* (Peking: Chung-yi ku-chi
ch'u-pan-she, 1986), pp. 162–164, 241–250.

39

occurrences of epidemics to the throne their motives were often to protect themselves from accusations of wrongdoing or incompetence, petition the court for relief, and gain permission to cancel obligations for labor services as well as remit taxes.[5] Finally, most sources almost certainly underreport the incidence of epidemics, often supplying the most data for capital cities.[6] Despite these drawbacks however, we still have ample evidence that Chekiang suffered from frequent outbreaks of epidemics, particularly during times of unrest, when vast numbers of people were on the move.

In considering the history of disease in Chekiang, it is also important to distinguish between diseases that were pandemic (occurring over a wide area and afflicting a high proportion of the populace), epidemic (afflicting many individuals within a community during a brief time span), and endemic (restricted to a particular region over an extended period of time). Pandemics and epidemics appear to have been relatively infrequent, the sources available indicating that they usually accompanied wars, famines, and other calamities, when masses of refugees poured into unfamiliar territory or when the natives of a region were in poor physical condition. Endemic diseases like smallpox and schistosomiasis were always present but apparently less fatal, inasmuch as the natives of a particular region had already built up a degree of resistance to the microparasites in their environment. These diseases struck at regular intervals but only claimed the weaker members of a community like the elderly and children. However, they could become epidemics when other calamities weakened the populace's resistance, when certain microparasites became more virulent, and when the weather caused some microparasites to flourish in larger numbers than usual. Under such circumstances, people could die of diseases so terrifying that they inspired worship of plague spirits yet not devastating enough to merit mention in a local gazetteer.

In his inspirational work entitled *Plagues and Peoples*, William H. McNeill utilized research done by epidemiologists and other scientists to explore how natural forces have influenced world history.

---

[5] See Hans Bielenstein, "An Interpretation of Portents in the *Ts'ien-han-shu* (*Ch'ien Han-shu* 前漢書)," *Bulletin of the Museum of Far Eastern Antiquities* 22 (1950): 127–143.

[6] One can often thumb through three or four pages of the "Treatise on Disasters and Anomalies" (*Tsai-yi chih* 災異志) of any Chekiang gazetteer before coming across one account of an epidemic. One reason for this is that epidemics often occurred in tandem with other disasters (especially famine) that weakened people's resistance to disease. It might be best to assume that epidemics were also present during times of numerous or particularly severe calamities (known in Chinese as "years when many things happened" [*ta-yu nien* 大有年]).

According to his work, while human beings act as "macroparasites" in consuming all manner of plants and animals, they also become the "food" of "microparasites" (germs) which infest their bodies, including those organisms that cause contagious diseases.[7] While most people can usually coexist with the microorganisms around them, a number of situations may arise which can disrupt this balance and cause large numbers of people to suddenly become infected by a particular microparasite. These include: 1) People migrating to another region becoming exposed to new microorganisms; 2) People indigenous to a region becoming infected by migrants carrying microorganisms the former have never been exposed to; and 3) Other natural disasters like flood and famine weakening people's resistance to microorganisms they could normally coexist with.[8]

Because the appearance of Marshal Wen's cult in Chekiang during the Southern Sung dynasty was in large part a result of Wen's ability to combat epidemics, I will place special emphasis on what we know of that dynasty's disease history. However, inasmuch as the continued growth of Wen's cult and festivals during the late imperial period also resulted in part from his continuing popularity throughout the province as a deity who protected against contagious diseases, I will also briefly explore the history of epidemics for that era as well.

The earliest recorded epidemics to afflict Chekiang disrupted attempts by Han Chinese from north China to settle in the south. Those who braved the dangers involved were painfully aware of what lay in store. The sources for that era describe the climate in the regions south of the Yangtze (known as Chiang-nan 江南) as being damp and humid, and warn that those who venture there will die young. Some also describe rivers full of plague-belching monsters like the Yü 蜮, which infected unsuspecting travelers by shooting them with poisonous pellets.[9] The first reports of epidemics in Chekiang occur in the "Treatise on the Five Phases" (*Wu-hsing chih* 五行志) of the *History of the Later Han* (*Hou Han shu*), which describes a series of outbreaks afflicting Kuei-chi (modern-day Shaohsing) in the years 37, 38 and 50 C.E.. Another epidemic ravaged Kuei-chi in 119, prompting the court to send medical supplies and wood for coffins to afflicted areas.

During the latter years of the T'ang dynasty, contagious diseases carried by foreign traders operating along the southeast

---

[7] See McNeill's introduction to *Plagues and Peoples* (New York: Anchor Books, 1976), pp. 5–13.

[8] *Ibid.*, pp. 31–68, 179–189.

[9] See Schafer, *The Vermillion Bird*, pp. 130–134, for a discussion of the impact of epidemics on the colonization of south China. This problem is also discussed in McNeill, *Plagues and Peoples*, pp. 75–80, 117–120.

China coast had a devastating impact on the province. More than half the population is said to have died from a series of epidemics which struck the Chiang-tung region (encompassing Kiangsu south of the Yangtze, Fukien, and Chekiang) in 762, while an epidemic that roared through eastern Chekiang in 806 also wiped out a large percentage of the populace. Other outbreaks in 832, 840, and 869 had less devastating but still fearful effects, especially in coastal cities like Ningpo and Wenchow. By the end of the ninth century the registered population of the former city had declined to less than ten percent of its 742 level. These unidentified epidemics continued to spread along trade routes as far north as Japan and Korea.[10]

An even more devastating series of epidemics ravaged Chekiang and its neighboring provinces during the Southern Sung. Twenty-seven major epidemics were recorded throughout the Southern Sung emperors' 150-year reign, with fifteen breaking out in Chekiang, thirteen of which struck Hangchow (again, we see that the sources tend to overreport incidence of epidemics in the capital). These epidemics appear to have in part been caused by the presence of large numbers of refugees fleeing the Jurchen invaders of north China, and later the constant warfare between Jurchen and Southern Sung forces which lasted until the 1160s.[11] Because these northern Chinese had not built up significant resistance to southern microparasites, their numbers were often decimated by disease after they moved south. They also carried diseases which the natives of Chekiang had not been exposed to, further aggravating the epidemiological crisis. According to one passage in the *History of the Sung (Sung shih)*:

> During the sixth month of the year 1131 there was a great epidemic in western Chekiang . . . The autumn and winter months also marked the start of a series of epidemics which ravaged Shaohsing Prefecture. The local officials recruited people to help feed gruel and administer medicines to the sick. Those who saved up to one hundred lives were allowed to become monks or nuns.[12]

Another account records that:

---

[10] See Twitchett, "Population and Pestilence," pp. 46–58.

[11] For an account of a religious specialist named Wang Kuang-ming 王光明 who cured soldiers suffering from an epidemic in south China, see *Sung shih, chüan* 462 (Peking: Chung-hua shu-chü, 1977), pp. 13530–13531.

[12] *Ibid., chüan* 62, p. 1370.

In the winter of 1164, between 200,000 and 300,000 refugees from the Huai River area fled the chaos there to the Chiang-nan region, building straw huts along the mountain valleys. Their exposure to the wet and cold caused extreme suffering, while epidemics claimed over half their lives . . . That year, many people in Chekiang suffering from famines were also afflicted by epidemics.[13]

The years 1195–1211 must have been especially terrifying for the people of Chekiang, as nine epidemics ravaged the province during that brief sixteen-year period. According to the *History of the Sung*, a major epidemic struck Hangchow in 1196, prompting the court to distribute free medicines to the poor and arrange for the burial of those who died.[14] These epidemics seem to have made a deep impression on Hung Mai (a native of Kiangsi), as his *I-chien chih* contains numerous stories of supernatural events related to the diseases which raged throughout southern China during those dark years. These include the story of the snake woman presented above, as well as an account of a virtuous citizen in Chia-hsing who worked with doctors to cure the sick through a combination of administering medicines and chanting Buddhist spells.[15]

The evidence in chapter 4 indicates that Marshal Wen's earliest temples in P'ing-yang and Hangchow were built during the epidemics mentioned above or shortly after they had abated. It is not surprising that Marshal Wen's cult arose during a time of rampant epidemics, as he specialized in controlling the diseases so many people feared. In fact, some sources explicitly state that his cult spread from Wenchow to Hangchow because the people of Hangchow invited Wen to come north and stop an epidemic (see chapter 4). People continued to worship Marshal Wen as a plague-fighting deity during later dynasties as well. Taoist liturgical texts, including works in the *Taoist Canon* and non-canonical liturgies in the possession of late imperial and modern Taoist priests, indicate that he continued to be invoked by religious specialists during epidemics. In addition, large-scale festivals featuring Wen in a plague-expelling role became an important part of the ritual calendar in many of Chekiang's major urban centers (see chapter 5).

The cult of Marshal Wen experienced a second period of growth during the early years of the Ch'ing dynasty, perhaps in part

---

[13] *Ibid.*.

[14] *Ibid.*, *chüan* 37, p. 719.

[15] ICC, pp. 892, 1044, 1074–1075, 1079, 1399, 1454, 1777–1778.

due to the devastation caused by epidemics during the late Ming. Many regions of China suffered from a series of epidemics during that time, calamities which played an important role in that dynasty's collapse. Some outbreaks have been identified as bubonic plague, dysentery, and typhus, but most simply had graphic names like "Big Head Fever" (*Ta-t'ou wen* 大頭瘟) or "Peep Sickness" (*T'an-t'ou ping* 探頭病) that do little in helping the historian define them. The natives of Chekiang and Kiangsu suffered from an epidemic called "Sheep's Wool Fever" (*Yang-mao wen* 羊毛瘟), so named because the afflicted were said to have sheep's wool on their bodies![16]

The late Ming epidemics occurred in tandem with other calamities, particularly drought and famine, the warfare of the 1640s serving to aggravate already miserable conditions. A passage in the 1687 edition of the *Jen-ho hsien-chih* states:

> In the year 1644, at the time of the Dragon Boat Festival, people heard a series of confusing reports that the invading armies [of the Manchus] had already reached Nanking. All the citizens [living in and around Hangchow] feared the soldiers like tigers, fleeing the city with their wives and children, as well as everything else they could carry. Some crossed the rivers and fled south; others hid in the remote mountains. Theirs was a bitter route, and in the heat and humidity of summer many suffered from cholera (*huo-luan* 霍亂) and malaria (*nueh-chi* 瘧疾)."[17]

A number of detailed accounts portray the horrific conditions in Chekiang during the 1640s, including the diary of Ch'i Piao-chia (1602–1645)[18] entitled *Ch'i Chung-min Kung jih-chi*, which chronicles epidemics in Shaohsing, and the *Tsai-huang chi-shih* 災荒記事 by Ch'en Ch'i-te 陳其德, which describes epidemics in Chia-hsing (see below).

Marshal Wen's cult continued to be popular well into the late nineteenth century in part because people worshipped him to check the spread of epidemics occurring during that time. A series of cholera

---

[16] See Dunstan, "Late Ming Epidemics," pp. 17–27; Elvin, *Pattern*, pp. 310–311. For an account of the devastation these diseases wrought in Chekiang, see Lin Chih-han (a native of Wu-ch'eng in Hu-chou during the K'ang-hsi reign), *Wen-yi ts'ui-yen* (Shanghai: K'o-hsüeh chi-shu ch'u-pan-she, 1989), pp. 89–109, 137–145.

[17] *JHHC* (1687), 27:35a-b. Although I have translated the terms *nüeh-chi* and *huo-luan* as malaria and cholera respectively, I do not assume that Chinese classifications of these diseases corresponded to past or present Western nosology.

[18] For biographical information on Ch'i, see *DMB*, pp. 218–219; and, *ECCP*, p. 126.

epidemics ravaged Chekiang during the 1820s, and like the outbreaks of the late T'ang, caused the greatest loss of life in the province's coastal cities. This time, the bearers of the disease were most likely traders and sailors from India and other nations of the Near East. From 1820 to 1822, cholera spread from Wenchow and Ningpo inland to market towns in the northern plains sub-region, persisting throughout these areas into the 1880s. Customs Medical Reports give a vivid picture of the effects of these epidemics in coastal regions, and these are supplemented by accounts in late Ch'ing sources.[19]

The Human Impact

It is difficult for the modern scholar to adequately fathom the devastating effects epidemics could have on a traditional society like China's, even with relatively recent memories of the post-World War I influenza epidemics and the graphic images of the cholera and dysentery epidemics in Rwanda and Zaire. During a serious outbreak, people watched helplessly as their loved ones died horrible and painful deaths, their bodies frequently being heaved into mass graves without benefit of proper mourning rituals. Epidemics were particularly terrifying because large numbers of people died of attacks by an invisible force. During droughts or floods, the cause of death could be visualized and readily understood, but death from contagious disease seemed inexplicable.

To understand the impact epidemic could have on the people of Chekiang, consider this vivid account by Ch'en Ch'i-te of an epidemic which struck T'ung-hsiang county in 1641:

> pestilence and diarrhea broke out together, and there were cases in which out of ten households five or six were consigned to their coffins. I do not know how many lacked coffins to which they might be consigned and, their

---

[19] For information on nineteenth-century epidemics in Chekiang, see Yü Yüeh (1821–1906), *Yu-t'ai hsien-kuan pi-chi* (1888), *chüan* 4, 11, 12 and 16. An overview of the nineteenth century cholera epidemics may be found in Imura Kozen, "Chihōshi ni kisaiseraretaru Shina ekirei ryakko," *Chūgai iji shimpo* (1936), part 3, pp. 30–39. On bubonic plague, see Carol Benedict, "Bubonic Plague in Nineteenth Century China," *Modern China* 14.2 (April 1988): 107–155; and, "Policing the Sick: Plague and the Origins of State Medicine in Late Imperial China," *Late Imperial China* 14.2 (Dec. 1993), 60–77. Benedict's forthcoming book, based on her 1992 dissertation, should shed even further light on these topics.

mourners but bluebottles, their graves but weeds and
rushes, were abandoned to the ever-flowing stream.[20]

Conditions became even worse during the summer of 1642.
According to Ch'en, nine out of every ten households were affected,
with no people being spared even in households having as many as
twenty members. At first, the dead were buried in coffins, and later,
wrapped up in bundles of grass. By the time the epidemic had reached
its peak, however, the bodies were simply left on their beds. Ch'en
claims that worms could be seen crawling in and out of numerous
houses, and that people dared not enter. The situation could only be
remedied by digging mass graves for between fifty and seventy
corpses. In a few months, nearly sixty such graves had been dug.[21]
    Under such horrific conditions, people sought a solution
through a number of different measures, including state or private
relief, traditional medical techniques, or a variety of ritual actions.

Relief Efforts

The Chinese state did what it could to provide succor to its subjects
during epidemics, and there are records of officials being sent to
afflicted areas to distribute free medicine as early as the Han dynasty.
Charitable infirmaries or sick wards were sponsored by Buddhist
monasteries up to the T'ang dynasty; however, the state assumed
control of these institutions following the Hui-ch'ang 會昌 persecution
of Buddhism in 845. Infirmaries called Peace and Relief Wards (An-chi
Fang 安濟坊) were established in China's major urban centers as part
of a national welfare program designed by the minister Ts'ai Ching
蔡京 (1046–1126) in 1102. These wards may have been modeled on the
Peace and Happiness Ward (An-lo Fang 安樂坊) established by Su
Shih (Tung-p'o) (1036–1101) in Hangchow in 1089, using 50 *taels* of his
own funds, as a response to the famine and epidemic of 1075–1076,
which reportedly killed 500,000 people in and around the city. The
government also promoted the establishment of charitable pharmacies
(*hui-min yao-chü* 惠民藥局), and these institutions could occasionally
be effective in saving lives. However, they were also targets of abuse
by corrupt officials, who shamelessly misappropriated medicines
meant for people in need.[22]

---

[20] See Dunstan, "Late Ming Epidemics," p. 17. The Chinese text may be found in
the *THHC* (1887), 20:8b–9a.

[21] *Ibid.*, p. 29. The Chinese text is in the *THHC* (1887), 20:9b–10a.

[22] See Angela Ki Che Leung, "Organized Medicine in Ming-Qing China: State

The Yüan dynasty proved particularly active in promoting the state's role in medical care, establishing the Supervisorate of Physicians (Kuan-yi t'i-chü-ssu 官醫提舉司) to regulate medical practitioners, and the Supervisorate of Medical Relief (Kuang-chi t'i-chü-ssu 廣濟提舉司) to oversee charitable pharmacies. Doctors also enjoyed higher official status than at any other time. In the realm of religion, the Yüan dynasty established Temples of the Three Emperors (San-huang Miao 三皇廟), where sages learned in medicine such as the legendary Yellow Emperor (Huang Ti 黃帝), Fu-hsi 伏義, and Shen-nung 神農 were worshipped.[23]

By the middle of the sixteenth century however, many of the institutions mentioned above had entered a period of decline, particularly the charitable pharmacies and the Temples of the Three Emperors. While the government continued to supply relief during times of calamities throughout the late imperial era,[24] local gentry and rich merchants assumed an increasing share of the burden. One of the first private charitable pharmacies was the Society for Broadening Benevolence (Kuang-jen Hui 廣仁會), founded by the Ming intellectual Yang Tung-ming 楊東明 (1548–1624; biography in *DMB*, pp. 1546–1547) in his home town of Yü-ch'eng in Honan. Other scholars such as Ch'i Piao-chia, Ch'en Lung-cheng 陳龍正 (1585–1645; *DMB*, pp. 174–176) and Kao P'an-lung 高攀龍 (1562–1626; *DMB*, pp. 700–710) also set up charitable institutions for the sick. During the early Ch'ing, two Yangchow commoners (perhaps salt merchants?) named Wang Tsao 王藻 and Chang Yang 張陽 established a dispensary in that city. Such efforts continued throughout the Ch'ing.[25]

---

and Private Medical Institutions in the Lower Yangzi Region," *Late Imperial China* 8.1 (June 1987): 135–137. I would like to thank Angela Leung for her help in directing me to useful materials while I was researching this part of the thesis. An overview of Sung relief efforts may be found in Wang Te-yi, *Sung-tai tsai-huang te chiu-chi cheng-ts'e* (Taipei: Chung-kuo hsüeh-shu chiang-chu wei-yüan-hui, 1970). See also James T.C. Liu, "Liu Tsai (1165–1238): His Philanthropy and Neo-Confucian Limitations," *Oriens Extremis* 25 (1978): 1–29; Hugh Scogin, "Poor Relief in Northern Sung China," *Oriens Extremis* 25 (1978): 30–46; and, Gernet, *Daily Life*, p. 68.

[23] See Robert Hymes, "Not Quite Gentlemen? Doctors in Sung and Yüan," *Chinese Science* 8 (1987): 9–76.

[24] See *Kuo-hsüeh pei-ts'uan*, *chüan* 21, pp. 8507–8598, as well as Chu Hsiung, *Chiu-huang huo-min pu-yi shu* (1443); Liu Shih-chiao, *Huang chu lüeh* (1608); and Yü Ju-wei, *Huang-cheng yao-lan* (1589). For an overview of relief efforts during the Ch'ing, see Pierre-Etienne Will, *Bureaucracy and Famine in Eighteenth-century China*, trans. Elborg Foster (Stanford: Stanford University Press, 1990); and Pierre-Etienne Will and R. Bin Wong, et. al., *Nourish the People. The State Granary System in China, 1650–1850* (Ann Arbor: University of Michigan Press, 1991).

[25] See Leung, "Organized Medicine," pp. 139–150; Joanna F. Handlin-Smith, "Benevolent Societies: The Reshaping of Charity During the Late Ming and Early

We know little about the actual prescriptions dispensed at these pharmacies, but it appears that they were only rarely based on the *shang-han* 傷寒 (Injurious Colds) and *wen-ping* 溫病 (Febrile Diseases) theories popular among many late imperial physicians.[26] Far more common were the prescriptions (often written in verse for easy memorization) found in almanacs and popular medical tracts. During epidemics, such prescriptions sometimes were posted outside for all to see; some are still reprinted and distributed free in Taiwan as an act of merit.[27] Even when medicine provided an effective cure, it was rarely utilized on a mass scale. Variolation (inoculation) against smallpox had been practiced in China since the Northern Sung, but never became widespread. Why this technological advance was not more fully taken advantage of remains one of the great mysteries of Chinese history of science.[28]

In late imperial Chekiang, government relief efforts often fell short of their goals due to corruption or neglect, while private efforts were limited in scope and often failed to aid significant numbers of the sick. Even when medicine was available, Chekiang natives continued to practice a wide range of religious responses for protection against epidemics. Rituals featuring Marshal Wen were but one of the many popular responses to an epidemic, as other forms of ritual action were available as well. Before exploring the case of Marshal Wen's cult and festival, I would like to describe some of these other responses.

Ch'ing," *JAS* 46.2 (June 1987): 309–338; and Yen Hsing-chen, "Ming-tai tsai-huang chiu-chi cheng-ts'e chih yen-chiu," (3 parts), *Hua-hsüeh yüeh-k'an*, 142 (Oct. 1983): 14–24; 144 (Dec. 1983): 23–34; and, 147 (March 1984): 40–48.

[26] See K. Chimin Wong and Wu Lien-teh, *History of Chinese Medicine* (Tientsin:, The Tientsin Press, Ltd., 1932), pp. 17–23, 32–34, 73–76; Paul Unschuld, *Medicine in China: A History of Ideas* (Berkeley: University of California Press, 1985), pp. 51–100, 168–179, 204–206; and Fan, *Chung-kuo yi-hsüeh shih-lüeh*, pp. 21–31, 41–47, 217–241. Helen Dunstan has analyzed some of the Wen-ping theories in her article on late Ming epidemics; see pp. 35–43. Marta Hanson, a Ph.D. candidate at the University of Pennsylvania, is currently writing a dissertation on Wen-ping theories.

[27] For examples of some prescriptions, see Chao Hsüeh-min (1719–1805), *Ch'uan-ya nei-wai-pien* (Hong Kong: Chiu-lung shih-yung shu-chü, 1957); Li Hsü (late Ming; a native of Shan-yin in Chekiang), *Chieh-an lao-jen man-pi* (Peking: Chung-hua shu-chü, 1982), 7:24b–25a; and Nieh Shang-heng (b. 1572), *Ch'i-hsiao yi-shu, hsia chüan*, 57a–58b, (Peking: Chung-yi ku-chi ch'u-pan-she, 1984), pp. 113–116. Chang Yen, *Chung-tou hsin-shu* (1760), 3:8a–19b, has a detailed description of the combined application of variolation and rituals used to cure smallpox. I wish to thank Charlotte Furth for this reference.

[28] See Donald R. Hopkins, *Princes and Peasants. Smallpox in History* (Chicago and London: University of Chicago Press, 1983), pp. 109–110, 114.

Spiritual Causes of Epidemics[29]

In order to understand the ritual responses to epidemics so frequently resorted to by the people of Chekiang, one must first attempt to understand popular explanations for these calamities. Members of the gentry and elite classes, as well as religious specialists, often interpreted epidemics using Five Phases (*wu-hsing* 五行) theories, and even those uneducated in such knowledge appear to have understood that epidemics could be linked to seasonal changes. As a result, the people of Chekiang staged numerous annual rituals as prophylactic measures before the summer months, when epidemics were considered likely to break out. At the same time however, rituals to expel epidemics could also be held as an apotropaic measure if an epidemic was already in progress.

What types of spiritual forces were conceived of as being responsible for causing epidemics? While cults to snake-women described in the previous chapter are frequently mentioned in pre-Sung anecdotal sources, anecdotal literature, stele inscriptions, and gazetteer accounts indicate that these deities appear to have been gradually superseded by the following two types of plague spirits: 1) Plague deities (commonly referred to as *wen-shen* 瘟神) belonging to the heavenly bureaucracy; and 2) Plague demons (*yi-kuei* 疫鬼), usually the souls of people who had died in epidemics. Plague deities were sent down to earth by the Jade Emperor in order to punish individual wrongdoers or sinful communities, while plague demons tended to go on uncontrollable rampages at random intervals, in order to kill victims to take their places. Plague deities and plague demons also differed iconographically, as can be seen from an examination of Figures 1 and 2 below. In terms of ritual action, the former were the objects of offering rituals (*chiao*), usually performed by Taoist priests, who implored the Jade Emperor and other Taoist deities to show mercy on the afflicted by recalling the plague gods sent to inflict their deadly punishment. Most of the violent apotropaic rites described below were designed to expel plague demons, spirits who were not

---

[29] Comparative material may be found in Charles-Edward Amory Winslow, *The Conquest of Epidemic Disease* (Madison: University of Wisconsin Press, 1971), pp. 3–39. For example, the Romans of Justinian's time believed in their own version of plague boats, in this case manned by black and headless men (p. 4). See also Terence Ranger & Paul Slack, eds., *Epidemics and Ideas. Essays on the Historical Perception of Pestilence* (Cambridge: Cambridge University Press, 1992); Keith Thomas, *Religion and the Decline of Magic* (New York: Charles Scribner's Sons, 1971), pp. 83–88, 111, 177–212, 469–492, 587–588, 593–594, 607, 610, 612–613 and 648–650; and, Valerie I.J. Flint, *The Rise of Magic in Early Medieval Europe* (Princeton: Princeton University Press, 1991), pp. 101–116 and 146–172.

part of the heavenly bureaucracy and therefore could be dealt with more roughly. Despite the clear differences between them, these types of plague spirits should not be seen as mutually exclusive. As I shall show in chapter 3, it was always possible for demons to become transformed into deities, and sometimes even vice versa. Although data concerning the growth of cults to plague spirits is hard to come by, it appears that temples dedicated to plague deities or deified plague demons did not begin to flourish until the Sung dynasty, while only a few temples dedicated to snake-women are mentioned in Sung and post-Sung sources.

Thus we see two very different and yet also overlapping views concerning the causes of epidemics. According to the first, epidemics were the end result of a fair yet harsh judicial process conducted by the heavenly bureaucracy. In this case, people had no choice but to repent and hope that the gods would be sufficiently moved by the merit of the religious specialists and the rituals they performed to rescind their deadly judgment. The other view saw epidemics as part of an ongoing battle between demonic forces outside the community and the spiritual forces meant to protect it. In this case, the entrie community fought for its own self-preservation through various exorcistic rituals, including boat expulsion rites. This conceptual overlap explains why the processions accompanying plague festivals simultaneously featured men and women dressed as criminals performing acts of penance, as well as others dressed as martial figures whose task was to capture and expel the demonic forces threatening the community. It also explains why plague festivals could include both offering rites and boat expulsion rituals.

There are two major groups of plague deities which have been worshipped in Chekiang and other parts of south China since the Sung dynasty, if not before: 1) The Five Commissioners of Epidemics (Wu-wen shih-che 五瘟使者; see Table 1 and Figure 1); and 2) The Twelve Year-Controlling Kings of Epidemics (Shih-erh chih-nien wen-wang 十二值年瘟王; see Table 2).[30]

Chekiang sources do not mention any cults to the Twelve Kings, although there is some information on the Five Commissioners.

---

[30] Ofuchi Ninji provides a brief yet penetrating analysis of the Five Commissioners and the Twelve Kings in his *Chūgokujin no shūkyō girei* (Tokyo: Fukutake Shoten, 1983), pp. 197–198. See also Liu Chih-wan, *T'ai-wan min-chien hsin-yang lun-chi* (Taipei: Lien-ching ch'u-pan shih-yeh kung-ssu, 1983), pp. 225–236, 242–244; Yin Teng-kuo, *Chung-kuo shen te ku-shih* (Taipei: Shih-chieh wen-wu ch'u-pan-she, 1984), pp. 91–100; and Katz, "P'ing-tung hsien Tung-kang chen te ying-wang chi-tien: T'ai-wan wen-shen yü wang-yeh hsin-yang chih fen-hsi," *Bulletin of the Institute of Ethnology, Academia Sinica* 70 (March 1991): 130–135 and 157–165.

These deities were worshipped during the Dragon Boat Festival in Hangchow, although there is no record of any temple to them in the city.[31] Wenchow boasted a large temple to these gods, which had been built in 1598, following a devastating series of epidemics, by the District Magistrate Lin Ying-hsiang 林應祥, a native of T'ung-an County (Fukien).[32]

Descriptions of the Five Commissioners may be found in works preserved in the *Taoist Canon* dating back to the Six Dynasties. These texts list their names,[33] their seasonal and directional correspondences, and the types of epidemics they could inflict. They also emphasize that knowledge of their names and the use of certain charms were essential in order to ward off their attacks.[34] One hagiographical compendium composed during the Yüan dynasty makes the as yet unsubstantiated claim that worship of the Five Commissioners on a national scale may have started during the Sui dynasty, when the emperor ordered temples established to them during an epidemic in the year 592 (sources on Sui history only record epidemics in the years 597 and 612). The text also notes that their collective birthday was celebrated on the fifth day of the fifth lunar month, the same day as the Dragon Boat Festival (this festival's links to epidemics will be discussed below).[35]

---

[31] See for example the Ming work *Hsi-tzu-hu shih-ts'ui yü-t'an* by Wang K'o-yü (1587-1643), in *WLCKTP*, volume 8, p. 5263.

[32] See *YCWCL* (1833), *chüan hsia*, 18b-19a; and *YCHC* (1882), 4:49a–b. For more on interaction between natives of Fukien and Wenchow, see Ch'en Hsüeh-wen, *Ming-ch'ing she-hui ching-chi shih yen-chiu* (Taipei: Tao-ho ch'u-pan-she, 1991), pp. 127–145. Information on the Five Commissioners' T'ung-an temple may be found in *Ch'üan-chou fu-chih* (1763), 16:70b; and *T'ung-an hsien-chih* (1929), 24:18b–19a. There is also data on a temple to these deities in Chen-hai (Ningpo Prefecture). See *Chen-hai hsien-chih* (1931), 14:7b–8a.

[33] Among them are historical figures such as Chung Shih-chi 鐘士季, whose biography is included in *chüan* 28 of the *Wei-chih* 魏志 (in the *San-kuo chih* 三國志). The most interesting figure of the lot is Chao Kung-ming 趙公明, who is not only a plague god but also the marshal of the North and the Martial God of Wealth. See *CKMCCS* (Hopeh: He-pei jen-min ch'u-pan-she, 1985), pp. 477-481, 625-632.

[34] These include the *Tao-yao ling-ch'i shen-kuei p'in-ching* (*TT* 875; *CT* 1201, 22a–b), and the *Nü-ch'ing kuei-lü* (*TT* 563; *CT* 790, 6:2). Research on early Taoist plague beliefs may be found in Li Feng-mao, "*Tao-tsang so shou tsao-ch'i tao-shu te wen-yi kuan*," *Bulletin of the Institute of Literature and Philosophy, Academia Sinica* 3 (March 1993): 1-38; and, Christine Mollier, *Une Apocalypse du Ve siècle — Étude du Dongyuan shenzhou jing* (Paris: Institut des Hautes Études Chinoises, 1991).

[35] See *Hsin-pien lien-hsiang sou-shen kuang-chi, hou-chi* 後集, # 31, pp. 125 and 128; *Hsin-k'o ch'u-hsiang tseng-pu sou-shen chi ta-ch'üan, chüan* 6, pp. 388–389; *San-chiao yüan-liu sheng-ti fo-tsu sou-shen ta-ch'üan, chüan* 4, pp. 152–153; *San-chiao yüan-liu sou-shen ta-ch'üan, chüan* 4, pp. 156–157; and, *Shih-shen, chüan* 10, p. 77.

Table 1. The Five Commissioners of Epidemics

Name	Season	Direction	Color
Chang Yüan-po 張元伯	Spring	East	Green
Liu Yüan-ta 劉元達	Summer	South	Red
Chao Kung-ming 趙公明	Autumn	West	White
Chung Shih-kuei 鐘士貴	Winter	North	Black
Shih Wen-yeh 史文業	——	Center	Yellow

Table 2. The Twelve Year-controlling Plague Kings

Name	Year (Associated Animal and Terrestrial Branch)
Chang Ch'üan (張全)	Year of the Rat (*tzu* 子)
Yü Wen (余文)	Year of the Ox (*ch'ou* 丑)
Hou Piao (侯彪)	Year of the Tiger (*yin* 寅)
Keng T'ung (耿通)	Year of the Hare (*mao* 卯)
Wu Yu (吳友)	Year of the Dragon (*ch'en* 辰)
Ho Chung (何仲)	Year of the Snake (*ssu* 巳)
Hsüeh Wen (薛溫)	Year of the Horse (*wu* 午)
Feng Li (封立)	Year of the Sheep (*wei* 未)
Chao Yü (趙玉)	Year of the Monkey (*shen* 申)
T'an Ch'i (譚起)	Year of the Cock (*yu* 酉)
Lu Te (盧德)	Year of the Dog (*hsü* 戌)
Lo Shih-yu (羅士友)	Year of the Pig (*hai* 亥)

Fig. 1 — The Five Commissioners of Epidemics. Reproduced from *San-chiao yüan-liu sou-shen ta-ch'üan*, p. 153.

Other sources such as the *I-chien chih* indicate that their cult did not begin to flourish in south China until the Sung.[36] By the late imperial period the Five Commissioners of Epidemics were being worshipped throughout China, usually on or around the Dragon Boat Festival.[37] A number of scholars have confused the Five Commissioners with other deities worshipped in groups of five, particularly the Five Manifestations (Wu-hsien 五顯), Five Interlocutors (Wu-t'ung 五通) and Five Saints (Wu-sheng 五聖).[38] Nevertheless, while some overlap may have occurred in the minds of some believers, the above-mentioned cults all have distinct iconographical and hagiographical features, and should not be seen as belonging to one single system.[39]

One of the Five Commissioners' largest cult centers was in Foochow, where they were worshipped using the title the Five Emperors (Wu-ti 五帝). It is not clear exactly when their cult spread to Foochow, but the people of this city held annual processions for the Five Emperors on or around the Dragon Boat Festival beginning in the year 1642, when the city was ravaged by a major epidemic. This festival, which culminated in the Five Emperors being expelled on burning plague boats, grew into the largest event in Foochow, surviving numerous attempts at persecution by the authorities.[40] Their cult spread from Fukien to Taiwan, where they are worshipped in a dozen or so temples under the title Great Emperors of the Five Blessings (Wu-fu ta-ti 五福大帝), this new title representing an attempt

---

[36] See *ICC*, p. 1808.

[37] Huang Shih, *Tuan-wu li-su shih* (Taipei: Ting-wen shu-chü, 1979), pp. 57–67.

[38] See for example Liu, *Min-chien hsin-yang*, p. 293.

[39] For a penetrating analysis of these cults, see Ursula-Angelika Cedzich, "Wu-t'ung: Zur bewegten Geschichte eines Kultes," in Gert Naundorf, ed., *Religion und Philosophie in Ostasien: Festschrift für Hans Steininger zum 65. Geburtstag* (Wurzburg: Könighausen & Neumann, 1985), pp. 33-60; and, Richard von Glahn, "The Enchantment of Wealth: The God Wutong in the Social History of Jiangnan," *HJAS* 51.2 (Dec. 1991): 651–714.

[40] See the Rev. Justus Doolittle, *The Social Life of the Chinese* (Singapore: Graham Brash (Pte) Ltd., 1986), pp. 157–167; 276–287; Lewis Hodous, *Folkways in China* (London: A Probsthain, 1929), pp. 212–214; and, Hsü Hsiao-wang, *Fu-chien min-chien hsin-yang yüan-liu* (Foochow: Fu-chien chiao-yü ch'u-pan-she, 1993), pp. 87–91, 93–98; and Ch'en Chien-ts'ai, ed., *Pa-min chang-ku ta-ch'üan* (Foochow: Fu-chien chiao-yü ch'u-pan-she, 1994), pp. 89–90, 263–264. The cult of the Five Emperors has continued to survive in Foochow despite the ravages of the Cultural Revolution. According to the *South China Morning Post* (March 15 1982), members of the Hung-liao Commune located in the suburbs of Foochow attacked party cadres who had torn down their temple to these deities. Eight people were injured, and the cadres' car set ablaze. Four ringleaders of this incident were arrested.

to conceal their original function of spreading epidemics.[41]

As for the Twelve Year-Controlling Kings of Epidemics, their worship does not seem to have gained significant popularity until the Northern Sung dynasty. These deities are first mentioned in a work written by the Taoist Yüan Miao-tsung (fl. 1086–1116) entitled *T'ai-shang chu-kuo chiu-min tsung-chen pi-yao*, in which they are referred to as the "Twelve Yearly Kings" (Shih-erh nien-wang 十二年王) (*TT* 986–987; *CT* 1227, 6:17). They originally seem to have been a nebulous group of deities, with no names assigned to them until the Ming, and then only in Taoist ritual texts like the *Fa-hai yi-chu* (*TT* 825–833; *CT* 1166, 44:5–8). The only non-canonical source describing their worship I have found today is the *I-chien chih*, which describes how a local magistrate destroyed their temple in Ch'ang-chou (Kiangsu), while also sending the spirit mediums who supported the temple into exile.[42] However, in modern Taiwan the popularity of the Twelve Kings (popularly known as the "Lords [Who Visit] Every Five Years" [Wu-nien ch'ien-sui 五年千歲]) far exceeds that of the Five Commissioners, with over two hundred temples having been built to them throughout the island. It is the Twelve Kings, not the Five Commissioners, who are the chief deities expelled during most of Taiwan's plague festivals.[43]

The Five Commissioners and Twelve Kings have one important point in common — they do not randomly inflict people with contagious diseases. Rather, they are members of the heavenly bureaucracy under the command of the Jade Emperor, who decides for himself which people or communities have performed evil deeds and deserve punishment. The idea that epidemics were a form of divine retribution dates back at least to the Han, if not before, and is expressed clearly in both Buddhist and Taoist texts from the medieval era.[44] Such beliefs were also highly prevalent during the Sung. Take

---

[41] See Ch'iu Te-tsai, *T'ai-wan miao-shen chuan* (Tou-nan: Tsung-ching hsiao-hsin-t'ung ch'u-pan-she, 1979), pp. 421–423; and, Cheng Chih-ming, "Wang-yeh ch'uan-shuo (shang)," *Min-su ch'ü-yi* 52 (March 1988): 20–21. Many Taiwanese confuse The Great Emperors of the Five Blessings with the Lords of the Five Halls (Wu-fu ch'ien-sui 五府千歲), whose most popular cult sites are at Nan-k'un-shen and Ma-tou in Tainan County. These two groups of deities are not identical, though, especially in terms of hagiography, iconography, and ritual function. See Katz, "P'ing-tung hsien Tung-kang chen te ying-wang chi-tien," pp. 130–135, 157–162.

[42] See *ICC*, pp. 1074–1075. Judith Boltz provides a stimulating analysis of this account in her article "Not by the Seal of Office Alone," p. 253, although she errs in identifying Ch'ang-chou as part of Chekiang.

[43] See Ch'iu, *Miao-shen chuan*, pp. 531–532; and Liu, *Min-chien hsin-yang*, pp. 285–401, esp. pp. 293–294, 303.

[44] See Erik Zürcher, "Prince Moonlight: Messianism and Eschatology in Early

for example a passage from the hagiography of the deity Wen-ch'ang entitled *The Book of Transformations of the Divine Lord of Tzu-t'ung* (1181), a work written when the epidemics ravaging south China during the Southern Sung were doing their worst. One section of chapter 12 reads:

> When both my parents died from an epidemic [referring to Wen-ch'ang's existence in a previous life], they caught this misery in summer, and suffered all the more. Every time I thought of the cruelty of the epidemic demons, my hatred for them cut to the bones. [He then uses spells to capture five demons] . . . [Having trapped them,] I rebuked them angrily, and was about to destroy their forms, when they pleaded, "We, your disciples, are born from the seasonal cycle and take form from the seasonal breaths. There are certain districts in which we roam, and certain people whom we afflict. Those who have a heavy accumulation of otherworldly offenses are visited with disaster, death comes to those whose heavenly lifespan is at an end. *We certainly do not dare to act on our own initiative . . .* If when we are spreading epidemics we see your honor's charm, we shall not dare to enter there" [italics mine].[45]

Another group of plague deities is the Five Emperors of Epidemics (*Wu-wen huang* 五瘟瘟) described in the late Ming novel *Feng-shen yen-yi* 封神演義. Chapters 57 and 58 of this novel portray them as having fought on the side of the Shang dynasty forces during their losing campaign against the Chou, using germ warfare to wreak havoc among their foes until their leader, Lü Yüeh 呂岳, was incinerated by Yang Jen's 楊任 fire fans. Although the Five Emperors have an important place in the literature and art of the late imperial

---

Medieval Chinese Buddhism," *T'oung Pao* 68 (1982): 1–58; Max Kaltenmark, "The Ideology of the T'ai-p'ing ching," in *Facets of Taoism*, pp. 19–45; Anna Seidel, "The Image of the Perfect Ruler in Early Taoist Messianism: Lao-tzu and Li Hung," *HR* 9.2/3 (Nov.–Feb. 1969–70): 216–247; and, Lin Fu-shih, "Shih-lun *T'ai-p'ing ching* te chi-ping kuan-nien," *Bulletin of the Institute of History and Philology, Academia Sinica* 62 (April 1993): 225–263.

[45] This translation is taken from Kleeman, *A God's Own Tale*, pp. 107–109. An illustration of this story may be found on p. 67 of Kleeman's book. Each spirit has animal features similar to those of the Five Commissioners portrayed in the murals of the Monastery for Preserving Tranquility (Pao-ning Ssu 寶寧寺), in Shansi. See *Pao-ning Ssu Ming-tai shui-lu hua* (Peking: Wen-wu ch'u-pan-she, 1985). The Five Emperors of Foochow also had animal features. See Ch'en, *Pa-min chang-ku*, p. 263.

period, I have yet to find any record of temples having been built for them in Chekiang or other parts of China.[46]

While the above-mentioned deities represented spiritual forces which used epidemics only as a means of punishing evil-doers, plague demons belonged to a more dangerous and uncontrollable class of spirits. These were a sub-class of vengeful demons (*li-kuei* 厲鬼; also known as "wronged souls" [*yüan-hun* 冤魂]), the souls of those who died premature or violent deaths and possessed the power to afflict others until they received sacrifices. Specifically, plague demons were viewed as the souls of those who had died during previous epidemics. These were a dreaded spiritual force, roaming the world in large bands in an attempt to find substitutes by infecting people with the very diseases that had claimed their own lives.[47] For example, chapter 10 of a late-Ming novel written by Teng Chih-mo (fl. 1566–1618) tells how the Perfected Man Sa (Sa Chen-jen 薩眞人)[48] expelled a marauding troupe of plague demons who had been terrorizing entire villages.[49] An illustration accompanying this story shows Sa performing thunder rites to exorcise these demons. The accompanying caption reads: "With a wave of his immortal fan, he instantly brings the sick man back to life; in a flash of thunder magic, he eradicates all the plague demons" (see Figure 2). Marshal Wen, who is portrayed in novels and folktales as having died by swallowing plague poison, may have originally been a plague demon. However, he ended up being worshipped as a deity who could control both plague deities and plague demons, the result of a process I shall discuss in detail in the next chapter.

---

[46] See Tseng Ch'in-liang, *T'ai-wan min-chien hsin-yang yü Feng-shen yen-yi chih pi-chiao yen-chiu* (Taipei: Hua-cheng ch'u-pan-she, 1987), pp. 133–137.

[47] Chinese plague demon beliefs have been aptly summarized in Liu, *Min-chien hsin-yang*, pp. 236–238. The most famous group of plague demons in ancient China was the trio of the sons of Chuan Hsü 顓頊 (grandson of the mythical Yellow Emperor). One powerful image of the way people represented plague demons may be found in Han Yü's poem entitled "Admonishing the Malaria Demons" (*ch'ien nueh-kuei* 譴瘧鬼). This has been translated in J. J. M. deGroot, *The Religious System of China* (Leiden: E. J. Brill, 1892–1910), volume 6, pp. 1054–1055. For Sung dynasty stories about plague demons, see *ICC*, pp. 327–328, 460, 660, 812–813.

[48] For more information on this deity, see *CKMCCS*, pp. 756–760.

[49] See Teng Chih-mo, *Wu-tai Sa chen-jen te-tao chou-tsao chi* (1603), in *Ku-pen hsiao-shuo ts'ung-k'an*, series 10, volume 5 (Peking: Chung-hua shu-chü, 1990), pp. 1990–2003.

Figure 2 — Perfected Man Sa Expels the Plague Demons. Reproduced from
Teng, *Chou-tsao chi*, pp. 1996-1997.

State-sponsored Rituals

The state attempted to cope with the threat of epidemics by making regular offerings at the Altar for Vengeful Souls (*li-t'an* 厲壇), which was part of the state cult (*ssu-tien* 祀典; literally "register of sacrifices"). These altars were established in the early years of the Ming dynasty, with the Hung-wu emperor (r. 1368–1398) decreeing in 1375 that one such altar be established in every community of one hundred households and sacrifices offered twice a year. The Manchus followed this system with some important modifications, ordering that an Altar for Vengeful Souls need only be erected in the northern suburb of each administrative center.   Late imperial ritual texts reveal officials petitioning these spirits to reward good citizens and punish evil ones. These altars do not appear to have been sites of popular worship, however, and occupied only a minor position in the state cult; in many places they eventually fell into ruin.[50]

On top of each Altar for Vengeful Souls was placed a tablet to the City God (*ch'eng-huang shen* 城隍神), a deity whose own temples were far more popular than the Altars for Vengeful Souls the officials were required to worship at. It is not certain when worship of the City God began, but by the T'ang and Sung dynasties it had developed into a major urban cult.[51] The Hung-wu emperor incorporated the City God into the state cult at the beginning of the Ming dynasty, and from that time on, officials would make offerings to this deity during all manner of calamities, at times resorting to flogging their statues when all else failed.[52] The country magistrate Tung Pang-cheng 董邦政, who served in Liu-ho (near Nanking) during the reign of the Chia-ching emperor (1522–1566) offered prayers to the City God during an epidemic, the texts of which are preserved in the "Belles-lettres"

---

[50] See Hsiao Kung-ch'üan, *Rural China: Imperial Control in the Nineteenth Century* (Seattle: University of Washington Press., 1960), pp. 220–224; Ch'ü T'ung-tsu, *Local Government in China Under the Ch'ing* (Cambridge, Mass: Harvard University Press, 1962), pp. 164–166; and, Romeyn Taylor, "Official and Popular Religion and the Political Organization of Chinese Society in the Ming," in Liu Kwang-ching, ed., *Orthodoxy in Late Imperial China* (Berkeley: University of California Press, 1990), pp. 126–157.

[51] See David Johnson, "The City God Cults of T'ang and Sung China," *HJAS* 45 (1985): 363–457; and, Valerie Hansen, "Gods on Walls: A Case of Indian Influence on Chinese Lay Religion?", in Ebrey and Gregory, eds., *Religion and Society in T'ang and Sung China*, pp. 194–206. See also *CKMCCS*, pp. 194–206.

[52] See Romeyn Taylor, "Ming T'ai-tsu and the Gods of Walls and Moats," *Ming Studies* 3 (1977): 31–49; and, Stephan Feuchtwang, "School-Temple and City God," in G. William Skinner ed., *The City in Late Imperial China* (Stanford: Stanford University Press, 1977), pp. 581–608.

(*yi-wen* 藝文) section of that county's gazetteer.[53] While no such documents survive for Chekiang, local sources clearly state that officials offered sacrifices to the City God during epidemics.[54]

The cult of the City God gained increasing popularity during late imperial times because he was seen as the arbiter of a region's fate, the spiritual equivalent of the district magistrate. As the magistrate could punish evil-doers or intercede with the emperor on behalf of the people, so could the City God inflict calamities or act as a go-between between the people and the Jade Emperor during times of crisis. One prayer text describes the City God's role thus: " . . . [All] vicious and evil persons will be reported by the spirits to the God of the City, thus causing their crimes to be disclosed and punished by the government . . . If their crimes are not disclosed, they will receive supernatural punishment; thus *all their family members will suffer from epidemics*, and they will have trouble in rearing their domestic animals, in farming, and in sericulture" (*italics mine*).[55]

Apart from these two cults, Chekiang local officials also offered sacrifices to other deities included in the register of sacrifices who were perceived to be particularly effective in controlling epidemics. For example, when the Ning-Shao Plain was ravaged by epidemics during the fifth and sixth lunar months of the year 1445, groups of officials, including Wang Ying 王瑛, Attendant of the Left in the Ministry of Rites (*Li-pu tso-shih lang* 禮部左侍郎), offered sacrifices at the temple of the mountain deity known as Nan-chen 南鎮 (Guardian of the South), which was located in the mountains near Shaohsing. The gazetteers from that area preserve some of the prayer texts used during these rituals, and contain many accounts of the miracles this deity performed during epidemics.[56] In addition, we shall

---

[53] *Liu-ho hsien-chih* (1646), 10:34a–b. For biographical data on Tung, see 4:22b, 52a, 54b.

[54] There are T'ang dynasty records of natives of Chin-yün County (Li-shui Prefecture) praying to the City God during epidemics; see Johnson, "City God," pp. 419–420. Additional data may also be found in *CCTC*, 217:5b–6b; and, Yeh Sheng (1420–1474), *Shui-tung jih-chi, chüan* 30 (Peking: Chung-hua shu-chü, 1980), pp. 296–297.

[55] See Ch'ü T'ung-tsu, *Law and Society in Traditional China* (Paris: Moulon, 1961), p. 211. The original of this text is in the *Ta-Ming hui-tien*, 94:151a–b. For more on the ideas underlying the belief that deities keep a close eye on people's moral qualities and administer rewards or punishments, see L.S. Yang, "The Concept of 'Pao' as a Basis for Social Relations in China," in John K. Fairbank, ed., *Chinese Thought and Institutions* (Chicago: University of Chicago Press, 1957), pp. 291-309; Wolfram Eberhard, *Guilt and Sin in Traditional China* (Berkeley: University of California Press, 1967); and Cynthia Brokaw, *The Ledgers of Merit and Demerit* (Princeton: Princeton University Press, 1991).

[56] See *KCTSCC*, "Shu-cheng," *chüan* 114; *SHFC* (1587), 19:10a–13a; *SHFC* (1719), 19:11a–16a; *SHFC* (1792), 36:21a–25b; and, *Shao-hsing hsien-chih tzu-liao, ti yi chi, Kuei-chi*

see in chapter 5 that officials would on occasion also make offerings to deities like Marshal Wen who were approved or tolerated by the state but not included in the register of sacrifices.

Popular Rituals

While the people of Chekiang did at times turn to state relief, traditional medicines or state-sponsored rites during epidemics, their primary recourse was to other forms of ritual activity — from holding a Buddhist fast for the dead to visiting a spirit medium in hopes of obtaining a cure. The popularity of such practices is reflected in the sections of local gazetteers describing an area's customs (*feng-su* 風俗). Take this somewhat stereotypical account from a Ch'ing-dynasty Hangchow gazetteer: "The people believe in spirit mediums and demons. When they fall ill, they turn solely to mediums and prayers for a cure." According to one county magistrate whose writings are preserved in the same work: "When the people are ill, they rely on spirit mediums and prayers. For this reason, [even] those who are aware of medicinal cures rarely desire them."[57] The popularity of ritual remedies can hardly be underestimated. In the words of the medical historian Paul Unschuld: "demonological healing was the most influential system" for most Chinese.[58]

In the search for ritual cures to their illnesses, the people of Chekiang turned to all sorts of religious specialists, including Buddhist monks and nuns, Taoist priests, local ritual masters, and/or spirit mediums. These religious specialists attempted to determine a disease's origins, and performed exorcisms if the cause turned out to be demonic. They could even supply prescriptions; in the case of the spirit medium these were often considered to come directly from the mouth of the god.[59] Private writings like the *I-chien chih* frequently

---

chih pu 會稽之部, tz'u-ssu chih 祠祀志, miao 廟, 1a–4a.

[57] See *HCFC* (1686), 6:19a–20a. For more descriptions of people preferring mediums to medicine, see *YCHC* (1882), 6:1b; *PYHC* (1915), 20:5b–6b; and, *Ch'ung-hsiu Che-chiang t'ung-chih kao* (1948), vol. 17:10b–12b and vol. 18:28b–29b.

[58] Unschuld, *Medicine in China*, p. 216.

[59] For an overview of Chinese healing, see Nathan Sivin, "Social Relations of Curing in Traditional China: Preliminary Considerations," *Nihon Ishigaku Zasshi* 23 (1977): 505–532. An analysis of ritual healing in ancient China may be found in Lin Fu-shih, "Shih-lun Han-tai te wu-shu yi-liao-fa chi ch'i kuan-nien chi-ch'u," *Shih-yüan*, 16 (Nov. 1987): 29–53, as well as his *Han-tai te wu-che* (Taipei: Tao-hsiang ch'u-pan-she, 1988). See also Chang Tzu-ch'en, *Chung-kuo wu-shu* (Shanghai: San-lien shu-chü, 1990); and, Sung Chao-lin, *Wu yü min-chien hsin-yang* (Peking: Chung-kuo hua-ch'iao ch'u-pan-she, 1990). The best anthropological studies of Chinese spirit mediums are

described such practices, although most authors claim that these rites were largely ineffective.[60]

The following account from the funerary inscription of Shen Tu 沈度 (1034–1094; a native of Wenchow) indicates that while he and some of his peers tended to look down on spirit mediums and their rituals, most natives preferred to consult them during epidemics:

> In viewing his lordship's conduct during his life, [one can see that] he was upright and upheld moral principles, not being befuddled by popular customs [*liu-su* 流俗]. The prefecture of Wenchow lies along the coast; its people have always believed in spirit mediums and priests [*wu-chu* 巫祝], and have many taboos [*chin-chi* 禁忌] — to the point where decent people become trapped in unrighteous behavior. In the spring, the epidemics [*ping-wen* 病瘟] come, and neighbors or relatives absolutely refuse to inquire after each other. If people die, their coffins are hurriedly placed in another room, which is sealed up and abandoned for one hundred days . . . In the early years of the Hsi-ning reign (1068–1078), there was a major epidemic in Wenchow. His lordhip's mother died, as did his female slaves [*nü-nu* 女奴]; many other members of his family were bedridden. Everybody was terrified, and followed the advice of the spirit mediums; only his lordship didn't care about these taboos.[61]

In addition to consulting local mediums, the people of Chekiang enjoyed a wide range of other ritual options for coping with epidemics.[62] Prophylactic rituals included the Great Exorcism, the Dragon Boat Festival, and the Double Ninth Festival, while apotropaic ones included Buddhist healing rites, as well as rites for feeding

---

Arthur Kleinman, *Patients and Healers in the Context of Culture* (Berkeley: University of California Press, 1980); Chang Hsün, *Chi-ping yü wen-hua* (Taipei: Tao-hsiang ch'u-pan-she, 1989); and A.J.A. Eliott, *Chinese Spirit Medium Cults in Singapore* (London: Royal Anthropological Institute, 1955).

[60] See *ICC*, pp. 986, 1076, 1429, 1558–1559 and 1736–1737. Research on Sung-dynasty mediums may be found in Nakamura, "Sōdai no hū," pp. 51–75; and, Wang Nien-shuang, "Nan-Sung wen-hsüeh chung chih min-chien hsin-yang" (M.A. thesis, National Cheng-chih University, 1980), pp. 71–125. For more on mediums in Chekiang, see Chiang Pin, *Wu-Yüeh min-chien hsin-yang min-su* (Shanghai: Shanghai wen-yi ch'u-pan-she, 1992), pp. 76–77.

[61] See Chou Hsing-chi, *Fu-chih chi, chüan 7, Ts'ung-shu chi-ch'eng* edition, p. 83.

[62] An overview of some of these rituals may be found in Chiang, *Wu-Yüeh min-chien hsin-yang*, pp. 171–294.

hungry ghosts (the latter were also performed during the Ghost Festival as a prophylactic measure).[63] Boat-burning rituals featuring the Five Commissioners and/or Marshal Wen were usually performed as apotropaic rituals.

The Great Exorcism (*Ta No* 大儺) may be the earliest known plague festival in China, dating back at least to the Shang-Chou era. The earliest accounts describe only court performances of the Great Exorcism held during the winter months, giving little information on popular versions of the festival. The Great Exorcism as celebrated at court was a violent and intense ritual, with youths under the command of an exorcist (*fang-hsiang shih* 方相氏) racing around the palace carrying torches and screaming imprecations at the top of their lungs in order to expel demonic creatures responsible for epidemics and other calamities.[64] Although it was an important part of court ritual through the medieval era, the Great Exorcism seems to have become less popular with China's emperors over time, with no mention of it in the dynastic histories following the T'ang.[65] There are some indications that the court form of the festival was briefly revived by the Southern Sung emperors,[66] but its grandeur does not appear to have equalled that of earlier dynasties. Post-T'ang sources, especially those from Chekiang and other southern provinces, rarely describe rituals called the Grand Exorcism, either as a court or a popular event. The only references to this rite in such works tend to describe its ancient forms, and give no indication as to whether it was still being practiced.[67] One important reason why the Great Exorcism may have been less popular in south China is that it was a *winter* festival; in the south, most plague expulsion festivals were held before the summer, as this was when epidemics were most likely to occur.

---

[63] See Stephen Teiser, *The Ghost Festival of Medieval China* (Princeton: Princeton University Press, 1988); and Robert P. Weller, *Unities and Diversities in Chinese Religion* (Seattle: University of Washington Press, 1987).

[64] One of the most thorough and penetrating analyses of the Great Exorcism may be found in Derk Bodde, *Festivals in Classical China* (Princeton: Princeton University Press, 1975), pp. 75–138. See also Chiang Hsiao-ch'in, *Ta No k'ao* (Taipei: Lan-t'ing shu-tien, 1988); Ch'en Yao-hung, et. al., *Chung-kuo No wen-hua* (Peking: Hsin-hua ch'u-pan-she, 1991).

[65] For more on the Great Exorcism as celebrated during the T'ang, see *Ch'üan T'ang-wen* (1814), 873:12a–14b and 896:6b–7a. I am grateful to Liu Shu-fen of the Institute of History and Philology, Academia Sinica, for showing me these passages.

[66] See *MLL, chüan* 6, pp. 181–182. See also *Tseng-pu Wu-lin chiu-shih*, p. 352. On Sung paintings of the Great Exorcism, see Sun Ching-ch'en, "Sung-tai Ta No t'u k'ao," *Wu-tao lun-ts'ung* 2 (1982): 62–71, and "Ta No t'u ming-shih pien," *Wen-wu* 210 (March 1982): 70–74.

[67] A good example of this is the account of the Great Exorcism by Wu Lai (1297–1340) in *chüan* 2 of his *Yüan-ying chi*.

The people of late imperial Chekiang did stage a number of year-end rituals designed to protect themselves from contagious diseases, but these do not appear to be linked to the Great Exorcism. For example, the people of Chia-hsing used to smear their faces with black paint and perform ritual dances in the streets,[68] while T'ai-chou natives held a midnight expulsion rite just after the lantern festival.[69] As for Hangchow, Ch'ing sources describe various masked dances performed during the Lunar New Year to expel demons.[70] People in Wenchow and other sites along the southeast coast (and later Taiwan) also staged nighttime exorcistic processions known as "night patrols" (*yeh-hsün* 夜巡) or "dark visitations" (*an-fang* 暗訪), either as prophylactic or apotropaic measures.[71] I have yet to determine whether such rituals derived from the Grand Exorcism, or, as is more likely, represented different local responses to the threat of epidemics.[72]

A number of dramatic performances have also been labelled "*No*," including those featuring Kuan Kung and the demon-quelling deity Chung K'uei 鍾馗,[73] as well as various other ritual dramas (frequently labelled by modern scholars as "*No* dramas" [*No-hsi* 儺戲]) still performed in parts of south and southwest China.[74] Some of the

---

[68] See *CHFC* (1600), 1:18a.

[69] See *CCFSCC*, p. 534.

[70] See *WLCKTP*, vol. 4, pp. 2173 and 2184. See also *JHHC* (1687), 5:23b–24a; and, T'ien Yi-heng (1524-1574), *Liu-ch'ing jih-cha*, *chüan* 19.

[71] See Yen Fang-tzu, "Lu-kang te wang-yeh yü an-fang ch'u-t'an," in Yü Kuang-hung, ed., *Lu-kang shu-ch'i jen-lei-hsüeh t'ien-ye kung-tso chiao-shih lun-wen-chi* (Nankang: Institute of Ethnology, Academia Sinica, 1993), pp. 75–108, as well as her M.A. thesis entitled "Lu-kang wang-ye hsin-yang te fa-chan hsing-t'ai" (National Tsing-hua University, 1994).

[72] See Hsiao Ping, *No cha chih feng. Ch'ang-chiang liu-yü tsung-chiao hsi-chü wen-hua* (Nanking: Chiang-su jen-min ch'u-pan-she, 1992).

[73] See Li Feng-mao, "Chung K'uei yü No-li chi ch'i hsi-chü," *Min-su ch'ü-yi*, 39 (1986): 69–99; and, Yung Sai-shing (Jung Shih-ch'eng), "Kuan-kung hsi te ch'ü-hsieh yi-yi," *Han-hsüeh yen-chiu*, 8.1 (June 1990): 609–626.

[74] See Li Ch'in-te, "No-li, No-wu, No-hsi," *Wen-shih chih-shih* 6 (1987), pp. 55–59. See also the following works by Tanaka Issei: *Chūgoku gōson saishi* (Tokyo: Tōyō bunka kenkyūjō, 1989), pp. 161–262; and, *Chūgoku fūkei engeki kenkyū* (Tokyo: Tōyō bunka kenkyūjō, 1993). Tanaka's works contain many photos of the performances. The Taiwanese journal *Min-su ch'ü-yi* has recently published a number of special issues (also with many photos) on exorcistic rituals and dramas supposedly called *No*. These include: *Chung-kuo no-hsi no wen-hua chuan-chi* 中國儺戲儺文化專輯 (#69–70, 1991); *Chung-kuo no wen-hua yü min-chien hsin-yang* 中國儺文化與民間信仰; (#82–83, 1993); and, *Chung-kuo no-hsi, no wen-hua kuo-chi yen-t'ao-hui lun-wen-chi* 中國儺戲儺文化國際研討會論文集 (#83–84, 1993). This journal has also begun to publish a series containing reprints of liturgical texts used in these ritual dramas accompanied by field reports about them, entitled *Min-su ch'ü-yi ts'ung-shu* 民俗曲藝叢書.

rituals mentioned above may have developed out of the Great Exorcism, but I would hesitate to use the term *No* describing them. This term has been all too loosely used to refer to all manner of exorcistic rituals (including Marshal Wen's festival) without critically examining their actual links to the Great Exorcism.[75] I would argue in favor of restricting the term *No*'s usage to the ancient Grand Exorcism ritual and other rites we can prove are directly related to it. As a general rule, it would be better to accept the autonyms most locals used in describing their plague expulsion rituals. For example, Wen's festival in late imperial Wenchow was known as the "Festival of [the Emperor of] the Eastern Peak" (*Tung-yüeh hui* 東嶽會),[76] while ritual dramas involving Chung K'uei performed in Hangchow and other parts of China and Taiwan were called "Chung K'uei Dances" (*t'iao Chung K'uei* 跳鍾馗).

The most important plague-prevention rite in Chekiang was the Dragon Boat Festival, held on an annual basis on the fifth day of the fifth lunar month. This date corresponds to the summer solstice, that time of year when the *yang* forces were considered to be strongest and the threat of disease had reached its peak.[77] Many scholars have claimed that the Dragon Boat Festival is a rite primarily linked to harvests and the cult of the loyal official Ch'ü Yüan 屈原 (ca. 300 B.C.E.),[78] but fail to take into account this festival's function of expelling epidemics. It might be more accurate to say that worship of Ch'ü Yüan simply became an important addition to this ancient festival, and that the Dragon Boat Festival not only commemorates him but also functions as a prophylactic rite against epidemics, with charms, herbs, and spells employed in a battle against the animal and spiritual forces that might make people ill.[79]

[75] See for example the *Tien-shih chai hua-pao* (chapter 5). The *T'ai-p'ing kuang-chi*, by Li Fang (925–996), et. al., *chüan* 86, has a passage calling dragon boat races a *"No"* ritual (*tou-ch'uan ch'ü-no* 鬥船驅儺). See also *Han-chou chih* (1817), 15:5a–b, for a description of boat expulsion rites performed during a so-called "*No*" in Szechwan.

[76] YCWCL (1833), *chüan shang*, 54b–55a; and, Tai Yü-sheng (fl. 1862–1874), *Ou-chiang chu-chih tz'u*, 2b–3a. The only copy of the latter text I have seen is in the Wenchow Provincial Library.

[77] For a discussion of theories about the Dragon Boat Festival, see Bodde, *Festivals*, pp. 289–302. Many important accounts of this event have been preserved in the *KCTSCC*, "Annual Works" (*Sui-kung* 歲貢), *chüan* 51–52.

[78] See Goran Aijmer, *The Dragon Boat Festival in the Hunan and Hupeh Plains: A Study in the Ceremonialism of Transplantation of Rice* (Stockholm: Ethnographical Museum of Sweden, 1964); and Wen I-to (1899–1946), *Wen I-to ch'üan chi* (Shanghai: K'ai-ming shu-tien, 1949), pp. 221–262. Eberhard notes the exorcistic nature of the festival, but fails to establish a clear link to epidemics. See *Local Cultures*, pp. 390–406.

[79] For a discussion of these practices, see Huang Shih, *Tuan-wu li-su shih* (Taipei: Ting-wen shu-chü, 1979), pp. 75–192. See also *Chung-kuo lung-chou wen-hua* (Hunan:

The boat expulsion rites that became an integral part of plague festivals in Chekiang and other provinces in south China may well have grown out of the Dragon Boat Festival, inasmuch as such rituals were usually held on or around its date since at least the Sung dynasty.[80] According to one source:

> [On the fifth day of the fifth lunar month] the people of Li-chou 澧州 (in Hunan) organize the Five Plague [Gods] Association (*Wu-wen she* 五瘟社). They bear flags and ritual items all [normally only] used by princes . . . They use supple wood to make a huge boat many tens of feet in length and identical to any ordinary vessel, decorated with the five colors (*wu-ts'ai* 五彩).[81] The people of the prefecture all have their names, birthdates, and the nature of the rite to be performed written in on a petition (*chuang* 狀).[82] This is placed on the boat, which is then floated away on the Li River. This custom is called "Sending Away Epidemics" (*sung-wen* 送瘟).[83]

Another contemporary work written by Fan Chih-ming, a native of Yüeh-yang in Hunan, describes how the locals made miniature dragon boats out of reeds and grass. These were then set afloat during the Dragon Boat Festival, in a rite also known as "Sending Away Epidemics."[84] Huang Chen (1213–1280), a local official who served in south China and wrote a number of memorials attacking popular customs, claimed that the natives of Fu-chou (Kiangsi) burned over one thousand such boats every year![85]

The Dragon Boat Festival continued to be associated with the expulsion of epidemics and other calamities during the Ming dynasty

San-huan ch'u-pan-she, 1991); and Chang Lun-tu and Huang Ching-chung, "Ching-tu, lung-chou yü lung-chou ching-tu chih yen-chiu," in *Chung-kuo min-chien wen-hua* (Shanghai: Hsüeh-lin ch'u-pan-she, 1991), volume 2, pp. 125–142.

[80] Huang, *Tuan-wu li-su shih*, pp. 57–67.

[81] Green, red, white, black, and yellow, corresponding to the Five Elements. In many regions of China, people wore five-colored threads as a prophylactic charm. See Huang, *Tuan-wu li-su*, pp. 151–164.

[82] This sounds similar to rituals in Taiwan; see Kristofer Schipper, "The Written Memorial in Taoist Ceremonies," in Arthur Wolf, ed., *Religion and Ritual in Chinese Society* (Stanford: Stanford University Press, 1974), pp. 309–324.

[83] See Chuang Ch'o, *Chi-lei pien* (1133), *shang chüan* (Peking: Chung-hua shu-chü, 1988), pp. 10–11. Note that this rite is not called a *No*!

[84] See Fan Chih-ming, *Yüeh-yang feng-t'u chi* (1935 edition), 24b–25a.

[85] See "Proclamation Forbidding Boat Festivals" (*Chin hua-ch'uan ying-hui pang* 禁划船迎會榜), in *Huang-shih jih-ch'ao*, 79:21b–22b, *Wen-yüan Ko Ssu-k'u chüan-shu* edition, pp. 823–824.

as well. One of the most detailed and lively accounts of the Dragon Boat Festival (as celebrated in Hunan) is the *Wu-ling ching-tu lüeh* 武陵競渡略, written by the late Ming literatus and statesman Yang Ssu-ch'ang 楊嗣昌 (1588–1641; *DMB*, pp. 1538–1542). This work contains the following passage:

> Now it is said that the boat race is customarily held to avert calamities. At the end of the racing the boats carry sacrificial animals, wine and paper coins, rowing straightly down-stream, where the animals and wine are cast into the water, the paper coins are burnt and spells are cited, so that pestilence and premature death would go away with the flowing water . . . About this time, the people have Taoist services for preventing conflagrations performed. If some are ill, they make paper boats in the same color as the dragon boat [to which their community team belongs] and burn them at the shore.[86]

A recently-discovered Ming woodblock print from Hunan provides further evidence that boat expulsion rites continued to be performed during the Dragon Boat Festival in Ming times. This work portrays the deities expelled on a plague boat shaped like a dragon boat. According to a brief inscription running accross the top of the print, these included the Five Commissioners of Epidemics and the Twelve Kings of Epidemics.[87]

Most plague festivals in Chekiang, especially those featuring boat expulsion rites, were celebrated on or around the Dragon Boat Festival. In the case of Wenchow, the Ming edition of the *P'ing-yang hsien-chih* states that: "During the fifth, eighth, and ninth lunar months, the people of each rural area hold dragon boat races and processions

---

[86] See Chao Wei-pang's annotated translation, "The Dragon Boat Race in Wu-ling, Hunan," *Folklore Studies* 2 (1943): 1–18, esp. pp. 9–11. Juliet Bredon and Igor Mitrophanow describe people floating burning lanterns from dragon boats during nocturnal water processions as a means to expel epidemics (unfortunately, the region where the rite was held is not given). See *The Moon Year* (Shanghai: Kelly and Walsh, Ltd., 1927), p. 307. This custom sounds similar to the rite of "floating the lanterns" (*fang shui-teng* 放水燈), performed during the Ghost Festival, the main difference being that the lantern ritual is performed to *invite* the souls of drowned people to a "feast for universal salvation" (*p'u-tu* 普度), not to expel them. See Duane Pang, "The *P'u-tu* Ritual," in Michael Saso and David W. Chappell, eds., *Buddhist and Taoist Studies I* (Honolulu: University of Hawaii Press, 1977), pp. 95–122; and, Liu, *Min-chien hsin-yang*, pp. 88–89, 134–135, 178–179, 221 and 370.

[87] See Lin Ho, *Chiu-ko yü Yüan-Hsiang wen-hua* (Shanghai: San-lien shu-tien, 1990), p. 153.

[*ching-tu sai-shen* 競渡賽神], claiming that these can expel epidemics." A note adds: "There is a saying: 'During an epidemic, when one hears the drum [warning people of the calamity?], [soon] someone to collect the money [for a dragon boat race] comes'." The text goes on to add that many quarrels broke out during these processions and boat races, and that some people lost their lives.[88] Sources for Hangchow reveal that plague gods were expelled during rites held on dragon boats, but do not say whether these vessels were torched, floated away, or kept for use year after year.[89] In Fukien, the fact that plague expulsion rites grew out of the Dragon Boat Festival might explain why the plague boats Justus Doolittle and Lewis Hodous observed in Foochow were shaped like dragon boats.

Another ritual activity originally connected with preventing epidemics was the Double Ninth Festival (Ch'ung-yang chieh 重陽節), during which people went for picnics in the mountains. One meaning of this act was to escape calamities afflicting the valleys, including pestilential vapors.[90] This event seems to have been celebrated less intensely than the other two festivals, and it is doubtful that many people were aware of the original meaning of their mountain excursions.

It is probably no coincidence that the three lunar months during which the above-mentioned festivals occurred (first, fifth, and ninth) were all considered inauspicious times of the year. Officials would not assume office, some butchers would cease slaughtering animals, and lay Buddhists would practice a vegetarian diet.[91]

Apart from the annual festivals described above, which were celebrated throughout China, local communities could also organize annual festivals to their protective deities in order to prevent outbreaks of epidemics. Annual festivals featuring Marshal Wen (discussed in detail in chapter 5) were but one of many such events to local deities celebrated throughout China, albeit one of the most popular in Chekiang. Other deities were also worshipped during local festivals in this province. For example, the people of Yü-yao (in Shaohsing Prefecture) attempted to ward off the threat of epidemics

---

[88] *PYHC* (1571), 1:20a; see also *PYHC* (1684), 4:3a.

[89] See *Tseng-pu Wu-lin chiu-shih*, p. 346; and *Hsi-tzu-hu shih-ts'ui yü-t'an*, *chung*中: 4a–b, in *WLCKTP*, vol. 8, p. 5263. See also Hsiao, *No cha chih feng*, pp. 293–295.

[90] See Bodde, *Festivals*, pp. 393–394; *KCTSCC*, "Annual Works," *chüan* 76–79; and, the writings of the late-Ming poet Chang Huang-yen in his *Chang Shui-ts'ang chi*, *chüan* 2.

[91] See Ku Yen-wu (1613–1682), *Jih-chih lu*, *chüan* 30, in *Jih-chih lu chi-shih* (Taipei: Shih-chieh shu-chü, 1968), pp. 710–712; and, Lang Ying (fl. 1566), *Ch'i-hsiu lei-kao*, *chüan* 45 (Peking: Chung-hua shu-chü, 1961), vol. 3, p. 75.

during an annual festival to the Emperor of the Eastern Peak held on his birthday, the twenty-eighth day of the third lunar month.[92] Such festivals were frequently marked by the presence of ritual dance troupes (often composed of beggars) who engaged in exorcistic performances designed to drive off plague demons.[93]

Other prophylactic rituals included staging a performance of the opera "Mu-lien Saves his Mother" (*Mu-lien chiu-mu* 目連救母), which, apart from presenting the Buddhist deity Mu-lien as a filial son, also features a number of scenes in which demons are exorcised. These performances, often staged during the Ghost Festival, were clearly both terrifying and exciting, and actors who played the demons to be expelled often did so at risk of life and limb. Consider this account of one performance in Shaohsing by Chang Tai 張岱 (1597–1684?):

> There were heavenly gods and earthly deities, Oxhead (*niu t'ou* 牛頭) and Horseface (*ma-mien* 馬面) . . . yakshas and rakshas, saws, grindstones and three-legged cauldrons, the Knife Mountain, the Icy [Pond], the Sword Tree, Yama's Palace . . . The audience was very uneasy; under the light of the lamps, the actors' faces had a demonic quality. In suites like "Summoning the Evil Ghosts of the Five Directions" (*Chao wu-fang o-kuei* 召五方惡鬼) and "Madame Liu Flees the Stage" (*Liu-shih t'ao-p'eng* 劉氏逃棚), ten thousand and more people all shouted at once.[94]

---

[92] See *Yü-yao hsien-chih* (1899), 5:2b–4b and 11:21b. For more on similar festivals throughout Chekiang, see Shang Tu, "Ch'ing-ch'ao Chiang-nan jen shu-t'ien chu-yi te su-hsin," in *Li-shih yüeh-k'an*, 19 (August 1989): 53–61; and, Chiang, *Wu-Yüeh min-chien hsin-yang*, pp. 421–470.

[93] For information on exorcistic dance troupes in Chekiang, see *Chiang-hsiang chieh-wu shih*, in *WLCKTP*, vol. 4, pp. 2214–2217; *Wu-lin tsa-shih shih*, in *WLCKTP*, vol. 12, pp. 7524–7529; and *JHHC* (1687), 5:24a.

[94] See Chang's *T'ao-an meng-yi*, 6:47–48. This passage has been translated in David Johnson, "Actions Speak Louder Than Words: The Cultural Significance of Chinese Ritual Opera," in Johnson, ed., *Ritual Opera, Operatic Ritual* (Berkeley: University of California Press, 1989), pp. 1–45, esp. p. 9. See also his "Scripted Performances in Chinese Culture: An Approach to the Analysis of Popular Literature," in *Han-hsüeh yen-chiu* 8.1 (June 1990): 37–55. Other studies of Chekiang Mu-lien operas include Lo P'ing, "Che-tung min-chien ya-chu — Ya Mu-lien," *Hsi-ch'ü yen-chiu* 16 (1985): 241–261; Hsü Hung-t'u, "Che-chiang sheng Tung-yang shih Han-jen sang-tsang yi-shih chi yi-shih chü tiao-ch'a," *Min-su ch'ü-yi* 84 (July 1993): 197–224; and, Chiang, *Wu-Yüeh min-chien hsin-yang*, pp. 368–388. A two-volume special issue of *Min-su ch'ü-yi* entitled *Mu-lien hsi chuan-chi* 目連戲專輯 was published in 1992 (#'s 77 and 78). For regulations in Hangchow attempting to control such performances, see *Wu-lin ts'ao*, in *WLCKTP*, vol. 4, p. 1881. Piet van der Loon's seminal essay "Les Origines Rituelles du

The exorcistic nature of Mu-lien dramas can be seen even more clearly in this twentieth-century account of "tranquility operas" (*p'ing-an hsi* 平安戲)[95] performed in Shaohsing during the fifth and sixth lunar months:

> [People watching the Mu-lien operas] put peach branches and peach leaves in their hair, which they say keep the ghosts away[96] . . . While the opera is being presented, many actors costumed as evil ghosts cavort around the base of the stage. At daybreak, they are driven underneath the stage. It is said that this means all the evil ghosts of the village have been driven away . . . [Those in the audience] must stay until dawn. If anyone leaves before the opera is over [i.e., while it is still dark], a real ghost will certainly follow them home.[97]

Apart from participating in prophylactic festivals, individuals could take extra measures to protect themselves by procuring a charm/talisman, either from a temple, a Taoist priest or Buddhist monk, a local priest, or a spirit medium. In addition, many people pasted images of the Door Gods on the doors of their houses during the New Year. Images of Chung K'uei or the First Heavenly Master Chang Tao-ling were also pasted on most doors during the Dragon Boat Festival.[98] Most charms were meant to be used before epidemics had begun, although others could be used to heal the sick during an

---

Théâtre Chinois," *Journal Asiatique* 265 (1977): 141–168, remains the finest introduction to Chinese ritual drama.

[95] While the dramas performed during Marshal Wen's festival in Wenchow were also called "tranquility operas", it is not clear if they included Mu-lien operas. For more on tranquility operas in Chekiang, see *Ch'ung-hsiu Che-chiang t'ung-chih kao* (1948), vol. 18:7a, and Hu P'u-an *Chung-hua ch'üan-kuo feng-su chih, hsia-p'ien, chüan* 4 "Che-chiang," pp. 48–49 (Chen-chou: Chung-chou ku-chi ch'u-pan-she reprint of 1923 edition, 1990).

[96] For the use of peachwood to exorcise demons, see Bodde, *Festivals*, pp. 128–137.

[97] Johnson, "Ritual Opera," p. 10. The writer Lu Hsün knew and participated in these Shaohsing rites; see Johnson, pp. 11–12. Hsü Hung-t'u has recently published a field report of another type of exorcistic ritual drama performed in Shaohsing. See "Jih fan chiu-lou, yeh yen Meng-chiang — Shao-hsing Meng-chiang hsi ch'u-t'an," *Min-su ch'ü-yi*, 92 (1994): 781–818.

[98] See Po Sung-nien, *Chung-kuo nien-hua shih* (Liaoning: Liao-ning mei-shu ch'u-pan-she, 1986); and, Po Sung-nien and David Johnson, *Domesticated Deities and Auspicious Emblems* (Berkeley: University of California Press, 1992), esp. pp. 105–147. See also Bodde, *Festivals*, pp. 127–138; Huang, *Tuan-wu li-su*, pp. 164–167; and, *CKMCCS*, pp. 222–247.

epidemic. Take, for example, the charm used to deceive plague spirits
contained in the collected works of Kao Lien 高濂 (fl. 1587; a native of
Ch'ien-t'ang) which reads *t'ien-hsing yi-kuo* 天行已過, literally "the
heavenly travellers have passed", in reference to the Five
Commissioners of Epidemics.[99] Almanacs contained charms for every
day of each lunar month which could be used to cure disease; nearly
identical charms may be found in almanacs on Taiwan today.[100]

The prophylactic rituals described above were all meant to
prevent outbreaks of contagious diseases; but what if they had failed
to work and an epidemic was raging through the community? Under
these circumstances, the people of Chekiang turned to a varied set of
apotropaic rituals, some of which have already been briefly mentioned
above. Some people would invite members of the Buddhist sangha to
perform rituals. As early as the Six Dynasties, the monk Chu Fa-kuang
竺法廣 (327–402) performed rites to heal the sick during an epidemic
in Chekiang, and the reformist monk Yün-ch'i Chu-hung 雲棲祩宏
(1535–1615) performed a Tantric rite to feed hungry ghosts (literally
"flaming mouths" [*yen-k'ou* 焰口]) near Hangchow during an epidemic
in 1588. In the year 1642, Ch'i Piao-chia summoned Buddhist monks to
hold ceremonies at his home in order to protect his family from that
year's pestilence.[101] On other occasions, expulsion rites involving local
deities could be held at Buddhist temples.[102] Ofuchi Ninji has shown
that some Buddhist liturgical collections dating from the Yüan
dynasty contain documents for use in boat expulsion rites, providing
tantalizing evidence that the Taoist rites so frequently performed in
south China during the late imperial period may have been linked to
Buddhist (perhaps Tantric?) ritual traditions.[103] As we shall see in the

---

[99] Kao Lien, *Tsun-sheng pa-chien*, 6:15a. See also Ch'en Hsiang-ch'un, "Examples
of Charms Against Epidemics With Short Explanations," *Folklore Studies* 1 (1942): 37–54.

[100] See *Tseng-pu Wan-pao ch'üan-shu* (1823; 1739 preface by Mao Huan-wen),
chüan 20; and Liu Ch'un-yi, *Liu-shih chia-ts'ang*, 5:25a–b. A fine introduction to these
almanacs may be found in Richard J. Smith's *Chinese Almanacs* (Hong Kong: Oxford
University Press, 1992). See also Sakai Tadao, "Confucianism and Popular Educational
Works," in Wm. Theodore deBary, ed., *Self and Society in Ming Thought* (New York:
Columbia University Press, 1970), pp. 331–338.

[101] See Erik Zürcher, *The Buddhist Conquest of China* (Leiden: E. J. Brill, 1959), pp.
144–145; Yü Chün-fang, *The Renewal of Buddhism in China: Chu-hung and the Late Ming
Synthesis* (New York: Columbia University Press, 1981), pp. 144–145; and Ch'i Piao-chia
(1602–1645), *Chi Chung-min kung jih-chi* (1642), 18b. For more on Buddhist healing, see
Paul Demieville *Buddhism and Healing*, trans. by Mark Tatz (Lanham, Md.: University
Press of America, 1985); and Raoul Birnbaum, *The Healing Buddha* (Boston and
Shaftesbury: Shambhala Publications, 1991).

[102] See *Su Tung-p'o chi*, *chüan* 33 (Taipei: Shang-wu yin-shu-kuan, 1967), p. 37;
and *CCFSCC*, p. 401.

[103] Ofuchi Ninji, *Shūkyō girei*, p. 197. See also Omura Seigai, *Mikkyō hattatsu shi*

following chapter, Marshal Wen's iconography appears to have been influenced by that of a Tantric Buddhist martial deity who specialized in expelling epidemics.

In addition to these rites, marionette performances were viewed as especially efficacious in expelling plague demons, perhaps because the patron deities of the marionette theatre are said to have expelled plague demons haunting the the T'ang emperor Hsüan-tsung (r. 712–756).[104] Ritual dances, such as the "Dance of the Five Fierce Ones" (*t'iao Wu-ch'ang* 跳五猖), were also held to expel demonic forces.[105]

Finally, people hired Taoist priests or ritual masters to perform plague expulsion rites, including those culminating in the burning or sending off of a boat. The *Taoist Canon* contains all manner of such rituals, among them the powerful *T'ai-shang san-wu pang-chiu chiao Wu-ti tuan-wen yi* (*TT* 566; *CT* 809), and a lantern ritual entitled *Cheng-yi wen-ssu pi-tu shen-teng yi* (*TT* 84; *CT* 209).[106] Numerous other plague expulsion rituals may be found in the *Tao-fa hui-yüan*, especially *chüan* 7–9, 46–49, 111–128 and 227–228. There were also non-canonical Taoist expulsion rites like the "Divine Lantern Rite for Relieving Epidemics" (*Jang-wen sheng-teng k'o*), included in *chüan* 14 of the *Shang-ch'ing ling-pao chi-tu ta-ch'eng chin-shu* (1432).[107] Plague expulsion rituals linked to the cult of Marshal Wen will be discussed in greater detail in chapter 5.

If apotropaic rituals failed to work, one could always try to trick those spirits who caused epidemics into leaving. This was often

---

(1918), a Chinese translation of which has been published in *Shih-chieh fo-chiao ming-chu i-ts'ung*, vols. 72–74 (Taipei: Hua-yü ch'u-pan-she, 1986), pp. 440–444, 547–548 and 830–831.

[104] See Schipper, "The Divine Jester, Some Remarks on the Gods of the Chinese Marionette Theatre," *Bulletin of the Institute of Ethnology, Academia Sinica*, 21 (Spring 1966): 81–95.

[105] See Chiang Yi-min, "Kuan-yü shen-wu 'T'iao Wu-ch'ang' ch'u-k'ao," *Wu-tao yi-shu* 13 (1985): 142–146; Yin Ya-chao, *Chung-kuo ku-wu yü min-wu yen-chiu* (Taipei: Kuan-ya wen-hua shih-yeh yu-hsien kung-ssu, 1991), pp. 256–267; Tanaka, *Chūgoku fūkei engeki kenkyū*, pp. 997–1022; Mao Keng-ju, "Wan-tung Nan-hsü-ho nan-an te 'T'iao Wu-ch'ang'" *Min-su ch'ü-yi*, 92 (Nov. 1994): 1093–1123; and, Chiang, *Wu-Yüeh min-chien hsin-yang*, pp. 466–467. The Five Fierce Ones may be related to a group of five plague demons by that name described in Wen's hagiography (see *TT* 557; *CT* 780:8a–9b).

[106] This may be an antecendent of the Five Thunder Lamps (*Wu-lei teng* 五雷燈) ritual performed in Taiwan at plague festivals. For the text of this rite, see Ofuchi, *Shūkyō girei*, pp. 383–386.

[107] This work is included in an important new collection of non-canonical Taoist texts entitled *Tsang-wai tao-shu* (Cheng-tu: Pa-shu shu-she, 1992), vol. 17, pp. 520–522. The entire *Shang-ch'ing ling-pao chi-tu ta-ch'eng chin-shu* fills volumes 16–17 of this collection.

done by celebrating the Lunar Chinese New Year during the summer months, in the hope that such spirits would think their tour of duty on earth had ended and go away. One fascinating story tells of a Kiangsu native named Hsü Kung-ting 徐公鼎, who in 1808 encountered five "plague commissioners" (*hsing-yi shih-che* 行疫使者; in all likelihood the Five Commissioners of Epidemics) while on his way to take up an official post in Ch'eng-tu. They told him they were also on their way to Ch'eng-tu, and would not leave until the New Year. This was during the third month; by the time Hsü reached Ch'eng-tu it was already the fourth month and people were dying at a rate of over eight hundred a day. Hsü ordered that the New Year be celebrated on the fifteenth day of the fifth lunar month, complete with fireworks and the Lantern Festival. After the celebrations, the epidemic ceased.[108]

Similar practices continue in China even in modern times. In the spring of 1988, some truck drivers in Heilungkiang stopped to let two snakes cross the road. These serpents turned into beautiful women, who thanked the men and informed them that many calamities would strike the area unless a second New Year was celebrated. This story spread quickly throughout northeast China, and many communities did in fact do as the snake-women had instructed.[109]

If all else failed, one could always attempt to coerce the plague deities into relenting. For example, the late-Ch'ing pictorial *Tien-shih chai hua-pao* contains a story of a Wenchow artisan who spent huge sums of money on offerings to the Five Commissioners of Epidemics in order to have his three sons cured, all to no avail. In a rage, the artisan stormed into the temple and decapitated all of the images.[110] Flagellating the image of a deity or exposing it to the elements was another ritual alternative (in ancient times human beings, particularly spirit mediums, were also used). However, such practices were usually connected with fertility and rain-making rituals, not the expulsion of epidemics.[111]

---

[108] See Ch'ien Yung (1759–1844), *Lü-yüan ts'ung-hua* (1825), *ts'ung-hua* 14, (Peking: Chung-hua shu-chü, 1983), pp. 380–381. See also Shang, "Chu-yi te su-hsin," pp. 56–57.

[109] This story was published in the April 22, 1988 issue of the *China Post*, an English-language newspaper in Taiwan. A friend of mine who lived in Tsingtao (Shantung) during the spring of 1988 reported having witnessed second New Year celebrations.

[110] See Shang, "Chu-yi te hsin-su," pp. 59–60. See also Alvin P. Cohen, "Coercing the Rain Deities in Ancient China," *HR* 17.3–4 (Feb.–May 1978): 244–265, for accounts of officials flogging or otherwise abusing images of deities who failed to respond to prayers for assistance.

[111] *Ibid.*; and Edward Schafer, "Ritual Exposure in Ancient China," *HJAS* 14

In the world of late imperial China, where medicine often proved ineffective against epidemics, and relief efforts only reached a small percentage of the populace, people usually turned to ritual remedies when contagious diseases struck. Even with the advent of more effective medical techniques, these rites have persisted in places like Hong Kong, Malaysia, and Taiwan, and have even reappeared in China.[112] In the case of modern festivals, this is because they influence local political systems, promote local commerce, express ethnic or kinship affiliations, and attract tourists, much as their late imperial predecessors did. One new wrinkle in these festivals is that they are now held in order to prevent all manner of calamities, not just epidemics. Today's plague deities have thus been transformed in the popular imagination into nebulous malevolent beings, informants describing them as spirits who cause floods or sink fishing boats. It seems logical to conclude therefore, that Chinese people throughout the world will continue to engage in these ritual actions, providing that political conditions permit.

(1951), 130–184.

[112] See David Jordan, "Changes in Postwar Taiwan and Their Impact on the Popular Practice of Religion," in C. Stevan Harrell and Huang Chün-chieh, eds., *Cultural Changes in Postwar Taiwan* (Boulder: Nestview Press, 1994), pp. 137–160; and Sung Kuang-yü, "Shih-lun ssu-shih nien lai T'ai-wan tsung-chiao te fa-chan," in Sung Kuang-yü, ed., *T'ai-wan ching-yen (2) — She-hui wen-hua p'ien* (Taipei: Tung-tu t'u-shu ku-fen yu-hsien kung-ssu, 1994), pp. 175–224. On religious conditions in modern China, see Julian F. Pas, ed. *The Turning of the Tide. Religion in China Today* (Hong Kong: Oxford University Press, 1989); and, Dean, *Taoist Ritual and Popular Cults*, pp. 3–6, 99–117 and 174–176.

THREE

The Hagiography of Marshal Wen[1]

In the temple, Wen mysterious events records;
Clad in black under the lamps, he reveals his true form.
"I'd rather drink the poison, and save a thousand souls;
My charms revive the people, and keep all creatures whole."

> —Ch'en Tsu-shou 陳祖綬, "Reverent Writings
> To Follow the Loyal and Defending King's
> Hagiography" (*Ching-shu Chung-ching
> Wang chuan hou* 敬書忠靖王傳後), in
> Huang T'i-fang, *A Brief Hagiography of the
> Loyal and Defending King (Wen Chung-ching
> Wang chuan lüeh)*[2]

We have seen in the previous chapter how over the centuries the
people of Chekiang developed a wide array of religious practices —
festivals, performances, processions, rituals, charms, even threats

---

[1] Some of the materials in this chapter have been published in my "Wen
Ch'iung — The God of Many Faces," *Han-hsüeh yen-chiu* 8.1 (1990): 183–219. I have also
been inspired by the work of Glen Dudbridge, who presents a stimulating analysis of
different versions of a deity's hagiography in his "Yü-ch'ih Chiung at An-yang: An
Eighth-Century Cult and Its Myths," *Asia Major*, Third Series, Volume III, Part 1 (1990):
27–49.

[2] A copy of this rare text (only 500 copies were printed) is preserved in the
Wenchow Provincial Library. According a postface written by the text's editor Huang
T'i-fang 黃體方, of whom we know nothing else besides his name, it was compiled in
1879. The hagiography of Wen in this text, written in 1771 by Chao Chia-chi 趙嘉楫 of
Jen-ho County (Hangchow) combines elements of the Wen's *Taoist Canon* hagiography
and popular folktales to be discussed in this chapter. Ch'en Tsu-shou was one of the
compilers of the 1882 edition of the *Yung-chia hsien-chih*, the title page of which lists him
as a Student by Purchase, Second Class (*tseng kung-sheng* 增貢生), who had also served
as a Subprefectural Magistrate (*t'ung-p'an* 通判). Ken Dean has an identical text in his
possession, which he graciously showed to me. See his "Manuscripts from Fujian," *CEA*
4 (1988): 222, #196.

against the gods — to protect themselves against epidemics. But amidst all these possibilities the cult of Marshal Wen remained one of the most popular recourses for those who feared contagious diseases. In the next few chapters, I will take a closer look at the evolution of his cult in Chekiang, as well as his festivals in Wenchow and Hangchow.

Before doing so, however, I intend to analyze a number of hagiographies about Marshal Wen in order to explore the various representations of this deity held by the people of Chekiang. Methodologically, this approach involves a major difficulty: determining the scope of the audience among which different versions of Wen's hagiography actually circulated. It is often difficult to assess what portion, if any, of the hagiographical writings available to us today was accessible to those who were illiterate or uninitiated into a religious tradition, and we often have the sneaking suspicion that what we read in extant written sources may not have corresponded exactly to the stories circulating among a deity's worshippers. Such suspicions are difficult to confirm, however, as the sources available usually reveal only the representations of religious specialists and/or members of the elite. While we may never be able to completely determine the representations of Marshal Wen held by most late imperial Chekiang natives, the survival of several different hagiographies written by people of varying backgrounds can help give us a sense of how a popular deity might be represented by members of different social groups.

For a deity like Marshal Wen, whose cult covered a large area of south China and existed for many centuries, one would expect differences in hagiographical texts to result from the influence of spatial and temporal factors. However, although significant variations do exist in the versions of Marshal Wen's hagiography available to us today, these cannot necessarily be explained along such lines; rather, the hagiographies seem to differ by the genre of the source materials consulted. Sung dynasty texts in the *Taoist Canon* depict Wen as a martial deity in the service of Taoist masters, his mission being to protect the Way and destroy all manner of illicit sacrifices (*yin-ssu*). Accounts written by members of the elite, including a stele inscription as well as a hagiography in the *Complete Compendium of Deities* (*Sou-shen ta-ch'üan* 搜神大全) collections portray him as a brilliant scholar but unsuccessful exam candidate who makes a vow to serve the Emperor of the Eastern Peak after his death. Popular novels, such as the *Journey to the North* (*Pei-yu chi*), and folktales that survive today claim that he sacrificed his own life in order that others might not die in an epidemic. Why do the various versions of Marshal Wen's hagiography differ so greatly, and what do these variations reveal about the nature of the sources that contain them? I will attempt to answer these questions in the pages below.

The origins of Marshal Wen's cult remain a mystery to this day. As many of the hagiographies discused below portray him as having serpentine features, it is possible that he represents the anthropomorphization of one of Chekiang's numerous plague-belching snake deities described in chapter 1. In addition, his iconography and even parts of his hagiography may have been influenced by the Tantric Buddhist martial deity and demon-queller named Āṭavaka or Āṭavika (A-t'o-p'o-chü 阿吒婆拘), also known as the Supreme Marshal (T'ai yüan-shuai 太元師) or the Supreme Marshal and Heavenly King (T'ai yüan-shuai ming-wang 太元師明王). Āṭavaka was originally an Indian non-Aryan deity whose name in Sanskrit literally means "demon of the wilds". He was eventually absorbed into Indian Buddhism, and is frequently mentioned in Tantric exorcistic liturgies as a subordinate of the Four Heavenly Kings. His cult appears to have been transmitted to China during the Six Dynasties, and spread to Japan through the efforts of Tantric monks during the late T'ang. This deity shares a number of iconographical features in common with Marshal Wen, inasmuch as both have green faces, red hair, and long ferocious teeth. Furthermore, one of Āṭavaka's favorite weapons is a wheel of fire, also a common feature of Wen's iconography.[3]

The earliest scriptures on Āṭavaka included in the *Buddhist Canon* were *dharani* sutras (collections of spells) translated into Chinese during the Liang dynasty (502–557). Such works place special emphasis on Āṭavaka's ability to destroy demons who spread epidemics.[4] Perhaps the most important and detailed account of this deity is presented in a scripture translated into Chinese by the T'ang dynasty Tantric Buddhist monk named Śubhakarsiṃha (Shan-wu-wei 善無畏; 637–735),[5] entitled *A-t'o-p'o-chü yüan-shuai ta-chiang shang-fo*

---

[3] See Mochizuki Shinkō, *Bukkyō dai jiten*, third edition, 10 volumes, (Kyoto: Sekai seiten kanko kyōkai, 1954–1971), pp. 1103, 3210–3212.

[4] See *A-t'o-p'o-chü kuei-shen ta-chiang shang-fo t'o-lo-ni shen-chou ching* (T 1237); and, *A-t'o-p'o-chü kuei-shen ta-chiang shang-fo t'o-lo-ni ching* (T 1238). Michel Strickmann has shown that many *dharani* sutras contained spells to be used against plague demons. See his "The *Consecration Sutra*: A Buddhist Book of Spells," in Robert E. Buswell, Jr., ed., *Chinese Buddhist Apocrypha* (Honolulu: University of Hawaii Press, 1990), pp. 75–118. Also see Hsiao Teng-fu, *Tao-chiao yü Mi-tsung* (Taipei: Hsin-wen-feng ch'u-pan-she, 1993).

[5] For more on T'ang Buddhism, see Stanley Weinstein, *Buddhism under the T'ang* (Cambridge: Cambridge University Press, 1987). Chou Yi-liang's "Tantrism in China," *HJAS* 8 (1945): 241–332 is a good Western language introduction to this topic. See also Raoul Birnbaum, *Studies on the Mysteries of Manjusri: A Group of East Asian*

t'o-lo-ni ching hsiu-hsing yi-kuei (*T* 1239; 3 *chüan*). This scripture presents Āṭavaka as an all-powerful protective deity to whom Śakyamuni Buddha designates the control of all demonic forces in the world (187c–188b, 190b–c). At one point in this scripture, Śakyamuni Buddha recounts the story of Āṭavaka's life, saying that he was a pilgrim who sacrificed his life to protect others from vicious bandits. Just before his death, he made a vow to protect others by appearing as a ferocious deity when summoned, and also composed a *gatha*. As we shall see below, the theme of self-sacrifice, vow to fight evil as a fierce deity, and composition of a *gatha* are all important features of Marshal Wen's hagiography. I have yet to determine whether Āṭavaka's iconography and hagiography influenced Marshal Wen's, and if so, to what degree. It is, of course, also possible that the features these deities share in common represent pure coincidence. Pending the discovery of convincing evidence to link the two, I can only hypothesize that Marshal Wen's similarities to Āṭavaka may represent one form of Tantric Buddhism's influence on Taoism (and local cults) described by scholars such as Michel Strickmann and Rolf Stein. Valerie Hansen has also shown that the cult of one of Āṭavaka's superiors in the Tantric hierarchy, the Heavenly King of the North Vaiśravaṇa (P'i-sha-men 毗沙門) may influenced the growth of the cult to the City God.[6]

The Marshal Wen of the Taoist Canon[7]

The earliest surviving version of Marshal Wen's hagiography portrays him as a martial Taoist deity whose function is the eradication of local deities considered "heterodox" (*hsieh*) or "licentious" (*yin*) by Taoist priests. Wen's hagiography in the *Taoist Canon*, entitled *The Biography of Grand Guardian Wen, Supreme Commander of Earth Spirits* (*Ti-ch'i shang-chiang Wen t'ai-pao chuan*; *TT* 557; *CT* 780), was edited and

---

Mandalas and their Traditional Symbolism, Society for the Study of Chinese Religions Monograph 2 (1983), pp. 9–36. A brief biography of Śubhakarasiṃha written by Charles D. Orech may be found in the *Encyclopedia of Religions* (New York: Macmillan Publishing Company, 1987), vol. 14, pp. 96–97.

[6] See Hansen, "Gods on Walls", pp. 76, 82, 87–88, 91, 98–100. She also points out that the some Buddhists adopted Kuan Kung as a monastic guardian (*ch'ieh-lan shen* 伽藍神); see pp. 88–90, 96.

[7] John Lagerwey, in chapter 14 of his book on Taoist ritual, provides a detailed summary of Wen Ch'iung's *Taoist Canon* hagiography, while Judith Boltz provides a briefer account of this text, as well as bibliographic notes. See Lagerwey, *Taoist Ritual in Chinese Society and History* (New York: Macmillan Publishing Company, 1987), pp. 241–245; and Boltz, *Survey*, pp. 97–99, notes 59 and 80.

compiled by a Divine Empyrean priest named Huang Kung-chin in 1274. According to a colophon preserved in the *Tao-fa hui-yüan*, Huang was a disciple of Liu Yü 劉玉 (fl. 1258), a renowned Divine Empyrean master of the Southern Sung.[8] In a foreword to a series of rituals invoking Marshal Wen, Huang gives an autobiographical account of his conversion to Taoism, stating that he was a Ch'an (Zen) Buddhist disciple for a number of years until 1247, when in desperation he used Taoist charms to perform a cure. This awakened his interest in Taoist self-cultivation, which he describes as "comprehending perfection and attaining the mysterious" (*t'ung-chen ta-hsüan* 通真達玄).[9] He later kowtowed to Liu as his master, and spent seven years studying charm writing and performance of rituals, plus an additional seven years engaging in Taoist meditation and alchemy (*TFHY* 253:3b-4b).

Huang's first exposure to rituals involving Marshal Wen known as "Earth Spirit Techniques" (*Ti-ch'i fa* 地祇法) also took place at this time. In later years, disturbed by the growing number of variations on the teachings he had learned, Huang resolved to compile Wen's hagiography and ritual texts in order to rectify the situation. As he writes:

> Because there are so many different schools, masters transmit different numbers of varying incantations and formulas [*chou-chueh* 咒訣], with counterfeits deviating from the true original core . . . Today the number of those studying Wen's ritual techniques steadily increases, yet the number of those successful in their efforts steadily declines, causing many to scorn the Earth Spirit Techniques. For these reasons, I composed this text and discussed with my comrades [*t'ung-chih* 同志] what I had done, entreating them to rectify any errors. (*TFHY* 253:3b).

Huang was certainly not alone in his concern with preserving "orthodox" ritual traditions. As I indicated in chapter 1, this was a major issue with most of the ritual movements which arose during the Sung dynasty.[10] Huang's desire to preserve an accurate record of

---

[8] For biographical information on Huang and Liu, see Boltz, *Survey*, pp. 30, 97–99, notes 59, 208 and 257.

[9] Many ritual specialists and healers appear to have begun their careers after being cured through rituals. For example, one descendant of the Sung imperial line named Chao Tzu-chü 趙子舉 became a ritual master after having been ritually cured of a severe affliction allegedly caused by a ghost. See Boltz, "Not by the Seal of Office Alone," pp. 256–257.

[10] Ritual specialists such as Pai Yü-ch'an even attempted to disseminate their

Marshal Wen's rituals may well have resulted from the chaotic conditions he experienced living in south China during the final years of the Southern Sung dynasty just before the Mongol conquest. Apart from believing that such rituals could actually aid people in need during those turbulent times, Huang may have desired to leave a record for posterity of what he saw as a valuable part of traditional Chinese culture.[11]

According to Huang's hagiography, Marshal Wen was a man named Wen Ch'iung who was born in Wenchow's P'ing-yang County during the T'ang dynasty. That his destiny was to be unusual was revealed even before his birth, as his mother became pregnant with him after dreaming of a huge sunwheel (*jih-lun* 日輪), approaching from the south and making a thunderous sound. He grew to a great height, and became known for his martial prowess. During the An Lu-shan Rebellion, he served under Kuo Tzu-yi 郭子儀 (697–781), often using a black vapor to rout his enemies. One day, Kuo had a dream in which Wen transformed himself into a huge one-horned black snake, and was so disturbed by this that he contemplated putting Wen to death. Wen became aware of this, and subsequently fled to the foot of Mt. T'ai, where he made his living as a butcher and a wine-seller[12] until the Taoist deity Master Ping-ling (Ping-ling Kung 炳靈公)[13] revealed to him that slaughtering animals offended the heavens. Inspired by his encounter with Master Ping-ling, Wen proposed entering the Temple of the Eastern Peak to practice Taoist self-cultivation, but Master Ping-ling told him that he lacked the potential to become an immortal (literally "immortal bones" [*hsien-ku* 仙骨])[14] and promptly disappeared. After puzzling things out, Wen did enter the temple, not as an ascetic questing for immortality but as a "Master of Contributions" (*hua-chu* 化主).[15] Wen served in the temple

ritual knowledge among local gentry. *Ibid.*, pp. 269–270.

[11] Such concerns also inspired many Neo-Confucian scholars living in Chekiang during this time to study and produce new editions of the Classics. See Sun K'o-k'uan, *Yüan-tai Han wen-hua chih huo-tung* (Taipei: Chung-hua shu-chü, 1968).

[12] According to the hagiographies of the Supreme Emperor of the Dark Heavens (Hsüan-t'ien shang-ti 玄天上帝) and the Patriarch of the Clear Stream (Ch'ing-shui tsu-shih 清水祖師) circulating in Taiwan today, both were butchers before taking up a religious life. See Chung Hua-ts'ao, *T'ai-wan ti-ch'ü shen-ming te yu-lai* (Taichung: T'ai-wan sheng wen-hsien wei-yüan-hui, 1987), pp. 101–105, 126–129; and Ch'iu, *T'ai-wan miao-shen chuan*, pp. 283–284, 454–457.

[13] A higher-ranking deity serving the Emperor of the Eastern Peak. According to some hagiographies, he was a son of the Emperor. See *CKMCCS*, pp. 291–296.

[14] It is said that an individual must have such bones to qualify as a Taoist priest. See Schipper, *The Taoist Body*, p. 58.

[15] An abbreviation of the expression "master in charge of begging for alms" (*hua-yüan chih chu* 化緣之主). Lagerwey interprets the term *hua-chu* as "chief of the

for a period of three years, after which a yellow-robed Taoist with dishevelled hair appeared before him, telling him that he was destined to serve the Emperor of the Eastern Peak in the afterlife and that he should set up a statue of himself inside the temple. After having been told by one of the temple's spirit mediums that he would enter the Emperor's service upon the transformation of his statue, Wen went to gaze at it every day. Thinking to poke fun at him, some of the apprentices in the temple painted his statue green and stuck tusks in its mouth. When, on the fifteenth day of the third lunar month, Wen came before his statue to burn incense (at the Hour of the Tiger = 3–5 a.m.), he was transformed into a deity on the spot, as were the mischievous apprentices, who became his servants.

Wen's body did not decay after his death (a sign that he had attained immortality), prompting the imperial court to enfeoff him as the Grand General of Manifest Virtue (Hsien-te ta chiang-chün 顯德大將軍). At the same time, the villagers who lived near the mountain proposed erecting a separate temple for him. He refused both honors, claiming that to accept them would violate his desire to "support the Orthodox Way" (*fu-ch'ih cheng-tao* 扶持正道) and going so far as to threaten to burn any temple built in his name. A year later, on the anniversary of his death, Wen received a post in the court of the Emperor of the Eastern Peak at the recommendation of Master Ping-ling, his responsibilities being to administer the registers of life and death.

In the year following the founding of the Sung dynasty (961), the people of Wenchow prayed to the Emperor of the Eastern Peak to end a drought. That same night, a flag appeared in the clouds with Wen Ch'iung's name on it, following which the rains came. Once again, grateful worshippers wanted to erect a temple for Wen and once again he refused, this time possessing one of the people and

---

mediums who communicate with the souls of the dead in the Temple of the Eastern Peak," while stating that *t'ai-pao* 太保 refers to "Taoist priests when they perform military rituals" (Lagerway, *Taoist Ritual*, p. 242). However, in Buddhism, *hua-chu* refers to a monk, an abbot (*chu-ch'ih* 住持), or a lay Buddhist responsible for soliciting contributions from the faithful. See Nakamura Hajime, *Bukkyōgo Dai Jiten* (Tokyo: Tokyo Shōseki, 1978), p. 290. In Sung dynasty Taoist temples, a *hua-chu* was most likely a Taoist monk or high-ranking temple worker. *T'ai-pao*, on the other hand, *was* used to refer to mediums in south China as early as the Sung. See Yü Yen (fl. 1260's), *Shu-chai yeh-hua*, 1:4b. This text can be found in vol. 37 of the *Hsü-chü chen-pen ts'ung-shu*, edited by Yen Yi-p'ing (Taipei: Yi-wen yin-shu-kuan, 1972). According to the *Sung-chiang fu-chih* (1884), 5:13a, "Male spirit-mediums [*nan-wu* 男巫] are called *t'ai-pao* ... females [*nü-wu* 女巫] are called [female] masters [*shih-niang* 師娘]." One should also consult Yi Hsi-chia, et. al., "T'ai-pao yü tso-she," in *Chung-kuo min-chien wen-hua*, volume 7, pp. 199–214.

revealing that he placed no value in temples, sacrifices, or titles. Wen claimed that he would prefer his meritorious acts be reported to the Supreme Emperor of the Dark Heavens in order to gain that deity's respect.[16] The locals did so, and also held a Taoist offering ritual in order to show their reverence for both deities.

In the waning years of the Northern Sung, the 30th Heavenly Master Chang Chi-hsien 張繼先 (ritual name (*fa-ming* 法名) = Hsü-ching 虛靖) (1092-1126)[17] visited Mt. T'ai and rewarded Wen for his "conversion to the Orthodox Way" (*kuei-i cheng-tao* 歸衣正道) by promoting him to the rank of Earth Spirit and bestowing various charms (*fu* 符) and seals (*chuan* 篆) on him, thereby creating a ritual technique (*fa* 法) which Taoist masters could use to expel demons and fight evil. Over the years, other Heavenly Masters and Taoist priests used Wen's ritual techniques or summoned Wen himself in their battles against "heterodox deities" (*hsieh-shen* 邪神) — many of whom were local deities who appear to have been awarded official titles! — in provinces such as Szechwan, Fukien, Chekiang, and Anhwei. In all these stories, Wen appears as a "ferocious general" (*meng-chiang* 猛將), his mission being to assist Heaven in making the Tao manifest by eradicating all demons. He frequently overcomes demons who spread epidemics, a function he continued to perform as a local deity in areas of Chekiang.

Over three-quarters of Marshal Wen's hagiography in the *Taoist Canon* is devoted to recounting these exploits against various "heterodox" cults in south China. During his travels in Fukien, a Taoist named Wu Tao-hsien 吳道顯 encountered a deity who used a form of sorcery known as "Gold Cocoon Ku Poison" (*chin-chien ku-tu* 金繭蠱毒) to control people by capturing their souls (*shou jen hun-p'o* 收人魂魄).[18] Travelling merchants in particular suffered greviously from his attacks. In order to destroy this evil deity, Wu utilized the Tantric Buddhist ritual technique of catoptromancy (summoning a deity by use of a mirror)[19] to call on Marshal Wen, as well as the T'ien-p'eng

---

[16] The Supreme Emperor of the Dark Heavens represents an anthropomorphization of the stellar deity known as the Dark Warrior (Hsüan-wu 玄武). For more on the growth of his cult, see chapter 4.

[17] Boltz, *Survey*, pp. 48, 63, 194–195; Sun K'o-k'uan, *Yüan-tai Tao-chiao chih fa-chan* (Taichung: Tung-hai University, 1968), pp. 33-41; Chuang Hung-yi, *Ming-tai Tao-chiao Cheng-i p'ai* (Taipei: Hsüeh-sheng shu-chü, 1986), pp. 36–43; and Chang Chi-yü, *T'ien-shih Tao shih-lüeh* (Peking: Hua-wen ch'u-pan-she, 1990), pp. 83–84, 196.

[18] See Feng Han-yi and John K. Shryock, "The Black Magic in China Known as Ku," *Journal of the American Oriental Society* 55 (1935): 1–30; and deGroot, *Religious System*, vol. 5, pp. 826–869.

[19] See chapter 5 of Michel Strickmann's draft *Magical Medicine*.

Incantation (T'ien-p'eng chou 天篷咒).[20] Wu used similar magic to destroy a Fukien temple to the Five Fierce Administrators of Epidemics (Wu-ch'ang wen-ssu 五猖瘟司;[21] see *TT* 557; *CT* 780:6b-10b for the above stories). There are also attempts to show Marshal Wen doing the work of the Heavenly Masters, such as when he assists the 30th Heavenly Master Chang Chi-hsien in annihilating the remnants of a demon horde at Ch'ing-ch'eng Shan 青城山 (near Ch'eng-tu) that had originally been defeated by the First Heavenly Master Chang Tao-ling (*Ibid.*, 3b–5b).[22]

A condensed version Marshal Wen's hagiography is located in Huang's preface to one of the ritual techniques for Wen entitled "The Secret Technique of Investigations and Summonses of Grand Guardian Wen of the Eastern Peak" (*Tung-yüeh Wen t'ai-pao k'ao-chao pi-fa; TFHY* 254). This text portrays Wen as developing an interest in Taoism as a young man, serving as a commander of the soldiers of the Emperor of the Eastern Peak. The text also claims that Wen aided another reputed leader of the Heavenly Master movement, the T'ang dynasty Taoist master Yeh Fa-shan 葉法善 (616–720/722?), in expelling plague demons who had been ravaging Szechwan. As no work on Yeh, including his hagiography in the *Taoist Canon* (*TT* 557; *CT* 779), mentions him as ever having used ritual techniques featuring Marshal Wen, Huang's claim probably represents an attempt to enhance the legitimacy of Wen's cult by extending its history back to the T'ang.

Throughout Marshal Wen's hagiography, Huang Kung-chin makes a great effort in attempting to link Wen to Heavenly Master Taoism. He places particular emphasis on the Heavenly Master Chang Chi-hsien, going so far as to list Chang as the chief ritual master of two of Marshal Wen's ritual techniques preserved in the *Tao-fa hui-yüan* (*chüan* 255–256). However, none of the biographical data on Chang Chi-hsien indicates that he practiced Marshal Wen's rites. As in the case of Yeh Fa-shan, Huang seems to have concocted this connection in order to enhance the status of Marshal Wen in the eyes of other

---

[20] For more on the T'ien-p'eng Incantation and its links to the cult of Marshal T'ien-p'eng, see *T'ai-shang tung-yüan Pei-ti T'ien-p'eng hu-ming hsiao-tsai shen-chou miao-ching* (*TT* 29 ; *CT* 53); and, *TFHY*, *chüan* 156–168, esp. 157:18, 159:3–11, 159:19–23 and 164. Like Marshal Wen, Marshal T'ien-p'eng was an exorcistic deity who served under the Supreme Emperor of the Dark Heavens.

[21] These may be related to the Five Fierce Ones (Wu-ch'ang) described in chapter 2.

[22] See the Ming-period *Han T'ien-shih chia-shih* (*TT* 1066: *CT* 1463), *chüan* 2; and Chao Tao-yi (fl. 1294–1307), *Li-shih chen-hsien t'i-tao t'ung-chien* (*TT* 139–148; *CT* 296), *chüan* 18 for accounts of Chang Tao-ling's exploits versus the demons of Ch'ing-ch'eng Shan.

Taoist priests. Evidence in the *Taoist Canon* indicates that Wen's ritual techniques were originally practiced by Divine Empyrean masters during the early years of the Southern Sung. These included Huang's master Liu Yü, as well as Liu's masters Hsü Hung-chi 徐洪季 and Lu Chün-po 盧君伯.[23] As Huang composed Wen's hagiography at a time when the Divine Empyrean movement was gradually being absorbed into the Heavenly Masters movement, this work may represent a conscious attempt to declare his loyalty to his new superiors. It is also possible that Huang's text was reworked by Heavenly Master Taoists of the Yüan or Ming dynasties.

The hagiography of Marshal Wen in the *Taoist Canon* is a text written by one Taoist for other Taoists; this is made clear in Huang's foreword. As a result of this, the theme of preserving "orthodox Taoism" is constantly stressed, not surprising for a work written when half of China had been lost to non-Han invaders, with the other half teetering on the brink of collapse. There is also great emphasis placed on the theme of deities knowing their places within the system. In his first encounter with Master Ping-ling, Wen is chided about his desire to become an immortal — such things are beyond his reach, he is told. Later, he refuses all honors offered by his worshippers and the imperial court, thus avoiding the trap of becoming a "heterodox" local deity like the ones he is under orders to destroy.

The sometimes polemical tone of Marshal Wen's hagiography in the *Taoist Canon*, with its emphasis on Wen's power to destroy various "heterodox" cults, may be due to Huang Kung-chin's desire to enchance the status of Wen's cult in the eyes of other Taoists. When Huang composed Wen's hagiography, he did so with very little regard for historical fact; thus we find Wen's ritual techniques first being practiced by the early twelfth-century Heavenly Master Chang Chi-hsien, only to be subsequently utilized by the Chen-tsung (r. 998–1023) period Taoist Wang Tsung-ching 王宗敬 and his disciple Wu Tao-hsien. Such anachronisms might best be explained by the fact that Huang Kung-chin was less concerned with writing a historical work than a didactic piece. For example, Huang launches a number of vicious attacks against the "heterodox" teachings of the Three Altars (San-t'an 三 壇) movement practiced by Hsü Wen 許溫 and Hao Pien 郝邊, although the identities of these men or the contents of their teachings remains unclear (*TT* 557; *CT* 780:3b and 11a). One of the most fascinating incidents involves a deity named King K'ang (K'ang Wang 康王); who had once been one of Wen's fellow earth spirits but

---

[23] See *TFHY* 253:3b–6b, 10a–12a. For research on Divine Empyrean lineages, see Strickmann, "Sōdai no raigi," pp. 19–21.

had turned to practicing evil, including spreading epidemics. He was captured by Wen, and received one hundred blows as punishment for his misdeeds (*Ibid.*, 13a–15a). However, most sources portray King K'ang as a deity nearly identical to Marshal Wen — a martial figure invoked to expel evil demons, including those who spread epidemics.[24] Some sources even claim that King K'ang was a Sung-dynasty war hero named K'ang Pao-yi 康保裔, who died fighting the Khitans in the year 1000.[25] Such wildly divergent perceptions of the same deity may reflect rivalries between different ritual movements, or between Taoism and local cults.

At the end of Wen's hagiography in the *Taoist Canon* is an addendum written by Huang, which opens with the earliest surviving story concerning Wen's links to epidemics. It reads:

> General Wen was loyal and upright, serving the Deities of the Peaks in protecting the cult [literally "incense fire" (*hsiang-huo* 香火)] of the Supreme Emperor of the Dark Heavens . . . One day the Northern Emperor [Pei-ti 北帝; probably a reference to the Lord of the Pole Star (Pei-chi hsing-chün 北極星君)] transmitted one thousand pills of plague poison (*wen-yao* 瘟藥) to the Emperor of the Eastern Peak, ordering him to deploy a commissioner to spread the plague [*ch'ien-shih hsing-wen* 遣使行瘟] . . .

> Upon receiving this edict, the Emperor of the Eastern Peak summoned Wen to spread the plague . . . Later, Wen thought things over, saying to himself: "One of these pills can kill thousands of people and harm thousands of households, not to mention that climatic currents (*ch'i-hou ch'uan-liu* 氣候傳流) will spread this poison even further. This will cause additional deaths . . . It would be better for me to die in place of all those thousands and save countless lives; if such is to be my fate, I would feel no bitterness." Thereupon he lifted his gaze towards heaven, faced north [because the order to spread the plague had originated with Pei-ti?], and swallowed all the pills. His body was instantly overcome by an unbearable burning sensation, and his belly ached. He then took burning incense and presented

---

[24] For information on the cult and hagiography of King K'ang, see *CKMCCS*, pp. 603–606. The *Chih-shun Chen-chiang chih* (1332), 8:2b–3a contains an account of this deity's exploits against epidemics.

[25] See *Chu-ting yü-wen* (1899), 2:22a–b, pp. 155–156. See also K'ang Pao-yi's biography in the *Sung shih*, *chüan* 446, pp. 13149–13152.

himself before the Emperor of the Eastern Peak, where he metamorphosized into a huge ferocious demon [*ta meng kuei* 大猛鬼]. Memorializing his acts, he lay prostrate and awaited his punishment. When the Northern Emperor heard of this incident, he immediately ordered an investigation, at which point the Emperor of the Eastern Peak could do nothing but clearly set out the facts of Wen's crime of disobedience in a memorial to the Northern Emperor. The latter deity ordered the Yu-sheng Yüan [右勝院; similar to the Right Tribunal (Yu-t'ai 右臺)?] to reprimand Wen, but because the Supreme Emperor of the Dark Heavens prized Wen . . . he submitted a memorial pleading for forgiveness of Wen's crimes. This was approved by the Northern Emperor, who ordered that Wen should solely serve the Supreme Emperor of the Dark Heavens in his missions of transforming [the people] through [Taoist] teachings and punishing demons.

Huang Kung-chin's relegation of this story to the addendum section of Wen's hagiography implies that he might have had some doubts as to its authenticity or inherent values. However, as we shall see below, it was stories similar to this one which appear to have enjoyed the greatest popularity among the people of Chekiang. This indicates that despite his polemical statements Huang was able to accept popular accounts of Wen's activities, albeit giving primacy to his own Taoist representation.

The Marshal Wen of the Stele Inscription

Quite a different vision of Marshal Wen emerges in a stele inscription dated 1355 which was composed for one of Wen's temples in Wenchow by the scholar-official Sung Lien 宋濂 (1310–1381; *DMB*, pp. 1225–1231). According to the inscription, a Wenchow Taoist named Ch'u Hsiang-hsi 儲祥曦 built Wen's temple in 1344, with Sung's text being written 11 years later.[26] Sung Lien was a native of Chekiang (born in Chin-hua; spent much of his life in P'u-chiang) who became

---

[26] The Temple of Boundless Numinosity (Kuang-ling Miao 廣靈廟) in P'ing-yang County also claims Sung's inscription was composed for it, although at present it appears that the Wenchow temple's claim bears greater weight (*PYHC* (1694), 7:9b). Even some Hangchow gazetteers record this inscription without noting its Wenchow connections, implying that Sung Lien composed it for a Marshal Wen temple there (see for example *HCFC* (1764), 28:23a–b).

one of the province's most renowned scholars. He represents the Chin-hua tradition of Neo-Confucian studies, whose members not only studied Confucian traditions but Taoist and Buddhist ones as well. Therefore, Sung felt free to compose stele inscriptions for a number of Buddhist and Taoist temples, including Marshal Wen's.[27] How he came to hear of Wen's Wenchow temple and whether he personally supported Wen's cult is unclear. Perhaps he composed the text as a favor to a friend in Wenchow. The fact that he was a native of Chekiang might also explain his support for this popular local cult.[28]

Although Sung's stele inscription postdates Wen's hagiography in the *Taoist Canon* by nearly a century, Sung indicates in a preface to his inscription that its contents may be as old or older.[29] There are a number of points where the two works overlap. For example, Wen is again portrayed as a T'ang figure whose conception occurred after his mother experienced a miraculous event. He also dies standing up (no mention is made of a statue) and is said to have served Yeh Fa-shan in the his campaign to rid Szechwan of various "noxious vapors" (*li-ch'i* 沴氣). An important difference between the two is that one of Wen's titles, The Mighty and Fierce Loyal and Pacifying King of Orthodox Blessings and Manifest Response (Cheng-fu hsien-ying wei-lieh chung-ching wang 正福顯應威列忠靖王), is not included in Huang's work. Most Chekiang gazetteers refer to Wen by an abbreviated form of this title — Chung-ching wang (Loyal and Defending King) — implying that it probably enjoyed greater popularity than those titles mentioned in Huang's hagiography. According to Sung Lien, Wen's titles were bestowed during the Sung. However, neither the *Sung shih*, *Sung hui-yao chi-kao*, nor *Sung ta chao-ling chi* provide any record of this, either because these sources are incomplete or because such titles were not granted by the imperial court but created by Marshal Wen's worshippers.

What is most striking about this version of Marshal Wen's hagiography is Sung's portrayal of Wen as a traditional Chinese scholar, not a martial figure. According to this text, Wen was born on the fifth day of the fifth lunar month (the date of Dragon Boat Festival)

---

[27] Sung also had connections with the Divine Empyrean movement, composing a biography of Mo Yüeh-ting, one of the movement's leading figures. See *Sung Wen-hsien kung ch'üan-chi* (53 *chüan*; *Ssu-pu pei-yao* edition), 9:19a–20a.

[28] Donald Sutton has explored the topic of literati support for popular deities in "A Case of Literati Piety: The Ma Yüan Cult from High-T'ang to High-Ch'ing," *Chinese Literature: Essays, Articles, Reviews* 11 (1989): 79–114. See also Leo Hak-Tung Chan, "Narrative as Argument: The *Yuewei caotang biji* and the Late Eighteenth-Century Elite Discourse on the Supernatural," *HJAS* 53.1 (June 1993): 25–62.

[29] Sung Lien refers to a "biographical account" he had seen, but neither gives its title nor describes its contents.

in the year 702.[30] The inscription supplies the names of both his parents — father = Wen Min-wang 溫民望; mother = Chang Tao-hui 張道輝 — and states that his father had passed the T'ang *ming-ching* 明經 exam. Unfortunately, the family was without an heir, and an apprehensive Tao-hui (like so many other women in traditional and modern China) made daily prayers to the gods (in this case, the Emperor on High *(shang-ti* 上帝); i.e., the Jade Emperor) to grant her a son and thus enable her to fulfill her marital obligations to her husband. Her prayers were answered one night when she dreamed of a huge deity descending from heaven carrying a fiery pearl in his hand (the pearl may be a variant of the sunwheel mentioned in the *Taoist Canon*). He revealed to her that he was "the essence of the great fire" *(ta-huo chih ching* 大火之精), and that he would enter her womb in order to be reborn.[31] Chang felt a red glow covering her body, while her innards emitted a faint glow. At this time, she became pregnant. When Wen was born, twenty-four seals written in a special "thunder script" *(chen-chuan* 震篆) were discovered under his left armpit, with half that total under the right one.

At age seven, Wen could perform the Steps of Yü *(Yü-pu* 禹步),[32] while by age fourteen he had already mastered the Five Confucian Classics, the writings of various other ancient philosophers, as well as the teachings of both Buddhist and Taoist masters. Despite having acquired such prodigious knowledge, he failed the *chin-shih* examination at age twenty-six. Greatly disappointed, he lay with his head on his desk and sighed, saying: "Since I am unable in this life to serve my ruler and the people, [I vow that] when I die I will serve as a deity at T'ai-shan, thereby ridding the world of all terrible plagues [*o-li* 惡癘]." Thereupon, he formulated 36 charms and transmitted them to others, saying: "With these you can master all the spirits in the world." When he had finished this task, he suddenly took the form of *yakṣa* (*yeh-ch'a* 夜叉), and died standing erect.

This text supplies important iconographical data about Wen, stating that he wore a red robe like that of an imperial prince and carried a jewelled sword. Riding a swift steed, he would assist Taoist priests performing rituals of interrogation and summoning (*ho-chao*

---

[30] The Ch'ing dynasty almanac *Yü-hsia chi* (1684) confirms that Wen's birthday was celebrated on this date; see *chüan shang*, 3b.

[31] Taoist priests often linked Wen to the fire element. See Lagerwey, *Taoist Ritual*, p. 244.

[32] This is one of numerous paces (*pu-fa* 步法; *pu-kang* 步罡) used to trace magic diagrams which are performed by Taoists in their rituals. See Poul Anderson, "The Practice of *bugang*: Historical Introduction," *CEA* 5 (1989-1990): 15–54.

劾召).[33] Later, grateful worshippers erected shrines to him and prayed for him to respond in times of trouble.

Wen is also portrayed as serving Taoist priests in this text, but the overall idea of the "system" he is fighting for differs greatly from that in the *Taoist Canon*. Wen's background is that of a broad-minded Chinese scholar who is well-versed in the teachings of Buddhism and Taoism. In fact, he seems remarkably similar to Sung Lien, who mastered many of these religions' texts in his childhood. The vow he utters prior to his transformation, while somewhat similar to that of Āṭavaka's, is also full of the idealistic Confucian rhetoric of a young man bent on serving the emperor and the people. While he does work at Mt. T'ai and assist the Taoist master Yeh Fa-shan, his overriding motive is to help bring peace and order to the world, not simply to preserve some sort of Taoist orthodoxy.

Sung Lien's inscription may also have aided the growth of Wen's cult in terms of providing a convincing rationale for gentry support. We find this in a long passage at the end of Wen's hagiography:

> . . . Many of the gentry claim that [Wen's hagiography] is extremely wierd and abtruse [*kuai shen chih chi* 怪神之極].[34] [In fact, such people] truly are unaware that . . . as there are vicious spirits who make people ill, so there must also be strong and upright spirits to expel [these evil creatures]. This is Heaven's unchanging way. The ancient sage-kings [*sheng-shen* 聖神; literally "sage-deities"] could internalize the way of Heaven to instruct the people. They made cauldrons engraved with all the spirits [*chu-ting hsiang-wu* 鑄鼎象物][35] to help the people recognize the divine and lascivious [*shen-chien* 神姦] and make them invulnerable against the attacks of all demons in the wild.[36] What can be done [today], when the vital essences have been depleted and customs debased [*ch'i-li su-wei* 氣漓俗微]? The arts of

---

[33] For a brief introduction to interrogation rituals, see John Lagerwey, "Les têtes des demons tombent par milliers," *L'Homme*, 101 (Jan.–March, 1987), 101–102.

[34] Sung is probably alluding to a passage in Book VII, line 20 of the *Lun-yü (Analects)*, which states that "The Master did not talk of wierd things, feats of strength, chaos, or the spirits" (*tzu pu-yü kuai li luan shen* 子不語怪力亂神). See Legge's translation (Oxford: Claredon Press, 1865–1895), vol. 1, p. 201.

[35] Sung is citing the *Tso-chuan*, the third year of Lord Hsüan (Hsüan-kung san nien 宣公三年 (605 B.C.E.)). See Legge's translation, vol. 5, pp. 291–293. Schipper also discusses this passage in *The Taoist Body*, pp. 175–176.

[36] Referred to as *ch'ih-mei wang-liang* 魑魅魍魎. For an analysis of the identities of these demons, see Bodde, *Festivals*, pp. 102–104.

controlling the forces of *yin* and *yang*, as well as
communicating with the gods [*t'ung shen-ming* 通神明]
have not been transmitted,[37] so that now disciples of
religious specialists [*fang-shih chih t'u* 方士之徒][38] have
misappropriated these subtle powers for their own use. The
ignorant in this world are unaware of the techniques
bequeathed by the sage-kings and say that these are part of
Taoism. Such people frequently deride these techniques as
deceitful and uncanonical. Alas! How is it possible that
these [arts once practiced by the sage-kings] have come to
be seen as deceitful?[39]

The hagiography of Marshal Wen, being full of demons and
accounts of exorcistic techniques, must have seemed to many
Neo-Confucian scholars exactly what Confucius warned his followers
to avoid. However, Sung Lien maintained that such an attitude
strongly contradicted the teachings of China's ancient sage-kings, who
not only believed that knowledge of spiritual forces should be made
available to all people but used such knowledge to instruct and
protect their subjects. In Sung's view, these teachings had been
corrupted through their misappropriation by various religious
specialists, who made such knowledge an esoteric part of their
traditions. According to Sung, a thorough understanding of the
processes which drive the universe will make one realize that it has
the ability to accommodate endless forms of existence, including
plague demons who make people sick and other spirits like Marshal
Wen who specialize in expelling them. Looked at in this light, Wen's
cult should no longer be seen as strange and unorthodox, but as a
necessary part of the cosmic order. Sung Lien's stele inscription would
have been important ammunition for those worshippers who wanted
to protect their cult from government suppression. Even if Wen had

---

[37] As they were in the days of the sage-kings, when all people could know of
the spirit world simply by gazing on the cauldrons referred to above.

[38] Often referred to as "magicians". See Kenneth J. Dewoskin, *Doctors, Diviners
and Magicians of Ancient China: Biographies of "Fang-shih"* (New York: Columbia
University Press, 1983).

[39] The text concludes with a poem describing Marshal Wen's exorcistic prowess
and the offerings presented by his worshippers. I have consulted the following versions
of Sung's inscription: *Sung Hsüeh-shih wen-chi* (40 *chüan; Ts'ung-shu chi-ch'eng* edition),
chüan 16, (Shanghai: Shang-wu yin-shu-kuan, 1939), pp. 560–561; and, *Sung Wen
hsien-kung ch'üan-chi*, 41:3b–4a. Sung's inscription has also been preserved in *chüan* 2 of
the *Chu-ting yü-wen*, as well as numerous Chekiang gazetteers. I wish to thank Lin
Fu-shih of the Institute of History and Philogy, Academia Sinica, for his assistance in
translating parts of Sung's inscription.

never been awarded an official title by the state, the support of a high-ranking scholar-official like Sung Lien gave Wen's cult a measure of prestige which may have protected it from persecution and even attracted support from both scholar-officials and other members of the gentry.

The Marshal Wen of the Complete Compendium[40]

The hagiography of Marshal Wen in the *Complete Compendium of the Deities of the Three Religions and their Origins (San-chiao yüan-liu sou-shen ta-ch'üan)* diverges even further from Huang Kung-chin's account. It is not clear whether this version of Wen's hagiography is older than the above two, or whether it circulated more widely.[41] This hagiography does follow Sung's stele inscription in including the following features: miraculous impregnation, birth on the fifth day of the fifth lunar month, failing the exams, and service of the Heavenly Masters as well as the Emperor of the Eastern Peak. Nevertheless, there are also some important differences, starting with the claim that Wen was born during the Han dynasty (in the year 142 C.E.). His family's residence is given as Whitestone Bridge (Pai-shih ch'iao 白石橋) in P'ing-yang,[42] and his mother made offerings to Lord Millet (Hou-t'u 后土) instead of the Emperor on High. She became pregnant with Wen after a visitation by one of the six *chia* 甲 spirits, who deposited a glowing pearl in her womb.

    The text states that Chang was pregnant for a period of twelve months, and that when she gave birth to Wen Ch'iung auspicious

----

[40] The *San-chiao yüan-liu sou-shen ta-ch'üan* (1909) represents Yeh Te-hui's reprinting of a seven *chüan* Ming edition entitled *San-chiao yüan-liu sheng-ti fo-tsu sou-shen ta-ch'üan*, a copy of which exists in the Naikaku Bunko in Tokyo. There are two other extant *Sou-shen* editions: 1) The Yüan-period *Hsin-pien lien-hsiang sou-shen kuang-chi*, which originally was part of the library of the bibliophile Mao Chin 毛晉 (1599–1659) and has been preserved in the Peking Library; and 2) The Ming-period *Hsin-k'o ch'u-hsiang tseng-pu sou-shen chi ta-ch'üan* (six *chüan*), preserved in both the Naikaku Bunko and the *Hsü Tao-tsang*. Yeh's work was published by Taiwan's Lien-ching Publishing Company in 1980, while the other three are included in the *Chung-kuo min-chien hsin-yang tzu-liao hui-pien* (Taipei: Hsüeh-sheng shu-chü, 1989). Wen's hagiography can only be found in the two *San-chiao* editions; I have yet to determine why the *Hsin-pien* and *Hsin-k'o* editions omit it.

[41] A number of later hagiographical anthologies also reproduce this version of Wen's hagiography, including *Chi-shuo ch'üan-chen hsü-pien* (1880), 14a–15a, pp. 35–37; and *Shih-shen* (1812), *chüan* 5, pp. 41–42.

[42] The 1915 edition of the *PYHC* mentions the earliest location of Wen's temple as having been at Whitestone Well (Pai-shih ching 白石井). See 45:12b.

clouds filled the room (indicating that an exceptional man had been born). The number of seals under Wen's armpits has increased to 40 (left = 24; right = 16), his studies do not include Buddhist and Taoist works, and he fails both civil and military exams. His vow reads: "As a man, I could not serve my ruler and aid the people; therefore [I vow that] after I die I will aid the Emperor [of the Eastern Peak?] in punishing evil and exterminating the wicked." He also composes a *gatha*, which reads:

> Filial piety forms the root,
> Loyalty and righteousness the core,
> I forgive in benevolence,
> Biased judgements abhor.
> By refining the pure,
> Perfection and mystery become whole,
> If you follow my Way,
> Could you not become an immortal?
> I follow by your side,
> Heeding summons or call.

As Wen was pondering what to do next, he suddenly spotted a dragon which dropped a pearl at his feet. He picked up the pearl and swallowed it, while the dragon danced and pranced in the sky, obstructing the sun with its body. Wen thereupon grasped the dragon and bent it into a circle, wrapping it around his arm. At the same time, his face turned green and his hair red. His body became blue in color, with his entire appearance fierce and imposing to behold. He then made a revelation, saying: "Whoever can practice my ritual techniques and chant my *gatha* will be able to bring blessings to the people and all things under heaven. In order to subjugate evil sprites, I will respond (*hsien-ying* 顯應) when called. Do not forget this."

When the Emperor of the Eastern Peak heard of Wen's awesome abilities, he summoned him to become his assistant. After having performed many meritorious acts, he was awarded a title by the Jade Emperor (The General of Manifest Martial Prowess who Aids the Spirits — Chief Military Administrator of Infantry and Cavalry). The Jade Emperor also presented him with a jade flower (*ch'iung-hua* 瓊花; said to confer immortality), a jade circlet, and a gold tablet inscribed with the words "The Carefree Man of the Empyrean" (*wu-chü hsiao-han* 無拘霄漢) in seal script. He was later installed as commander of all the forces of the Five Peaks (Wu-yüeh 五嶽), and was the only marshal permitted an audience before the Jade Emperor.

According to the *Complete Compendium*, Wen received "bloody" meat offerings (*hsüeh-shih*; as opposed to the vegetarian offerings sacrificed by Buddhist and Taoist specialists to their deities) at Wenchow, where he was both feared and respected by the locals. The 36th Heavenly Master Chang Tsung-yen 張宗演 (1244–1291)[43] drafted the forces of the Five Peaks to carry out his own set of ritual techniques, establishing a group of ten grand guardians (*t'ai-pao*) with Wen as their leader. He also ordered temples enshrining their images to be built. One such temple was built in Hangchow during the thirteenth century (see chapter 4), although its links to the Heavenly Master movement have yet to be determined.

The *Complete Compendium* hagiography also gives a great deal of information concerning Marshal Wen's iconography, portraying him as grasping a steel baton (*chien* 簡) in his right hand and a jade circlet in his left (see Figure 3). Father Henri Doré summarizes Wen's *Complete Compendium* hagiography in his account of Wen's cult in Kiangsu. However, the color illustration he supplies labels Wen as a "Heavenly King" (*t'ien-wang* 天王),[44] and shows him holding a *mace* in his *left* hand and the jade circlet in his *right*.[45] The iconography of Marshal Wen in Taiwan features even more variations. In altar scrolls used by Taoists in Tainan, Wen is depicted holding a sword with both hands. In the Kaohsiung-Pingtung region of southern Taiwan, Taoist scrolls of Wen I have seen follow the *Complete Compendium* system, showing him holding the ring in his left hand and the baton in his right.

Although Marshal Wen is once again portrayed as being in the service of the Emperor of the Eastern Peak and Taoist priests, the overwhelming emphasis of his hagiography in the *Complete Compendium* is not on his role as a defender of Taoism but on his ambition to aid all people by fighting the forces of evil. The Confucian nature of his scholarship receives greater emphasis than in Sung's stele inscription, as do the ideals of filial piety and loyalty to the state which lead off his *gatha*. In fact, the hagiographies of Marshal Wen presented in Sung's stele inscription and the *Complete Compendium* seem to be

---

[43] See Boltz, *Survey*, p. 58, note 248; and Chuang, *Ming-tai tao-chiao*, pp. 43–46, 53, 80.

[44] Some papier maché statues of Wen used during *chiao* rites in Taiwan portray him as holding a lute. This probably results from a confusion of his iconography with that of the Eastern Heavenly King Dhrtarashtra, who carries a lute.

[45] Doré claims to have seen a statue of Wen iconographically similar to the illustration at a rural temple about three miles east of Ju-kao in Kiangsu province. See his *Researches into Chinese Superstitions*, D.J. Finn trans. (Shanghai: T'usewei Printing Press, 1931), vol. 9, pp. 204–206. This temple might be the one listed in the *Ju-kao hsien-chih* (1808), 3:61b–62b.

Fig. 3 — Marshal Wen. Reproduced from *San-chiao yüan-liu sou-shen ta-ch'üan* (1909), *chüan* 5 .

addressing the issue of how scholars frustrated in their ambition to serve the state could use Taoism to further their ideals of bringing peace and harmony to the world. It could be argued that this was an important goal of many literati who joined Taoist movements during times of political instability, including those who became members of the Mao Shan movement during the Six Dynasties era and the Perfect Realization movement during the Chin and Yüan dynasties.[46]

Popular Representations of Marshal Wen

While each of the various versions of Marshal Wen's hagiography presented above has its own unique points, they all share one thing in common: that is, they go to great pains to explain why Wen's iconography is so demonic. With a green face, red hair, and sometimes even protruding fangs, Wen seems more like a rampaging demon than a deity who staunchly defends some Taoist or Confucian order. According to the *Taoist Canon* account, two mischievous assistants were responsible for Wen's having such features. Sung's stele inscription merely states that Wen died suddenly while standing up, while the *Complete Compendium* cites the ingestion of a pearl as the cause. Popular hagiographies reveal a different cause for Wen's transformation. They agree that his mutation was caused by something he swallowed, but it was not a pearl — it was plague poison.

Most stories linking Marshal Wen to epidemics portray him as someone who prevents plague deities or plague demons from doing their deadly deeds. The oldest surviving version of such a tale has been preserved in chapter 19 of the novel *Journey to the North*, which was edited and published by the Fukien publisher Yü Hsiang-tou 余象斗 (fl. 1588–1609) during the late Ming.[47] It states that the Stove God of a certain village reported to the Jade Emperor that all the inhabitants of that place persistently engaged in evil deeds. Livid with rage, the Jade Emperor summoned one of the Five Commissioners of Epidemics, Chung Shih-kuei (in charge of epidemics occurring during

---

[46] This point is eloquently stated by Sun K'o-k'uan in his book *Yüan-tai Tao-chiao chih fa-chan*, as well as his *Yüan-tai Han wen-hua chih huo-tung*. For more on Taoism's links to the Chin-Yüan elite, see Ch'en Yüan, *Nan-Sung ch'u Ho-pei hsin Tao-chiao k'ao* (Peking: Chung-hua shu-chü, 1941), pp. 20–26.

[47] This work has been studied and translated by Gary Seaman. See "The Divine Authorship of the *Pei-yu chi*," *JAS* 45.3 (May 1985): 483–497; and, *Journey to the North* (Stanford: Stanford University Press, 1988).

the winter months),[48] and ordered him to use plague poison to exterminate all the village's inhabitants. Chung took his poison down to the Earth God of the village, and instructed him to scatter it in every well the next morning during the Hour of the Snake (9–11 a.m.). On hearing this, the Earth God petitioned Chung, saying:

> It is true that the people are a sorry lot and should be wiped out. But there is one man, named Hsiao Ch'iung 蕭瓊,[49] who makes a living selling beancurd. He is of good heart, and frequently plants virtuous roots [*shan-ken* 善招; *kusāla-mūla*], making great efforts in performing charitable works. This man cannot be harmed. The Commissioner replied: "The good can be saved; the rest cannot be bargained for." After having received the plague poison, the Earth God decided to warn Hsiao of the impending calamity and transformed himself into an old man. Soon he ran into Hsiao, who had gone to a well to draw water for making beancurd. The Earth God stood behind him and said: "You had better take some extra water. Tomorrow at the Hour of the Snake all the water will be poisoned and those who drink it will perish. Don't you drink it!" Terrified by this warning from an unseen source Hsiao thought: "If a deity sent by Heaven is to poison the wells tomorrow and kill all the people, can I conceal what I know and preserve my own life? I would rather die myself and save the lives of the villagers; such an act would add to this old man's hidden merit" [*yin-te* 陰德; believed to bring rewards in this life or the next] . . .

The story goes on to recount how Hsiao Ch'iung went to the vilage well the very next day to confirm the Earth God's warning. Before long, he spotted an old man approaching the well with a packet of poison in his hand. Just when the old man was about to cast its contents into the waters, Hsiao charged forward, snatched the packet away, and swallowed the lot. He died on the spot, his body turning black all over.

The Earth God was terrified at this turn of events, and promptly took Hsiao's three *yang* and seven *yin* souls (*san-hun ch'i-p'o* 三魂七魄) to present to the Jade Emperor. Deeply moved by Hsiao's spirit of self-sacrifice, the Jade Emperor ordered Hsiao to be enfeoffed

---

[48] He was known as Chung Shih-chi in ancient times (see chapter 2).

[49] This is the surname given in most late imperial editions of the novel I have seen. However, some modern Taiwanese editors of this work give his surname as Lei, as does Seaman's translation.

as the Mighty Spirit and Marshal of Epidemics (Wei-ling Wen yüan-shuai 威靈瘟元帥; here the character *wen* 瘟 means epidemics), and bestowed on him a hat, a jade flower, and a golden tablet inscribed with the characters "The Carefree Man of the Divine Empyrean" (see Figure 4). Hsiao persuaded the Jade Emperor to spare the villagers, and used a dream to warn them to change their evil ways. He later served the Supreme Emperor of the Dark Heavens.[50]

Although the surname of the deity featured in this story has changed, there is little doubt that he is in fact Marshal Wen, because his name, iconography and hagiography are strikingly similar to those presented in other texts, not to mention the fact that he also serves the Supreme Emperor of the Dark Heavens. The fact that his surname has changed may be due to the influence of spirit mediums.[51] In Wenchow, his surname is said to have been Lin 林 or Ling 凌;[52] some Shaohsing sources also give Wen's surname as Lin.[53] There is a deity named Lin Hung 林洪 (also known as Marshal Lin) worshipped at Lin-hai (T'ai-chou), whose cult is said to have arisen during the Five Dynasties era. Lin's hagiography states that he had drunk water from a pool which had been poisoned by a dragon. Wen's hagiography may have experienced a degree of overlap with Lin's, but the relationship between these two cults has yet to be determined.[54]

Of all the hagiographical accounts concerning Marshal Wen, those recounting his attempts to prevent epidemics appear to have had the widest circulation. According to an account by the late Ch'ing

---

[50] This combined summary/translation is based on the *Ming dynasty Pei-fang chen-wu tsu-shih hsüan-t'ien shang-ti ch'u-shen chih-chuan*, in *Ku-pen hsiao-shuo ts'ung-k'an*, series 9, volume 1, pp. 191-194. Seaman's translation of this story may be found in *Journey to the North*, pp. 175-177.

[51] In Taiwan, spirit mediums may be largely responsible for creating the 132 different surnames of the Lords (*wang-yeh*) who populate that island's temples. See my "P'ing-tung hsien Tung-kang chen te ying-wang chi-tien," pp. 177-178. For more on the links between spirit-mediums and the cult of the Lords, see Maejime Shinji, "Taiwan no onyakugami, ōya, to sōō no fushū ni tsuite," *Minzokugaku kenkyū*, 4.4 (Oct. 1937): 39-47; Liu, *Min-chien hsin-yang*, pp. 225-228; Cheng Chih-ming, "Wang-yeh ch'uan-shuo (hsia)," *Min-su ch'ü-yi* 53 (June 1988): 101-118; Norma Diamond, *K'un Shen: A Taiwan Villag* (New York: Holt, Rinehart and Winston, 1969), pp. 93-94; Katherine Gould-Martin, "Medical Systems in a Taiwanese village: *ong-ia-kong* (*wang-yeh-kung* 王爺公), the Plague God as Modern Physician," in Arthur Kleinman, et. al., eds., *Medicine in Chinese Cultures: Comparative Studies of Health Care in Chinese and Other Societies* (Washington, DC: U. S. Dept. of H. E. W., 1975), pp. 115-141; and Huang Yu-hsing, *P'eng-hu te min-chien hsin-yang* (Taipei, 1992), pp. 82-122.

[52] See WCFC (1765), *chüan* 9; and, WCFSC, p. 27.

[53] See CCFSCC, p. 328

[54] See *T'ai-chou fu-chih* (1926), 54:4a; *Lin-hai hsien-chih* (1683), 2:13b; and *Lin-hai hsien-chih* (1935), 12:3a.

100

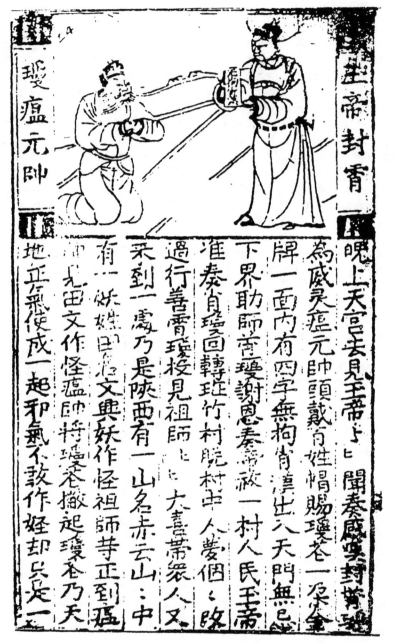

Fig. 4 — Hsiao Ch'iung is Appointed Marshal of Epidemics. Reproduced from *Pei-fang chen-wu tsu-shih hsüan-t'ien shang-ti ch'u-shen chih-chuan*, p. 194.

writer Fan Tsu-shu:

> One night [Marshal Wen] overheard demons putting
> plague poison in a well, and, thinking to rescue the
> populace, he threw himself in. When they fished his body
> out the next day, it had turned black all over, and they
> knew that he had been poisoned.[55]

In Shaohsing, a serpent was responsible for poisoning the waters, while in both Li-shui and Chia-hsing plague demons are blamed.[56] The Reverend Hampden C. DuBose describes a similar story of a deity worshipped in Soochow, and provides a black and white illustration similar to that of Doré's; however, no surname of the deity is given.[57]

One common thread running through all these tales is the link between epidemics and well-poisoning, a theme familiar to those who have studied events surrounding the Black Death in Europe. Wells have always been one of the centers of Chinese life, part of the water-supply and irrigation systems and also a social center where people congregated while drawing water or doing laundry. Wells are also places where drownings occurred, both accidental and intentional, and consequently were conceived of as sites full of spiritual power.[58] For example, Fang Shao (1066–?) Presents the following account of the process of well-boring as it was practiced in eleventh-century Chekiang:

> According to ancient techniques, when boring a well one
> should store up many tens of buckets of water and place
> them where one is thinking of digging. If at night one sees a

[55] Fan Tsu-shu, *The Lost Customs of Hangchow* (*Hang-su yi-feng*) (1864). I have used a recent reprint of a 1928 punctuated edition published in Hangchow, edited by Hung Ju-sung (Shanghai: Wen-yi ch'u-pan-she, 1989). A different edition of Fan's work has also been preserved in vol. 30 of the *Sui-shih hsi-su tzu-liao hui-pien* (Taipei: Yi-wen yin-shu-kuan, 1970). The differences between Sung's stele inscription and Fan's account were of great interest to literati living in Hangchow. For example, Wang T'ung claims that Sung's inscription differed from Fan's account because Fan recorded tales told by Hangchow natives (*WLFSC*, 7:49a).

[56] See *CCFSCC*, pp. 277, 328, 578. A variant of the Li-shui story may be found in Wolfram Eberhard, *Erzählungsgut aus Südost-China* (Berlin: Walter de Gruyter, 1966), pp. 267 and 272. See also *WLFSC*, 7:46a–49b.

[57] See Rev. Hampden C. DuBose, *The Dragon, Image, and Demon* (New York: A. C. Armstrong and Son, 1887), pp. 220–221.

[58] On wells in rural China, see Arthur Smith, *Village Life in China* (New York: F. H. Rovell Co., 1899), pp. 28–31. A number of stories involving wells and spirits can be found in *ICC*, pp. 456–458, 1472–1474. People also drank water from wells during epidemics as a *cure*; see *Chiang-hsi t'ung-chih* (1881), 73:16a–b and 74:26b.

star of unusual largeness in the water, one will certainly
strike a sweet spring. When Fan Wen-cheng Kung 范文正公
[Fan Chung-yen 范仲淹 (989–1052)] had a well dredged at
his residence, they first put many pounds of *ch'ing-chu*
[青朮; *podophyllum versipella*] into it, in order to ward off
febrile vapors [*pi wen-ch'i* 辟溫氣].[59]

Wells were also conceived of as sources of the plague in the West, and
during the Black Death thousands of Jews were persecuted on
trumped-up charges of well-poisoning.[60]

Contemporary Folktales in Taiwan

Stories of deities like Marshal Wen drinking plague poison or
preventing people from falling victim to poisoned waters have also
spread to Taiwan, although their protagonist is not Wen Ch'iung but
various Lords. One of Taiwan's most popular Lords, Ch'ih Wang-yeh
池王爺, appears in many different versions of these stories, one of the
most widely circulated reading as follows:

> Lord Ch'ih [Ch'ih-fu ch'ien-sui 池府千歲] had the
> taboo name [*hui* 諱] of Meng-piao 夢彪 and was a native of
> Ch'en-liu 陳留 [in Honan]. Born during the Sui-T'ang era,
> he had all the qualities of a literatus and a benevolent heart
> ... After the T'ang Emperor Kao-tsu [r. 618–626] overthrew
> the Sui, Ch'ih was appointed as Prefectural Magistrate
> [*chih-fu* 知府], at which post he loved the people as dearly
> as his life.
>   During his tenure, a plague god [*wen-yi shen*
> 瘟疫神] received a decree from the Jade Emperor to

---

[59] Fang Shao, *Po-chai pien, chüan* 2 (Peking: Chung-hua shu-chü, 1983), p.11. The
term "febrile vapors" is often used in conjunction with other compounds meaning
"epidemics." In the chapter entitled "Ming-yi" 命義 (The Meaning of Fate) of Wang
Ch'ung's Han dynasty work *Lun Heng*, there is a passage which reads: "In years when
famines occur, the roads are full of starving people; during epidemics caused by febrile
vapors (*wen-ch'i li-yi* 溫氣癘疫), thousands of families are wiped out." Alfred Forke
translates *wen-ch'i* as "malarial exhalations" in his translation of the *Lun Heng*, (New
York: Paragon Book Gallery, 1962), p. 136. For additional information on prophylactic
measures involving wells, see the Southern Sung ritual calendar entitled *Yang-sheng
yüeh-lan*. This has been photographically reproduced in Mitsuo Moriya, *Chūgoku ko
saijiki no kenkyū* (Tokyo: Teikaku shōin, 1963), p. 474.

[60] See Philip Ziegler, *The Black Death* (New York: Harper and Row, 1969), pp.
97–109.

transform himself into a member of the scholar-official class [*shih-jen* 世人] and head to the area under Ch'ih's jurisdiction. On his arrival, he entered the prefectural yamen and engaged Ch'ih in conversation, during which they found that they saw eye to eye on many issues. Later, they became the closest of friends [*chih-chi* 知己].

One day while they were feasting together, the plague god let it slip that the real nature of his mission was to spread the plague. Ch'ih was horrified when he heard this, and asked the deity: "And by what means will you spread this poison?" Thereupon the plague god took a packet of plague powder [*wen-yi fen* 瘟疫粉] from out of his bag, saying:"I have decided that tomorrow I will scatter this powder in the wells of each village." "Might I have a look?"' Lord Ch'ih asked, to which the god replied: "Since we are best friends, it can do no harm." Lord Ch'ih took the packet in his hands and untied it, following which he swallowed all of the powder. The effects of the poison manifested themselves immediately, as his face became covered with black blotches [*hei-pan* 黑斑] and his eyes bulged out.

Everyone in the prefectural city was deeply moved by Lord Ch'ih's love for them and his act of self-sacrifice, and were terribly saddened by his death. After Ch'ih's ascent to Heaven, the Jade Emperor enfeoffed him as an Inspector in Place of Heaven [*tai-t'ien hsün-shou* 代天巡狩].[61]

Many similar tales continue to circulate in Taiwan today, the vast majority of which appear to be linked to the *Journey to the North* story. Although most Taiwanese stories claim that the deity who saved others from epidemics had the surname Ch'ih, this deity may in fact be related to Marshal Wen. Cheng Chih-ming has speculated that Lord Ch'ih's surname may be based on the fact that in one story he throws himself into a pool (*ch'ih* 池) of poisoned water, his floating corpse warning the people not to drink it (a similar story about a deity named Lin Hung also circulated at Lin-hai; see above).[62] Other scholars have argued that Lord Ch'ih is actually the Taiwanese hero

---

[61] This folktale has been recorded by Cheng Chih-ming in his "Wang-yeh ch'uan-shuo" (hsia), 104, 110–111. For more on local gods interceding on behalf of their communities, see Stephan Feuchtwang, *The Imperial Metaphor. Popular Religion in China* (London and New York: Routledge, 1992), pp. 58–59. On the *hsün-shou* (Imperial Tours of Inspection), see Howard Wechsler, *Offerings of Jade and Silk* (New Haven: Yale University Press, 1985), pp. 161–169.

[62] See Cheng, "Wang-yeh ch'uan-shuo" (hsia), 110–113.

Koxinga (Cheng Ch'eng-kung 鄭成功),[63] but Koxinga has nothing in common with other Marshal Wen or Lord Ch'ih, either hagiographically or iconographically. Of Taiwan's 700-plus Lord temples, at least 131 enshrine Ch'ih as the sole main deity (chu-shen 主神). If one were to include all the temples in which Ch'ih is worshipped along with other Lords as a group of main deities, or as a subsidiary deity (p'ei-shen 陪神), the number of temples enshrining him would exceed half of all the Lords temples on the island.[64]

There is one significant difference between these popular stories from China and Taiwan and Huang Kung-chin's account of Marshal Wen swallowing plague poison presented in the Taoist Canon: that is, in Huang's version Wen is portrayed as a deity with the power to inflict others with epidemics, even though he declines to use it. Despite Wen's strong sense of compassion, however, one still wonders whether he might have originally been worshipped as a spirit capable of spreading epidemics, particularly in the initial period of his cult's growth. There are a number of reasons to suspect that this may have been the case. For one thing, Wen's birthday is celebrated on the date of the Dragon Boat Festival, the traditional time for expelling epidemics in south China and also the birthday of the Five Commissioners of Epidemics. Wen also serves the Emperor of the Eastern Peak, a deity who is not only responsible for one of the courts in the underworld but also governs all manner of other deities, including plague gods.[65] There are records of people in north China worshipping a deity named the Marshal of Epidemics (Wen's title in the Journey to the North) who had a green face and red hair, including a passage in The Story of the Stone (Hung-lou meng).[66] He is also called the Marshal of Epidemics in some Chekiang folktales. It is even possible that the use of the character wen 溫 (meaning "warm"; also a Chinese

[63] See Ts'ai Hsiang-hui, T'ai-wan te wang-yeh yü Ma-tsu (Taipei: T'ai-yüan ch'u-pan-she, 1989), pp. 84–86. I have critiqued Ts'ai's methods and conclusions in a review of his book published in Hsin Shih-hsüeh (New History) 1.1 (March 1990): 155–162.

[64] Ch'iu, Miao-shen chuan, pp. 588–602.

[65] See for example the Southern Sung Taoist scripture entitled T'ai-shang shuo hsüan-t'ien ta-sheng Chen-wu pen-chuan shen-chou miao-ching (TT 530–531; CT 754), 5:18a–19a. For more on this text, see Boltz, Survey, pp. 87–88.

[66] See the translation by David Hawkes (Harmondsworth: Penguin Books, 1973–1986), vol. 2, p. 275. For more on the cult of Marshal Wen in north China, see Amano Genosuke, Chūgoku nōgyō keizairon (Tokyo: Ryūkai shosha, 1978), vol. 3, p. 290; and, Li Ching-han, Ting-hsien kai-k'uang tiao-ch'a (Peking: Chung-hua p'ing-min chiao-yü ts'u-chin-hui, 1934), p. 431. For more on the religion of Ting-hsien (in Hopeh), an area extensively researched by ethnographers during the 1930's, see Sidney Gamble, Ting Hsien: A North China Rural Community (Stanford: Stanford University Press, 1968), pp. 371–425.

surname) instead of *wen* 瘟 ("fevers" or "epidemics") in Marshal Wen's titles may have been due to his cult's deep roots in Wenchow.[67]

In addition to this, the *Taoist Canon* version of Marshal Wen's hagiography mentions that he could transform himself into a snake and belch forth black fog to overcome his foes. As I have shown in chapter 1, snakes with the power to harm others using poisonous vapors they spat out were an important part of the folklore of south China. While these snake-like features were quickly expunged from later versions of Wen's hagiography and iconography, their presence in the earliest known version of his hagiography indicates that at least some worshippers saw him as a potentially dangerous spirit with the power to infect others.

As Wen's cult continued to grow, however, the nature of his links to epidemics appears to have undergone a change. In analyzing the development of Wen's hagiography, it is important to remember that plague deities should be divided into two types: those that spread epidemics (*hsing-wen* 行瘟), and those that expel them (*ch'ü-wen* 驅瘟; *chu-yi* 逐疫).[68] It appears that while Marshal Wen may originally have been represented as a demon who could spread epidemics, he eventually became worshipped as a deity with the power to prevent them. Even though some of his titles retained the character *wen* (epidemics), I have not found any evidence to indicate that he was viewed as a deity who could spread contagious diseases. I have yet to determine how Wen became transformed from a demon into a deity, but the process involved may have been somewhat similar to what frequently occurs in Taiwan. Field data on a number of cults there, including those of some Lords, indicates that the souls of those who die premature or violent deaths, and prove powerful enough to resist attempts at exorcism, are considered to be "vengeful ghosts" (*li-kuei*).[69] Such research also reveals that if such a spirit can acquire an individual identity, and also proves efficacious when approached by worshippers, it may end up being worshipped as a deity.[70]

---

[67] The authors of a twentieth-century work entitled *Wen-chou feng-su chi* (*WCFSC*) claim that this was the case (see Appendix A).

[68] See Katz, "P'ing-tung hsien Tung-kang chen te ying-wang chi-tien," 131–135, 173–176. See also Li Feng-mao's recent article entitled "Hsing-wen yü sung-wen — Tao-chiao yü min-chung wen-yi kuan te chiao-liu ho fen-ch'i," in *Proceedings of the International Conference on Popular Beliefs and Chinese Culture*, volume 1, pp. 373–422.

[69] I have discussed the worship of vengeful ghosts in imperial China and modern Taiwan in "P'ing-tung hsien Tung-kang chen te ying-wang chi-tien," 112–113, 173–176. Important historical data may also be found in Lin Fu-shih, "Shih shih Shui-hu-ti Ch'in-chien chung te 'li' yü 'ting-sha'," *Shih-yüan*, 15 (1986): 2–38.

[70] See C. Stevan Harrell, "When a Ghost Becomes a God," in Wolf, ed., *Religion and Ritual in Chinese Society*, pp. 193-206; David Jordan, *Gods, Ghosts and Ancestors. Folk*

The numerous versions of Wen's hagiography presented above all reveal that he had died young (before marrying and fulfilling his Confucian obligation of fathering descendants), and in a highly unusual or violent fashion. This implies that he was originally conceived of as a vengeful ghost with the power to harm individuals or communities by infecting them with contagious diseases. Furthermore, the novel *Journey to the North* and other sources indicate that Marshal Wen may originally have been a plague demon lacking any individualistic features, as seen in his title "Marshal of Epidemics". The fact that his surname frequently changed also hints at such the nebulous nature of his identity. Wen appears to have acquired a clear hagiography and iconogaphy only by the Sung dynasty, and it is probably no coincidence that his first temples were built at that time.

Taoism and the Hagiographies of Local Deities

We have seen that Marshal Wen was a deity who enjoyed great popularity among both Taoist priests and all manner of lay believers in Chekiang. One important question which has yet to be addressed, however, involves the degree to which each group's representation of Wen could interact with the others, and the ways in which such interaction occurred. One approach to answering this question involves analyzing the relationship between Taoist hagiographies of local deities and non-Taoist ones.

Those scholars researching Taoism have made significant contributions to our understanding of Chinese religion, through both fieldwork and the study of previously unused or under-utilized materials in the *Taoist Canon*. At the same time, however, the work of many scholars in this field, excellent though it may be, has failed to fully account for the complex interaction that occured between Taoism and local cults. Some scholars argue that Taoism represented a "higher" or "elevated" form of Chinese popular religion which played a major role in shaping the latter's growth.[71] Others claim that there was a sharp distinction between the beliefs of Taoist priests and lay worshippers (see below). In the case of hagiography, some scholars researching Taoism have concluded that this distinction resulted in the existence of two separate haiographical traditions, and that even when interaction between Taoist and popular hagiographies of a local deity

---

Religion in a Taiwanese Village (Stanford: Stanford University Press, 1972), pp. 164–171; and Katz, "Demons or Deities? — The *Wangye* of Taiwan," 201–204.

[71] See Schipper, *The Taoist Body*, pp. 2, 7–8, 69, 86 (note 48) and 89.

occurred, it resulted in the former's dominance over the latter. However, the description of Marshal Wen's various hagiographies presented above suggests that the relationship between Taoist and popular hagiographies was neither so clear-cut nor so one-sided.

In commenting on the relationship between Taoism and local cults in medieval China, Kristofer Schipper claims that: "In its scriptural expression T'ang Taoism drew a very clear line between local cults and saints and the 'pure' theology of the Tao. Cults to deified local heroes were expressly forbidden."[72] This view has greatly influenced the work of social historians like Valerie Hansen, who concludes, based on Schipper's ideas, that: "These spirit emissaries [recorded in a Taoist priest's register (*lu* 錄) and summoned in rituals] remained exclusively within the province of ordained Taoism. Lay people did not worship them."[73] Such a statement is simply not true; one need only examine the cult of Marshal Wen to see that deities worshipped by Taoist priests could also be popular on the local level. Furthermore, evidence presented above and in chapter 4 also indicates that deities absorbed into Taoism like Marshal Wen were often exactly those deified local heroes Taoists were supposedly forbidden to worship.

This tendency to neglect the interaction between Taoism and local cults appears in the works of other scholars as well. For example, in their studies of Marshal Wen, both Judith Boltz and John Lagerwey focus exclusively on the hagiography by Huang Kung-chin, ignoring the numerous other versions presented above.[74] Such an oversight clearly reflects the fact that these scholars have made the beliefs and practices of Taoist priests the major emphasis of their research. As a result, they have sometimes unwittingly accepted the worldview of the Taoists they study, suggesting that these religious specialists and members of a local community lived in separate worlds in terms of the deities they worshipped, the rituals they performed, and the hagiographies they recounted. While it is true that Taoism is a largely esoteric religion, and that Taoist priests often have a more sophisticated interpretation of rituals, the deities involved, and their symbolism than the uninitiated, it would be unwise to stress these

---

[72] Kristofer Schipper, "Taoist Ritual and Local Cults of the T'ang Dynasty," p. 831.

[73] Hansen, *Changing Gods*, p. 26.

[74] See Lagerwey, *Taoist Ritual*, pp. 241–245; and Boltz, *Survey*, pp. 97–99. Valerie Hansen cites Marshal Wen's *Taoist Canon* hagiography as an example of Taoist attitudes toward popular deities, but appears unaware of the existence of other non-canonical hagiographies. See "Gods on Walls," p. 98.

differences to the point where it becomes difficult to see the significant areas of interaction between Taoism and local cults.

Scholars have long been aware of the esoteric nature of Taoism and the fact that most Chinese were unaware of or did not fully understand the beliefs and practices contained in the *Taoist Canon.* Unfortunately, this had led them to conclude that Taoist beliefs often failed to interact with those of the general populace. For example, in an article entitled "The Mythology of Modern China," Henri Maspero gives the following analysis of gods of illnesses and healing gods:

> The *tao-shih* [Taoist priests] have a Ministry of Epidemics composed of the five gods who preside over the epidemics of the five cardinal directions and the four seasons [i.e., the Five Commissioners of Epidemics]. But these are divinities who are objects of worship only among Taoist sorcerers, who give them various names and titles according to the regions and schools to which they belong.[75]

This statement represents an over-simplification of the facts. While Taoist priests do tend to have a more profound degree of knowledge concerning such deities than most members of the populace,[76] this does not mean that such deities could not also be worshipped by lay believers. In general, it might be useful to divide those deities worshipped by Taoist priests into the following two types: 1) Those either created to fit certain cosmological or hierarchical schemes or who became known to Taoist priests through divine revelation (e.g., the Three Pure Ones or various stellar deities); and 2) Those co-opted from local cults (e.g., the Emperor of the Eastern Peak or Marshal Wen). This second group of deities often ended up being worshipped by both Taoist priests and members of a local community.

A number of scholars have recently argued that this type of interaction between Taoism and local cults represents a new religious phenomenon which occurred during the Sung dynasty. For example, Pat Ebrey and Peter Gregory claim that scholar-officials, Taoists, and Buddhists generally opposed local cults throughout the Six Dynasties era, adopting "strategies of appropriation" only by the T'ang and Sung

---

[75] Henri Maspero, *Taoism and Chinese Religion*, trans. Frank Kierman, (Amherst: University of Massachusetts Press, 1981), p. 173.

[76] Maspero also notes that the same situation holds true in the cases of the Ministry of Medicine and the Ministry for the Expulsion of Evil Influences, inasmuch as the names of their members are usually known only to Taoist priests.

dynasties.[77] Valerie Hansen presents a similar argument, stating that the pre-T'ang relationship between organized religions and local gods was one marked by conflict.[78] In his study of the cult of Wen-ch'ang, Terry Kleeman attempts to prove that any interaction between what he postulates as two ritual continuums — sacrificial (state and local cults) and institutionalized (Taoism and Buddhism) — did not occur until the Sung.[79] In fact, such interaction was nothing new. Rolf Stein's research on medieval Taoism and popular religion (cited by all the authors mentioned above) has demonstrated that while Six Dynasties Taoists did oppose and even attempt to suppress certain local cults they also tolerated a variety of local deities and even adopted some into their own movements.[80]

In considering this problem, it might be useful to view Taoist attempts to influence Chinese local cults as bearing some resemblances to the early Christian practice of converting popular local deities into saints while transforming their hagiographies (as well as iconographies and rituals) to fit the criteria of Christianity.[81] As Christian church tried to absorb the ancient cults to various nature and tutelary spirits and transform these deities into more acceptable saints, so Taoist movements from the Six Dynasties onwards strove to mold those local gods whose cults could not be eradicated into deities conforming to Taoist norms. However, as Rolf Stein has noted, this process could work both ways, with Taoist hagiography, iconography, and ritual often being influenced by the very cults its priests attempted to destroy. As Stein so eloquently put it: "In many specific cases popular customs and/or beliefs have been borrowed from or adopted by a great religion. Rather than posing the chronological question of which happened first [a question that usually cannot be solved], it is better to envisage a ceaseless coming and going."[82]

Once one accepts the fact that considerable interaction between Taoism and local cults had been constantly occurring since at least the Six Dynasites, the next question involves the degree to which Taoist representations of a local deity could influence popular ones,

---

[77] See Ebrey and Gregory, "The Religious and Historical Landscape," p. 28.

[78] Hansen, "Gods on Walls," p. 76.

[79] Kleeman, "Expansion of the Wen-ch'ang Cult," p. 62. In his more recent book, Kleeman argues that interaction between Taiosm and local cults had always occured, but that it "accelerated" during the Sung. See *A God's Own Tale*, p. 44.

[80] Stein, "Religious Taoism and Popular Religion," pp. 59, 68–71, 74–76 and 80.

[81] See for example Peter Brown, *The Cult of the Saints. Its Rise and Function in Latin Christianity* (Chicago: University of Chicago Press, 1981), esp. chapter 6; and Robert Hertz, "St. Besse: a Study of an Alpine cult," Stephen Wilson trans., in Wilson ed., *Saints and their Cults* (Cambridge: Cambridge University Press, 1983), pp. 55–100.

[82] See Stein "Religious Taoism and Popular Religion," pp. 53–54.

and vice versa. Regarding this important problem, scholars researching Taoism have tended to focus solely on the former process, not to mention exaggerate its effects. For example, in his study of the hagiography of Marshal Wen, John Lagerwey claims that Taoist representations of Wen had a profound impact on popular ones, in large part because "the complex world of Chinese religion is an epistemologically structured hierarchy."[83] To him, the significance of Wen's *Taoist Canon* hagiography is its revelation that:

> there was a clear demarcation between those principalities and powers which recognized and those which did not recognize the authority of the immortal officials of the Orthodox Way. . . . Henceforth, all power in heaven and on earth was in the hands of Chang Tao-ling and his successors, and all powers had either to enroll in his ranks, that is, support and protect the Orthodox Way, join the System, perform public services, or else "go into the opposition" and so expose themselves to constant persecution.[84]

Lagerwey seems to believe in the existence of a ritual system with a capital "S", consisting of a hierarchy of spirit mediums on the bottom, ritual masters in the middle, and Taoist priests at the top.[85] While it is highly unlikely that the majority of religious specialists (not to mention lay worshippers) in late imperial China saw themselves as part of such a system, it is clear that some Taoists favored the establishment of such a hierarchy, and used the hagiography of Marshal Wen as a means to state their case.

Terry Kleeman adopts a view similar to Lagerwey's in his dissertation on the cult of Wen-ch'ang, arguing that popular representations of local deities ended up being "subordinated" to Taoist ones.[86] However, despite such assertions, he and Lagerwey have yet to provide convincing evidence that Taoist representations of popular deities significantly influenced those of people who were not initiated into Taoism. As Hansen notes," their [Taoist priests'] claims alone did not mean that the laity accepted the rankings

---

[83] Lagerwey, *Taoist Ritual*, p. 251.

[84] *Ibid.*, p. 246.

[85] *Ibid.*, pp. 249, 251–252. See also Schipper, *The Taoist Body*, pp. 44–60.

[86] See Kleeman, "Wenchang and the Viper: The Creation of a Chinese National God", Ph.D. thesis (UC Berkeley, 1988), pp. 130–132. This discussion is not included in his new book.

[formulated by Taoists]".[87]

Kleeman has also argued in a recent article that: " . . . during the Sung Taoism claimed a role of caretaker in relation to the popular pantheon, a role it maintains to this day."[88] While some Sung Taoists may have attempted to assume such a mantle, the degree to which they have succeeded is less clear. As I shall show in the next two chapters, cults like Marshal Wen's could expand and develop elaborate festivals without necessarily requiring consistent and active supervision by Taoist priests. In Taiwan today, cults to popular deities like Ma-tsu 媽祖 (the Goddess of the Sea) or various Lords like Lord Ch'ih have also flourished with little apparent support or leadership on the part of Taoist priests, apart from their participating in some rites performed during festivals.

Still other scholars have claimed that Taoism brought about the "universalization" of local deities by transforming their hagiographies and iconographies. In his fascinating study of Taoism and local cults in Fukien, Ken Dean emphasizes that the composition of Taoist scriptures in classical Chinese identifying a local god as a Taoist astral deity represented a "major step" in this universalization process.[89] Taking the cults of the Great Emperor who Protects Life (Pao-sheng ta-ti 保生大帝) and the Reverent Lord of Broad Compassion (Kuang-tse tsun-wang 廣澤尊王 known as Sage King Kuo [Kuo sheng-wang 郭聖王]) as his examples, Dean claims that the compilation of such scriptures was part of "an effort by local leaders working with Taoist and Buddhist specialists to transcend localism."[90] However, no such scriptures appear to have been composed for Marshal Wen, and the spread of his cult and hagiography throughout parts of south China and Taiwan appears to have been largely due to the influence of popular novels and folktales, not just hagiographies composed by local leaders and Taoist priests. Even if a Taoist scripture in classical Chinese had been composed for Wen, one wonders how widely it might have circulated, as no convincing evidence has been supplied to date that proves that Taoist scriptures played a major role in the spread of the cult of Marshal Wen or any of the cults Dean has studied.

In attempting to determine whether Taoist hagiographical scriptures could actually further a cult's universalization, it is

---

[87] Hansen, "Gods on Walls," p. 76. Robert Weller has also demonstrated the limited popularity of religious specialists' views in his *Unities and Diversities*, pp. 64, 90–124.

[88] Kleeman, "Expansion of the Wen-ch'ang Cult," p. 62.

[89] Dean, *Taoist Ritual and Popular Cults*, p. 18.

[90] *Ibid.*, p. 82.

important to keep in mind David Johnson's discussion of the factors affecting the degree to which a particular text could circulate and influence the mentalities of its readers (or listeners). As he has convincingly shown, any social historical evaluation of these problems must be based on an in-depth understanding of a text's author, intended audience, and actual audience.[91] It is also important to remember that Taoist scriptures were not read as works of literature but performed during rituals. This means that any analysis of their meaning must at the very least take into account the fact that any performance inevitably involves a number of speech events which contribute to its contextualization, including past performances, readings of texts, reports, critiques, challenges, subsequent performances, etc.[92] In addition, it is also important to consider the problem of what anthropologists and scholars of literature refer to as a text's "reception." As W.F. Hanks points out: "For an anthropology of text, this research [on a text's reception] helps to emphasize the sociocultural encounter between text and audience [and therefore author and audience], the institutional and ideological formation of ways of reading, [and] the imposition of interpretations."[93] While the lack of data usually prevents the social historian of late imperial China from conducting analyses of the depth Hanks' arguments suggest, it is essential to at least consider these problems and their implications when evaluating the influence a particular text might have had.

I am not attempting to deny the important role Taoist priests played in the growth of local cults like Marshal Wen's (see the following chapter), nor would I reject the importance of the study of Taoist hagiographies of local deities. Nevertheless, I think it is important to emphasize that Taoist priests might not have been able to influence the representations of local deities to the extent that some scholars have claimed. In the case of Marshal Wen's hagiography, Huang Kung-chin's *Taoist Canon* version is undeniably an important source for studying Taoist representations of Wen, but appears to have had a limited impact on other non-Taoist representations. Even though Sung Lien's stele inscription and the *Complete Compendium* hagiography do link Wen to the Heavenly Master movement, these

---

[91] See David Johnson, "Communication, Class, and Consciousness in Late Imperial China," in Johnson, et. al., eds. *Popular Culture in Late Imperial China* (Berkeley: University of California Press, 1985), pp. 40–43.

[92] For more on these problems, see Richard Bauman and Charles L. Briggs, "Poetics and Performance as Critical Perspectives on Language and Social Life," *American Review of Anthropology* 19 (1990): 60–61, 67.

[93] W.F. Hanks, "Text and Textuality," *American Review of Anthropology* 18 (1989): 113.

works tend to place greater emphasis on his adherence to Confucian ideals. As for the *Journey to the North* and later folktales, these give only the merest hint of Wen's links to Heavenly Master Taoism. Even Huang, a self-professed stickler for "orthodoxy," included popular representations of Wen in his hagiography (albeit in the addendum) in the story of Wen's swallowing plague pills.

The evidence on the numerous versions of Marshal Wen's hagiography presented above indicates that the issue of Taoism's influence on local cults should be treated with extreme caution. At the same time, however, it would also be a mistake to lump all non-Taoist representations of Wen into that nebulous category of "popular religion." This is because a wide range of social groups participated in local cults like Wen's, including scholar-officials, members of the gentry and local elite, merchants, peasants, and even beggars. In recent years, the analysis of the beliefs of people from a broad range of social classes has been of great interest to scholars of Chinese culture, with much pioneering work being done in this area.[94] Prasenjit Duara has attempted to explain the existence of different beliefs by using the concept of the "superscription" of symbols, which he explains as: "a modality of symbolic evolution [whereby] cultural symbols are able to lend continuity at one level to changing social groups and interests even as the symbols undergo transformations."[95] Using the cult of Kuan Kung as an example, he argues that superscription involved a conscious effort on the part of the state to assert its power over popular deities and their worshippers by superscribing its hegemony over the symbolism of local cults.[96]

Duara's theory of superscription works very well when analyzing a deity like Kuan Kung, whose hagiography has a definable original text (in this case the *Record of the Three Kingdoms* [*San-kuo chih*]) and who was included in the register of sacrifices (*ssu-tien*). However, one cannot necessarily apply this concept so readily in the case of a deity like Marshal Wen, who was not a historical figure with a biography in the standard histories and whose cult does not appear to have been greatly influenced by the state. Furthermore, the concept of superscription (which literally means to add new material to an extant text) postulates a progressive or linear generation of new versions of a hagiography, failing to account for the simultaneous

---

[94] For an overview of these issues, see Catherine Bell, "Religion and Chinese Culture: Toward an Assessment of 'Popular Religion'," *HR* 29 (1989): 35–57.

[95] See Prasenjit Duara, "Superscribing Symbols: The Myth of Guandi, Chinese God of War," *JAS* 47.4 (Nov. 1988): 778–795.

[96] Prasenjit Duara, *Culture, Power and the State. Rural North China, 1900–1942* (Stanford: Stanford University Press, 1988), pp. 138–148.

creation of various versions by different people. If one were to hypothesize that Wen's hagiography started as a folktale, was absorbed into Taoism, and later recorded by literati, that would be superscription. However, the evidence above indicates that more than one version of Wen's hagiography circulated simultaneously as his cult arose. I would tentatively call such a phenomenon 'cogeneration' of beliefs. Cogeneration may not have occurred in the case of every Chinese deity, nor does it rule out the existence of superscription, for as Wen's cult spread new material was added to older legends. In the case of this cult, the simultaneous use of both concepts can help us understand how differing representations of a deity evolve over time.

These two concepts — superscription and cogeneration — imply an ongoing interaction between different representations of the same deity. More importantly, they allow for both upward and downward interaction, and also suggest that while Chinese society was strongly hierarchical, it was by no means composed of insulated groups of people whose representations of a deity's hagiography were unknown to others. It is clear that there was a continuous exchange of ideas, values, and beliefs between different groups of people in late imperial China, something perhaps comparable to the richocheting back and forth of the echo of a yodel off the sides of a mountain. I would tentatively call such a process of interaction the 'reverberation' of beliefs, a concept inspired in part by Stein's description of "a ceaseless coming and going" (see above). As the sound of the echo varies with each rebound, so do ideas, values, and beliefs change as they pass from person to person. However, as in the case of cogeneration, different beliefs prove able to coexist.[97]

The concept of reverberation can also be applied to other problems in the study of Chinese religion besides that of a deity's hagiography. For example, in their introduction to *Religion and Society in T'ang and Sung China*, Peter Gregory and Pat Ebrey note that what they define as the "four traditions" (Buddhism, Taoism, Confucianism, and popular religion) "were in constant interaction."[98] Such interaction may in fact have been a form of reverberation, representing the constant flow to and fro of various beliefs and practices. Reverberation may also be used to study what Judith Berling in the same volume describes as the "channels of connection" in Sung dynasty religion.[99] The interaction between different individuals, traditions, and cult

---

[97] The concepts of cogeneration and reverberation may be similar to a number of concepts in textual studies, including cohesion, cointerpretation, mutual adjustment, and reinforcement. See Hanks, "Text and Textuality," 103.

[98] See "The Religious and Historical Landscape," p. 12.

[99] Berling, "Channels of Connection," p. 307.

centers that she portrays in her paper all appear to be different forms of reverberation.

Another advantage of this concept is that it allows us to view the interaction between different individuals or groups in a more balanced light. Many sinologists, apparently influenced by Marxist historiography, have tended to view any interaction between more powerful and less powerful individuals or groups as a form of cultural "hegemony." David Johnson, for example, draws on the writings of Antonio Gramsci to argue that: "cultural integration . . . is not the natural result of the interaction of people between each other and with their traditions but the willed product of a particular class."[100] Duara's description of superscription also implies a form of hegemony, in that representations of popular deities end up being imposed by the state. Scholars like Terry Kleeman and John Lagerwey also appear to view the interaction between Taoism and local cults as hegemonic, inasmuch as they argue that Taoist versions of a deity's hagiography could dominate local ones. James Watson's work on the Ma-tsu cult provides a more balanced analysis of such interaction, revealing that different individuals or groups could preserve their own representations of a deity in spite of state/elite attempts at hegemony (or standardization). However, he fails to discuss the interaction between different representations.[101]

My analysis of Marshal Wen's hagiography has shown that interaction and integration in late imperial China involved much more than cultural hegemony. Although classically educated scholars-turned-Taoist-priests like Huang Kung-chin, as well as scholar-officials like Sung Lien, composed hagiographies of Wen reflecting their own agendas, such hagiographies had only a limited influence on popular representations of Wen, and clearly failed to cause the latter's subordination. On the contrary, we have seen that popular representations of Wen very different from those presented by Huang and Sung also existed, and that these men could even draw on such representations of Wen in their own writings. Such a process of reverberation between different versions of a deity's hagiography does not appear to have been unusual in late imperial China, as Glen

---

[100] See Johnson, "Communication, Class, and Consciousness," p. 48.

[101] James Watson, "Standardizing the Gods: The Promotion of T'ien Hou ('Empress of Heaven') Along the South China Coast, 960–1960," in Johnson, et. al eds., *Popular Culture in Late Imperial China*, pp. 310–313, 315–322. Robert Weller explores the problem of how such interaction can constitute a form of resistance in *Resistance, Chaos and Control in China* (Seattle: University of Washington Press, 1994).

Dudbridge has shown in his masterful analysis of the Miao-shan 妙善 legend.[102]

  If one applies the concepts of cogeneration and reverberation to the study of Wen's hagiography, one can discard the idea that any one particular text represents a "standard" hagiography which dominates all others. Inasmuch as the late imperial Chinese lived in an open and dynamic society, one would expect a constant interchange of ideas, values, and beliefs. Variations would arise as each group or individual participated in such interaction, yet people and the ideas they embraced could exist side by side in a community. It appears, therefore, that the concepts of cogeneration and reverberation can help us develop what Catherine Bell has termed a "third stage" interpretation of Chinese popular beliefs, one that allows for a degree of diversity inside the larger unity we describe as Chinese culture.[103]

---

  [102] Glen Dudbridge, *The Legend of Miao-shan* (Oxford: Oxford University Press, 1978).

  [103] Bell, "Religion and Chinese Culture," 43.

FOUR

The Spread of Marshal Wen's Cult

Diversity of beliefs, spirits worshipped, and rituals practiced is perhaps the most striking characteristic of Chinese religion. But this very diversity — one could even say fluidity of beliefs — also resulted in the rapid rise and equally rapid fall of many different gods and spirits. Once a deity was viewed as ineffectual, people would simply cease to worship it, switching easily to one of numerous other deities available to them (or, in certain cases, simply creating a new deity). Thus the long survival of the cult to Marshal Wen and its development into one of Chekiang's most famous festivals was in fact an achievement of some note.

What helped ensure the success of Wen's cult? Generally speaking, four factors contributed to the survival and growth of religious cults in late imperial China (and continue to play a role today): 1) A continuous stream of miracles performed by the cult's deity; 2) Efficient management of the temple and its finances; 3) The presence of powerful and respected religious specialists, be they Taoist priests, Buddhist monks, or local specialists (particularly spirit mediums); and 4) Support from members of the gentry and local elite classes. Few cults were able to survive unless they met these requirements.

In a cult's early stages of existence, its deity competed with other deities to attract new worshippers by performing miracles. In most cases, the more frequent and spectacular the miracles were, the better the cult fared. As few deities could perform miracles without being summoned or commanded by ritual specialists, these people played a major role in keeping the cult alive. Spirit mediums were of the utmost importance, because deities depended on them to communicate with believers. Mediums also attracted supporters by interpreting dreams and performing cures in the names of the deities possessing them.

Temples were usually built only after a deity had gained a large or diverse enough following for sufficient funds to be raised for such a project. Such buildings were among the most significant features of late imperial cults. The sacred landscape of that era, not to mention modern-day Hong Kong, Taiwan, and other overseas Chinese communities, was dotted with all manner of cult sites, ranging from fledgling shrines to developing temples to enormous festival and pilgrimage centers. Many new deities didn't even have buildings of their own, starting off as images on the altars of a few devotees or the cult's religious specialists. However, while providing some measure of permanence, temples did not in themselves guarantee a cult's success. The late imperial sacred landscape was also full of large numbers of abandoned temples belonging to gods whose popularity had declined.

As a cult gained increasing numbers of supporters through its deity's steady performance of miracles, its temple also grew in size and grandeur. However, as its activities became known to members of the officialdom, the cult ran the risk of being classified as an "illicit sacrifice" (yin-ssu). For a cult to survive official investigations or be awarded a title, support by members of the local elite, particularly the gentry, could prove critical. Such men also composed the various documents required to submit a petition for a title.

At the same time, however, elite support and state recognition alone were not enough to help a cult survive; money was also essential for supporting various cult activities. Most cults faced periodic crises in the form of their temples' destruction during natural calamities or warfare. Money was necessary to build, maintain, and rebuild the cult's temple, as well as pay for annual birthday rites and festivals. Members of the gentry often contributed money to support local cults, but they frequently shied away from the day-to-day management of a temple, as this was considered beneath their dignity. More often than not, it was members of the local elite, particularly merchants, who paid for the cult's upkeep and ran its affairs. Merchants also played an important role in a cult's spread by founding temples in the places where they conducted business (see below).

For a cult to survive and become the focus of a festival or pilgrimage network, all the factors mentioned above had to come into play. This is reflected in the spread of Marshal Wen's cult throughout Chekiang (see Map 5). In analyzing this process however, it is important to remember that the sources available (in most cases local gazetteers) only tell us the date when one of Wen's temples was founded, not when his cult started to become popular. Because popular deities like Marshal Wen could attract worshippers long before being worshipped in temples, the construction of a temple to

Map 5 — Marshal Wen's Cult Sites in Chekiang

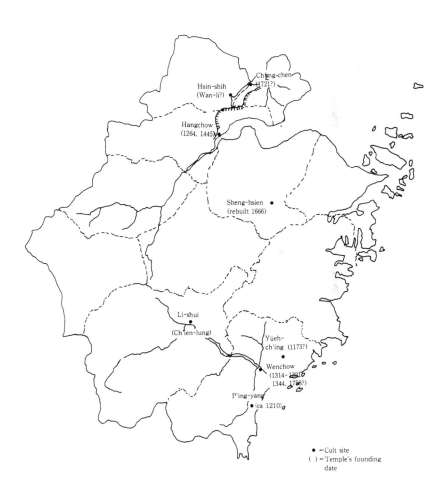

Ch'eng-chen
(1721?)

Hsin-shih
(Wan-li?)

Hangchow
(1264, 1445)

Sheng-hsien
(rebuilt 1666)

Li-shui
(Ch'ien-lung)

Yüeh-
ch'ing (1173?)

Wenchow
(1314-1316,
1344, 1755?)

P'ing-yang
(ca 1210)

● = Cult site
( ) = Temple's founding
date

25   0   25   50   75   100
km

Wen in a particular area does not necessarily mean that his cult had suddenly become popular there, but merely that his worshippers had not acquired the resources to build a temple until that time.

While most sources indicate that Marshal Wen's oldest temple in Chekiang was founded in P'ing-yang, some members of the local elite in Yüeh-ch'ing County (also in Wenchow Prefecture) claimed that Wen's temple at Tung-kao Shan 東皋山 was his oldest cult site. According to Ch'ing editions of the county gazetteer, Wen's temple at Yüeh-ch'ing was built during the 1170s at the instigation of no less a figure than Chu Hsi (1130–1200). These sources also contain an account of the temple's reconstruction attributed to Chu, dated the eighteenth day of the eighth lunar month in the year 1173. It describes a dream Chu had one night after giving lectures at Tung-kao Shan, the contents of which bear a striking resemblance to the more popular forms of Marshal Wen's hagiography. A figure with a green face and red hair appeared before Chu, giving his surname as Wen and stating that he had lived during the T'ang dynasty. While travelling on Tung-kao Shan, Wen had encountered a heavenly officer (*t'ien-tsao* 天曹) who poured plague poison in a well in order to wipe out the local populace. Wen drank the poisoned waters and died, prompting the grateful populace to build a temple to him there. As Wen's temple had fallen into disrepair, Chu ordered his friends and students to have it rebuilt. After being destroyed during the Taiping Rebellion, this temple was rebuilt once again during the T'ung-chih reign (1862–1874) the reconstruction project being led by the supernumerary government student (*tseng-sheng*)[1] Ts'ai Tu-kuang 蔡篤光 and a commoner named Hsü Ping-hsin 徐丙新.[2] The gazetteer also mentions a postface for Chu's account written in 1550 by the tribute student (*kung-sheng* 貢生) Hsü Shih-piao 徐世鑣.[3] More could be learned if Hsü's *Tung-shan chi* 東山集 could be examined, but this text has been lost.[4]

Did Chu in fact compose this inscription? It is not included in his collected writings or any other source apart from the Yüeh-ch'ing

---

[1] This is an abbreviated form of the title *tseng-kuang sheng-yüan* 增廣生員. *Tseng-sheng* enjoyed the same privileges as *sheng-yüan*, but did not receive government stipends.

[2] See *Yüeh-ch'ing hsien-chih* (1901), 3:23b-24a. This text also mentions another temple dedicated to Wen at Nine Ox Mountain (Chiu-niu Shan 九牛山) (3:23b; no founding date is given). Data on Wen's temple at Tung-kao Shan may also be found in the 1685 edition of the county gazetteer (7:4b–5a).

[3] For biographical data, see *Yüeh-ch'ing hsien-chih* (1685), 4:26b and 5:17b; and *Yüeh-ch'ing hsien-chih* (1901), 8:80a–b and 10:30a.

[4] *Yüeh-ch'ing hsien-chih* (1901), 11:81a. See also *Wen-chou ching-chi chih,* Sun Yi-jang (1848–1908), ed., (Hangchow: Che-chiang sheng-li t'u-shu-kuan, 1921), 28:14b.

gazetteers. Chu Hsi was travelling through southern Chekiang in 1173, taking advantage of his temporary loss of favor at court to recruit disciples along the southeast coast. As his biography states that he had been in T'ai-chou Prefecture in the fifth lunar month of 1173, a trip to nearby Yüeh-ch'ing would not have been out of the question.[5] There was also an academy (*shu-yüan* 書院) at Tung-kao Shan where Chu Hsi is said to have given lectures.[6] As Linda Walton has shown, many academies were built near or even at temples or monasteries, although whether this was the case with the Tung-kao Shan academy has yet to be determined.[7]

Based on the evidence presented above, I would hesitate to conclude that Chu Hsi did in fact dream of Marshal Wen and was subsequently moved to help found his temple and write the account mentioned above. Apart from the fact that this inscription is not included in Chu's collected writings, the sources indicate that all activity surrounding Wen's cult at Yüeh-ch'ing appears to have occurred during the Ming-Ch'ing era, not as early as the Sung dynasty. The seven-hundred year gap between the supposed founding of Wen's temple and its first restoration is also highly suspicious, as most temples with histories covering many centuries underwent numerous restorations. The fact that Hsü's postface dates from the sixteenth century, and the earliest account of the temple from the seventeenth century, also casts doubt on the validity of the Yüeh-ch'ing elite's claim that Chu Hsi composed an inscription for Wen's temple. Such a work was more likely an elaborate forgery composed to enchance the prestige of Marshal Wen's cult in Yüeh-ch'ing, perhaps due to competition with other nearby cult sites in P'ing-yang, Wenchow, and Li-shui.[8]

Wen's earliest cult site in Chekiang was probably the Temple of Boundless Numinosity (Kuang-ling Miao 廣靈廟), also known as the Temple of the Grand Guardian (T'ai-pao Miao 太保廟). This temple, located in Wenchow's P'ing-yang County near Whitestone Well (Pai-shih ching 白石井), was founded by a scholar-official named Lin T'ang-fu 林鐺夫. Lin was awarded the *chin-shih* degree in 1210,

---

[5] See *Chu-tzu nien-p'u*, Wang Mao-hung (1668–1741), ed., (Taipei: Shih-chieh shu-chü, 1968), pp. 54 and 273.

[6] See *Yüeh-ch'ing hsien-chih* (1901), 4:34a; WCFC (1756), 7:20b; and *Ta-ming yi-t'ung chih*, Li Hsien (1408–1467), et. al., ed. and comp., *Wen-yüan Ko Ssu-k'u ch'üan-shu* edition, 48:10a.

[7] See Linda Walton, "Southern Sung Academies as Sacred Places," in Ebrey and Gregory, ed., *Religion and Society in T'ang and Sung China*, pp. 349–352.

[8] Valerie Hansen has examined the use of forged inscriptions by rival cult groups in Sung-dynasty Hu-chou. See *Changing Gods*, pp. 113–127.

and later served as a Recorder in the Court of Imperial Sacrifices (*T'ai-chang ssu pu* 太常四簿).[9] Why a scholar-official like Lin would build a temple to Marshal Wen remains a mystery, but his position in the Court of Imperial Sacrifices indicates that he had some knowledge of ritual matters. He might even have used his position to help the people of P'ing-yang apply for one of the titles Wen is said to have been awarded in his hagiographies, although Sung sources provide no record of any such event. A second temple to Wen was later built outside the city's Western Gate (no date is given). A set of fingerprints impressed on the temple's walls are said to have been made by Wen after drinking the plague poison intended to infect the local populace.[10]

Wen's cult appears to have had strong roots in P'ing-yang, as is indicated by the fact that his temple was founded by a member of the local gentry. Local gazetteers claim that Wen was born in P'ing-yang, and some even include Wen's hagiography composed by Sung Lien in the chapter entitled "Biographies of Immortals and Monks" (*Hsien-shih chuan* 仙釋傳) in the section on T'ang individuals, indicating that the editors viewed Marshal Wen as a historical figure.[11]

We do not know the identity of the founder of Marshal Wen's first temple in Wenchow city, the Temple to the Loyal and Defending King (Chung-ching Wang Miao 忠靖王廟), which was constructed during the Yen-yu reign (1314–1321) on a lane near the Eight Immortals Tower (Pa-hsien Lou 八仙樓), a traditional medicine shop which still exists in Wenchow today. However, the second Chung-ching Wang temple (for which Sung Lien composed his stele inscription), built near a large hill called Hua-kai Shan 華蓋山 during the late Yüan dynasty,[12] was said to have been founded by a Taoist named Ch'u Hsiang-hsi, about whom nothing is known apart from the fact that he was a Wenchow native. A third temple was later built at

---

[9] For biographical data on Lin, see *WCFC* (1756), 19:37a; and *PYHC* (1915), 28:29a.

[10] For information on Wen's P'ing-yang temples, see *CCTC* (1736), 225:11a and 13b; *PYHC* (1571), 6:3a; *WCFC* (1605), 4:15a; *PYHC* (1684), 7:9b; *PYHC* (1760), *chüan* 9; and, *PYHC* (1915), 45:12b. The 1915 gazetteer provides a map showing Wen's temple as having been located on Whitestone Road (Pai-shih chieh 白石街). There was a King of Boundless Numinosity (Kuang-ling Wang 廣靈王) worshipped in Ningpo, but this was a deity surnamed Pao 鮑 and should not be confused with Wen. See Hansen, *Changing Gods*, p. 76. This deity also had a temple in Li-shui; see *Chin-yün hsien-chih* (1767), 3:2b.

[11] See *PYHC* (1684), 12:7a-b; *PYHC* (1760), *chüan* 17; and *PYHC* (1915), 47:1b–2a.

[12] While most Wenchow gazetteers state that this temple was built in the early years of the Ming dynasty, the data from Sung Lien's 1355 stele inscription indicates that the date of this temple's construction was 1344 (see chapter 3).

Hsün-chi Shan 巽吉山 in 1758 (again, the identity of the founder is unknown).[13]

The earliest Marshal Wen temple in Hangchow was constructed in 1264. Like Wen's temple in P'ing-yang, it was called the Temple of Boundless Numinosity or Temple of the Grand Guardian, indicating that it probably was a branch temple of Wen's P'ing-yang temple. Most Sung sources list it alongside other temples considered to be from outside Hangchow prefecture (*chün-wai hsing-tz'u* 郡外行祠), thus confirming its outside origins. This temple was built near the Muddy Water Locks (Hun-shui cha 渾水閘) in Ch'ien-t'ang County (see Map 6). Most gazetteers state that this dyke burst in the ninth month of 1264, prompting the villagers and their elders to construct a temple to Wen and his nine fellow grand guardians.[14] The locals also petitioned the Southern Sung court to award the title of marquis (*hou* 侯) to these deities. This request was granted in the year 1269.[15]

One account in the 1736 edition of the Chekiang provincial gazetteer presents a different version of these events. It states that Marshal Wen was summoned from Wenchow to quell numerous calamities (including epidemics) afflicting the people of Hangchow in the year 1227. He had succeeded, and was about to return to Wenchow, when his palanquin suddenly became too heavy to lift. People said that this indicated Wen's desire to stay in Hangchow, and

---

[13] For data on these temples, see CCTC (1736), 225:3b–4a; WCFC (1605), 4:6a; WCFC (1756), 9:4b–5b; YCHC (1566), 4:5a–b; and, YCHC (1682), 3:51a–b. The late Ch'ing edition of the Yung-chia county gazetteer states that Marshal Wen's temple at Hsün-chi Shan was built in 1344 (YCHC (1882), 4:31a–32a). This seems rather unlikely due to the fact that no earlier sources mention such a temple, including an eighteenth-century account of Wen's festival which states that at the time only two temples to Wen existed in Wenchow (see chapter 5). I would argue that the editors of the 1882 edition of the YCHC confused the temple at Hsün-chi Shan with the one built by the Taoist Ch'u Hsiang-hsi in 1344. It is of course possible that people near Hsün-chi Shan worshipped Wen in a household shrine as early as the 1340's, but I have found no evidence to support such a hypothesis.

[14] These ten grand guardians are mentioned in a number of sources, including Wen's *Complete Compendium* hagiography; Chiang Chün (late Ming), *Ch'i-hai so-t'an chi*, 12:3a; and, *Tseng-pu Wu-lin chiu-shih*, 3:15a–b, in *Wen-yüan Ko Ssu-k'u ch'üan-shu*, vol. 590, p. 346.

[15] See MLL, *chüan* 14, p. 253; HCLAC (1274), 73:16b; CCTC (1736), 217:7b; HCFC (1579), 47:28a; HCFC (1764), 8:9a; and HCFC (1922): 9:32a. The *Sung shih* and *Sung hui-yao chi-kao* contain no record of this title having been awarded, but these sources are not comprehensive, and the latter only records titles awarded before the 1230s. If titles had been awarded, marquis would have been the first one, followed by duke (*kung*) and king (*wang*); see Hansen, *Changing Gods*, pp. 80–81.

124

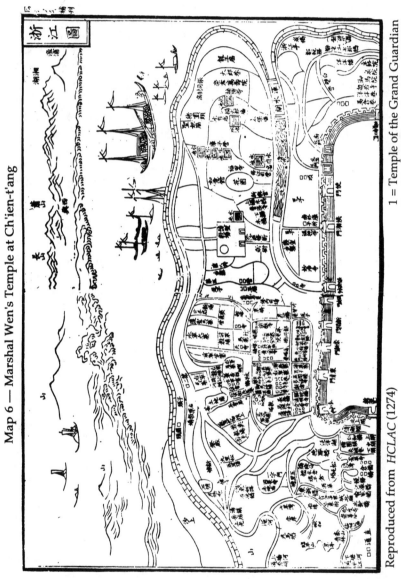

Map 6 — Marshal Wen's Temple at Ch'ien-t'ang

Reproduced from *HCLAC* (1274)

1 = Temple of the Grand Guardian
2 = Muddy Water Locks

built a temple for him on the spot soon afterwards.[16]

There are a number of problems with this account. First of all, no Hangchow gazetteer I have seen contains it. Secondly, Wen's Ch'ien-t'ang temple was built in 1264, not 1227. A Taoist cloister later converted into a temple for Marshal Wen was constructed at West Lake in 1227 (see below), and it appears that the editors of the Ch'ing provincial gazetteer confused the histories of these two temples. Nevertheless, as the founding of Wen's West Lake temple appears to have had nothing to do with natural disasters, this account may be elaborating on the events surrounding the founding of the Temple of Boundless Numinosity in Ch'ien-t'ang. If nothing else, it shows that some Ch'ing residents of Hangchow believed that Marshal Wen had been brought to their city from Wenchow in order to help them cope with calamities such as epidemics.

There is a great deal of evidence which indicates that the Temple of Boundless Numinosity in Hangchow may have been founded by Wenchow merchants, particularly since trade between these two cities had increased dramatically by the Southern Sung. Wenchow's supply of rice came mainly from Hangchow, while Wenchow products such as seafood, oranges, lacquer, and paper were shipped north to Hangchow via T'ai-chou, Ningpo, and Yü-yao along coastal trade routes.[17] Most of these goods were sold at markets located near the Muddy Water Locks.[18] Merchants from southern China had begun to form guilds (*hang-hui* 行會) and erect guild halls (*hui-kuan* 會館) in Hangchow by the Southern Sung, gaining renown for their charitable works.[19] As many temples also doubled as guild halls,[20] it is possible that Hangchow's Temple of Boundless

---

[16] See *CCTC* (1736), 217:15a. These events are also described in the *WLFSC*, 7:46b.

[17] See Chou, *Wen-chou kang-shih*, pp. 13 and 18; Lin, *Nan Sung tu-ch'eng*, pp. 261 and 262; *Tu-ch'eng chi-sheng*, p. 100; and, *MLL*, *chüan* 12, p. 236 and *chüan* 13, p. 241. Hangchow, Ning-po, and Wenchow were all part of a large network of Maritime Trade Supervisorates (*shih-po ssu* 市舶司) established during the Sung.

[18] See Lin, *Nan Sung ku-tu*, p. 263; and, *HCLAC* (1274), 19:18a, 39:20b and 39:22b.

[19] See Gernet, *Daily Life*, pp. 87–88; Ch'üan, *Chung-kuo hang-hui*, pp. 93–94; and *MLL*, *chüan* 18, p. 294. For more on guild members' involvment in religious and charitable activities throughout China, see Ch'üan, *Chung-kuo hang-hui*, pp. 57–62, 112–120.

[20] The most well-known guild halls/temples are the T'ien-hou Kung 天后宮 (Ma-tsu) for Fukien merchants and the Wan-shou Kung 萬壽宮 (Hsü Ching-yang) for Kiangsi merchants. See Ho Ping-ti, "The Geographic Distribution of *hui-kuan* (Landsmannschaften) in the Central and Upper Yangtze Provinces — with Special Reference to Interregional Migrations," *Tsing Hua Journal of Chinese Studies*, New Series V, Number 2 (Dec. 1966): 125; and Ho Ping-ti, *Chung-kuo hui-kuan shih lun* (Taipei:

Numinosity may have been founded by Wenchow or P'ing-yang merchants and even served as their guild hall.[21] At the same time however, it is also important to remember that Taoist priests used trade routes (as did Buddhist monks, doctors, migrants, etc),[22] and should also be considered as possible temple founders. As we shall see below, the subsequent spread of Marshal Wen's cult in the Hang-Chia-Hu sub-region may also have been aided by merchants, albeit this time from Hangchow.

The growth of Marshal Wen's other temple in Hangchow, a Taoist monastery known as the Temple of Manifest Virtue (Ching-te Kuan 旌德觀), was largely due to the efforts of Taoist priests. Numerous Taoist monasteries were built in Hangchow during the Southern Sung dynasty, which indicates that religion's strength there at that time.[23] This monastery was originally a Taoist cloister named the Taoist Monastery of the Jade Dawn (Yü-ch'en Tao-yüan 玉晨道院). It was located behind a Shrine to Local Worthies (Hsien-hsien Tz'u 先賢祠) constructed along Su [Tung-p'o]'s Dike (Su T'i 蘇堤) at West Lake by the prefectural magistrate Yüan Chao 袁昭 in 1227.[24] The Taoist cloister was subsequently renamed the Temple of Manifest Virtue (the date this occurred is unclear).[25] Its proximity to Yüan's Shrine to Local Worthies caused some confusion among later gazetteer editors, who referred to both sites using the characters for "manifest virtue" (ching-te 旌德).

Although the Temple of Manifest Virtue was destroyed in the chaos accompanying the fall of the Southern Sung, it was soon rebuilt in the Ward of Preserving Peace (Pao-an fang 保安坊), only to be destroyed again when the Yüan dynasty collapsed. Reconstruction did not commence until the mid-Ming, when the Taoist Hsü Tao-ch'ang

---

Hsüeh-sheng shu-chü, 1966), p. 64.

[21] A Wenchow guild hall existed in Hangchow by the late Ch'ing, but I have not been able to find any evidence concerning the date of its founding. See Ho, *Chung-kuo hui-kuan*, p. 44; *Hang-chou ti-fang chih tzu-liao, ti yi, erh chi* (Hangchow: Che-chiang jen-min ch'u-pan-she, 1987), p. 58; and Hsü Ch'ing-hsiang, *Hang-chou wang-shih t'an* (Peking: Hsin-hua ch'u-pan-she, 1993), pp. 15-17.

[22] See Barend ter Haar, "The Genesis and Spread of Temple Cults in Fukien," in E.B. Vermeer, ed., *Development and Decline of Fukien Province in the 17th and 18th Centuries* (Leiden: E. J. Brill, 1990), p. 354.

[23] Lin, *Nan Sung tu-ch'eng*, pp. 165–168.

[24] See his *Ch'ien-t'ang hsien-hsien chuan-tsan*, in vol. 1 of the *WLCKTP*, pp. 68–83. A Ningpo native, Yüan was awarded the *chin-shih* degree in 1187, but assigned to Hangchow only in 1220, relatively late his career. See *Sung shih*, chüan 415, pp. 12451–12452; and *CCTC* (1736), 110:25b, 113:16a, 114:15a, 159:16a, and 237:23b.

[25] See *MLL*, chüan 12, pp. 228–229; chüan 14, p. 250; and, chüan 15, p. 257. See also *HCLAC* (1274), 75:11a–b.

許道昌 led efforts to have a temple built for Marshal Wen in 1445. Further work was undertaken in the year 1475 by Hsü's disciple Shih Chih-chung 史志中, who received help from the Administration Vice Commissioner (*ts'an-cheng* 參政) Chang Huan 張寰 and the Assistant Surveillance Commissioner (*an-ch'a ch'ien-shih* 按察僉事) Li Hsien 李巘 (1419–1493). During the late seventeenth century, Wen's temple was rebuilt at the same site, which by then had become the heart of one of Hangchow's commercial districts. This temple also became a major festival center around this time (see chapter 5).[26]

Although the sources describing Marshal Wen's cult during the Sung and Yüan are few and far between, it is clear that his cult was merely one of many struggling to survive in cities like Wenchow and Hangchow during that era. The increasing popularity of Wen's cult at these sites, as well as the second phase of his cult's spread throughout the province, occurred during the Ming-Ch'ing era.[27] In the Hang-Chia-Hu sub-region, this new growth of Wen's cult may have been largely the result of a new period of economic development. Chekiang and its surrounding provinces entered a period of great prosperity during the sixteenth through eighteenth centuries, only briefly interrupted during the Manchu conquest of the 1640s.[28] The most important trend shaping Chekiang's economic history at that time was the province's development as the heartland of south China's sericulture. The collapse of land prices, and technical improvements in the design of looms, caused capital to be redirected towards the production of silk and cotton, which supplanted rice as the staple crop in the Hang-Chia-Hu sub-region. As commercialization picked up steam, more and more farmers turned their rice paddies into mulberry orchards, earning three to six times

---

[26] For data on the Temple of Manifest Virtue, *CTHC* (1609), *chi-chih* 紀事, 26b–28a and 58a; *HCFC* (1579), 47:17b–20a; *HCFC* (1686), 16:34b–36b and 35:34a, *HCFC* (1764), 28:22b–23b, *HCFC* (1922), 9:20b–21a, 10:1a–2b and 34:12b–13a; *Hsi-hu chih* (1734), 10:9b–10a and 14:17a–21a; and, *Hu-shan pien-lan* (1875), 3:3b–4a. Most of the relevant information concerning this temple, including entries in rare Ming gazetteers, has been collected in the *WLFHC*, vol. 4, pp. 269–292.

[27] For a stimulating analysis of the socioeconomic changes affecting south China and their impact on local cults, see von Glahn, "The Enchantment of Wealth," pp. 677–704.

[28] For a review of the socioeconomic changes occuring during the late Ming/early Ch'ing period, see Evelyn Rawski, "Economic and Social Foundations of Late Imperial China," in *Popular Culture in Late Imperial China*, pp. 3–33. On the eighteenth century, see Susan Naquin and Evelyn Rawski, *Chinese Society in the Eighteenth Century* (New Haven: Yale University Press, 1987), pp. 97–106, 147–158, 167–176.

more profit.[29] As for Wenchow and its neighboring prefectures, silk and cotton were also important crops, but this region also featured the intense production of oranges, sweet potatoes and various aquacultural products. The porcelain, lacquer, paper, fishing and ship-building industries also continued to flourish there throughout the late imperial era.[30]

The commercialization of Chekiang during the late Ming/early Ch'ing may be one factor behind the increased merchant support for Marshal Wen's cult at that time. Wen is said to have helped his own cause by aiding Wenchow merchants in their travels. One such weary individual stopped to rest at a temple to Marshal Wen (its exact location is not given), after first having asked permission to do so through divination. During the night, his money was pinched by a young ruffian, who hid it in an earthenware wine jug. Wen appeared to the merchant in a dream and told him where the money was, prompting him to offer lavish sacrifices to Wen upon his return to Wenchow.[31]

In Hangchow, Wen also used a dream to attract new worshippers among merchants. His temple in the Ward of Preserving Peace had burned to the ground in 1666, and shortly thereafter Wen revealed himself in a dream to a man named Wang Te-sheng 王德盛. The nature of this dream is not known, but Wang was so moved by the blessings Wen subsequently provided him that he contributed large amounts of money to buy materials for the temple's reconstruction, and it was soon rebuilt as good as new.[32] Wang's social status is not indicated, but most late imperial people who had enough money to help pay for the reconstruction of a major temple but who were not identified as gentry usually belonged to the merchant class.

---

[29] On the Ming-Ch'ing silk and cotton industries, see Nishijima Sadao, "The Foundation of the Early Cotton Industry," in Linda Grove and Christian Daniels, eds., *State and Society in China: Japanese Perspectives on Ming-Qing Social and Economic History* (Tokyo: University of Tokyo Press, 1984), pp. 17–78; and, Lin, *Che-chiang ching-chi wen-hua shih*, pp. 71–76. See also Chiang Chao-ch'eng, "Lun Ming-Ch'ing Hang-Chia-Hu ti-ch'ü ts'an-sang ssu-chih-yeh te chung-yao ti-wei," *HCTHHP* 18.4 (Dec. 1988): 11–25, and "Ming-Ch'ing shih-ch'i Hang-Chia-Hu ti-ch'ü hsiang-chen ching-chi shih-t'an," *Chung-kuo she-hui ching-chi shih yen-chiu* (1986): 62–72. One should also consult the many essays on this topic in Ch'en, *Ming-Ch'ing she-hui ching-chi shih yen-chiu*, esp. pp. 23–52, 147–183 and 371–384. The English botanist Robert Fortune visited the Hu-chou silk country in the 1850's, presenting a detailed and colorful picture of the industry in his *A Residence Among the Chinese* (London: J. Murray, 1857), pp. 339–378.

[30] See Ch'en, *Ming-Ch'ing she-hui ching-chi shih yen-chiu*, pp. 127–145.

[31] See Chiang, *Ch'i-hai so-t'an chi*, 12:7a.

[32] *HCFC* (1764), 28:22b–23a.

The spread of Marshal Wen's cul*
Wenchow and Hangchow also appears
merchant support. The late imperial periou
growth of Wen's cult in the Hang-Chia-Hu sub-ι
from Hangchow to a number of sites along trade routε
merchant activity. We do not know when Wen's culι
Hu-chou, but his festival at Hsin-shih in Te-ch'ing County was
at a Buddhist monastery named the Chüeh-hai ssu 覺海寺 (foundeu
815), which was rebuilt early in the Wan-li reign using funds raised by
the townspeople. Wen may have entered the monastery's pantheon at
that time.[33] Hsin-shih was a major market town in the Hang-Chia-Hu
sub-region, with links to both Hangchow and Ch'ing-chen (a Marshal
Wen cult site in T'ung-hsiang County, Chia-hsing Prefecture; see
below). The Chüeh-hai ssu was located along the town's main river
and near a bridge, which may indicate one factor behind merchant
support.[34]

Marshal Wen was worshipped at Ch'ing-chen in a Branch
Temple of the Emperor of the Eastern Peak (Tung-yüeh hsing-kung
東嶽行宮) which was built at the site in 1721 (the date Wen's cult had
spread to Ch'ing-chen is not given). This Branch Temple was part of
the temple complex belonging to the Taoist Monastery of Refining
Perfection (Hsiu-chen Kuan 修眞觀), which was founded in 998. This
monastery had the clearest links to merchants, being located across
from a market for Hangchow goods which was named after it. This
market was close to the town's southern gate, the Nan-ch'ang Men
南昌門, through which all water traffic to Hangchow passed.[35]
Ch'ing-chen was located along the border between Chia-hsing and
Hu-chou prefectures, lying across the river from Wu-chen (Hu-chou)
and being located along a major water route between Hangchow and
Hsin-shih.[36] The fact that this monastery was able to attract merchant
support may also be seen in the construction of a temple to the God of
Wealth (Ts'ai-shen 財神), which was erected by cloth merchants

---

[33] See *Hu-chou fu-chih ch'ien-pien* (1649), 5:15b–16a; *TCHC* (1673), 3:21a; *CCTC* (1736), 229:14a; *Hu-chou fu-chih* (1870), 28:26a; *Te-ch'ing hsien hsü-chih* (1808), 2:6b; and, *Te-ch'ing hsien hsin-chih* (1923), 3:21a. For more on Wen's festival at Hsin-shih, see *CCFSCC*, p. 401.

[34] See *TCHC* (1673), 2:4a; and, Fan Shu-chih, *Ming-Ch'ing Chiang-nan shih-chen t'an-wei* (Shanghai: Fu-tan ta-hsüeh ch'u-pan-she, 1990), pp. 455–457.

[35] See Fan, *Chiang-nan shih-chen*, pp. 452–456; *Chia-hsing fu ch'eng-chen ching-chi shih tzu-liao ts'uan* (Chia-hsing: Chia-hsing t'u-shu-kuan, 1985), pp. 299–371; and Chang Yung-yao, et. al., "Chia-hsing mi-shih hsi-su tiao-ch'a," in *Chung-kuo min-chien wen-hua* (Shanghai: Hsüeh-lin ch'u-pan-she 1994), volume 14, pp. 48–65.

[36] Fan, *Chiang-nan shih-chen*, pp. 456–457.

ably from Hangchow).[37]

Another temple to Marshal Wen with possible links to merchants was located in Hu-yeh, a thriving market town about nine kilometers north of the Hangchow metropolitan area (the date of the temple's founding is not given). The earliest records of this temple date from twentieth-century sources, which state that representatives from this temple participated in Wen's festival in Hangchow (see chapter 5).[38]

There is, unfortunately, no evidence that even hints at the identities of Marshal Wen's worshippers in Sheng-hsien (Shaohsing Prefecture). An old temple to Wen (the founding date is not given) destroyed during the Manchu conquest was moved from its original location (unknown) to a new site at the county seat and rebuilt in 1666.[39] This temple was subsequently rebuilt twice during the nineteenth century, once in 1818 and once during the reign of the Hsien-feng emperor (1851–1861).[40] According to the modern edition of the local gazetteer, Wen's festival at Sheng-hsien had become the leading ritual event for the locals by the Republican era.[41]

Apart from merchants, the other group of people who played an important role in the spread of Wen's cult during the Ming-Ch'ing era were members of the scholar-official class. I have described above how Marshal Wen's oldest temple in P'ing-yang was founded by Lin T'ang-fu, a Sung bureaucrat, while Ming officials and Taoist priests helped rebuild Wen's main temple in Hangchow. By the Ch'ing dynasty, support by scholar-officials had become even more common. For example, Brigade General (*tsung-ping* 總兵) Li Hua 李華 [42] ordered the P'ing-yang County Magistrate Chin Yi-chün 金以竣[43] to add a pavilion to the temple compound.[44] Another example of scholar-official support is the case of a temple to Marshal Wen erected at Yu-shan in Li-shui (Ch'u-chou Prefecture) during the middle of the reign of Ch'ien-lung emperor (1736-1795), located at the former mountain villa of the Sung-dynasty Supervising Secretary

---

[37] See *CHFC* (1600), 4:23b; *CHFC* (1681), 7:35a; *THHC* (1887), 5:26a–b; and *Wu-ch'ing chen-chih* (1760), 6:9b. For more on the cult of the God of Wealth in south China, see von Glahn, "The Enchantment of Wealth," pp. 651–714.

[38] See *Hang-chou shih hsin-chih kao* (1948), *chüan mo* 卷末, 2a; and, *HCFC* (1922), 9:21a.

[39] See *SHFC* (1792), 36:59b; and, *SHC* (1684), 6:4b.

[40] *SHC* (1934), 7:7a.

[41] *SHC* (Hangchow: Che-chiang jen-min ch'u-pan-she, 1989), p. 534. For more on this festival, see *CCFSCC*, pp. 277–278.

[42] For biographical data, see *WCFC* (1756), 18:38a.

[43] He served from 1694–1696; see *PYHC* (1915), 26:12a.

[44] See *CCTC* (1736), 217:15b; and, *PYHC* (1915), 45:12b.

(*chi-shih-chung* 給事中) Wang Hsin 王信.[45] According to the nineteenth-century edition of the county gazetteer, Wen's was one of three cults moved to Ch'u-chou from P'ing-yang by a group of military officials, following their transfer to Ch'u-chou. Wen's temple was also known as the Temple of the Grand Guardian, a further sign of its links to P'ing-yang. It was rebuilt using funds raised by the locals in 1867, having been destroyed during the Taiping Rebellion.[46]

The support of scholar-officials also enabled Wen's cult to thrive in places where it had first been established during the Sung-Yüan era. In Wenchow, men like Ch'en Tsu-shou composed poems about Marshal Wen (like the one at the beginning of chapter 3) and helped sponsor hagiographical collections like the *Brief Hagiography*. As for Hangchow, the Governor-General (*tsung-tu* 總督) Li Wei 李衛 (1687–1738) composed an inscription carved on one of the pillars in Wen's Temple of Manifest Virtue. Li's face had been scarred by smallpox, and this may in part explain his interest in a deity renowned for his powers of healing contagious diseases.[47] Scholar-officials also played important roles in Wen's festivals in Hangchow and Wenchow (see chapter 5).

Most of Marshal Wen's new temples in Chekiang (with the possible exception of the one in Sheng-hsien) share one thing in common — they were located in commercial centers, particularly market towns. While the founders or supporters of Marshal Wen's temples are rarely named, it appears that Taoist priests did not play as important a role in the growth of these temples as they had during the Sung to mid-Ming period. It was merchants and/or scholar-officials who were usually behind the growth of Marshal Wen's cult during the late imperial era. In the case of those temples founded in the Hang-Chia-Hu sub-region, these merchants may have been based in Hangchow, traveling throughout the region by means of various water routes as they conducted their business.

The Spread of Marshal Wen's Cult Outside Chekiang

Although a detailed examination of the spread of Wen's cult throughout China is beyond the scope of this work, a survey of local

---

[45] For more on Wang's life and career, see his biography in the *Sung shih, chüan* 400, pp. 12139–12143.

[46] See *LSHC* (1846), 5:5a; and, *LSHC* (1926), 5:34b. A large-scale festival to Wen subsequently arose in Li-shui, although it is not clear when this occurred. See *CCFSCC*, p. 578.

[47] See *ECCP*, pp. 720–721.

gazetteers and epigraphic materials has yielded considerable data on this subject. Of particular interest is the fact that while Taoist priests and ritual masters living outside Chekiang frequently invoked Wen in their rituals, only a few temples to him appear to have been constructed in these areas. The reasons for this phenomenon are unclear; I discuss some possibilities below.

Marshal Wen was the main deity of a temple located in Soochow, which local gazetteers claim dates back to the Sung dynasty.[48] This may be the temple mentioned by the Reverend Hampden C. DuBose in his account of a deity who saved the people of Soochow from being poisoned by plague gods (see chapter 3). Henri Doré also mentions a temple to Marshal Wen in Ju-kao (see chapter 3), but its age and the circumstances behind its founding are not included in local gazetteer accounts.[49] Marshal Wen remains an important deity in rituals performed by Taoist priests in Shanghai's Temple of the Eastern Peak, but is only a subsidiary deity in the temple's divine hierarchy.[50] There is some evidence that Marshal Wen's cult spread further north from Kiangsu to Hopeh (see chapter 3), but I have yet to find any evidence as to how this occurred.

Taoists and other religious specialists in Szechwan also invoked Marshal Wen in their rituals. One late-Ch'ing collection of non-canonical Taoist liturgical materials recently discovered in Ch'eng-tu's Erh-hsien An 二仙庵, entitled the *Kuang-ch'eng yi-chih*, contains texts of a number of plague expulsion rites featuring Wen as a deity to be summoned when epidemics were raging out of control.[51] Unfortunately, I have not been able to determine how such liturgical texts might have been performed. An image of Marshal Wen is also included in a scroll given to Mr. Brian Harland in Szechwan in 1946, although it is unclear how this scroll might have been used in local rituals.[52] No temples to Marshal Wen appear to have been built in Szechwan.

---

[48] See *Chiang-nan t'ung-chih* (1684), 33:9a; and, *Su-chou fu-chih* (1691), 36:37a.

[49] See *Ju-kao hsien-chih* (1808), 3:61b–62b.

[50] See Chu Chien-ming, "Tung-yüeh miao 'Fa-fu' k'o-yi ch'eng-shih yü kao-kung fa-shih tsai pien-shen fa-fu chung te kung-neng," *Min-su ch'ü-yi* 91 (Sept. 1994): 465–502.

[51] The *Kuang-ch'eng yi-chih* may be found in volumes 13–15 of the *Tsang-wai tao-shu*. Texts in which Wen is summoned include the *Tung-yüan cheng-ch'ao ch'üan-chi*, 9a; *Ho-wen ch'ien-chou ch'üan-chi*, 2a; and *Ho-wen cheng-ch'ao chi* (1886), 4a.

[52] A portion of this scroll adorns the cover of Joseph Needham's *Science and Civilization in China*. Wen was also portrayed in the Yung-lo Kung 永樂宮 murals (Shansi), but was not worshipped in that temple. A painting of Wen is still worshipped in the White Cloud Monastery (Pai-yün Kuan 白雲觀) in Peking.

Marshal Wen's cult also spread southwards to Fukien, with a large temple to both him and a deity named Marshal K'ang being erected near Foochow next to a Temple of the Eastern Peak.[53] This temple was said to have existed since the Sung dynasty, although the exact date of its founding is unclear. Both Wen and K'ang served the Emperor of the Eastern Peak, and were probably originally worshipped as subsidiary deities in the local Temple of the Eastern Peak. It appears that local worshippers built a separate temple for them as their cult became increasingly popular. These two deities are said to have performed a number of miracles, particularly helping to fend off a series of pirate incursions during the late Ming.[54]

Marshal Wen's cult also appears to have spread along the southern coast of Fukien, attaining greatest prominence in T'ung-an County of Ch'üan-chou Prefecture. However, by the time Wen's cult had begun to flourish in that area, people had apparently begun to worship him as a Lord (*wang-yeh*), with his surname changing from Wen to Ch'ih.[55] Lord Ch'ih's temple in T'ung-an was built on Wu-chia chieh 五甲街. The county gazetteer states that his cult spread to T'ung-an after he revealed himself to members of the local community (probably through a dream or spirit medium) and later caused a statue of himself to mysteriously appear.[56]

Despite the differences in surname and title, Marshal Wen and Lord Ch'ih should probably be considered as two forms of the same deity, especially because their hagiographies and iconographies are nearly identical (see chapter 3). Like Marshal Wen, Lord Ch'ih was also represented as a martial figure (in this case, a military *chin-shih*) who specialized in curing diseases. The change in Wen's surname to Ch'ih (it had also changed to Lin and Ling in parts of Chekiang; see chapter 3) was probably due to the influence of spirit mediums, who according to the Republican edition of the T'ung-an county gazetteer were frequently possessed by Lord Ch'ih.[57] One important factor which may have led to the confusion between Marshal Wen and Lord

---

[53] Hagiographical sources indicate that Marshal K'ang was a legendary figure renowned for his kindness towards all living things, later being awarded the title "Benevolent Sage Marshal" (Jen-sheng yüan-shuai 仁聖元帥). See *Shih-shen* (1812), *chüan* 1, p. 8; *San-chiao yüan-liu sheng-ti fo-tsu sou-shen ta-ch'üan*, *chüan* 5, pp. 235–236; and, *CKMCCS*, pp. 347–348.

[54] See *Fu-chien t'ung-chih, t'an-miao chih* (1938), 5a–b; *Min-Hou hsien-chih* (1933), 17:1b and 22:1b; and *Chu-ting yü-wen* (1899), 2:22a, p. 155.

[55] For more on Lord Ch'ih's cult in Ch'üan-chou, see Ts'ai, *T'ai-wan te wang-yeh yü ma-tsu*, pp. 60–63; and, Ch'en Keng and Wu An-hui, eds., *Hsia-men min-su* (Hsia-men: Lu-chiang ch'u-pan-she, 1993), pp. 149–153.

[56] See *T'ung-an hsien-chih* (1929), 24:20b.

[57] *Ibid.*, 22:6b–7a.

Ch'ih is that by late imperial times Wen was commonly known only by his title Loyal and Defending King (Chung-ching Wang), not Marshal Wen (Wen Yüan-shuai). As this title ends with the character *wang*, people might have addressed him using the honorific "Lord" (*wang-yeh*). For example, during the Wenchow festival he was referred to as the "great king" (*ta-wang* 大王; see chapter 5), a form of address also used for the Lords of Fukien and Taiwan.

The cult of Lord Ch'ih appears to have spread to Taiwan via Quemoy (Chin-men) and the Pescadores (P'eng-hu), both of which were settled by large numbers of T'ung-an natives during the Ch'ing dynasty.[58] Natives of the Pescadores later brought Lord Ch'ih's cult with them to Tainan, and it spread from there throughout most of the island.[59] Today, Lord Ch'ih is the most popular of all the Lords worshipped in Taiwan, with over one hundred temples featuring him as their main deity, including forty-three in Tainan County.

Marshal Wen is worshipped in his original form by Taoist priests in Taiwan as the guardian of the eastern side of the altar. He is also popularly worshipped as a marshal of the Eastern Legion (*tung-ying* 東營) of the Five Legions (*wu-ying* 五營), whose mission is to guard the house, neighborhood, village, town, etc. against incursions from demonic forces.[60] The only temple on Taiwan in which Marshal Wen is worshipped as the main deity is the Ching-yang Kung 景陽宮 (in Shui-lin Township, Yunlin County), but he is frequently worshipped as a subsidiary deity in temples to the Emperor of the Eastern Peak and the Supreme Emperor of the Dark Heavens. There is a deity named Lord Wen (Wen Wang-yeh 溫王爺) who is also widely worshipped throughout Taiwan. He is the main deity of at least sixty temples, his cult being most popular in Pingtung County (fifteen temples). One of his oldest and largest temples on the island is located in Tung-kang (East Haven), a large fishing port in Pingtung where I have conducted extensive fieldwork.[61] However, because Lord Wen's hagiography and iconography differ greatly from those of Marshal Wen (and Lord Ch'ih), I would hesitate to conclude that Marshal Wen

---

[58] For data on Lord Ch'ih's cult in Quemoy, see *Chin-men chih* (1836), p. 58; and, *Hsin Chin-men chih* (1959), pp. 288, 296, 302, 305 and 306. For the Pescadores, see Liu, *Min-chien hsin-yang*, pp. 229, 260–261.

[59] See Liu, *Min-chien hsin-yang*, pp. 260–268.

[60] See Jordan, *Gods, Ghosts and Ancestors*, pp. 50–51, 56 and 133; and, Huang Wen-po, *T'ai-wan min-chien hsin-yang chien-wen lu* (Hsin-ying: T'ai-nan hsien-li wen-hua chung-hsin, 1988), pp. 14–17.

[61] See Katz, "P'ing-tung hsien Tung-kang chen te ying-wang chi-tien"; and Katz, "Welcoming the Lords and the Pacification of Plagues: The Relationship between Taoism and Local Cults," presented at the Association of Asian Studies Annual Meeting, Boston, March 24–27, 1994.

and Lord Wen are the same deity.[62] A Lords' temple in Taihsi (Yunlin County), the Wu-t'iao Kang An-hsi Fu 五滌港安西府, contains an image of Lord Wen which does conform to Marshal Wen's iconography, but he is only a subsidiary deity and local worshippers appear unaware of his hagiography.

At this point, some readers might wonder why Marshal Wen's cult failed to develop into a national cult like those to deities such as Kuan Kung and the Emperor of the Eastern Peak. One key factor may have been that Wen's cult failed to gain imperial sanction. Even though scholar-officials like Sung Lien and Li Wei supported his cult, there is no evidence that Wen was ever awarded an official title or incorporated into the register of sacrifices, and by the end of the Ch'ing his cult had become a target of state suppression (see chapter 5).

One important Taoist and popular deity who did gain imperial support was the Supreme Emperor of the Dark Heavens, originally worshipped as a stellar deity known as the Dark Warrior (Hsüan-wu) and the guardian spirit of the north. During the T'ang dynasty, Taoist priests transformed the Dark Warrior into a martial deity who specialized in exorcising demons, and it was these men who promoted his cult to the Northern Sung and early Ming emperors. The Dark Warrior became the God of War during the Sung dynasty, with the Chen-tsung emperor (r. 998–1022) changing this deity's name to Chen-wu 眞武 to avoid the taboo against using his own name, Hsüan-lang 玄郎. Imperial support during the Ming by the Yung-lo emperor (r. 1403–1424) contributed to the rapid growth of cult sites to Chen-wu like Wu-tang Shan (in northern Hupeh) and the spread of this cult to other regions of China.[63]

Another Taoist/popular deity whose cult spread throughout China as a result of imperial support was that of Marshal Wen's overlord, the Emperor of the Eastern Peak. Originally a local mountain god at the sacred site of Mt. T'ai (T'ai-shan), his cult gained increasing

---

[62] It is possible that Lord Wen represents another transformation of Marshal Wen brought about by spirit mediums, but I have found no evidence to support such a hypothesis.

[63] Many of the important sources concerning this cult may be found in *CKMCCS*, pp. 62–82. See also Seaman, "Divine Authorship," pp. 483–495; Willem A. Grootaers, "The Hagiography of the Chinese God Chen-wu," *Folklore Studies* 11 (1952): 139–181; and Anna Seidel, "A Taoist Immortal of the Ming Dynasty: Chang San-feng," in William Th. deBary, ed., *Self and Society in Ming Thought* (New York: Columbia Univeristy Press, 1970), pp. 492–496. For more on the cult's primary sacred site, Wu-tang Shan, see John Lagerwey, "The Pilgrimage to Wu-tang Shan," in Susan Naquin and Yü Chün-fang, eds., *Pilgrims and Sacred Sites in China* (Berkeley: University of California Press, 1992), pp. 293–332.

popularity as this site came to be linked to the entrance to the underworld. The deity of Mt. T'ai became worshipped as the overseer of the registers of life and death, and eventually became transformed into one of the Ten Kings of Hell.[64] Politically, Mt. T'ai became a powerful symbol of imperial legitimacy, where emperors who considered themselves worthy would perform the *feng* 封 and *shan* 禪 sacrifices. Therefore, successive emperors awarded the god of Mt. T'ai more and more prestigious titles, culminating in that of the Emperor of the Eastern Peak in 1011. This deity was also an important spirit in the Taoist pantheon, who controlled a vast hierarchy of spirits, including Marshal Wen.[65] The cult of the Emperor of the Eastern Peak, was incorporated into the register of sacrifices during the T'ang-Sung era, and temples to this deity were built throughout China during the late imperial era.[66] Unfortunately, these were also among the first temples targeted for destruction during Nationalist and Communist "anti-superstition" campaigns.[67]

Marshal Wen was frequently worshipped as a subsidiary deity in temples to the Supreme Emperor of the Dark Heavens and the Emperor of the Eastern Peak, both in Chekiang and other parts of China. For example, sources from Ming-dynasty Wenchow indicate that Wen and his fellow grand guardians were enshrined in that city's Temple of the Eastern Peak,[68] while in Taiwan, he is frequently worshipped in temples to the Supreme Emperor of the Dark Heaven

[64] See Stephen F. Teiser, "The Growth of Purgatory," in *Religion and Society in T'ang and Sung China*, pp. 115–145, and *The Scripture of the Ten Kings* (Honolulu: University of Hawaii Press, 1994).

[65] See Anne S. Goodrich, *The Peking Temple of the Eastern Peak: The Tung-yüeh Miao in Peking and its Lore*, (Nagoya: Monumenta Serica, 1964).

[66] See Chavannes, *Le T'ai Chan*; Goodrich, *Temple of the Eastern Peak*; Wechsler, *Offerings of Jade and Silk*, pp. 170–194; Ono Shihei, "Taisan kara Hōto e," *Bunka* 27 (1963): 80–111; Sakai Tadao, "Taisan shinkō no kenkyū," *Shichō* 7 (1937): 70–118; Yüan Ai-kuo, *T'ai-shan shen wen-hua* (T'ai-an: Shan-tung ta-hsüeh ch'u-pan-she, 1991); and Liu Hui, *T'ai-shan tsung-chiao yen-chiu* (Peking: Wen-wu ch'u-pan-she, 1994). Data on the Temple to the Eastern Peak in Hangchow may be found in Lin Yung-chung and Chang Sung-shou, *Lao Tung-yüeh. Miao-hui tiao-ch'a pao-kao* (Hangchow: Che-chiang yin-shua-chü, 1936); and Hsia T'ing-yü, "Kuan-yü Hang-chou Tung-yüeh miao," *Chung-shan ta-hsüeh min-su chou-k'an* 41 and 42 (1929): 27–78.

[67] A description and analysis of the Nationalist anti-superstition campaigns may be found in Prasenjit Duara's article entitled "Knowledge and Power in the Discourse of Modernity: The Campaigns against Popular Religion in Early Twentieth-Century China," *JAS*, 50.1 (Feb. 1991): 67–83. Numerous articles on the impact of the Cultural Revolution on Chinese popular religion may be found in Pas, ed., *The Turning of the Tide*.

[68] See for example Chiang, *Ch'i-hai so-t'an chi*, 12:3a. Wen was also a subsidiary deity in Ch'ing-chen's temple to the Emperor of the Eastern Peak (see above), although whether or not other grand guardians were also worshipped there is unknown.

(see above). As gazetteer and epigraphic accounts of temples rarely list subsidiary deities by name, it is difficult to determine how many such temples contained statues of Marshal Wen and how prominently he figured in a given temple's divine hierarchy. I have yet to determine why so few temples featured Wen as a main deity, but this does seem to indicate that his cult rarely attained the degree of popularity necessary to inspire people to pay for and build temples to him.

Another reason that Wen's cult failed to attain prominence on the national level may have been that he proved unable to supplant other plague-fighting deities worshipped outside of Chekiang. Data presented in chapter 2 reveals that people in Kiangsu tended to worship the City God during epidemics, while in Foochow, the Five Commissioners of Epidemics (Five Emperors) were the objects of plague expulsion rituals. In southern Fukien and Taiwan, numerous Lords (including Lord Ch'ih) were worshipped as divine guardians against epidemics, but so were the Great Emperor who Preserves Life, Kuan Kung, and even Ma-tsu.[69] In the case of Szechwan, Terry Kleeman has shown that Wen-ch'ang was worshipped there as the Patriarch of Epidemic Demons (Wen-tsu 瘟祖), probably due to the influence of stories about him like the one discussed in chapter 2.[70]

In addition, the cult of Marshal Wen might have spread more widely and gained greater prominence if he had been worshipped as the patron deity of a particular group of merchants. Ho Ping-ti and Barend ter Haar have shown that guild members built temples to their patron deities throughout China in the places they traveled to and did business in,[71] while Farzeen Baldrian-Hussein has demonstrated the important role tradespeople played in the spread of the cult of Lü Tung-pin 呂洞賓 during the Sung dynasty.[72] Although Marshal Wen was worshipped by merchants, such as the Wenchow merchant whose money he helped recover or the Hangchow merchant Wang Te-sheng, he did not become the patron deity of a particular guild or merchant association. If, for example, Hangchow silk merchants had adopted Wen as one of their patron gods, his cult might have spread on a much

---

[69] See Sung Kuang-yü, "T'ai-wan jih-chü ch'u-ch'i te wen-yi yü ying-shen," in Li Yih-yüan, et. al., eds., *K'ao-ku yü li-shih wen-hua* (Taipei: Cheng-chung ch'u-pan-she, 1991), pp. 305–330.

[70] Kleeman, *A God's Own Tale*, p. 43.

[71] See Ho, "Geographic Distribution", p. 125; and, ter Haar, "Genesis and Spread," pp. 349–396.

[72] See Farzeen Baldrian-Hussein, "Lü Tung-pin in Northern Sung Literature," *CEA* 2 (1986), 133–169.

larger scale than it did.[73]

The final factor preventing Wen's cult from becoming a national cult was pure luck. If Wen had provided divine assistance to an imperial envoy (like Ma-tsu) or the emperor himself (like the Supreme Emperor of the Dark Heavens), his cult's ascendancy would have been assured.

Taoism and the Spread of Local Cults

The evidence presented above reveals that Taoist priests played an important role in the spread of Marshal Wen's cult, particularly during the initial phase of its growth. Of the four Marshal Wen temples constructed in Hangchow and Wenchow before the Ch'ing dynasty, two were built or restored by Taoist priests and one was built by a scholar-official (it is not clear whether or not the founder of the other temple was a Taoist). Further evidence for Taoist priests popularizing the cult of Marshal Wen may be found in a late Ming Wenchow gazetteer, which tells of a Sung dynasty Taoist named Huang Liang-wu 黃良晤 who resided in the Perfect Flower Monastery (Chen-hua Kuan 眞華觀) and was skilled in Five Thunder ritual techniques (*Wu-lei fa*). He was also a prodigious drinker, and one day as he lay on the floor in his cups, someone came into the temple to ask for a charm. Huang looked at Wen's statue and said: "Go to the home of the afflicted person." The sick person was immediately cured.[74]

Marshal Wen's *Taoist Canon* hagiography also indicates that Taoist priests spread Wen's cult by performing rituals to him during their travels.[75] It is surely no coincidence that the cult of Marshal Wen spread from Chekiang to some of the same provinces (Kiangsu and Fukien) to which, his *Taoist Canon* hagiography claims, Taoists performing his ritual techniques had journeyed. The question of why temples dedicated to Marshal Wen tended to be built long after Taoist priests visited these areas has yet to be resolved. This may well be because Marshal Wen belonged to that class of deities worshipped by

[73] For more on patron deities, see Kuo Li-ch'eng, *Hang-shen yen-chiu* (Taipei: Kuo-li pien-yi-kuan, Chung-hua ts'ung-shu wei-yüan-hui, 1967); and, Li Ch'iao, *Chung-kuo hang-yeh-shen ch'ung-pai* (Peking: Chung-kuo hua-ch'iao ch'u-pan-she, 1990).

[74] See WCFC (1605), 13:56b–57a; YCFC (1882), 36:22a. This Taoist monastery was first constructed during the mid-eighth century; see WCFC (1605), 4:21b. It was later restored during the reign of the K'ang-hsi emperor (1662–1722); see CCTC (1736), 234:3a. Marshal Wen appears to have been a subsidiary deity in this temple, though the date of his inclusion in its pantheon is not known.

[75] For more on this phenomenon, see Boltz, "Not by the Seal of Office Alone," p. 269.

Taoist priests and recorded in their liturgical texts, but rarely enshrined as a main deity of their temples. Thus, Taoist priests could spread his cult throughout China without necessarily founding temples to him.

Even when a gazetteer states that a Taoist priest "built" a temple, one should not take this to mean that he did the work with his own bare hands, or even shelled out most of the money involved. Taoist priests did initiate and/or supervise temple construction projects, and often raised much of the necessary funding. However, unless a Taoist priest could find a generous patron (usually a merchant or scholar-official, as in the case of Hsü Tao-ch'ang and his disciples) to support a temple's construction, work usually proceeded in stops and starts, and could take many years (even decades) to complete. Temples whose construction was supervised and/or supported by scholar-officials, the gentry, or members of the local elite tended to be completed at a faster pace.[76]

The important role Taoist priests played in the spread of local cults to deities like Marshal Wen has only recently come to be fully appreciated by social historians. For example, while Valerie Hansen does note that religious specialists were also important supporters of local cults,[77] her reliance on anecdotes and epigraphic sources at the expense of data in the *Taoist Canon* caused her to overemphasize the role of merchants and scholar-officials in the growth of such cults.[78] Terry Kleeman, on the other hand, has clearly shown that Taoist priests helped spread the cult of Wen-ch'ang from Szechwan to Chekiang during the Sung, founding temples to him in major urban center, such as Ningpo and Hangchow.[79]

Ken Dean has advanced an even bolder argument, claiming that " Taoism provides the liturgical framework which enables local cults to expand and develop," a process which supposedly involves Taoist priests "channeling" what Piet van der Loon has labeled China's "shamanistic substratum."[80] Dean also states that the standardization of the canonization process for local deities usually occurred within a framework provided by the Taoist liturgical

---

[76] See Wolfram Eberhard, "Temple-Building Activities in Medieval and Modern China: An Experimental Study," *Monumenta Serica* 23 (1964): 312–317.

[77] See Hansen, *Changing Gods*, p. 139, note 7.

[78] She has recently modified her position in "Gods on Walls," pp. 108–109 (note 88).

[79] Kleeman, "Expansion of the Wen-ch'ang Cult," pp. 58–59.

[80] Dean, *Taoist Ritual and Popular Cults*, p. 17. The concept of a Taoist "liturgical framework" was first formulated by Kristofer Schipper, particularly in his "Taoist Ritual and Local Cults".

tradition.[81] Dean never clarifies whether or not Taoism played a significant role in the development of most local cults in China, but the evidence he supplies regarding the growth of the three cults his book focuses on (those of the Great Emperor who Protects Life [Pao-sheng ta-ti], the Reverent Lord of Broad Compassion [Kuang-tse tsun-wang], and the Patriarch of the Clear Stream [Ch'ing-shui tsu-shih]) unfortunately does not support his theories. While Taoist priests did contribute to the formation of hagiographical traditions surrounding the former two deities, by composing scriptures about them, the growth and spread of their cults appears to have been largely due to the support of scholar-officials, merchants, and members of powerful lineages.[82] The case of the Patriarch of the Clear Stream is even more interesting, as many of his cult's supporters were not Taoist priests but Buddhist monks.[83] Dean's analysis does work to a certain extent in the case of cults to deities such as Marshal Wen or the Supreme Emperor of the Dark Heavens; however, the issue of whether the growth of these cults occurred within a Taoist liturgical framework has yet to be resolved (see chapter 5).

It is also important to remember that even when Taoist priests did contribute significantly to the spread of a deity's cult, such cults rarely flourished over the long term without the additional support of members of the scholar-officials, gentry, or elite classes. The evidence presented above indicates that this was the case not only for the cult of Marshal Wen, but also for the very cults Dean has researched. The resulting competition between different groups for control of a cult could even result in occasional tensions between cult members. In the case of the Lords of Taiwan for example, certain rituals once performed by Taoist priests are occasionally performed by members of the temple committee, causing these two groups to argue over who should perform which ritual in what location and at what time.[84]

A particularly vivid account of the struggle between different worshippers for control of a popular cult involves the cult of Wong Tai Sin (Huang Ta-hsien 黃大仙), which enjoys immense popularity in Hong Kong. Wong's cult was initially brought to Hong Kong from Kwangtung in 1915 by religious specialists who appear to have been Taoists. However, the cult's rapid growth following World War II was largely due to the efforts of a new group of leaders, members of the Tung Wah (Tung-hua 東華) charitable organization, who took over the

---

[81] *Ibid.*, p. 37.

[82] *Ibid.*, pp. 83–89, 134–135 and 142–143.

[83] *Ibid.*, pp. 120–129.

[84] For more on this problem, see Katz, "Welcoming the Lords and the Pacification of Plagues."

management of the cult in 1956. Although their efforts resulted in the rapid expansion of Wong's cult, their decision to eliminate planchette divination rituals (*fu-chi* 扶乩) at the temple caused considerable chagrin among many of the cult's early members.[85]

I have yet to determine the extent to which such tensions may have accompanied the growth of Marshal Wen's cult, but the differing representations of Wen presented in the previous chapter may indicate one potential source of tension between different cult members. James Watson's analysis of the Ma-tsu cult has also revealed that attempts by different groups of believers in Hong Kong's New Territories to control her cult and festival could even result in outbreaks of violence (he does not mention Taoist priests, though).[86] No such violence appears to have accompanied the growth of Marshal Wen's cult, although we do know that a wide range of groups participated in Wen's cult and festivals during the late imperial era. Tension between these groups might have contributed to the performance of rituals known as "filing indictments" during Wen's festival in Wenchow (see below), but further research is needed to clarify this problem. Suffice it to say that Taoist priests were but one of many groups attempting to assert their authority over popular local cults, and that the success or failure of each group's efforts can only be determined through detailed case studies.

---

[85] See Graeme Lang and Lars Regvald, *The Rise of a Refugee God. Hong Kong's Wong Tai Sin* (Hong Kong: Oxford University Press, 1993), pp. 10–70.

[86] Watson, "Standardizing the Gods," pp. 311–313 and 318–320.

FIVE

The Festival of Marshal Wen in Wenchow and Hangchow

Believing in ghosts and revering mediums was not by chance,
Even now, illicit sacrifices perpetually are enhanced;
Expelling the plague demons; who knows whither to?
The plague boat floats along in its seaborne dance.

—Tai Yü-sheng, *Ou-chiang chu-chih tz'u*

Historical Background

As we saw in the previous chapter, the spread of Marshal Wen's cult throughout Chekiang during the late imperial era was linked to the province's economic development. Extant cults to Wen in Wenchow and Hangchow also experienced a period of increasing popularity at that time, and large-scale festivals to him in these cities began to be held. The sources we have on Wen's festivals in Wenchow and Hangchow are mostly from the mid- to late-Ch'ing dynasty, but it is clear that a festival of the size and stature described in these sources did not suddenly appear then but was the result of a long period of growth, probably beginning during the late Ming. While it is impossible to determine with any degree of certainty all of the factors leading to the growth of Wen's festivals in these cities, they probably included the socioeconomic changes Wenchow and Hangchow were experiencing during the late imperial era.

Coastal areas of south China (including Wenchow) underwent a period of decline during the early and mid-Ming periods due to the state's restrictions on trade, and later suffered terribly during the forced coastal evacuations of the early Ch'ing and a second ban on trade that lasted until the conquest of Taiwan in 1683. By the eighteenth century, however, a thriving foreign trade in silk and tea had helped spark a revitalization of Chekiang's coastal regions. From the early eighteenth century to the Opium War in 1840, over 6,200 ships traveled trade routes between Chekiang (Ningpo) and Japan (Nagasaki), with silks taking up seventy percent of the cargo space in their holds. In addition, a 1759 memorial reported that between 200,000 and 330,000 catties (*chin* 斤; one catty = approx. 1.32 pounds) of Hu-chou silk passed through Canton (via ports such as Wenchow, Ningpo and Ch'üan-chou) on its way to customers in Southeast Asia and the West, with customs duties raking in an estimated 800,000 *taels* (*liang* 兩; one *tael* = approx. 1.3 ounces of silver) of revenue a year.[1] Ningpo grew into a major entrepôt of coastal and overseas trade (esp. with Japan), while Wenchow flourished as an important transshipment port between Foochow and Ningpo.[2]

Ningpo, Hangchow, and Wenchow all became treaty ports in the years following the Opium War, ranking thirteenth, fifteenth, and twenty-fourth respectively in terms of the net value of trade they handled. Ningpo also grew into an important banking center. Links between Ningpo and Wenchow became even stronger during this period, with Ningpo merchants establishing a large guild hall in Wenchow and developing into one of the most powerful interest groups in the city.[3]

Hangchow's continuing prosperity during the Ming-Ch'ing era was in large part due to its silk industry. The number of looms operated by the state-controlled Weaving and Dyeing Service (Chih-jan chü 織染局) of Hangchow increased from 385 in 1694 to 600 in 1745, with a work force of over 2,000 laborers. If one includes private industry as well, the city of Hangchow contained 3,000 looms. It also boasted huge temples in which the God of the Looms (Chi-shen 機神) was worshipped.[4] Many large and elaborate festivals had been staged in Hangchow since at least the Southern Sung dynasty,[5] but the late imperial era appears to have witnessed the growth of new festivals sponsored by up-and-coming young merchants. Whether Marshal Wen's was one of these has yet to be determined, but it

---

[1] See Chiang, "Ts'an-sang ssu-chih-yeh," pp. 17–20, 23.

[2] See Chu Te-lan, "Ch'ing k'ai hai-ling hou te Chung-Jih Ch'ang-ch'i mao-yi shang yü kuo-nei yen-hai mao-yi," in Chang Yen-hsien, ed., *Chung-kuo hai-yang fa-chan shih lun-wen-chi* (Nankang: Sun Yat-sen Institute of Social Sciences, 1988), vol. 3, pp. 369–416; and, Chou, *Wen-chou kang-shih*, pp. 29, 31 and 34. For research on Ningpo, see Shiba Yoshinobu, "Ningpo and Its Hinterland," in Skinner, *City*, pp. 391–439.

[3] Chou, *Wen-chou kang-shih*, pp. 34–37.

[4] See *Yüan-Ming-Ch'ing ming-ch'eng Hang-chou* (Hangchow: Che-chiang jen-min ch'u-pan-she, 1990), pp. 157–243.

[5] See for example Gernet, *Daily Life*, pp. 185–197.

clearly did develop into an important ritual and commercial event for Hangchow merchants by the eighteenth century (see below).

Hangchow experienced great hardship during the collapse of Ch'ing China in the nineteenth century.[6] The Taiping Rebellion, which erupted in southwest China in 1850 under the leadership of the fanatic Christian convert Hung Hsiu-ch'üan 洪秀全, proved devastating to the city. The rebels stormed through Chekiang in the early 1860s, with the northern plains sub-region bearing the brunt of the blow. The devastation wrought by the rebels reduced Chekiang's registered population by nearly half, from just over thirty million in 1851 to eighteen million in 1873, with the northern plains sub-region suffering the worst losses.[7] Hangchow endured a horrific two-month siege before being sacked and burned in 1861, with the rebels reducing nine-tenths of the city to utter ruin and butchering four-fifths of the populace. It is said that the canals were so full of the bodies of terrified citizens who had taken their own lives that there was no room for others to jump in. An American visiting the city forty years later observed that "there still remain great tracts of land unoccupied, on which formerly stood handsome buildings or the homes of many thousands of people".[8]

The traumatic changes Chekiang and the rest of China were experiencing during the nineteenth century took their toll on Marshal Wen's cult and festival, particularly in Hangchow. Wen's festival there never fully recovered from the effects of the massive destruction wrought by the Taiping rebels. In addition, vigorous "anti-superstition" campaigns led by zealous late Ch'ing and early Republican era officials sounded the death knell for Wen's Hangchow festival. Wen's cult and festival in Wenchow were able to survive the fall of the Ch'ing however, perhaps due to their deeper roots in the area.

---

[6] For a study of the region's nineteenth-century history, see Li Kuo-ch'i, *Chung-kuo hsien-tai-hua te ch'ü-yü yen-chiu: Che-Min-T'ai ti-ch'ü* (Nankang: Institute of Modern History, 1982), pp. 37–42, 57–58, 71–72.

[7] See Mary B. Rankin, *Elite Activism and Political Transformation in China, Zhejiang Province, 1865–1911* (Stanford: Stanford University Press, 1986), pp. 54–62.

[8] See Frederick D. Cloud, *Hangchow: The "City of Heaven"* (Shanghai: Presbyterian Mission Press, 1906), pp. 7–8; Hsü Ying-p'u, *Liang-che shih-shih ts'ung-k'ao* (Hangchow: Che-chiang ku-chi ch'u-pan-she, 1988) pp. 139–247; and, Kathryn Bernhardt, *Rents, Taxes and Peasant Resistance. The Lower Yangtze Region, 1840–1950* (Stanford: Stanford University Press, 1992), esp. pp. 84–160.

Marshal Wen's Festival in Wenchow[9]

It is difficult to determine with any certainty the age of Marshal Wen's festival in Wenchow, which was held annually during the third lunar month as a prophylactic ritual, and occasionally staged as an apotropaic rite when an epidemic raged. The earliest record of Wen's festival there dates from the eighteenth century, but its origins are certainly older than that. As early as the Sung dynasty, people in Wenchow had probably begun to invoke Wen in rituals meant to expel plague demons afflicting individuals (see below), but there is no evidence as to when and how large-scale festivals to Wen developed. I can only speculate that Wen's festival in Wenchow may have arisen during the late Ming, when a renewed influx of foreign trade revitalized the city's economy, and when Wen's cult gained increasing support among merchants and scholar-officials.

Because Marshal Wen's hagiography stated that he had thwarted the efforts of plague deities to spread epidemics by poisoning the wells, people believed that he possessed special powers to combat contagious diseases. There are a number of Southern Sung and Yüan dynasty liturgical texts in the *Taoist Canon* in which Wen is invoked to expel plague demons, particularly those belonging to the Divine Empyrean ritual movement. While it is impossible to prove that such rites may have been performed in Wenchow, the fact that this movement had its origins in the Wenchow area and enjoyed great popularity there indicates that such a possibility should not be considered too remote.

The first rites invoking Marshal Wen were not meant to be held during large-scale festivals but to meet the needs of individual believers, a fact which may reflect the limited growth Wen's cult had achieved during the Sung and Yüan dynasties.[10] For example, "The Great Ritual Technique of the Earth Spirit Marshal Wen" (*Ti-ch'i Wen yüan-shuai ta-fa* 地祇溫元帥大法 ; *TFHY, chüan* 256), portrays Wen as a

---

[9] While doing fieldwork in Wenchow in October 1989, I met Yeh Ta-ping, a local scholar who has also been researching the festival of Marshal Wen in Wenchow. He has recently published two important articles on this topic entitled "Wen Yüan-shuai hsin-yang yü Tung-yüeh miao-hui," *Min-su ch'ü-yi*, 72/73 (1991): 102–128; and, "Wen-chou Tung-yüeh miao-hui p'o-hsi," in *Chung-kuo min-chien wen-hua* (Shanghai: Hsüeh-lin ch'u-pan-she, 1992), volume 5, pp. 235–251.

[10] In *The Taoist Body*, Kristofer Schipper states that: "The manuscripts of the *tao-shih* [Taoist priests] are exclusively liturgical [they never pertain to individual worship]" (p. 60). However, the evidence in the *Tao-fa hui-yüan* indicates that such a claim may have its limits, unless of course one chooses to treat these rituals as non-Taoist (Judith Boltz and Piet van der Loon consider the *Tao-fa hui-yüan* to be a Taoist work).

deity who aids individuals in distress. This text opens with a document entitled "A Secret Edict for Expelling Epidemics" (*Ch'ien-wen pi-chih* 遣瘟祕旨), which describes a boat ritual that was to be performed for someone afflicted by a contagious disease. According to the instructions accompanying this text, the ritual master performing the ritual should " visualize Marshal Wen aboard a painted boat. Wen captures and holds all the plague demons, whom he forces onto the boat, locking up the entire lot" (*TFHY* 256:1a–b). The description of this concludes with an expulsion spell to be chanted by the ritual master, part of which reads:

> Oh emperors of heavenly plagues, I am accompanied by the Jade
>   Emperor's General [Wen] Ch'iung;
> Oh emperors of earthly plagues, I possess a writ of the heavenly
>   codes . . .
> I know your surnames, I know your given names,
> If you do not leave at once, your forms will be destroyed by thunder
>   axes . . .
> If you disobey my commands, you will be sliced up into little pieces
>   (*TFHY* 256:1b–2a).

At the ritual's conclusion, the boat was either set afloat or burned.

A more elaborate ritual may be found in *chüan* 220 of the *Tao-fa hui-yüan*, entitled "The Divine Empyrean Rite for Banishing Plagues and Sending Off the Boat" (*Shen-hsiao ch'ien-wen sung-ch'uan yi* 神霄遣瘟送船儀). This rite also portrays Marshal Wen (and numerous other members of the Divine Empyrean pantheon) as plague-fighting deities, and resembles the "Secret Edict" in both structure and function. The Sending off the Boat ritual appears to be the antecedent of the "Pacification of Plagues" (*Ho-wen* 和瘟) ritual performed in Taiwan today. Both rites open with passages describing the causes of epidemics, include a feast for all manner of plague gods and plague demons, feature the reading of a memorial in which the gods are asked to forgive sinful behavior and recall the plague spirits, and conclude with all plague spirits being forced onto a plague boat which is then burned. The Sending off the Boat rite was also originally designed to be performed for individuals, but later versions (including the Pacification of Plagues) appear to have been reworked in order to accompany large-scale plague expulsion festivals.[11]

---

[11] For more on the nature and history of plague expulsion rites, see Ofuchi, *Shūkyō girei*, pp. 197–198, 383–391, 1008–1059; Katz, "P'ing-tung Hsien Tung-kang Chen te sung-wang yi-shih: Ho-wen," *Bulletin of Institute of Ethnology, Academia Sinica — Field Materials*, Occasional Series 2 (March 1990): 93–106; Katz, "Welcoming the Lords and

The earliest description of Marshal Wen's festival in
Wenchow, describing annual prophylactic rites performed during the
third lunar month, may be found in the 1761 edition of the *Yung-chia
hsien-chih* (*chüan* 13).[12] It opens with a summary of Sung Lien's stele
inscription, but goes on to state that:

> Nowadays, the people invite the [Loyal and Protecting]
> King [*ch'ing-wang* 請王][13] to leave his temple and go on
> patrol [*ch'u-miao hsün-hsing* 出廟巡行][14] inside and outside
> the city every year during the beginning of the third lunar
> month. The purpose of this is to expel epidemics [*ch'ü
> wen-yi* 驅瘟疫]. Wen's temples [at Hua-kai Shan and
> Pa-hsien Lou] take turns in organizing the procession
> [*lun-ch'u* 輪出]. On the day the procession starts, tents are
> erected and lanterns strung out all along the streets, making
> them alive with color. Men and women can intermingle,
> and friends and relatives come from distant places to visit
> and watch the fun. Along the streets through which
> Marshal Wen passes, groups of ten or twenty families set
> up as many as seven or eight square tables, on which they
> display the three offerings [*san-sheng* 三牲],[15] as well as
> many candies and fruit, incense and candles. These families
> kowtow, offer libations and read memorials.[16] They also
> burn spirit money. These offerings are called 'roadside
> sacrifices' [*lu-chi* 路祭] . . . When it rains, [the deities in the
> procession] temporarily take shelter at various temples
> [along the route] . . . After returning to the temple, each
> neighborhood [*li* 里] gathers together to erect a stage and
> [hire actors] to perform many dramas. These are called

the Pacification of Plagues"; and, Li Feng-mao, "Tung-kang wang-ch'uan, Ho-wen, yü
sung-wang hsi-su chih yen-chiu" *Tung-fang tsung-chiao* 3 (1993): 229–265.

[12] This account is reproduced and expanded upon in a passage contained in the
Yung-chia wen-chien lu.

[13] A similar ritual also known as *ch'ing-wang* is performed during plague
festivals in Taiwan. See Liu, *Min-chien hsin-yang*, pp. 355–358.

[14] In many parts of southern Taiwan, such processions are often called "tours of
inspection in place of heaven" (*tai-t'ien hsün-shou* 代天巡狩). On the historical origins of
tours of inspection, see Wechsler, *Offerings of Jade and Silk*, pp. 161–169.

[15] These consisted of oxen, sheep, and pigs. In modern Taiwan however, they
usually include pigs, chicken, and fish.

[16] On rituals involving the reading of a memorial, see Schipper, "The Written
Memorial," pp. 309–324. Other sources mentioned below indicate that these memorials
were read by Taoist priests.

"tranquillity operas" [*p'ing-an hsi*].[17] People lavishly spend hundreds and thousands [of *taels*?] without any regrets. If during a year of poor harvests the festival is not held, many people will fall ill, which is blamed on the fact that Marshal Wen didn't go out on patrol that year. This custom has passed down through the generations without change, and the officials have never been able to prohibit it.[18]

This description of Marshal Wen's festival reveals that it performed a number of important social functions. First of all, it brought families and neighbors together in communal worship. Secondly, it stimulated commercial activity in the form of some merchants selling offerings for the roadside sacrifices and others selling goods to all the visitors who flocked to Wenchow during the festival.[19] These and other aspects of the festival are treated in greater detail in a mid twentieth-century manuscript entitled *the Treatise on Wenchow Customs* (*Wen-chou feng-su chih* (*WCFSC*)). I have provided a complete annotated translation of the passages describing the festival of Marshal Wen in Appendix A; here I will simply summarize the main points presented in the text.

Marshal Wen's festival was always preceded by an event known as "Blocking the Road with Blessings" (Lan-chieh Fu 攔街福),[20] which began on the first day of the second lunar month in the Ward of Health and Happiness (K'ang-lo Fang 康樂坊) and extended into the third lunar month. During this period, different neighborhoods took turns holding huge feasts, staging dramatic performances, and inviting Taoists to perform offering services (*ta-chiao* 打醮).[21] The streets were bedecked with lanterns and flowers, as the people of each neighborhood displayed their finery in attempts to surpass their neighbors. There were also offerings for hungry ghosts, and an atmosphere of prosperity and rejoicing prevailed.[22]

---

[17] See chapter 2 for a discussion of tranquility operas. These probably included performances of Mu-lien operas.

[18] See *YCWCL*, *chüan shang*, 32a–33a.

[19] Wu Cheng-han has provided a stimulating presentation of these functions in his "Temple Fairs", pp. 66–157. See also the essays in Kao Chan-hsiang, ed., *Lun Miao-hui wen-hua* (Peking: Wen-hua yi-shu ch'u-pan-she, 1992).

[20] The *Treatise* notes that the name of this event may be related to the similar-sounding term *lan-chieh hu* 攔街虎, which literally means "the tiger that blocks the road", in other words a robber. Unfortunately, they do not provide further details.

[21] See Chiang, *Wu-Yüeh min-chien hsin-yang*, p. 517.

[22] See *WCFSC*, pp. 25–27. See also *Ch'ung-hsiu Che-chiang t'ung-chih kao* (1948), vol. 18:4b. For a description of the Blocking the Road festival in P'ing-yang, see *PYHC* (1915), 20:6a–b. A similar festival, known as "Making Displays in the Five Wards" (*pai*

The *Treatise*'s account of Marshal Wen's third month festival opens with a description of his hagiography, iconography, and temples. The three temples to Marshal Wen in Wenchow described in chapter 4 took turns staging the festival, each term running for a period of two years. The dates on which the festival was to be celebrated were determined by divination using "moonblocks" (*kao-pei* 筶杯)[23] thrown by the temple chairmen (*miao-tung* 廟董). When the dates had been determined, proclamations written on red paper were posted throughout the city, and the citizens engaged in a massive clean-up effort.

The procession was the high point of the festival, lasting over one week. It was divided into three sections: front station (*t'ou-chan* 頭站), second station (*erh-chan* 二站), and third station (*san-chan* 三站 ; also referred to as rear station [*hou-chan* 後站]).

Lamp-bearers and musicians carrying a huge gong led the front station, which also featured men carrying giant placards on which were inscribed the words "expel fevers and drive off epidemics" (*ch'ü-wen chu-yi* 驅瘟逐疫). They were followed by beggars impersonating the Five Demons (*Wu-kuei* 五鬼),[24] as well as a huge puppet of the deity Fang-hsiang Shih (from the ancient Great Exorcism) which was also borne by a beggar. This deity had four gold eyes and carried a huge spear,[25] which he used to keep the Five Demons in line.

The second station consisted of many people dressed in black and wearing tall hats, called "deities who clear the road" (*k'ai-lu shen* 開路神).[26] People who dressed as these deities were required to make a

---

wu-fang 擺五坊), was also celebrated in Ch'ing-liu City of Ting-chou Prefecture (northern Fukien), where it was also followed by plague expulsion rituals, including a boat-burning rite. See Ch'en, *Pa-min chang-ku ta-ch'üan*, pp. 59–60.

[23] For a description of this and other forms of divination, see Richard J. Smith, *Fortune-tellers and Philosophers. Divination in Traditional Chinese Society* (Boulder: Westview Press, 1991); Emily Martin Ahern, *Chinese Ritual and Politics* (Cambridge: Cambridge University Press, 1981), pp. 43–74; and Jordan, *Gods, Ghosts and Ancestors*, pp. 66–77.

[24] These are considered to be associated with the five directions (*wu-fang* 五方) of Five Phases theory, and are occasionally identified as the Five Commissioners of Epidemics.

[25] For more on this deity and its iconography, see Bodde, *Festivals*, pp. 77–84; *CKMCCS*, 483–485; and Anna Seidel, "Traces of Han Religion in Funerary Texts Found in Tombs," in Akizuki Kanei, ed., *Dōkyō to shūkyō bunka* (Tokyo: Hirakawa, 1987), pp. 21–57.

[26] See *CCFSCC*, pp. 277–278 and 401 for descriptions of similar troups in other parts of Chekiang. These performers seem similar to the Eight Family Generals (*Pa-chia chiang* 八家將) and Lord Seven, Lord Eight (*Ch'i-yeh* 七爺 , *Pa-yeh* 八爺) troupes in Taiwan. See Shih Wan-shou, "Chia-chiang T'uan — T'ien jen ho yi te hsün-pu tsu-chih,"

vow (*hsü-yüan* 許願)[27] and pay a sum of money to participate. These deities were followed by a group of people on horseback dressed as the stars of the Big Dipper, as well as four people carrying huge containers of burning incense. A martial figure known as "the marshal who supervises the troupes (in the procession)" (*ya-tui yüan-shuai* 押隊元帥) brought up the rear, sitting in a palanquin and dressed in gold-colored clothes. He carried a flag of command (*ling-ch'i* 令旗), and was accompanied by four guards (also played by beggars) carrying huge halberds called "horse-beheading knives" (*chan-ma tao* 斬馬刀). The man who played the marshal could neither move nor talk, and was often mistaken for a statue by children. Those portraying the marshal and the seven stars of the Big Dipper also had to make a vow in order to participate. The former had to hire his four guards, while the latter supplied their own horses.

The rear station consisted of people known as "criminals" (*fan-jen* 犯人) or "sinners" (*tsui-jen* 罪人). These were mostly men, but women and children could also join in. They dressed in red,[28] wore cangues, carried chains, and painted their faces. The experience of dressing as a criminal or sinner was apparently so moving that many shed tears as they processed. The more devout ones even hung incense burners from their flesh by hooks. People also participated as criminals or sinners after making a vow, which they usually did due to illness or fear that they hadn't expiated sins committed in the past.[29] According to the text, their goal in performing this role was to rely on

---

T'ai-nan wen-hua 22 (1986): 48–65; and, Donald Sutton, "Ritual Drama and Moral Order: Interpreting the Gods' Festival Troupes of Southern Taiwan," *JAS* 49.3 (Aug. 1990): 535–554.

[27] In Taiwan, making a vow usually entails the worshipper's promising to serve a deity in return for divine assistance. The act of serving a deity after a miracle has been performed is called "fulfilling a vow" (*huan-yüan* 還願). For more on people in late imperial Chekiang making vows when ill, see *Ch'ung-hsiu Che-chiang t'ung-chih kao* (1948), vol. 17:11a–b.

[28] Condemned criminals in late imperial China usually wore red at their executions.

[29] For accounts of "criminals" in the festivals of Chekiang's neighboring provinces, see John K. Shryock, *The Temples of Anking* (Paris: J. K. Sheyock, 1931), p. 105; *Chü-jung hsien-chih* (1904), 66:5; and *Ch'ang-Chao ho chih* (1898), 6:7. One of the most detailed and colorful accounts of exorcistic Processions (in Fukien) may be found in deGroot, *Religious System*, vol. 6, pp. 980–990. These events included handcuffed children, sometimes in cages. People dressed as criminals invariably participate in the plague festivals I have seen in Taiwan. They usually dress in black, wear cardboard cangues, and carry light chains. Some also carry brooms which they use to sweep the streets as they march (a form of service to the gods). People in Taiwan who dress as criminals usually do so as part of making a vow (*hsü-yüan*), fulfilling a vow (*huan-yüan*), or atoning for previous sins (*shu-tsui* 贖罪).

the power of the Loyal and Defending King to expunge past faults and prevent disasters in this life.

The criminals and sinners were followed by four "civil and martial judges (*wen-wu p'an-kuan* 文武判官),[30] four "generals on duty in the palace" (*chih-tien chiang-chün* 值殿將軍), and eight eunuchs. Marshal Wen rode an imperial palanquin in the place of honor at the rear of the procession.

The *Treatise* also contains an elaborate description of the etiquette followed in determining ritual interaction between different deities. Members of Wen's and other temple committees, known as "managers" (*ssu-shih* 司事), also marched in the procession, and there were professionals trained in etiquette who accompanied them in order to smooth out any disputes that arose en route. The rites that were performed at temples during the procession depended on the rank of their main deity. For example, if the procession passed a temple whose deity had the title of "emperor" (*ti*; a higher rank than Wen's), members of Wen's temple committee would have to present Wen's name card (*ming-p'ien* 名片) in order for Wen to be able to enter and pay his respects. If the deity was a king (*wang*; equal to Wen), members of both temple committees would exchange incense. If the deity held a rank below Wen's, its temple committee members would have to go out and offer incense at Wen's palanquin. There were similar rituals that had to be followed if the procession had to seek shelter in a temple along the route during a rain storm.[31]

The text also describes the goods offered at the roadside sacrifices and the fine wares people displayed outside their houses when the procession passed. People competed in presenting elaborate displays of wealth, especially the owners of shops along the procession route. Huge feasts were held, dramas were performed, and a festive atmosphere reigned.

On the evening before the final day of the festival the rite of "filing indictments" (*fang-kao* 放告) was held in the western suburbs, at the military training grounds. This rite invoked Wen's function as a deity in the subterranean bureaucracy administered by the Emperor of the Eastern Peak. Placards were pasted up all over the city during the day telling people who "bore resentment or held hatred" (*han-yüan yin-hen* 含冤飲恨) to file a complaint with the underworld (*kao yin-chuang* 告陰狀). A temporary structure was erected, to which Wen

---

[30] For more on the exorcistic role these "judges" played in processions, see Bredon and Mitrophanow, *The Moon Year*, pp. 312–313; and de Groot, *Religious System*, vol. 6, p. 980.

[31] This emphasis on etiquette was also an important part of festivals to the Five Emperors in Foochow. See Hsü, *Fu-chien min-chien hsin-yang*, pp. 94–95.

was brought in his palanquin. He was flanked by the marshal who supervises the troupes, while the criminals and sinners filled the hall. People dressed as assistants and yamen runners lined up in formation and hollered "The Great King has entered the hall!" (ta-wang sheng-t'ang 大王升堂) when Wen arrived. After much kneeling and bowing, people who had complaints were allowed to enter. They wore mourning garments and their hair was disheveled. Screaming cries of "Injustice!" (yüan-wang 冤枉), they would attempt to present a written complaint to Wen, but could only do so after having been beaten back two times. This document was then burned and the validity of the grievance was acknowledged. According to the authors of the Treatise, some of the accused died soon after this rite was performed![32]

The actual expulsion rites were held on the final day of the festival during a 24-hour procession which passed through the largest streets of the city. No roadside sacrifices were offered during this procession, but people did burn incense along the route. The goal of this procession was for Marshal Wen to capture and expel any plague demons lingering in the area which had not left of their own free will. The procession entered the city through the southern gate at midnight, with all the criminals and sinners (except the children) lighting torches and racing through the city behind Wen's palanquin. This rite to expel epidemics, somewhat reminiscent of the Grand Exorcism, lasted until dawn.[33]

Boat Expulsion Rites in Wenchow

Rituals involving the expulsion of a plague boat were not held at regular intervals but whenever an epidemic struck. According to the editors of the Treatise, such a catastrophe would prompt the city's elders to meet at the temple to Wenchow's most renowned local hero,

---

[32] Similar rites were performed in City God temples throughout China. See, for example, the Rev. J. MacGowan, Chinese Folklore Tales (London: Macmillan and Co., 1910), pp. 139–140. Such rites often featured the ritual beheading of a chicken. Hsia Chih-ch'ien has explored the topic of divine trials and ordeals in his Shen-p'an (Shanghai: San-lien shu-tien, 1990). For a description of the insane being put on trial in the Temple of the Eastern Peak, see Ch'ung-hsiu Che-chiang t'ung-chih kao (1948), vol. 17:12b. Plague festivals held in Taiwan feature similar ceremonies in which people can submit documents to plague deities, with men dressed as clerks and yamen runners playing a supervisory role. However, in some parts of Taiwan, indictments are not allowed to be filed, as community leaders fear this would spark social unrest! See Liu, Min-chien hsin-yang, pp. 353–370, esp. pp. 365–366.

[33] This description is taken from the WCFSC, pp. 27–35. A briefer account may be found in the YCHC (1882), 6:6a.

the King Eastern of Ou (Tung-Ou Wang 東甌王),[34] to organize Wen's festival and raise funds to pay for it, which the terrified populace gladly contributed. Much of the money was used to erect a mammoth altar and hire Taoist priests to perform an elaborate ritual known as the Great Offering Under the Heavens (*Lo-t'ien ta-chiao* 羅天大醮),[35] which lasted all week. Before the Great Offering started, the managers of the King of Eastern Ou's temple would send out formal notices to the temple committees of Wenchow's other major temples, including Wen's, directing each to raise money to pay for the festival. As in the third month festival, people cleaned the streets to prepare for the procession.

A large plague boat made of a bamboo frame covered with paper was set up in front of the Temple of the King of Eastern Ou. In it were placed miniature pieces of furniture and tools made of paper, as well as food and spirit money. Over ten feet long and seven feet wide, with three masts, it was built along the lines of the sampans that regularly plied the waters off south China.

On the day the festival was to begin, all the deities involved (a total of ten) arrived in their palanquins in reverse order of rank, starting with the City God. The final deity to arrive was the Great Emperor Hua-kuang 華光,[36] who received a special invitation via a runner dispatched by the King of Eastern Ou. After all the deities had arrived and been seated according to rank, tea and snacks were served.

Shortly afterwards, the Taoists and temple committee members serving at the altar brought out the tablets (*p'ai-wei* 牌位) representing Taoism's highest deities, the Three Pure Ones,[37] which all the deities in the temple went out to welcome. The Taoists then summoned Marshal Wen to receive his orders. He was issued an

---

[34] This king was named Kou Yao 句搖, and he was a descendant of the famous King of Yüeh named Kou Chien 句踐 (r. 497–465 B.C.E.). Because Kou Yao aided the first Han emperor Liu Pang in his conquest of the Ch'in dynasty, he was granted a kingdom in Wenchow (then known as Eastern Ou) and awarded the title King of the Eastern Oceans (Tung-hai Wang 東海王) in 193 B.C.E. His kingdom was short-lived, though, being conquered by the Han emperors a few years later. See *Shih-chi, chüan* 114, pp. 2979–2980; and *Han shu, chüan* 95, pp. 3859–3860. Despite the fact that Kou Yao's official title was King of the Eastern Oceans, he was popularly known as the King of Eastern Ou.

[35] The prologue of the novel *The Water Margin (Shui-hu chuan*水滸傳) contains the story of a *Lo-t'ien ta-chiao* which was held when an epidemic ravaged Kaifeng during the Northern Sung. The *Taoist Canon* contains some of the liturgical texts used during such offerings, but these do not include plague expulsion rites.

[36] For more on this deity, and its links with the cult of the Five Interlocutors (Wu-t'ung), see Cedzich, "Wu-t'ung," pp. 33–60.

[37] In the offering rituals performed in Fukien and Taiwan, the Three Pure Ones and other Taoist deities are usually represented in scroll paintings.

"arrow of command" (*ling-chien* 令箭)[38] by the Three Pure Ones, after which he left through the main gate to lead the procession, while the other deities returned to their respective temples. For the next six days, the Taoists chanted scriptures and performed rituals in the temple, while Wen led the procession to expel epidemics.

Every official in the city attended the temple rites. The biggest responsibility rested on the shoulders of the Yung-chia county magistrate, who had to offer a memorial to the Emperor of Heaven (*T'ien-ti* 天帝; most likely the Jade Emperor). The text of this document consisted of a statement in which the magistrate reproved himself for having been morally inadequate, thereby provoking Heaven's wrath and making the populace suffer for his failures. In order to atone, he stated his willingness to accept responsibility for his crimes, and entreated the Emperor on High (i.e. Emperor of Heaven) to show mercy towards the local populace.[39] After the text was read, the Taoists ascended a nine-level platform, blowing horns and pacing the Steps of Yu. They then opened a gourd out of which poured yellow smoke that set the memorial ablaze.

The procession itself was identical to that staged during the third lunar month, except that the roadside sacrifices consisted of purely vegetarian foods and the procession did not stop if it rained.

After the sixth day of the procession, Wen and the other deities returned to the temple of the King of Eastern Ou and took their assigned places. According to the text, they then conferred with the plague deities responsible for the epidemic, asking them to leave Wenchow. At evening, when it was high tide, ten people would carry the plague boat out through the temple's northern gate, followed by a huge crowd bearing torches. They raced through a dark and silent city,[40] through the Gate Overlooking the River (Wang-chiang Men 望江門), and up to the banks of the Ou River. At this point, the boat was placed on a raft covered with dry grass and other flammable objects, and towed out to sea by a sampan manned by a "marshal"

---

[38] According to the authors of the *WCFSC*, this "arrow" should have resembled a jade tablet with a pointed top (*yen-kuei* 琰圭), but in fact was shaped like a large *kuei* 圭, a jade tablet with a square base and pointed top used in official ceremonies in ancient China. They blame the Taoists for this confusion.

[39] The Taoist rituals performed during plague festivals in Taiwan contain the reading of a Heavenly Pardon (*t'ien-she* 天赦), which describes the community's sins and concludes with a plea to the Jade Emperor for forgiveness. See Katz, "P'ing-tung hsien Tung-kang chen te sung-wang yi-shih." A similar text is contained in the Divine Empyrean boat expulsion rite described in this chapter.

[40] During the expulsion, all lamps were doused and no one dared to talk. In this respect, Wenchow's expulsion rites resembled the "Dark Visitation" (*an-fang*) rituals in Lukang which have been studied by Yen Fang-tzu (see chapter 2).

played by a beggar. The boat was set alight and allowed to drift out to sea. All the deities returned to the Temple of the King of Tung-Ou, and Wen turned in his arrow of command to the Three Pure Ones, thereby marking the conclusion of the festival.[41]

There are also a number of accounts of boat expulsion rites performed in Wenchow that do not mention Marshal Wen by name but are clearly describing his festival. One such description in the *Yung-chia wen-chien lu* states that:

> In Yung-chia clear and rainy seasons vary, and periods of hot and cold are hard to predict. The people suffer from seasonal illnesses, and good doctors are few . . . [During epidemics], the people raise money and set up a ritual altar, engaging in rites which last anywhere from three to seven days. Before these start, the people build a large paper boat, filling it with countless quantities of money and treasures made of paper. As soon as the rites have concluded, they take the boat to the estuary and float it away using a wooden raft. When the boat is afloat, they set it afire and let the winds blow it out to sea; to where, no one knows. The masses believe that this rite results in expelling plague demons and curing all illnesses.[42]

According to the early twentieth-century pictorial *Wu Yu-ju hua-pao* (1909),[43] an epidemic occurring in the autumn of that year became so virulent that the people decided to erect a Buddhist altar for the celebration of a land and water mass (*shui-lu hui* 水陸會),[44] while also inviting certain local deities (probably those mentioned in the *Treatise*, including Wen) to patrol the city for seven days and nights. Officials presented a memorial and made offerings of incense, imploring the gods to take pity on the people of Wenchow. One large and five small boats were constructed and filled with many exquisite objects, and were burned outside the city's northern gate on the final day of the festival at the Hour of the Pig (9:00 - 11:00 p.m.) (see Figure 5). While

---

[41] A similar description of Wen's involvement in Wenchow boat expulsion festivals may be found in CCFSCC, pp. 216–217.

[42] See YCWCL, *chüan hsia*, 19a.

[43] See *Wu Yu-ju hua-pao, feng-su t'u-shuo, shang*, page 8. *Hua-pao* (also written as *hua-pao* 畫報) were pictorials popular in the late nineteenth and early twentieth centuries which recorded actual events by means of a full-page illustration often accompanied by a detailed caption.

[44] For more on this rite see Teiser, *Ghost Festival*, pp. 108–112; and, Makita Tairyo, "Surikue shōkō," *Tōhō shūkyō*, 12 (July 1957): 14–33.

Fig. 5 — Boat-burning Festival at Wenchow. Reproduced from *Wu Yu-ju hua-pao* (1909).

Marshal Wen is not mentioned by name, the description of this festival corresponds almost exactly to that in the *Treatise*. The omission of Wen's name probably represents oversight or ignorance on the part of the pictorial's author(s).

I have not been able to locate any record of when Marshal Wen's festival ceased to be celebrated in Wenchow. It survived the chaos marking the fall of the Ch'ing dynasty, and informants in Wenchow told me that people stopped celebrating Wen's festival only during the tumultuous years of the Second World War. Although all of Wen's temples in Wenchow and P'ing-yang were destroyed during the Cultural Revolution, some people in Wenchow have begun to worship his image in their homes. These men and women told me that they planned to rebuild his temple if conditions permitted.[45] Whether Marshal Wen's festival in Wenchow will ever be celebrated again, and if so on what scale, remains to be seen.

Rituals involving the expulsion of plague demons by means of a boat flourished throughout south China. Boat expulsion rites could be performed for individuals or families, but more usually were staged on behalf of the entire community. Various forms of these ritual flourished in a number of provinces, including Chekiang,[46] Fukien,[47] Kiangsu,[48] Kiangsi,[49] Hunan,[50]

---

[45] The revival of Wen's cult in P'ing-yang has apparently progressed even further, as informants from the area report that his temple there has been rebuilt.

[46] For data on boat expulsion rites to individuals in Chekiang, see PYHC (1684), 4:5b; and, CCFSCC, p. 583. For accounts of boat expulsion festivals in other parts of Chekiang besides Wenchow, see CCFSCC, pp. 277–278, 328, 401, 460, 534 and 578; Yü Yüeh, *Yu-t'ai hsien-kuan pi-chi* (1888), 12:2b–3a; Hsü Hung-t'u, "No-hsi te ch'i-yüan, liu-hsiang chi ch'i tsai Che-chiang te yi-tsung," in *Chung-kuo min-chien wen-hua* (Shanghai: Hsüeh-lin ch'u-pan-she, 1994), volume 13, pp. 165–166; and Hsü Ch'un-lei, "T'ung-hsiang shen-ko kai-shu," in *Chung-kuo min-chien wen-hua*, volume 14, p. 197.

[47] See *Ch'üan-chou chiu feng-su tzu-liao hui-pien* (Ch'üan-chou: Ch'üan-chou min-cheng chü, 1985), pp. 17, 23, 26 and 123; Ts'ai, *Wang-yeh yü Ma-tsu*, pp. 45–59; Hsü, *Fu-chien min-chien hsin-yang*, pp. 92–100. Shih Yi-lung, "T'ung-an Lü-ts'u te wang-yeh hsin-yang," in Chuang Ying-chang and P'an Ying-hai, ed., *T'ai-wan yü Fu-chien she-hui wen-hua yen-chiu lun-wen-chi* (Nankang: Institute of Ethnology, 1994), pp. 183–212; Doolittle, *Social Life of the Chinese*, vol. 1, pp. 156–167 and 267–287; Hodous, *Folkways in China*, pp. 212–214; and, Dean, "Notes on Two Taoist *Jiao* Observed in Zhangzhou in December, 1985," *CEA* 2 (1986): 202–204.

[48] See Li T'i-chai (1794-1867) *Chen-chou chu-chih tz'u* (Taipei: Chung-hua ts'ung-shu wei-yüan-hui, 1958), pp. 37–38 and 52; and, Bredon and Mitrophanow, *The Moon Year*, pp. 471–473.

[49] Huang, *Huang-shih jih ch'ao*, 79:21b–22b.

[50] See Chao, "The Dragon Boat Race," pp. 1–18; Chuang, *Chi-lei pien*, pp. 10–11; Fan, *Yüeh-yang feng-t'u chi*, 24b–25a; and, Lin, *Chiu-ko yü Yüan-Hsiang wen-hua*, p. 153.

Szechwan,[51] Kweichow,[52] and Yunnan.[53] They also spread to Hong Kong and Taiwan.[54] Boat expulsion rites are also performed throughout Asia in places such as Korea[55] and Tibet,[56] as well as parts of Southeast Asia.[57] I have not yet been able to determine the common points and possible interconnections between these rituals, but hope to pursue these questions in future research.

⟿7 *Marshal Wen's Festival in Hangchow*

Although the earliest descriptions of Marshal Wen's festival in Hangchow also date from the eighteenth century, one late Ming account in a local gazetteer concerning the growth of festivals (referred to as "inviting the gods and competing among associations" [*ying-shen sai-hui* 迎神賽會]) in Hangchow's Jen-ho County (located inside the city limits) may reveal some of the factors involved in the growth of Marshal Wen's own festival. This account reads:

> In Jen-ho, this custom [of staging festivals] began at Ch'u Dike (Ch'u T'ang 褚塘). During the end of the Ch'eng-hua reign period (1465–1487), there was a man named Lu 魯 who lived in this neighborhood. He was a clever and

---

[51] For rites to individuals see Wang Yao, "Chiang-pei hsien Shu-chia hsiang Ta-t'ang ts'un Hu-chai te 'Ying-mao t'i-tai' chi-yi tiao-ch'a," *Min-su ch'ü-yi* 90 (July 1994): 321–354. An account of boat expulsion festivals may be found in *Han-chou chih* (1817), 15:5a–b.

[52] *Ta-ting fu-chih* (1849), 14:20b.

[53] See Francis L.K. Hsü, *Exorcising the Troublemakers: Magic, Science, and Culture* (Westport, Conn.: Greenwood Press, 1983), pp. 73–83.

[54] An account of boat expulsion rites for individuals in Hong Kong may be found in Valentine R. Burkhardt, *Chinese Creeds and Customs* (Hong Kong: South China Morning Post, Ltd., 1958), vol. 3, p. 74. Boat expulsion festivals in Hong Kong are described in James Hayes, *The Rural Communities of Hong Kong: Studies and Themes* (New York: Oxford University Press, 1983), pp. 153–164. The best overview of the history of boat expulsion rites in Taiwan remains Liu, *Min-chien hsin-yang*, pp. 286–294.

[55] Christian Deschamps, "Deux Fêtes de Village en Corée," *CEA* 2 (1986): 172–181, esp. 176-177.

[56] Marion H. Duncan, *Customs and Superstitions of Tibetans* (London: The Mitre Press, 1964), pp. 206–207.

[57] See James G. Frazer, *The Golden Bough* (New York: Avenal Books, 1980 rpt. of 1890 edition), vol. 2, pp. 185–189; Cheu Hock Tong, *The Nine Emperor Gods. A Study of Chinese Spirit-medium Cults* (Singapore: Times Books International, 1988), pp. 152–154; and Tan Chee-Beng, "Chinese Religion and Local Communities in Malaysia," in Tan Chee-Beng, ed., *The Preservation and Adaptation of Tradition: Studies of Chinese Religious Expression in Southeast Asia, Contributions to Southeast Asian Ethnography* 9 (Dec. 1990): 7–8 and 17–18.

opportunistic fellow, who liked to admire beautiful things. This was a time of successive peaceful reigns, and the region was prosperous.[58] Therefore, he proposed that on the thirteenth day of the seventh lunar month, the birthday of Marquis Ch'u [Ch'u Hou 褚侯],[59] the people should establish an association to celebrate this event. He gathered together the sons of rich families [*fu-chia tzu-ti* 富家子弟], each man paying a sum from his own pocket to decorate all manner of floats [*t'ai-ko* 臺閣];[60] various other associations [*she*] also helped in this effort. These floats were extremely beautiful, and everybody was full of enthusiasm. Such things had never been heard of before . . . so when the people who lived inside and outside the city heard of this, they all came to watch the festival. In this way, the young men of other areas were moved by their admiration of the festival to start copying it just a couple of years later.

The leading festivals were Ch'u's and that of the Temple of One Thousand Victories [Ch'ien-sheng Miao 千勝廟; celebrated on the fifteenth day of the ninth lunar month].[61] . . . Second to these was the festival of the Emperor Hua-kuang's Temple [Hua-kuang Miao 華光廟; 9/28],[62] . . . followed by the festival of Lord Yen's Temple [Yen-kung Miao 晏公廟; 10/13].[63] The people who lived around these four temples held their festivals on these fixed

---

[58] On Jen-ho's thriving markets, see *JHHC* (1549), 1:27a–31a.

[59] He was named Ch'u Sui-liang 褚遂良, and lived during the T'ang dynasty. See *JHHC* (1549), 9:12a–13a. For data on his temples, see 7:20b–22a, 25a–26b; and *WLFHC*, vol. 5, pp. 328–355.

[60] According to the *Wu-lin chiu-shih*, these were mobile platforms made of wood and metal which featured images of all manner of deities and demons that moved through the air. See *chüan* 3, p. 378. See also *Ch'ung-hsiu Che-chiang t'ung-chih kao* (1948), vol. 16:6b–7a.

[61] This temple was dedicated to the T'ang general Chang Hsün 張巡 (709–757), who was cruelly put to death defending the city of Sui-yang (in Honan) against An Lu-shan's forces. For more on his cult, see *CKMCCS*, pp. 593–599. Data on Chang's temple in Jen-ho may be found in *JHHC* (1594), 7:19a–20a; *CCTC* (1561), 19:4b–5a; *CCTC* (1736), 217:23a and 224:34a; *HCFC* (1579), 47:21a–23b; *HCFC* (1784), 7:8b, 9:29b and 9:32b; and *HCFC* (1922), 11:1b, 12:21a, 13:3b, 13:8b, 13:14b and 13:20b. For an account of a festival to Chang in Chekiang, see *CCFSCC*, pp. 103–104. Chang's cult was sometimes confused with Wen's because both military men said to have fought against An Lu-shan; see *Chu-ting yü-wen* (1899), 2:15a–17b.

[62] See *JHHC* (1687), 5:24b–25a; *HCFC* (1922), 11:34b; and, *WLFHC*, vol. 1, pp. 147–159. For another account of the festival, see *T'ang-ch'i chih-lüeh* (1769), *chüan hsia*, 18b–18a. This text is preserved in the *WLCKTP*, vol. 1, pp. 571–572.

[63] See *JHHC* (1549), 7:31b.

dates, and these events became more and more wondrous with each staging.

In 1494, the Hua-kuang festival was held again [fu-chü 復舉].[64] Apart from the floats made by various associations, there were also children from the Huai-nan and Yangchow regions who would ascend tall poles and perform all manner of dances and acrobatic tricks, frequently flinging themselves into the air as if wings had sprouted from their armpits. The people were both terrified and wonder-struck.

. . . One year it happened that Secretary Wu [Wu Chu-shih 吳主事] wanted to see [these children perform] and went out with his wife and children to watch, promising a large reward if the performers would display their skills to their fullest. Because people heard of this before the performance had begun, they crowded onto a bridge near the Northern Gate [Pei-hsin Kuan 北新關] to watch. Who expected that the bridge couldn't hold all these people? . . . When people started to yell "The bridge is collapsing!" those who heard ran this way and that in a panic. As the roads were jammed with spectators, over thirty people were trampled to death, while those who were shoved into the water [and drowned] numbered even more.[65]

At that time, the censorial official [hsün-shih kuan 巡士官] felt pity for all the innocents who had perished and ordered an investigation. The performers were punished, and this custom was abolished. As for Wu, he was demoted. From this time on, when any officials encountered these child performances,[66] they would immediately forbid them.[67]

This text is highly significant in that it links the growth of festivals to the economic growth occurring in and around Hangchow during the Ming dynasty (see chapter 4). As people acquired more money to spend, many contributed to organizing festivals as an

---

[64] Meaning that the cult had been temporarily suppressed?

[65] For another account of this incident, see Ting Ping (1832–1899), Pei-kuo shih-chang (1897), chuan shang, 34b–35a. This text is preserved in the WLCKTP, vol. 12, pp. 8007–8008. Biographical data on Ting may be found in ECCP, pp. 726–727.

[66] It seems that attempts to ban such child performers were not very successful!

[67] The entire passage may be found in the JHHC (1549), 13:37b–38b. It is also preserved in later gazetteers, such as the JHHC (1687), 27:24b–26a, and the HCFC (1922), 75:10b–11b.

expression of local pride and prosperity. Furthermore, this account indicates that merchant support may have been a major factor behind the growth of these festivals. While the text does not actually call Lu and his friends merchants, it does reveal that they were young men from rich families with pocket money of their own, who do not appear to have belonged to the gentry class. Finally, this text shows how popular such festivals could become in a short period of time, as well as the problems that could occur as huge crowds jammed the streets to watch the fun.

The biggest problem with this account is its claim that these festivals were something new to Hangchow. This is difficult to accept in light of the colorful descriptions of festivals preserved in Southern Sung sources like the *Meng-liang lu* and the *Wu-lin chiu-shih*. Perhaps these earlier events had suffered a period of decline following the collapse of the Southern Sung, and were only revived or replaced during the fifteenth century. Another possibility is that the Ming festivals were somewhat different from their Southern Sung predecessors, but there is not enough data on which to base a comparison. Nevertheless, it does seem reasonable to conclude that the peace and prosperity of the mid- to late-Ming helped stimulate the growth of new and perhaps more elaborate festivals.

Marshal Wen's festival had probably begun to be celebrated in Hangchow during this period as well, particularly as his main temple in Hangchow was also rebuilt during that time. However, as in the case of his festival in Wenchow, the earliest source dates from the eighteenth century. This is a poem by Liang Yü-sheng 梁玉繩 (1745–1819),[68] most likely written during the late eighteenth century, which states that Wen's festival was held during the fifth lunar month as a prophylactic measure to prevent the outbreak of epidemic fevers during the hot summer months. Liang's poem has a detailed description of the wonders of the procession, the banquets that were held along the route, as well as the plays and marionette shows performed. Merchants vied to outdo each other in displaying their finery, and huge crowds jammed the city to worship and join the fun. Liang also mentions various martial troupes, as well as people marching in the procession who appear similar to the sinners and criminals of Wenchow, and who also practiced self-mortification by hanging incense burners from their arms with hooks.[69] As Liang was writing about a festival which was celebrated on a massive scale by

---

[68] For biographical data, see *ECCP*, pp. 505–506.

[69] This poem has been preserved in Liang's *Ch'ing-pai shih-chi* (1800), 27:10b–11a. See also *WLFSC*, 7:47a–b; *HCFC* (1922), 76:26b–27a, and *WLFHC*, vol. 4, p. 289.

the late eighteenth century, it would be safe to assume that it had begun to be celebrated long before then. Similar festivals were also staged throughout Kiangsu, although whether or not they were related to Wen's festival is unclear.[70]

Apart from Liang's work, a number of late Ch'ing poems or their prefaces also contain brief descriptions of Marshal Wen's festival in Hangchow. For example, the *Wu-lin feng-su chi* contains a song about the festival of Marshal Wen written by Ch'en Yi-ch'i 陳一麒 (fl. 1832–1842), which lauds Wen's abilities as a demon-devouring exorcist and compares Wen's festival to the ancient Great Exorcism.[71] Wang Tan-hsü 王丹墀 describes how women would dress in their best clothes and families show off their finest possessions in a display that sounds similar to Wenchow's Blocking the Road with Blessings festival,[72] while a brief prose passage in the *Hang-tu tsa-yung* 杭都雜詠 states that people came from the outlying villages to participate in the festival.[73] Two poems in the *Hang-tu tsa-yung* are also about Wen's festival. One, by Ts'ao Chin-liu 曹金籀 (fl. 1862–1874) describes the event's festive atmosphere; the other, by Chang Shih 張鉽, provides many striking images of children wearing cangues, performers entertaining the crowds, and the streets bedecked with lanterns.[74] All the above-mentioned sources agree that the purpose of Wen's festival was to prevent outbreaks of epidemics.

The Lost Customs of Hangchow (*Hang-su yi-feng*), composed by Fan Tsu-shu in 1864 following the Taiping Rebellion, has the most thorough account of Wen's festival in Hangchow (an annotated translation is provided in Appendix B). Like the *Treatise on Wenchow Customs*, this work opens with a brief version of Wen's hagiography (see chapter 3), as well as a description of the temple network which

---

[70] See Kung Wei (1704–1769), *Ch'ao-lin pi-t'an* (Peking: Chung-hua shu-chü, 1981), *chüan* 2, pp. 34–35.

[71] WLFSC, 7:46a–47a. The original of this text is in Juan Yüan (1764–1849) ed., *Ku-ching ching-she hsü-chi*, *chüan* 7, a work named after the Ku-ching ching-she 詁經精社 (Retreat for Researching the Classics) founded by Juan in Hangchow in 1801. Ch'en Yi-ch'i was one of the 183 students belonging to this academy. For more on Juan's life, see ECCP, pp. 399–402. I wish to thank Professor Hsü Shuo-fang 徐朔方 of Hangchow University for information he supplied regarding Juan's writings.

[72] See WLFSC, 7:49b.

[73] This account has been preserved in the WLFHC, vol. 4, p. 278. The *Hang-tu tsa-yung* has been lost (personal communication from Hsü Shuo-fang).

[74] Ibid., p. 287. A poem by Shu Shao-yen in the *Wu-lin hsin-nien tsa-yung* (1775), 37b, describes lanterns being displayed at the Temple of Manifest Virtue during the New Year's festival. See WLCKTP, vol. 4, p. 2170. See also Ting Ping, *Hsü Tung-ho chao-ko* (1894), 18b–19a, in WLCKTP, vol. 10, pp. 6728–6729.

supported his festival.[75] While Wen's birthday was celebrated on the eighteenth day of the fifth lunar month, the procession commenced on the sixteenth,[76] its goal being to "capture epidemic [demons]" (shou-wen 收瘟). Staff from the yamens of the Provincial Governor and other officials participated in the procession, and even local jailors and yamen runners took part. The procession was the largest in the city, and included stilt-walkers, musicians, people carrying lanterns and banners, children dressed as characters from popular stories, etc. In addition to the yamen personnel, there were also people dressed as soldiers, civil and martial judges (wen-wu p'an 文武判), eight generals (pa-chiang 八將; similar to Taiwan's pa-chia chiang 八家將 troupes?), and criminals.[77]

Fan's account stresses the intense efforts made to keep quarrels from erupting during the procession. Each association hired its own palanquin bearers from among those who carried sedan chairs for a living. It took forty to fifty men to bear Wen's palanquin, each dressed in ceremonial hats and gowns. These men would surrender the palanquin to another group of bearers at fixed points along the procession's route; according to the text, they dared not go one step further.

Marshal Wen was accompanied by an adjutant (chung-chün 中軍) surnamed Yang 楊, a deity who rode in a smaller palanquin. He had a white, beardless face and was clad in a white robe, under which he wore the armor of a general.[78] People would cease talking as their palanquins passed as a sign of fear and respect.

Fan's account concludes with a description of the festive atmosphere that prevailed, with the streets decorated with lanterns and people enjoying the finest foods. Large sums of money circulated during this time, with both merchants and peddlers making a tidy profit.[79]

The late Ch'ing literatus Yü Yüeh (1821–1906) included a brief article on Wen's festival in his collected writings. One interesting aspect of this work is its claim that the procession always hurried past

[75] This network, which also included Wen's temple in Hu-yeh, is also described in the HCFC (1922), 9:20b–21a.
[76] See also Chung Yü-lung (1880–1970), Shuo Hang-chou (Hangchow: Che-chiang jen-min ch'u-pan-she, 1983), p. 326.
[77] See also the Hsi-hu yu-lan chih, yü chüan 餘卷 20:7b, in WLCKTP, vol. 10, p. 6306.
[78] I have been unable to identify this figure.
[79] Hang-su yi-feng, pp. 15–17. Abbreviated versions of Fan's account may be found in the WLFSC, 7:47b–48b; and HCFC (1922), 76:27a–28a. The Tien-shih chai hua-pao (1884) also contains an abbreviated account of Fan's text, as well as an illustration (see Figure 6).

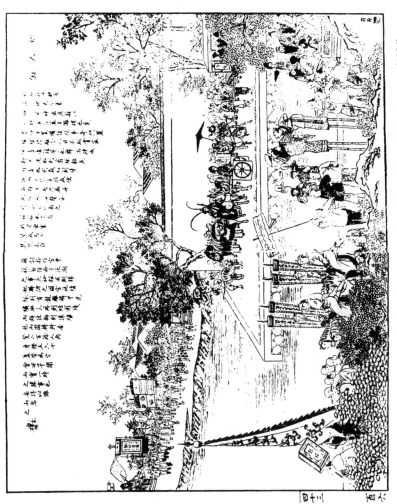

Fig. 6 — Marshal Wen's Festival in Hangchow. Reproduced from *Tien-shih chai hua-pao* (1884).

the former residence of Hsü Ch'ao 徐潮 (1647–1715),[80] a high-ranking official of the early Ch'ing, because of his alleged power over spiritual forces.[81]

Marshal Wen's festival in Hangchow appears to have experienced a period of rapid decline during the late Ch'ing, and largely ceased to be celebrated following the Taiping Rebellion (hence its inclusion in Fan Tsu-shu's work on "lost customs"). It also didn't help that Grand Coordinator (*hsün-fu* 巡撫) Yang Ch'ang-chün 楊昌濬 had attempted to outlaw all festivals in Hangchow (including Wen's) during his tenure in the 1850s because he considered such events a waste of money. According to Republican-era sources, the festival was briefly revived in 1899, but soon collapsed after being banned by Vice Censor-in-Chief T'an (T'an Chung-ch'eng 譚中丞) following disturbances during the procession. It took widespread epidemics in the year 1902 for the festival to be celebrated again, but even that only lasted for a few years.[82] Most people I talked to in Hangchow did not remember Marshal Wen's temples or festival, the only exception being an old Taoist master I met in a temple overlooking West Lake dedicated to the Six Dynasties Taoist practitioner Ko Hung 葛洪 (283–343). Under these circumstances, it seems unlikely that Marshal Wen's cult will ever reappear in Hangchow.

Marshal Wen's festivals in Wenchow and Hangchow appear to have been highly similar to each other, the only major differences being that Hangchow's festival was held during the fifth lunar month and that boat burning rites do not appear to have been performed there during epidemics (they could have coincided with the Dragon Boat Festival though; see chapter 2). Overall, the similarities between the two cities' festivals far outnumber the differences. In both cities, festivals to Marshal Wen were usually prophylactic in nature, but could also be staged when epidemics were in progress. Both featured

---

[80] For biographical data on Hsü, see *ECCP*, p. 602. Gazetteer biographies have been conveniently gathered together in the *WLFHC*, vol. 4, pp. 296–300.

[81] See Yü, *Yu-t'ai hsien-kuan*, 16:2a. Biographical data on Yü may be found in *ECCP*, pp. 944–945. This event is also alluded to in a poem included in the *Wu-lin tsa-shih shih*, 6b. See *WLCKTP*, vol. 12, p. 7525.

[82] See *Hang-su yi-ch'ing ts'ui-chin* (1903), in *Chung-kuo shih-hsüeh ts'ung-shu* (Taipei: Hsüeh-sheng shu-chü, 1987), vol. 32, p. 12; and, *HCFC* (1922), 75:11b and 76:28a. See also Day, *Chinese Peasant Cults*, pp. 191-194 for translations of some Republican-era government decrees banning local cults. These do not mention Marshal Wen, but do include plague gods (*wen-shen*). For more information on attempts to ban festivals throughout China during the late imperial era, see the mid-Ch'ing work entitled *Liu-pu ch'eng-yü, hsing-pu* 刑部, (Hangchow: Ku-chi ch'u-pan-she, 1987), p. 138; and *Yüan Ming Ch'ing san-tai chin-hui hsiao-shuo hsi-ch'ü shih-liao* Wang Li-ch'i comp., (Peking: Tso-chia ch'u-pan-she, 1958), pp. 87–138.

the participation of a full range of social classes, from high-ranking scholar-officials down to itinerant beggars. Both brimmed with bureaucratic and martial symbolism, and both were occasions for people to engage in acts of penance and even self-mortification to expiate previous sins.

Many of the rituals performed during Marshal Wen's festivals appear to have been cathartic in nature in the sense that they conformed to the original sense of the Greek *katharsis*, meaning to remove dirt or a blemish (*katharma*) for the purpose of making oneself, an object, or one's environment pure (*katharos*).[83] Such festivals may also be considered cathartic in a ritual sense, inasmuch as they were purification rites designed to rid the individual or community of impure or unclean forces.[84] In Wenchow, cathartic rites included the *fang-kao* ritual, the torch-lit procession held on the last night of the third month festival, and the burning of the plague boat. The entire Hangchow procession also appears to have been a cathartic ritual in that it was designed to purify the city and its inhabitants. Cathartic elements in the rituals mentioned above include the symbolism of numbers in both the selection of both purifying agents and sacrificial victims (Three Pure Ones, three sacrifices (*san-sheng*), Five Commissioners of Epidemics, etc.), the idea that communal defilement involved illness or even death, and the use of cathartic substances such as fire (torches, boat burning) and incense (burned in temples and along the procession's route; also hung from the arms of sinners or criminals). Water might have served as an additional cathartic element, inasmuch as the plague boat burned at Wenchow was floated on the Ou River before being set afire. In addition, the act of dressing up as a criminal or sinner, as well as the expiatory rites performed by local officials, might also be considered cathartic because the public recitation (or admission) of transgressions was believed to purge the individual or community of guilt and counter the pollution brought about by immoral acts.

In many cultures, cathartic rituals involve the sacrifice of a substitute to which polluting forces have been transferred — the scapegoat. Some scholars believe that rituals involving scapegoats represent an attempt to relieve social tensions by directing communal anger towards an individual or group seen as being responsible for

---

[83] See E.R. Dodds, *The Greeks and the Irrational* (Berkeley: University of California Press, 1955).

[84] Robert Parker, *Miasma: Pollution and Purification in Early Greek Religion* (Oxford: Oxford University Press, 1983). See also Henri Hubert and Marcel Mauss, *Sacrifice*, trans. by H.D. Walls (Chicago: University of Chicago Press, 1964 (1899)), pp. 36–38.

calamities that have occurred. For example, René Girard has theorized that violent tendencies that would tear a community apart are redirected onto this defenseless surrogate victim during rituals.[85] Did the people of late imperial Chekiang single out scapegoats, as well as practice rites involving the expulsion of such victims? There is little evidence that this was the case. Although one Chinese scholar has claimed that the plague boat itself served as a scapegoat,[86] I would argue that the plague expulsion rituals described above, including those featuring a boat, were designed to deal with the spiritual forces conceived of as being responsible for epidemics. Plague deities had to be feasted and then entreated to leave, while plague demons were violently expelled during exorcistic rituals. In both cases, these plague spirits do not appear to have been conceived of as scapegoats but rather as powerful spiritual forces whose arrival had to be dealt with by the most efficacious ritual means available.

The people of late imperial Chekiang also do not appear to have viewed protective deities or the ritual specialists invoking them as potential scapegoats, and did not attempt to punish those considered ineffective. There are no records of officials flogging or burning images of Marshal Wen (although one bereaved father decapitated images of the Five Commissioners when they failed to heal his son; see chapter 2), nor is there any evidence of exposing spirit mediums as was done in ancient China.[87] Ritual violence also does not seem to have been directed against potential human scapegoats such as beggars or itinerant religious specialists, who were frequently persecuted during sorcery panics.[88] Furthermore, no ritual action appears to have been taken against the Yung-chia magistrate, despite the fact that he had to publicly admit that his own moral failings had caused the gods to inflict epidemics on the populace. The *fang-kao* indictment ritual might be considered an attempt to identify and punish scapegoats, inasmuch as it involved naming individuals accused of wrongdoing. However, there is no evidence that the

---

[85] See Rene Girard, *Violence and the Sacred*, trans. by Patrick Gregory, (Baltimore and London: The Johns Hopkins University Press, 1979 (1972)). See also Jonathan N. Lipman and C. Stevan Harrell, eds. *Violence in China* (Albany, NY: SUNY Press, 1990), esp. Harrell's introductory chapter. Unfortunately, this book does not address the issue of ritual violence in China.

[86] Hsiao, *No-Cha chih feng*, 290–295.

[87] See Cohen, "Coercing the Rain Deities," 244–265; and Schafer, "Ritual Exposure," 130–184.

[88] See Philip A. Kuhn, *Soulstealers. The Chinese Sorcery Scare of 1768* (Cambridge, Mass: Harvard University Press, 1991), pp. 1–29, 94–118; and, Barend ter Haar, *The White Lotus Teachings in Chinese Religious History* (Leiden: E.J. Bill, 1992), pp. 173–174, 180–181, 268–272 and 281–285.

accused were actually punished (either ritually or physically) during the festival. Marshal Wen merely acknowledged receiving the plaintiff's accusation, the implication being that the accused would receive his or her just desserts at a later date.

The presence of so many cathartic rituals being held alongside celebratory and sacrificial ones indicates that Marshal Wen's festivals in Wenchow and Hangchow had the potential to both strengthen and at the same time challenge these cities' social cohesion. Friends, acquaintances, and relatives gathered together for feasts, with social relations being reaffirmed along the lines proposed by anthropologists such as Emile Durkheim (1858–1917) and A.R. Radcliffe-Brown (1881–1955).[89] At the same time however, certain social tensions could also surface, the result of people competing against their neighbors, harboring resentment toward injustices done to them, or having guilt feelings about their own misdeeds. Festivals in late imperial China often sparked conflicts between different interest groups, and could even erupt into full-scale riots, although this does not appear to have been the case in Wenchow or Hangchow.[90] The same is true of certain festivals in Taiwan today.[91] This does not necessarily mean that the performance of cathartic rites could make some festivals more violent than others, but it does seem clear that these events had the potential to tear the fabric of Chinese society as well as to mend or reinforce it. However, it also seems true that any social damage resulting from festivals was probably only temporary, and failed to threaten the social order as a whole. One could even say that Marshal Wen's festival, by allowing the temporary airing of grievances and at times perhaps even encouraging their eventual settlement, ended up supporting the existence of the established social order.[92]

Marshal Wen's festivals certainly provided a dazzling array of contrasts. On the one hand, there were elaborate symbols of wealth, prosperity, and a general feeling of well-being expressed in the lavish

---

[89] See Emile Durkheim, *The Elementary Forms of the Religious Life*, trans. by Joseph W. Swain (London: George Allen and Unwin, 1957 (1915)); and, A.R. Radcliffe Brown, "Religion and Society," in *Structure and Function in Primitive Society* (New York: The Free Press, 1965), pp. 153–177.

[90] See Wu, "Temple Fairs", pp. 97–101; and, William T. Rowe, *Hankow. Conflict and Community in a Chinese City, 1796–1895* (Stanford: Stanford University Press, 1989), pp. 201–206.

[91] See Weller, *Unities and Diversities*, pp. 75–77 and 81–83.

[92] For more on this problem, see Lewis A. Coser, *The Functions of Social Conflict* (New York: The Free Press, 1956). See also Mikhail Bakhtin, *Rabelais and his World*, trans. Hélène Iswolsky (Bloomington: Indiana University Press, 1984 (1965)); and Umberto Eco, "The Frames of Cosmic 'Freedom'," in Thomas A. Sebeok, ed., *Carnival!* In *Approaches to Semiotics*, number 64 (Berlin: Mouton Publishers, 1964), pp. 1–9.

offerings and expensive products displayed during the procession. On the other hand, the poorest of the poor also marched alongside wealthier members of the community, and local tensions bubbled to the surface during the procession and the *fang-kao* indictment rites. People cleaned the streets in order to display the community's ritual purity only to have those same streets filled by beggars and people expressing their polluted state who called themselves "criminals" and "sinners."[93] The community was also considered polluted by the presence of dangerous plague demons on the loose that had to be rounded up and expelled by Marshal Wen.

The presence of contradictory symbols during rituals, as well as the temporary reversal of order which often accompanies the performance of rituals, has been extensively analyzed by scholars such as Victor Turner (1920–1983), who developed the ideas presented by Arnold van Gennep (1873–1957) in *The Rites of Passage* (1909) to theorize that rituals feature a liminal or liminoid phase during which established social structures are reversed and people enjoy a temporary form of harmonious equality known as "communitas."[94] In the case of Marshal Wen's festivals however, it appears that neither liminal nor liminoid phenomena occurred, much less any form of communitas. Perhaps this is because such festivals were not rites of passage like marriages or funerals, despite the fact that the community was believed to be transformed from a polluted state to a purified one in the course of the festival. Even though beggars did participate, their presence does not appear to have encouraged any liminality, inasmuch as they could not assume prestigious roles and were only allowed to dress up as demons or low-ranking deities.[95] It might be better to view the rituals of Wen's festivals as being rites of affliction, but in the case of late imperial Chekiang this can only be considered a

---

[93] See Mary Douglas, *Purity and Danger* (London: Routledge and Kegan Paul, 1966) for a discussion of these concepts.

[94] Turner's best-known work on this subject is *The Ritual Process. Structure and Anti-structure* (Ithaca: Cornell University Press, 1969). One should also consult "Liminal to Liminoid, in Play, Flow, and Ritual: An Essay in Comparative Sociology," *Rice University Studies* (Special Issue on the Anthropological Study of Human Play) 60.3 (1974): 53–92; and Victor Turner and Edith Turner, *Image and Pilgrimage in Christian Culture* (New York: Columbia University Press, 1978).

[95] P. Steven Sangren has expressed some doubt as to whether Turner's ideas may be used in the study of Chinese religion, especially pilgrimage. See his *History and Magical Power in a Chinese Community* (Stanford: Stanford University Press, 1987), pp. 189–194. James Wilkerson has argued in favor of the critical application of Turner's theories in his "Self-referential Performances: Victor Turner and Theoretical Issues in Chinese Performative Genre," *Min-su ch'ü-yi* 90 (July 1994): 99–146.

tentative hypothesis pending the discovery of further evidence.[96] Field work on plague festivals in modern Taiwan has revealed that they do feature numerous rites of affliction.[97]

All in all, it seems that Marshal Wen's festivals in Chekiang were as complex as the culture and society they were a part of. The reader might find it contradictory to purify a city's streets only to have them subsequently filled by people representing the most polluted elements of the community, or for conflicts to break out during a supposedly festive event. Perhaps such phenomena may best be explained as due to the fact that one important function of most rituals is to express and even shape the mentalities of the individuals or societies performing them. As Ronald Grimes has noted, "It [ritual] is not a bastion of social conservatism whose symbols merely condense cultural values. Rather it holds the generating source of culture and structure."[98] We see such a process at work in the cults and festivals of many popular Chinese deities, such as the cult of Ma-tsu.[99] One finds a similar mix of emotions and values in traditional European festivals as well.[100]

Taoist Rituals and Local Festivals

One particularly striking aspect of Marshal Wen's festivals in both Wenchow and Hangchow is the relatively limited role played by Taoist priests. Apart from officiating at the Great Offering held at Wenchow during epidemics, the only other role they played in Wen's

---

[96] The best examples of Turner's work on social dramas and rites of affliction may be found in his *Schism and Continuity in an African Society: A Study of Ndembu Village Life* (Manchester: Manchester University Press, 1957); *The Forest of Symbols* (Ithaca: Cornell University Press, 1967), pp. 9–11; *The Drums of Affliction* (Oxford: Oxford University Press, 1968), pp. 15–16, 89–127; *Dramas, Fields, and Metaphors. Symbolic Action in Human Society* (Ithaca and London: Cornell University Press, 1974), pp. 23–59; *On the Edge of Bush* (Tucson, Ariz.: University of Arizona Press, 1985), pp. 119–150 and 227–246; and *The Anthropology of Performance* (New York: PAJ Publications, 1986), pp. 33–71. Ronald L. Grimes analyzes Turner's work on social dramas in "Victor Turner's Social Drama and T.S. Eliot's Ritual Drama," *Anthropologica* N.S. 27.1–2 (1985): 79–100.

[97] See Katz, "The Pacification of Plagues: A Chinese Rite of Affliction," *Journal of Ritual Studies* (forthcoming).

[98] Ronald L. Grimes, "Ritual Studies: Two Models," *Religious Studies Review* 2 (1976): 13–25.

[99] See Watson, "Standardizing the Gods," pp. 292–324.

[100] See Peter Burke, *Popular Culture in Early Modern Europe* (Aldershot: Wildwood House, Ltd., 1988), pp. 178–204; and Emmanuel Le Roy Ladurie, *Carnival in Romans* (New York: George Braziller, 1980).

festivals involved reading memorials for lay worshippers during the roadside sacrifices held during the third month festival in Wenchow. Even more remarkable is the fact that Taoist priests are not mentioned at all in descriptions of Wen's festival in Hangchow. One factor behind this lack of data concerning Taoist priests and their rituals could be the biases of literati writers, who frequently overlooked or downplayed the important of Taoist rituals performed during local festivals. However, since most accounts of festivals do at least mention Taoist rituals if they were performed, it seems reasonable to conclude that Taoist priests had little influence on Marshal Wen's festival as celebrated in Chekiang during the Ch'ing, even though they played a significant role in the spread of his cult throughout the province during previous dynasties.

Such a conclusion is at odds with the arguments put forth by other scholars researching the influence of Taoism on local cults. For example, in an important article on the T'ang dynasty cult of Hsü Sun 許遜 (Hsü Ching-yang [239–292/374?]) and its links to Taoism, Kristofer Schipper states that Taoist ritual should be seen as "transcending local traditions" because it is "highly literate in nature and expression."[101] According to Schipper, local and regional leaders *not* belonging to what he calls the "literati class" chose to sponsor Taoist rituals during local festivals because such acts enabled them to increase their status. Schipper states that:

> For them, Taoist liturgy provided a religious consecration of their political power, otherwise unrecognized by the official administration . . . [T]his leadership confirmed and enhanced its position through elaborate and solemn rites of investiture. In conclusion we may therefore propose that the connection of local cults with Taoist ritual implies the upgrading and emancipation of local power structures, and not the downgrading or popularization of Taoism.[102]

I would certainly agree with Schipper's argument that Taoism did not necessarily suffer any form of downgrading as a result of its interaction with local cults. It is also true that local leaders did (and sometimes still do) attempt to enhance their status by sponsoring Taoist rituals. However, Schipper fails to clearly define what types of

---

[101] Schipper, "Taoist Ritual and Local Cults", p. 833. Dean also argues that the compilation of Taoist scriptures for local deities represented elite attempts to "transcend localism." See *Taoist Ritual and Popular Cults*, p. 82. For additional data on Hsü's cult, see Boltz, *Survey*, pp. 70–78 and 197–199; and, *CKMCCS*, pp. 846–859.

[102] Schipper, "Taoist Ritual and Local Cults," pp. 833–834.

individuals should be included in his so-called "literati class" which failed to lead local and regional society (all classically educated people? members of the gentry only? scholar-officials only?). More importantly, he implies that only Taoist rituals enabled local and regional leaders to increase their status. I would argue that Schipper's exclusion of members of the literati as local and regional leaders seems highly arbitrary, particularly since the work of Valerie Hansen and other scholars has clearly shown that local and regional leaders who supported local cults included all manner of classically educated individuals, be they members of the local elite or local gentry, or even scholar-officials.[103] As for Schipper's emphasis on the importance of Taoist rituals to such leaders, I would argue that not only Taoist but also *other* rituals provided them with opportunities to solidify and even strengthen their status in the eyes of both the state and members of the local community. In fact, the desire of local and regional leaders to sponsor all manner of rituals probably reflected their desire to acquire what Pierre Bourdieu refers to as "symbolic capital" (see Conclusion). It scarcely mattered to them whether the ritual in question was performed by Taoist priests, Buddhist monks or nuns, or members of local ritual traditions. What was more important was that the rituals and the specialists performing them be considered efficacious and legitimate.

Finally, it is important to keep in mind that the "upgrading and emancipation of local cults" Schipper describes could be achieved by other means than performing Taoist (or other) rituals. Scholars like Hansen and James Watson have convincingly shown that in addition to sponsoring rituals, community leaders also attempted to persuade the state to award official titles for popular deities, both to augment the cult's status and to increase their own aura of legitimacy in the local community.[104] Therefore, it might be more accurate to say that although Taoist rituals could at times play an important role in the growth and even legitimization of local cults and festivals, they were but one of many options available to a cult's supporters desiring to accomplish such goals.

Another scholar who has thoroughly explored the relationship between Taoist ritual and local cults is Ken Dean. As he states in the introduction to his new book, one of the main goals of his research has been to clarify "the still poorly defined relationship between . . .

---

[103] See for example Hansen, *Changing Gods*, pp. 95–104, 118–126 and 144–146; and Dean *Taoist Ritual and Popular Cults*, pp. 87–88 and 123–126.

[104] See Hansen, *Changing Gods*, pp. 82–84 and 103–104; and, Watson, "Standardizing the Gods," pp. 313–315.

popular cults and Taoist liturgy."[105] He attempts to accomplish this goal by using the concept of "the Taoist liturgical framework" to analyze this relationship,[106] arguing that Taoist liturgy plays a predominant role in "structuring" cult worship.[107] He also claims that Taoist priests performing rituals in local temples lie at the center of a ritual "structure" featuring processions, dramatic performances, and family/community sacrifices, and that Taoist priests frequently lead the processions held during festivals.[108] Dean's concept of the Taoist liturgical framework provides an important means of analyzing the relationship between Taoism and local cults. In addition, he has provided convincing evidence that this framework does play a role at some of the cult sites in Fujian he has studied, particularly during offering rituals.[109] However, the descriptions of Marshal Wen's festivals presented above indicate that Taoism in Chekiang province may not have attained the same level of influence it apparently did in Fukien, especially since many of the rituals performed during Wen's festivals did not feature Taoist priests. As for Taoist priests being at the "center" of a festival, this may have happened during the Great Offering held during Wenchow's expulsion rites, but the evidence is far from convincing. In addition, the reading of memorials by Taoist priests during roadside sacrifices does not seem to have placed them at the center of the festival. Taoist priests also did not participate in the processions at Hangchow or Wenchow, much less lead them (the same is also true for festivals I have witnessed in Taiwan). This means that Dean's arguments, while generally suitable for describing the relationship between Taoism and local cults in coastal areas of southern Fukien, should be applied with considerable caution in other parts of China, including Chekiang.

---

[105] Dean, *Taoist Ritual and Popular Cults*, p. 12.

[106] Schipper also uses the term "liturgical framework" in his work on T'ang local cults. See his "Taoist Ritual and Local Cults," p. 833. Schipper's and Dean's use of the term "liturgy" is based on the Greek *leitourgia*, meaning a public service to the gods.

[107] Dean, *Taoist Ritual and Popular Cults*, p. 14.

[108] *Ibid.*, pp. 13 and 17.

[109] *Ibid.*, pp. 50–53.

Conclusion

The description of the cult of Marshal Wen presented above provides important insights into the ways local cults arose and expanded in late imperial China. We have seen how Wen's cult grew from a local cult in P'ing-yang to a regional cult covering much of Chekiang province. This growth was based on a number of key historical factors, starting with the existence of climatic and epidemiological conditions which made Chekiang hospitable to cults of plague-expelling deities. The spread of Wen's cult throughout Chekiang was also facilitated by the creation of a rich and varied hagiographical literature about him, making knowledge of his abilities accessible to a wide range of believers. The participation of all types of people with different social backgrounds and concerns also aided the growth of Wen's cult throughout Chekiang. Finally, the establishment of festivals seen as being able to prevent epidemics while also allowing expressions of guilt and demands for rectifications of wrongs encouraged the cult's staying power in sites like Wenchow and Hangchow.

The main goal of this work has been to analyze the complex relationship between Taoism and local cults. As I have shown above, Taoist priests could play important roles in the growth of local cults, particularly in terms of compiling hagiographies of popular local deities, organizing the construction of temples to them, transmitting their cults beyond local boundaries, and performing rituals at their festivals. At the same time, however, I believe that it is essential not to overstate the influence Taoist priests exerted over local cults, or uncritically accept their claims regarding this interaction. Taoist priests did compose hagiographies in an attempt to transform certain local deities into "orthodox" Taoist ones. They also tried to control local temples and assert their authority over the rituals associated with local cults. However, the evidence presented above reveals that their efforts achieved only a limited degree of success. Popular representations of local deities appear to have been very different from those held by Taoist priests, while the affairs of most local temples were decided by lay members of their temple committees. Although Taoist priests did preside over many important rituals associated with local festivals, particularly offering rites, many other rituals (especially those associated with processions) remained well beyond their control.

In addition to the relationship between Taoism and local cults, however, a number of other important questions, particularly those pertaining to the social aspects of Wen's cult, need to be addressed before we can hope to fully appreciate its historical significance. Therefore, I intend to devote the remainder of the conclusion to exploring a number of ideas only briefly touched on in the chapters above, especially symbolic capital and the public sphere. The focus of the discussion below will thus be on the second goal of this book mentioned in the Introduction: combining the disciplines of Chinese religious and social history in order to achieve a more thorough understanding of Chinese cults and festivals. I should emphasize, however, what follows does not represent a set of definitive conclusions, but merely tentative hypotheses based on the data I have been able to collect to date.

Who Supported Marshal Wen's Cult?

Determining the identities of those men and women who supported local cults is of primary importance to the social historian. Unfortunately, in the case of the cult of Marshal Wen and many other late imperial cults, very little data survives which allows us to research this problem in depth. Even in the few cases where names of cult supporters are listed, I have only been able to find biographical data on high-ranking scholar-officials. Rubbings of the steles from Hangchow and Wenchow bearing Sung Lien's inscription would have proved invaluable, inasmuch as these would probably have listed the names of cult supporters and even the amounts of money they donated, but none have survived. Nevertheless, the evidence presented above reveals that people representing a wide range of social classes supported Marshal Wen's cult and festival.

The most prominent group of Wen's supporters, and that for which the most data survives, were the gentry and scholar officials. Wen's oldest temple in P'ing-yang was founded by a member of the Court of Imperial Sacrifices, while military officials provided important support for Wen's cult at sites like Li-shui and Hangchow.

High-ranking officials such as Sung Lien and Li Wei played a critical role in the growth of Wen's cult by writing hagiographical stele inscriptions about Wen and making donations to his temples. In offering such visible demonstrations of their support for Wen's cult, these men provided it with an aura of legitimacy which helped protect it against being labeled "heterodox" or "illicit".

Merchants and other members of the local elite were another important group who supported the cult of Marshal Wen, and along with the gentry and scholar-officials, appear to have been largely responsible for its continued spread throughout Chekiang during the Ming-Ch'ing era. Although none of these men left a record explaining their motives for supporting Wen's cult, they appear to have viewed him as a deity who could protect their lives and their business interests, especially during their travels. Like the young entrepreneurs of fifteenth-century Hangchow, merchants probably also supported Wen's festival because the market fairs held then enabled them to earn a profit.

Little is known about the people who actually managed Wen's festivals — members of the temple committee. Page eight of Wen's *Brief Hagiography* lists the names of the members of the temple committee of Marshal Wen's temple at Hua-kai Shan for the year 1879. I have not been able to find any biographical data on these men, but two of them held the *sheng-yüan* degree while the rest were commoners. This corresponds to informant accounts which state that the upper gentry considered managing temple affairs to be beneath their dignity, and that most of the temple committee's posts were filled by community elders, merchants, and lower degree holders. Such men generally had to make a large donation to the temple for the honor of serving on its committee, and also were responsible for leading efforts to raise money for festivals and temple construction projects, contributing the necessary funds out of their own pockets if necessary.[1]

Why were these men willing to invest the large amounts of time and money required to support Wen's cult and festival? Apart from devotion to Wen as a protective deity, their efforts may have been linked to their desire to acquire what Pierre Bourdieu has called

---

[1] For information on the composition and function of temple committees, see Sangren, *History and Magical Power*, pp. 58–60; Stephan Feuchtwang, "City Temples in Taipei Under Three Regimes," in Mark Elvin and G. William Skinner, eds., *The Chinese City Between Two Worlds* (Stanford: Stanford University Press, 1974), pp. 263–303; and Wang Shih-ch'ing, "Religious Organization in the History of a Chinese Town," in Wolf, *Religion and Ritual*, pp. 71–92.

"symbolic capital". As Bourdieu notes in his *Outline of a Theory in Practice*, the acquisition of symbolic capital involves:

> the work of reproducing established relations — through feasts, ceremonies, exchanges of gifts, visits or courtesies, and, above all, marriages — which is no less vital to the existence of the group than the reproduction of the economic bases of its existence.[2]

Bourdieu was not thinking of late imperial China when he developed this theory, and indeed some of his ideas do not seem applicable here. For example, Chekiang does not appear to have had an "ancient economy" threatened by a severe climate or the threat of tribal warfare.[3] In spite of these drawbacks though, Bourdieu's work is of immense value because it reveals that an individual's or community's assets include not only material goods but also relationships which have to be maintained, if not strengthened, in order to survive.[4]

In a recently-published paper on Taiwan's local elites, I attempted to determine the means they used to establish and then maintain a degree of power and influence in community life. Achieving this goal involved the acquisition of two types of capital — economic and symbolic — the former referring to material wealth and the latter to an individual's honor and prestige (in other words, face) in the community. Elite families in Taiwan (and China as well) attempted to amass economic capital by educating their sons and diversifying their investments. Marrying one's children to those from other leading families involved exchanges of both economic and symbolic capital, while supporting temple construction projects or festivals entailed considerable expense of economic capital in order to acquire additional symbolic capital. It appears that while the gentry also supported important local temples, such men rarely ran temple affairs directly, preferring to exert control via intermediaries. The day-to-day business of running the temple appears to have left to members of the elite, who found such work particularly valuable in the process of acquiring symbolic capital.[5] The quest for symbolic capital may well have been one factor behind elite support of Marshal

---

[2] Pierre Bourdieu, *Outline of a Theory in Practice* (Cambridge: Cambridge University Press, 1977), p. 171.

[3] *Ibid.*, p. 179.

[4] *Ibid.*, pp. 178, 180–181.

[5] See Katz, "Commerce, Marriage and Ritual: Elite Strategies in Tung-kang During the Twentieth Century," in Chuang and P'an, eds., *T'ai-wan yü Fu-chien she-hui wen-hua yen-chiu lun-wen-chi*, pp. 127–165.

Wen's festivals in Hangchow and Wenchow, but further evidence is needed before a definitive conclusion can be reached.[6]

The other important group of people who supported Wen's cult and festival were Taoist priests. Although their influence on his cult appears to have waned over time, they played a critical role in the early growth and spread of his cult. In the case of Taoists like Huang Kung-chin, their support of Wen's cult appears to have been based on their representation of him as a martial deity who supported "orthodox" Taoism against local cults they considered "licentious" or "heterodox." The representations of Wen other Taoists held are less clear, although their liturgical texts portray him as a powerful and efficacious deity to be invoked in plague expulsion rituals. Rituals involving Wen were also part of the "intellectual property" possessed by religious specialists which could influence their relations with other members of the community and also increase their overall prestige.[7]

Apart from these groups, however, people often considered social outcasts played a prominent role in Wen's festivals. The most obvious were beggars and yamen runners, many of whom dressed up as the demons marching in the procession. These men were often paid for their services, as opposed to other participants who joined the procession as part of a vow they had made. Beggars in particular have always had a dual nature in Chinese culture, at times considered dangerous outsiders yet also seen as figures with special powers who could work wonders for those who treated them well.[8] It is not clear whether the participation of beggars in such a prestigious festival was a source of tension or something considered a necessary evil. Beggars were invariably hired, though, because dressing up as demons was

---

[6] Timothy Brook also discusses the late Ming gentry's attempts to acquire symbolic capital by supporting religious activities in his *Praying for Power: Buddhism and the Formation of Gentry Society in Late-Ming China* (Cambridge, Mass.: Harvard University Press, 1993), pp. 19–20.

[7] See James Wilkerson, "The 'Ritual Master' and his 'Temple Corporation' Rituals," in *Proceedings of the International Conference on Popular Beliefs and Chinese Culture*, volume 2, pp. 475, 477–479. See also Simon Harrison, "Ritual as Intellectual Property," *Man* N.S. (1992): 225–243.

[8] See David Schak, *A Chinese Beggars' Den: Poverty and Mobility in an Underclass Community* (Pittsburgh: University of Pittsburgh Press, 1988), as well as his earlier essay "Images of Beggars in Chinese Culture," in Sarah Allan and Alvin P. Cohen, eds., *Legend, Lore and Religion in China: Essays in Honor of Wolfram Eberhard on his 70th Birthday* (San Francisco: Chinese Materials Center, 1979), pp. 109–133. A fine introduction to the history of beggars in China may be found in Ch'ü Yen-pin, *Chung-kuo ch'i-kai shih* (Shanghai: Wen-yi ch'u-pan-she, 1990), while Jen Chien and Lei Fang desribe their ritual powers in *Chung-kuo kai-pang* (Nanking: Chiang-su ku-chi ch'u-pan-she, 1993), pp. 75–88. Philip Kuhn describes beggars as being linked to sorcery in the popular imagination in *Soulstealers*, pp. 115–118.

considered a dangerous and polluting job that nobody else would willingly assume. Other more prestigious roles in the procession were played by people who had the money to pay for such an honor.

Cults, Festivals, and the Public Sphere in Late Imperial China

Some might wonder why I choose bring up the public sphere in a book on late imperial Chinese religion, particularly since the storm of debate over this issue appears to be just dying down. My main reason for doing so is that many scholars on both sides of this debate have generally ignored or underestimated the importance of religion in Chinese public life. This is in large part the unintended result of their desire to show that China possessed a public sphere similar to that which developed in the West — one in which religion played a largely insignificant role. For example, William Rowe's interest in the public sphere appears to derive from his attempt to overturn Max Weber's arguments on Chinese cities and show that modern Chinese cities shared many elements in common with Western ones,[9] while other scholars have explained the failure of China's democracy movement in 1989 by pointing to the absence of civil society or a public sphere.[10] In either case, the issue of the public nature of many Chinese religious activities does not find a place in their arguments.

Other scholars have argued that the concept of the public sphere may be of limited use in studying Chinese history, pointing out that when the German social philosopher Jürgen Habermas formulated this concept, he viewed the rise of the public sphere as intimately linked to the growth of democracy in Western European cities during the seventeenth and eighteenth centuries.[11] He therefore emphasized that such a concept was temporally and culturally specific, and should not be used in the study of other societies.[12] This has prompted scholars such as Philip Huang to describe the search for a Chinese public sphere as "poignant,"[13] and to conclude that: "the

---

[9] See in particular his introduction to *Hankow: Commerce and Society in a Chinese City, 1796–1889* (Stanford: Stanford University Press, 1984), pp. 1–14. See also Rowe, "The Public Sphere in Modern China," *Modern China* 16.3 (July 1990): 309–310, 326.

[10] For an analysis of this problem, see Frederic Wakeman, Jr., "The Civil Society and Public Sphere Debate: Western Reflections on Chinese Political Culture," *Modern China* 19.2 (April 1993): 108–111 and 133–134.

[11] Jürgen Habermas, *The Structural Transformation of the Public Sphere*, trans. by Thomas Burger with the assistance of Frederick Lawrence (Cambridge, Mass.: Harvard University Press, 1989), pp. 81–87, 398.

[12] *Ibid.*, pp. xvii-xviii.

[13] Philip C.C. Huang, "The Paradigmatic Crisis in Chinese Studies: Paradoxes in

notion of a bourgeois public sphere is much too historically specific to be a guide for analyzing China."[14] Frederic Wakeman has also pointed out that, despite the expansion of China's public realm following the turn of the century, the result has not been the expected rise of civic power but rather the expansion of state coercive power.[15] Here too, however, the debate is marked by the failure to consider religion as a key facet of Chinese society, which exerted a profound influence on a community's public life.

I wish to emphasize that the goal of this book is not to show whether or not modern Chinese society possessed civil society or a public sphere in the Western senses of these terms. The finest scholars in the field have researched this issue in great detail over the past few years, and their efforts have made a significant contribution towards our understanding of Chinese society. For example, scholars such as William Rowe, Mary Rankin, R. Keith Schoppa, and David Strand have explored the relationship between the Chinese concept of "public" (*kung* 公) and its Western counterpart, while also locating elements of civil society and the public sphere in modern Chinese society.[16] At the same time, however, I do wish to emphasize that one of the most important realms of public activity in late imperial China and modern China prior to 1949, not to mention Chinese communities in Taiwan, Hong Kong, and overseas today, centered/centers on popular cults and festivals like those to Marshal Wen. This means that any discussion of civil society or the public sphere in China should not be considered complete until it has taken into the account the immense importance of religious activities in Chinese public life.

For example, while many scholars searching for a Chinese civil society or public sphere have rightly emphasized that corporate groups and voluntary associations formed independent of the state could be important components thereof, their research has tended to focus on organizations such as guilds, native place associations, and lineages, the unfortunate result being that they have largely overlooked what Martin Yang has described as "religious groupings such as temple societies, deity cults, monasteries, and secret

---

Social and Economic History," *Modern China* 17.3 (July 1991): 321.

[14] Huang, "The Third Realm," 222.

[15] See Wakeman, "The Civil Society and Public Sphere Debate," 111–112 and 133–134.

[16] See Rowe, "The Public Sphere in Modern China," 314–325; and, "The Problem of 'Civil Society' in Late Imperial China," *Modern China* 19.2 (April 1993): 143–153. See also Rankin, *Elite Activism*, pp. 15, 102–110; Schoppa, *Chinese Elites and Political Change*, pp. 7–8; and David Strand, *Rickshaw Beijing: City People and Politics in 1920s China* (Berkeley: University of California Press, 1989), pp. 6–8, 100–102, 167–172 and 225.

societies."[17] Although temple societies and deity cults are usually not voluntary but ascriptive, this does not affect their significant role in public affairs. In fact, the evidence presented in the chapters above has shown that religious activities associated with local cults like Marshal Wen's clearly conform to Mary Rankin's definition of "public" in that they involved "the institutionalized, extrabureaucratic management of matters considered important by both the community and the state."[18] However, Rankin chooses to exclude religious activities from her definition by labeling them as private (*ssu* 私), in contrast with the official administration (*kuan* 官) and public management by elites (*kung*).[19] Such an analysis overlooks the fact that temples and festivals like Wen's were run by sophisticated organizations outside the imperial bureaucracy, and that their religious activities were both intensely supported by local communities and intently scrutinized by the state.

There are numerous other cases in which the use of data pertaining to local cults and festivals like Marshal Wen's can benefit social historians researching Chinese public life. Take for example some of the "constituent elements" of civil society in China discussed by William Rowe, particularly those of public institutions and public management, sites for the discussion of public affairs, and autonomous organizations. Regarding the first of these constituent elements, Rowe describes organizations like charitable granaries (*she-ts'ang* 社倉) and orphanages (*yü-ying t'ang* 育嬰堂) as being important public organizations subject to public management. However, he fails to take into account the fact that temples and other religious organizations supported and/or engaged in these and numerous other charitable activities throughout Chinese history, especially famine relief, education, bridge construction, and roadbuilding projects.[20] Recent scholarship has also shown that a large number of sectarian groups also pursued such charitable works.[21]

---

[17] See Martin Yang, "Between State and Society: the Construction of Corporateness in a Chinese Socialist Factory," *Australian Journal of Chinese Affairs* 22 (1989): 35–36.

[18] Rankin, *Elite Activism*, p. 15.

[19] *Ibid.*

[20] See for example Jacques Gernet, *Les aspects économiques du Bouddhisme dans la Société Chinoise du Ve au Xe Siècle* (Paris: École Française d'Extrême Orient, 1956); Robert Hymes, *Statesmen and Gentlemen: The Elite of Fu-chou, Chiang-hsi in Northern and Southern Sung* (Cambridge: Cambridge University Press, 1986), pp. 174–176, 182–183; Leung, "Organized Medicine," 134–136; and Lang and Regvald, *The Rise of a Refugee God*, pp. 14–15, 23–29 and 40–42.

[21] See ter Haar, *The White Lotus Teachings*, pp. 24–28.

More importantly, many late imperial and modern Chinese temples deserve consideration as public institutions, particularly Buddhist and Taoist "public monasteries" (*shih-fang ts'ung-lin* 十方叢林), which were considered to be the common property of the Buddhist sangha or ordained Taoist priests,[22] as well as the "public temples" (*kung-miao* 公廟) of neighborhood, village or regional cults.[23] Such institutions were built and maintained using public funds from donations, while festivals were funded by contributions from all households in a specific locality.[24] Prasenjit Duara has shown that many villages in north China had no large-scale social organizations apart from those belonging to the village temple, that the temple and its possessions were seen as public property belonging to the village, that members of the temple committee also ran village finances and dealt with village affairs, and that such men took over the new secular village organizations formed during China's modernization process.[25] There is also the fascinating case of the Pescadores (P'eng-hu), where the property of temple corporations (literally known as "public companies" [*kung-ssu* 公司!]) used to (and in some cases still does) include shares (*fen* 份) in the means of aquacultural production such as tidal basins used by the community for seaweed gathering.[26] How often such arrangements occurred throughout different parts of China and Taiwan has yet to be fully understood, but they do reveal the important role public institutions such as temples could play in a community's public life.

As for the second constituent element of civil society in China — sites for the discussion of public affairs — Rowe only considers urban teahouses and wineshops as being capable of stimulating the debate of public issues similar to that of European cafes or coffee houses.[27] I would argue that although teahouses and wineshops were of considerable importance in providing a setting for the discussion of

[22] See Holmes Welch, *The Practice of Chinese Buddhism, 1900–1950* (Cambridge, Mass.: Harvard University Press, 1967), pp. 3–4, 129–141 and 444–449; and, Yoshioka Yoshitoyo, "Taoist Monastic Life," in Welch and Seidel, eds., *Facets of Taoism*, pp. 229-230.

[23] See Sangren, *History and Magical Power*, pp. 61–86.

[24] See Alvin Cohen, "Fiscal Remarks on Some Folk Religion Temples in Taiwan," *Monumenta Serica* 32 (1976): 85–158; and Eberhard, "Temple-building Activities".

[25] Duara, *Culture, Power, and the State*, pp. 119, 137–138 and 148–149.

[26] See James Wilkerson, "The 'Ritual Master'," pp. 481–483 and 494–510; and "Rural Village Temples in the P'enghu Islands and their Late Imperial Corporate Organization," in *Proceedings of the Conference on Temples and Popular Culture*, (Taipei: Center for Chinese Studies, 1995), volume 1, pp. 67–95.

[27] Rowe, "Civil Society in Late Imperial China," 146.

issues of public interest, such matters were also frequently contested in the realm of popular religion. Although temples appear to have little in common with European cafes and coffee shops, they did provide a public space available to all citizens in which opinions, beliefs, and values could be formed and debated. Furthermore, the rituals, dramas, and ritual-dramas performed during festivals played a significant role in shaping popular mentalities,[28] while the murals that graced a temple's walls possessed a clear didactic function which could influence public mores.[29] Festivals in particular provided a public arena in which different groups attempted to shape and manipulate public opinion. Take for example the festival of Marshal Wen, during which the wealthy citizens of Wenchow and Hangchow showed off their most prized possessions in order to win the respect of their neighbors, while temple committee members and prominent citizens marched in the procession as an expression of both their high status and proper moral conduct. Wen's festivals also allowed those who felt that they had been wronged to accuse their enemies in public, while those burdened with feelings of guilt or sin openly (and often painfully) performed penance in front of the entire community.

In their contradictory symbolic expressions of prosperity and poverty, health and affliction, solidarity and discord, festivals like those to Marshal Wen appear to have been similar to what Edward Muir terms "civic rituals" in that they represented:

> commentaries on the city, its internal dynamics, and its relationship with the outside world . . . [Such] rituals illustrated an ideal arrangement of human relationships, created a homily that stimulated or altered some formal political and social ideas, and provided a medium for discourse among . . . the literate elite and the masses. Although civic rituals served the rulers' interests they were not just propaganda and did not pass messages in only one direction.[30]

---

[28] See Tanaka Issei, "The Social and Historical Context of Ming-Ch'ing Local Drama," in Johnson, et. al., eds., *Popular Culture in Late Imperial China*, pp. 143–160; and, Johnson, "Actions Speak Louder than Words," pp. 1–9, 29–32.

[29] See Katz, "The Function of Temple Murals in Imperial China: The Case of the Yung-lo Kung," *Journal of Chinese Religions* 21 (Fall 1993): 45–68.

[30] See Edward Muir, *Civic Ritual in Renaissance Venice* (Princeton: Princeton University Press, 1981), p. 5. See also W.R. Connor, "Tribes, Festivals and Processions: Civic Ceremonial and Political Manipulation in Archaic Greece," *Journal of Hellenic Studies*, cvii (1987): 40–50.

In considering the public nature of rituals performed at temples or during festivals, it might be helpful to treat these events as performances that brought differing representations and conflicting ideologies into a public space where they could be examined critically. Such performances had the potential to shape speech, influence behavior, and generally contribute to the construction and assumption of social power.[31] When viewed in this light, it becomes apparent that the activities associated with temples and festivals may have had a greater influence on Chinese social and political life than has been assumed. For example, Prasenjit Duara has shown that public activities associated with temples could play a crucial role in the creation of local norms and the establishment of local power.[32] In addition, Steven Sangren's work on Ma-tsu cults in modern Taiwan reveals that supporting her temples provides an opportunity for individuals and interest groups (including the state) to legitimize their power in the eyes of the community,[33] while pilgrimages play a key role in the creation of individual or communal identity.[34] Finally, by allowing for the multi-directional exchange of ideas, representations, and values, Chinese cults and festivals may well have contributed to the process of reverberation described in chapter 3.

Finally, Rowe's highly stimulating discussion of autonomous organizations, based largely on his own work on guilds and philanthropic associations in late imperial Hankow,[35] fails to take into account the fact that temple committees represented another type of autonomous organization which exercised great power over neighborhood and local affairs (see above). In addition, the relationship between temples and the state was not all that different from that which he describes for the organizations mentioned above. Like guilds and philanthropic associations, temple cults could not survive for long if they went against the will of the state (unless of course they were too insignificant to be bothered with or the state had become particularly weak). Once guilds and philanthropic associations had attained a significant degree of influence, they

---

[31] This is far too complex an issue to address in full here, especially since I have only just begun to study it. I do intend to focus on this problem in future research. For a summary and analysis of research on the cultural significance of performances, see Bauman and Briggs, "Poetics and Performance," 59–88. Clifford Geertz explores the interrelationship between performance, religion, politics, and social conduct in his *Negara: The Theatre State in Nineteenth Century Bali* (Princeton: Princeton University Press, 1980).

[32] Duara, *Culture, Power, and the State*, pp. 26–41, 118–149.

[33] Sangren, *History and Magical Power*, pp. 207–227.

[34] *Ibid.*, pp. 187–206.

[35] Rowe, "Civil Society in Late Imperial China," 146–148.

applied for state sanction by being put "on the record" (*tsai-an* 在案). Similarly, once temples to popular deities like Wen had grown to the point where they might attract the attention of the state, their members would enlist members of the gentry or elite classes to compose hagiographical texts and temple steles, as well as assist in applying for an official title for the temple's main deity (see chapters 3 and 4).

Based on the evidence presented above, I would argue that temples and festivals represented an important part of what Philip C.C. Huang has termed China's "third realm" — a space between state and society in which both interacted. Huang has pointed out that Habermas describes the public sphere as occupying two rather different spaces: 1) An intermediate space where state and society interact; and 2) An independent space which evolved in opposition to the state.[36] Huang goes on to argue that while China may not have possessed a public sphere in Habermas' sense of the word, the idea of a third space located between state and society and in which both interact can be of considerable value to scholars studying Chinese social history.[37] However, despite the fact that his arguments are highly convincing, in his attempt to locate the third realm Huang pays too little attention to the importance of temples and festivals. For example, Huang states that during the Ch'ing dynasty the third realm lay somewhere between the formal state-run legal system and informal customary practices for dispute resolution, with most lawsuits being resolved in their middle stages.[38] Such an analysis, while helpful in conceptualizing the third realm, ignores the fact that late imperial Chinese often resorted to temple rituals after other customary practices had failed to work but before filing a formal lawsuit. The *fang-kao* indictment ritual of Marshal Wen's festival in Wenchow is but one example. Staged during the city's biggest festival and before the leading members of the community, it allowed for the public expression and attempted resolution of grievances which had not been resolved through other customary means but which do not appear to have reached the magistrate's yamen. People throughout China who were involved in disputes might also make a public oath or undergo an ordeal in order to satisfy the community of the righteousness of their cause.[39] Businessmen and politicians in Taiwan still do so today. One could also consider the case of Peasant Shen

---

[36] Huang, "The Third Realm," 219.

[37] *Ibid.*, 223–224.

[38] *Ibid.*, 226–227. See also Kathryn Bernhardt and Philip C.C. Huang, eds., *Civil Law in Qing and Republican China* (Stanford: Stanford University Press, 1994).

[39] See Hsia, *Shen-p'an.*

discussed by Philip Kuhn: tormented and cheated by the sons of his deceased older half-brother, Shen did not go to the authorities but filed a complaint with the King of the Underworld by burning a yellow paper petition in his temple.[40] Village leaders in north China also punished local offenders by thrashing them in the presence of the gods inside their temples.[41]

Huang's discussion of subcounty administration could also have benefited from a greater appreciation of the importance of religion in local communities. While Huang is certainly correct that unsalaried quasi-officials such as *hsiang-pao* 鄉保 or *p'ai-t'ou* 牌頭 occupied key positions between state and society,[42] the same could also be said for the managers of religious associations, men known as "association heads" (*hui-shou*), "incense heads" (*hsiang-shou* 香首), or "general managers" (*tsung-li* 總理). While such men did not collect taxes (unless of course they also served as *hsiang-pao* or *p'ai-t'ou*), they did gather levies for temple construction projects and festivals. Furthermore, like their quasi-official counterparts, they also coordinated public services such as water control and defense.[43] Finally, while Huang shows that public functions performed by the gentry also formed an important part of the third realm,[44] he fails to note that their support of and participation in public services such as famine relief, water control, defense, etc., was often linked to their support of religious organizations. For example, Timothy Brook has shown that the late-Ming gentry in Chekiang actively patronized Buddhism and supported that religion's charitable activities in order to "publicize" the merit they had obtained and even acquire a share of symbolic capital.[45]

If one accepts the importance of religion in Chinese public life, an important implication is that the temporal scope of the debate on the Chinese public sphere needs to be expanded back to at least the late imperial era, if not earlier.[46] This is because many phenomena

---

[40] Kuhn, *Soulstealers*, p. 3.

[41] Duara, *Culture, Power, and the State*, p. 138.

[42] Huang, "The Third Realm," 227. See also Huang, *The Peasant Economy and Social Change in North China* (Stanford: Stanford University Press, 1985), pp. 224–248.

[43] Duara, *Culture, Power, and the State*, pp. 119, 137–138.

[44] Huang, "The Third Realm," 227–228.

[45] See Brook, *Praying for Power*, pp. 13–15, 23–29, 54–126 and 316–321. See also his "Family Continuity and Cultural Hegemony: The Gentry of Ningpo, 1368–1911," in Esherick and Rankin, eds., *Chinese Local Elites*, pp. 43–47.

[46] Robert Hymes and Conrad Schirokauer argue that a notion similar to Rankin's concept of "public space" began to emerge as early as the Southern Sung dynasty. See "Introduction," in Hymes and Schirokauer, eds. *Ordering the World. Approaches to State and Society in Sung Dynasty China* (Berkeley: University of California

associated with the public sphere in modern China, particularly elite activism and autonomous organizations, were also important elements of the societies of those times. For example, Hoyt Cleveland Tillman has argued that academies and granaries functioned as "middle level" institutions between state and society during the Sung dynasty.[47] Furthermore, as we saw in chapters 4 and 5, the growth of Marshal Wen's cult in late imperial Chekiang was linked to growing activism on the part of local elites, while autonomous organizations such as the committees managing Wen's temples exerted considerable influence over affairs directly affecting the lives of the citizens of Wenchow and Hangchow. Such phenomena may have become even more significant in modern times, but it would be a mistake to deny their importance during earlier eras as well.

The idea that state and society in traditional China interacted via the realm of religion and ritual is not a new one. Over a decade ago, Kristofer Schipper stated that:

> for more than two thousand years of history, [Taoism] remained the typical and coherent expression of the Chinese religion, of its *she-hui* ["the congregation of the Earth God"], that is the society vis-à-vis the state. Its liturgy provided the context within which the politico-religious structures of non-official China were formed.[48]

Although Schipper once again exaggerates the influence of Taoism on local society, he is correct in seeing the importance of cults and festivals in facilitating interaction between the imperial state and local society. Ken Dean presents a similar analysis in his work on Taoism and local cults in Fukien, pointing out that while Taoist ritual there draws on many imperial symbols, it also possesses its own unique interpretation of them which conforms to local mores.[49]

One social historian of modern China who has also considered the role of religion in the relationship between state and society is Prasenjit Duara. He maintains that temples made up a key element of what he has termed the "cultural nexus of power," that is, the matrix of hierarchical institutions (including temples) and networks

---

Press, 1993), pp. 51–56.

[47] See Tillman, "Intellectuals and Officials in Action: Academies and Granaries in Sung China," *Asia Major*, Third series, Volume IV, Part II (1991), 1–14. See also the essays by Angela Leung, James T.C. Liu, and Hugh Scogin cited above, which describe elite activism in public affairs during the Sung dynasty.

[48] Schipper, *The Taoist Body*, p. 15.

[49] Dean, *Taoist Ritual and Popular Cults*, pp. 53, 99–117 and 181–186.

(including temple and festival networks) "within which legitimacy and authority were produced, represented, and reproduced."[50] Duara's research also reveals that temples were among the most important symbols various interest groups (including the state) attempted to manipulate in order to achieve their goals.[51] Taking the cult of the Dragon King in north China as his example, he demonstrates that this deity's temples provided a framework for the creation and transformation of local alliances. At the same time, he also shows how the state attempted to manipulate this important symbol by adopting the cult of the Dragon King into the register of sacrifices.[52] Duara further explores the state's attempt to mold local symbols by superscribing the cult of Kuan Kung (see chapter 3), and concludes that his cult " brought together villagers, their elite leaders, and the state in a shared universe".[53]

My work attempts to take these arguments one step further by showing that cults to popular deities like Marshal Wen, whose followers included both religious specialists and lay believers, may well have been an integral part of China's third realm in the sense of occupying a public space between state and society which both attempted to influence while failing to totally control. Marshal Wen's cult could not have survived without the support, or at least the acceptance, of scholar-officials representing the state, but it is clear that their representations of this deity never completely supplanted (or superscribed) more popular ones. Wen's festivals provided a stage for the expression of local concerns and the attempted resolution of local conflicts, but also featured the participation of scholar-officials and the prominent display of symbols representing imperial authority. Such evidence makes it abundantly clear that local cults and festivals in late imperial China not only addressed the religious concerns of their supporters but also provided one important means for facilitating the ongoing interaction between state and society.

---

[50] Duara, *Culture, Power, and the State*, pp. 5–6, 15, 26 and 40. Sangren has also portrayed the overlap between ritual, economic and administrative systems in *History and Magical Power*, pp. 105–126.

[51] Duara, *Culture, Power, and the State*, pp. 24–25.

[52] *Ibid.*, pp. 34–35, 39.

[53] *Ibid.*, p. 250.

APPENDIX A

The Festival in Wenchow

What follows is a translation of two passages in the *Treatise on Wenchow Customs* (*WCFSC*), a work written during the mid-twentieth century based on both historical documents and the recollections of local elders. The first passage concerns Marshal Wen's festival as celebrated during the third lunar month. The second is about boat expulsion rites featuring Marshal Wen that were held when epidemics occurred. Sites mentioned in the text which can be identified have been assigned a number indicated on Map 7. I have not translated the authors' notes, which generally include comments on certain aspects of the festival as well as its origins.

pp. 27-35 — Worshipping the Eastern Peak
on the Third Day of the Third Lunar Month

"Worship the Eastern Peak on the third day of the third lunar month." This is a saying constantly on the lips of the people of Wenchow. However, the date of the festival is not on the third, and the deity invited is the Loyal and Defending King (Marshal Wen), not the God of T'ai-shan (the Emperor of the Eastern Peak). Why doesn't this saying conform to reality? Here is an explanation.

The Loyal and Defending King was named Ling Ch'iung 凌瓊,[1] and was a resident of P'ing-yang County. There is a temple to him in P'ing-yang known as the Temple of the Grand Guardian, whose deity is called Lord Grand Guardian (T'ai-pao yeh 太保爺).[2] The P'ing-yang county gazetteer describes him, and there is even a book about him.[3] According to folktales, this deity was once a

---

[1] This name was also used by some of my informants in Wenchow. The change in Wen's surname probably reflects the influence of spirit mediums (see chapters 3 and 4).

[2] For more on the use of the word *yeh* as an indication of respect, see Katz, "Demons or Deities?" pp. 203–204.

[3] Prcbably an allusion to the *Wen Chung-ching Wang chuan-lüeh*.

Map 7 — Late Imperial Wenchow

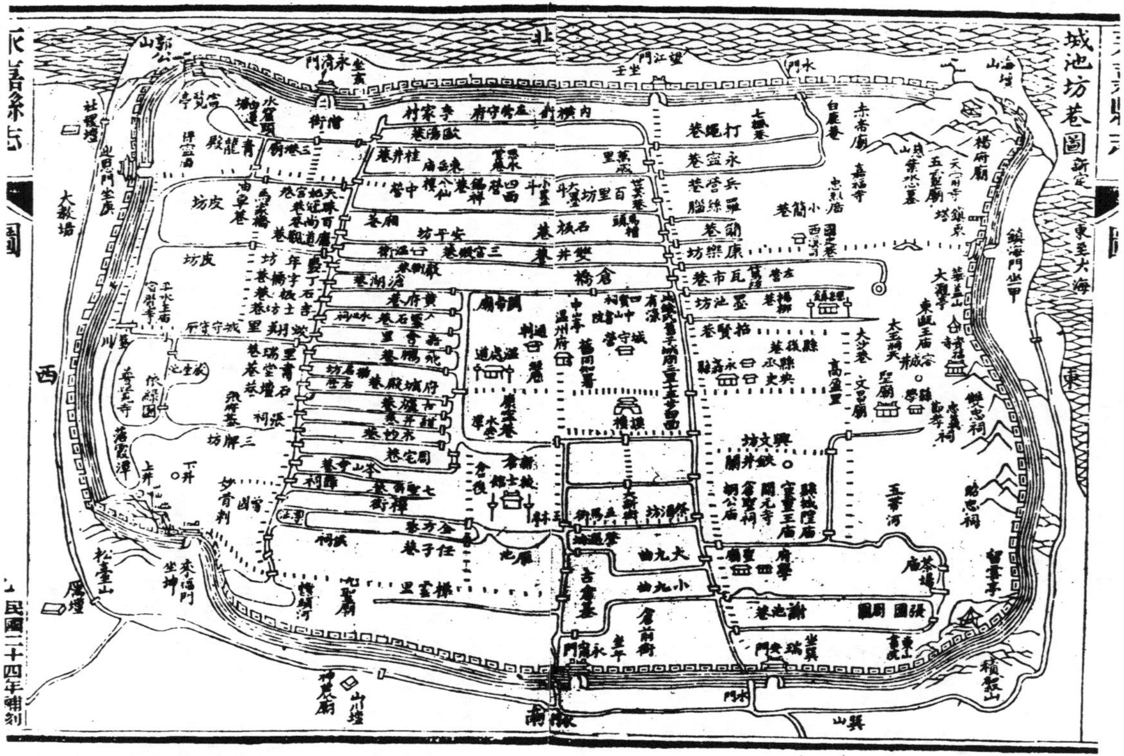

Reproduced from *YCHC* (1882).

government student (*hsiu-ts'ai* 秀才)[4] who took his *chin-shih* exams in the same year as Liu Yin 劉隱 (874-911) and Huang Ch'ao 皇巢 (d. 884);[5] none of them passed. One dark night, he heard two demons talking by the well outside his window, saying that since many people drank from this well, putting it (plague poison) in the well would be very effective. When Ling went out to take a look, he couldn't see a thing, and suddenly realized that those two were in fact plague demons (*yi-kuei*). He arose early in the morning, and stood guard by the well to prevent people from drinking the water. But as nobody believed his story, Ling threw himself into the well and died, proving that he hadn't lied. When they pulled out his body, it had turned dark blue.

Because of these events, Ling was worshipped as a deity who expelled epidemics, and his statues all have blue faces. He was enfeoffed as the Loyal and Defending King, and served as a marshal in the forces of the Emperor of the Eastern Peak. He was also one of the four heavenly generals.[6] Because he lived in Wenchow (Prefecture), and was a deity who could expel epidemics, he was granted the surname Wen and called Marshal Wen. In feudal times, it was the Heavenly Master Chang who memorialized to the emperor for a deity to be granted a surname. Therefore, this story comes from Taoism. As for the book about Marshal Wen, few people have it because the festival hasn't been held in a long time. For more details, see the P'ing-yang county gazetteer.

There are three temples to the Loyal and Defending King, the first being at the foot of Hua-kai Shan (#1 on map). Because it is next to the temple of the King of Eastern Ou (#2) and is small by comparison, it is known as the "Small Temple". The second temple is at the foot of Hsün-chi Shan, and the third is at Pa-hsien Lou (#3). These three temples take turns organizing the procession, with each term running two years and the entire cycle lasting six years. The festival's dates are determined during the first ten-day period of the third lunar month, when the temple chairmen use divining blocks to ask Wen. The chairmen will follow Wen's decision, no matter whether the date is auspicious or inauspicious. Because this procession is an

---

[4] This is an anachronism, as no such title was used during the T'ang.

[5] It would have been impossible for Liu Yin and Huang Ch'ao to have taken their *chin-shih* exams in the same year.

[6] These are: Marshal Wen (Ch'iung, who guards against demons from the East), Marshal K'ang (South), Marshal Ma (Sheng; West), and Marshal Chao (Kung-ming; North). See Ma Shu-t'ien, *Hua-hsia chu-shen* (Peking: Yen-shan ch'u-pan-she, 1990), pp. 109–116.

exorcism and rite of purification,[7] it will certainly bring supreme peace (*t'ai-p'ing* 太平); whether the date is auspicious or inauspicious is of no relevance. For example, even if the blocks come up with a day of destruction (*ta-p'o jih* 大破日), day of death (*shou-ssu jih* 受死日) or day of heavenly stars (*t'ien-kang jih* 天罡日), if no disasters occur people will say that this was because Wen's might had destroyed all calamities; if there are disasters, that would confirm what the blocks had indicated. Contrariwise, if the blocks had indicated an auspicious date and things ended up going wrong, this would mean that people needed to make greater efforts to attain supreme peace. As a result (of these explanations), the festival is always considered efficacious.

As for the saying "worship the Eastern Peak on the third day of the third lunar month," this is a result of literati creating refined sayings to amuse themselves. They believe that Wen's festival is linked to the ancient Lustration Festival (see note 7). Another explanation will be given below (pages 32-33 of the *WCFSC* contain a long note examining the similarities between the Wenchow plague festival and the Lustration Festival).

After the date of the festival has been determined, the chairmen write up placards on red paper announcing the procession of the Loyal and Defending King, and have them posted on every gate and street in the city of Wenchow so that all will know.[8] All the citizens sweep the streets and engage in a general clean-up. One or two days before the festival starts, a man is hired and given the title "Controller of Talismans" (*fu-ssu* 符司). He wears armor and a helmet, and carries a long bamboo pole. While the streets are being cleaned, he attaches to the bamboo a piece of blue cloth with the words "Clean the streets!" (*ch'ing-ching chieh-ch'ü* 清靜街衢) pasted on with yellow paper. Grass is burned next to all toilets (*mao-k'eng* 茅坑) to purify them. These events are referred to as "The Controller cleaning the streets" (*fu-ssu ching-chieh* 符司淨街). Every family participates in the clean-up before Wen's procession as a sign of reverence, and to preserve supreme peace.

The procession troupes are divided into three groups: the front station, second station, and third station (also referred to as rear station). They consist of:

---

[7] The authors call it a "festival of purgation and lustration" (*fu-hsi* 祓禊). For more on these rites, see Bodde, *Festivals*, pp. 273–288. These rites were also celebrated during the third lunar month, usually on the first *ssu* 巳 day. According to the *Yung-chia hsien-chih* (1882), 6:6a, this was also the date of Wen's festival.

[8] This assumes that at least one person in each neighborhood could read these announcements out loud to his or her neighbors.

Front Station: Leading off are people carrying a pair of lanterns hung from tall poles, two street cleaning banners and tiger rampant banners, as well as a pair of huge gongs, each borne by two people. Men carrying six pairs of placards follow. These read: "Silence!" (*su-ching* 肅靜), "Keep Back!" (*pi-hui* 避迴), "Working for Heaven to Change the World" (*tai-t'ien hsing-hua* 代天行化), "Heaven's Gate is Never Sealed" (*t'ien-men wu-chin* 天門無盡), "Expel Epidemics" (*ch'ü-wen chu-yi*), "Bestowing Blessings and Granting Favor" (*hsi-fu hsiang-hsiang* 錫福降祥), and "The Loyal and Defending Sage King" (*Chung-ching sheng-wang* 忠靖聖王). Others hold many other banners of all sizes and shapes, as well as numerous umbrellas. Umbrellas used during the day are made of satin, while those used at night are made of gauze; these latter ones have lanterns inside which are lit during the evening.

The first station also includes five beggars who are hired to dress as the Five Demons. Bringing up the rear is a giant puppet dressed in black with an immensely huge head. The head is made by pasting strips of bamboo together, and has four golden eyes; the body is also made of bamboo. A beggar is hired to stand inside it and carry it along the route. The puppet's stomach is covered by a Diagram of the Supreme Ultimate (*T'ai-chi t'u* 太極圖) made of gauze through which the bearer looks to find his way. He holds a long spear, and wears tiger-head shoes and socks. This puppet is called the Exorcist,[9] and its responsibility is to watch over the Five Demons. The Exorcist is much larger than an ordinary man; there is a local saying which refers to him as "The great man of the double third" (*san-yüeh-san ta-jen* 三月三大人). (A note follows explaining the origins of the Exorcist.) The Exorcist is also called "the deity who clears the road" (*k'ai-lu shen*), but is different from the *k'ai-lu shen* of the second station.

Second Station: First come men bearing a pair of small gongs, followed by a troupe of vast numbers of people on horseback dressed in black and wearing huge hats made of black gauze and over a foot long; these are called *k'ai-lu shen*. All of these people had to make a vow and pay a contribution before they could march as *k'ai-lu shen*. Then come people dressed as the Seven Stars of the Big Dipper, also on horseback and with their faces painted different shades of vermilion. They hold steel tridents, and are of evil (*hsiung-o* 凶惡) appearance many times worse than that presented in dramas.[10] It is said that they are seven demonic stars (*sha-hsing* 煞星) who are vicious deities (*hsiung-shen* 凶神). Why use evil spirits to bring peace? This

---

[9] This description of the Exorcist is strikingly similar to those provided in descriptions of the Great Exorcism; see Bodde, *Festivals*, pp. 77–84.

[10] I am not sure which dramas feature these deities; perhaps Mu-lien operas?

probably stems from the idea of using evil to control evil ("set a demon to catch a demon") as expressed in a summons written by Ch'en K'ung-chang 陳孔璋 (Ch'en Lin; d. 217 C.E.), which reads: "The skill of the eagle or the hound lies in their teeth and claws."[11]

Bringing up the rear of the second station are four people dressed in yellow carrying a pavilion with an incense burner inside, accompanied by the "marshal who oversees the troupes (in the procession)". He has a gold spear and gold helmet, and wears golden armor covered by a martial ceremonial robe of the type worn by officials (*mang-p'ao* 蟒袍). His clothes are called "civil and martial armor" (*wen-wu chia* 文武甲). The marshal rides an open imperial palanquin, and carries a flag of command. Next to the palanquin march four people dressed as guards carrying a huge "horse-beheading sword". The marshal must not look around, nor may he talk, causing some children watching the procession to mistake him for a deity's statue and worship him.

The Seven Stars and the marshal must first make a vow before being allowed to join the procession. The former must prepare their own horses, and the latter must hire his four guards. These guards are all played by beggars, who are fed and paid for their work.

At meals sponsored by the temple, a distinction is made between the "small crowd" (*hsiao-chung* 小眾) and "large crowd" (*ta-chung* 大眾). The former consists of those who made contributions and the temple managers, and their food is slightly better than that of the large crowd, which consists of people (i.e., beggars) hired for the procession.

Rear Station: This begins with a pair of people wearing black hats who beat small gongs, followed by more people carrying placards. Next comes a huge mob of "sinners" and "criminals", mostly played by males . . . (part of the text has been obliterated) . . . and children who walk along the street; this is called "dressing as sinners" (*pan tsui-jen* 扮罪人). Others wear red clothes, and their hands are shackled; some even bear cangues and chains. Yamen runners holding keys lead them along. Some even paint tears and snot on their faces, which appear sallow and white. The streets seem to be full of demons. This is called "dressing as criminals" (*pan fan-jen* 扮犯人).

There are also seven and eight year-old children dressed in silk and with faces painted like those of martial figures from dramas. Some ride horses which are led along by others. Others ride in gorgeous prisoner cages which are borne aloft by others. These

---

[11] See *Ch'en K'ung-chang chi*, 2:2b. This text has been preserved in the *Chien-an ch'i-tzu chi*, compiled by the Ming scholars Yang Te-chou, et. al. (Taipei: Chung-hua shu-chü, 1971).

children sit on piles of silks, with candies and cookies placed in front of them.[12] All of these are called sinners. These sinners (who don't have to walk) are usually played by children. However, even some forty or fifty year-old adults also ride in these cages, and are also said to be "dressing as sinners."

Other people ride in a prisoners' cart filled only with grass. These people bear cangues and chains, and are considered to have committed particularly heinous crimes. This is also referred to as "dressing as criminals".

Another type of participant wears a short jacket made of silk and wraps a white garment around his waist. His or her arms are left bare, and into these hooks are stuck from which hang incense burners suspended by two-foot long red ropes. This is called "flesh-sticking incense" (*cha-jou hsiang* 紮肉香).[13] These people form their own troupe, but are also considered to be "dressing as criminals."

Sinners and criminals are all people who have made a vow to participate in the procession because they or a family member is ill, or faces impending danger because of sins from a previous life which have not yet been atoned for. By dressing as sinners or criminals they can draw on the power of the Loyal and Defending King to expiate their sins and prevent disasters in this life.

Following the sinners and criminals are two people dressed as servants bearing incense burners, as well as four civil and martial judges and four generals on duty in the palace. Then come people carrying two warning placards and one huge umbrella. There is also a troupe of musicians, as well as eight eunuchs.

Bringing up the rear of the entire procession (in the place of honor) is Wen's imperial palanquin, which is followed by a man bearing a fan made of feathers. At each corner of the palanquin walks Wen's honor guard (*yi-chang* 儀仗), four men dressed as a martial figures from dramas who bear banners during the day and hold lamps at night. The palanquin itself is magnificent and resplendent, and requires eight people to carry it. The temple managers accompany the palanquin, wearing hats and robes which are tucked in at the waist. There is also a professional trained in local etiquette who wears

---

[12] Children play similar roles in some processions I have seen in southern Taiwan, but instead of being carried in prisoner cages they sit atop a massive wooden centipede, which is either carried or pushed on wheels. They are called "centipede troupes" (*wu-kung chen* 蜈蚣陣) and are considered highly auspicious, despite the centipede's originally negative symbol as one of the five poisonous creatures to be expelled during the Dragon Boat Festival.

[13] For more on this practice, see *Ch'ung-hsiu Che-chiang t'ung-chih kao* (1948), vol. 18:37a–b.

everyday clothes and guides the palanquin as it goes forward and back, left and right. If the palanquin encounters any hindrance (somebody blocking the route), he yells: "Take heed and step aside!" Those people (he admonishes) all give way.

After Wen and his honor guard set out, if they pass other temples along the route they will perform different ceremonies depending on that deity's rank. In the case of deities with the title emperor, like the Sage Emperor Lord Kuan (Kuan-sheng ti-chün 關聖帝君) or the Great Emperor Hua-kuang, who rank higher than king (Wen's rank), the managers of their temples will seal the gates and put out a placard reading "Keep Back!" The managers of Wen's temple must thereupon present Wen's name card to gain entry. In the case of deities who also have been awarded the title king, the managers of both temples will exchange incense. Temple managers of deities who rank lower than Wen must go out to Wen's palanquin and offer incense as a sign of respect.

If it starts to rain, everybody should seek shelter in the nearest temple. At such a time, the ceremonies performed not only vary by the temple deity's official rank but by the wealth of the temple. If the temple in question is without property and the street it lies on is impoverished, it cannot afford to entertain Wen, who must therefore remain outside its gates. If the temple has property and the neighborhood surrounding it is well off, then its temple managers will go out and present a formal invitation in the name of that deity inviting Wen to enter the temple. This is called "An Invitation for a Meeting" (*hui-ch'ing* 會請). If the temple deity's rank is higher than Wen's, Wen's forward palanquin bearers should squat down a little, and the rear bearers should stand up higher. In this way, Wen's statue is said to be "bowing down as if entering a nobleman's gate." The higher-ranking deity need only come out to the lower front steps to welcome Wen. If both deities are of equal rank, the temple deity will go out to invite Wen in a ceremony resembling the ancient rite of the eastern and western steps (*tung-hsi chieh* 東西階).[14] If the deity in question ranks below Wen, he or she must go out and bow down as if inviting an honored guest. The host temple should offer sacrifices and stage dramatic performances, and as this requires considerable expense, it is essential for Wen to seek shelter in the wealthier temples during a rainstorm.

All the people living along the streets through which Wen's procession passes offer roadside sacrifices. A tall platform is erected at

---

[14] This is an allusion to the rules of etiquette for receiving guests. See *Li-chi* (*The Book of Rites*), Legge trans., pp. 71–72.

the mouth of the street, on which are placed a table and chairs covered with tiger skins. An incense burner to the Loyal and Defending King is set upon the table, and in front of it are placed offerings consisting of five bowls of fruits and cakes, a pot of tea, and candles. Six tables covered with offerings are also set up on the street in front of the platform. Taoists read memorials while those who paid for the sacrifices and the local temple managers kneel in worship. The sacrifices include all manner of delicacies, including pig's heads, fish, chickens, ducks, geese, flowers, and antiques. The lavishness of these offerings is taken as an indication of wealth or poverty.

In addition to paying for these sacrifices, each household must also make glutinous rice dumplings, and they compete to see whose are the finest and most remarkable. Some dumplings are so small and delicate as to resemble lustrous pearls, and receive great praise from all the people. Some women are so skilled in making them that they are awarded silver plaques during the festival.

Of all the displays of wealth held during these festival days, those along the avenue running north to south are the finest, extending for miles from house to house. Huge tents are erected, from which are suspended colorful lanterns, ancient toys, marvelous flowers, and splendid jades. Red candles are lit behind curtains, and sounds of musical performances fill the air. During the festival, one can see old gramophones (*liu-sheng chi-ch'i* 留聲機器), fountains (*lung p'en-shui* 龍噴水), Western-style watches, projectors(?) (*huan-teng* 幻燈), animal and bird specimens, and ancient timepieces. Every seventh or eighth house displays some remarkable artwork for all to admire, and local elders offer opinions (as to which is finest).

(This passage is followed by a note on whether such displays are wasteful or pleasurable; the authors settle on the latter.)

While the displays on the other streets are not as magnificent as those on the main avenue, multicolored lanterns bedeck the entire city. In addition to this, the people of any street through which the procession passes will surely display their finest wares. This is especially true for the Eastern Gate district, which stages an elaborate amateur marionette show (*ch'uan-k'o hsi* 串客戲),[15] and the Western Walls district, which erects colored towers (*ts'ai-lou* 彩樓).[16] These colored floats are decorated like the palaces in which gods and immortals reside, and the elaborateness of their decorations can be

---

[15] I am following the definition provided in the *Chung-kuo hsi-ch'ü ch'ü-yi tz'u-tien* (Shanghai: Shang-hai tz'u-shu ch'u-pan-she, 1983), p. 62; see also *Ch'ung-hsiu Che-chiang t'ung-chih kao* (1948), vol. 16:26b–27b.

[16] These may have resembled the floats (*t'ai-ko*) used in Hangchow festivals, or the elaborate pavillions set up during offering rituals in Taiwan.

grasped from their name; it would be difficult to describe them in only a few words. As for the puppet shows, these were staged on a moving float atop a tall platform covered with colored cloth at its base. Performers hide inside this structure, and on top are placed paper figures over two feet high. The puppeteers manipulate these figures so that they fight, ride horses, travel on boats, worship, laugh and cry just like real people. The scripts are identical (to those used for plays), and what is performed is based on the dramas of the theatrical world. Such performances and displays all require great skill which is rarely seen.

When the procession reaches the western suburbs, the rite of filing indictments (*fang-kao*) is staged. First a placard announcing the filing of indictments is posted at the local parade grounds. This announcement is in fact a document written in the name of the Loyal and Defending King, which summons all people who have been wronged or bear a grievance to file a complaint with the underworld bureaucracy so that the King can intercede for them. Wen's palanquin enters the parade grounds, and he is taken out, given a Taoist priest's robe (*yü-yi* 羽衣), and carried in a chair borne by four temple managers. Three strings of firecrackers are set off, and the four men start running, fierce expressions on their faces. After Wen's statue enters the parade grounds, tea is presented and his clothes are changed. At this point, a yamen runner bellows: "The great king has entered the hall!" Three more firecrackers are set off, and a drum is beaten three times. All the judges and yamen runners stand in formation and set up two placards reading "File Indictments" and "Submit Documents" (*t'ou-wen* 投文). Wen's statue is slowly borne out through the Griffin Gate (*Ch'i-lin men* 麒麟門) and seated in the center of the hall. The marshal who oversees the troupes sits at his left, and the Seven Stars, criminals, sinners, justices, and yamen runners all stand in orderly formation in the hall.

When all has been prepared, the senior runner gives a yell, prompting all the criminals to kneel down and worship; at the second yell, the sinners do so too. At the third yell, the plaintiff enters the hall dressed in mourning clothes, with his or her hair in disarray.[17] Holding incense and carrying an indictment written on yellow paper, he or she screams: "Injustice! Lord of the Eastern Peak, I implore you to right this wrong!" The plaintiff is driven back by the judges, but continues to press forward, in tears, not being allowed to approach Wen until the third attempt. The plaintiff then kneels down and offers Wen the indictment, crying continuously to the point of exhaustion

---

[17] As opposed to being tied neatly in a queue.

while presenting the facts of the grievance. Following this, the senior runner burns the indictment in the incense burner (to transmit it to the heavens), saying, "The Sage-King knows now," and advising the plaintiff to retire.

These events truly represent traditional society. For the Loyal and Defending King to settle actual disputes is nonsense, but this was something 90% of the people believed in. The injustices described in the indictments must have occurred, for who would have dared to lie in front of Wen? Those who witnessed these rites invariably shed tears, for such tragic events were indeed common in traditional society. Were such grievances redressed? There are no detailed records, but some say that those indicted did in fact die! This is probably because the guilty party was fully aware of the evil he or she had committed, and died of fear and shame. Such events made people believe even more deeply in Wen's miraculous powers.

The final event of the festival is a procession of inspection which lasts one day and night. This procession of inspection is similar to the procession held during the initial stage of the festival, but they are spoken of as distinct events because the rituals involved vary. On this final day, Wen makes another tour of the city, but the route is shorter than that of the first six days. For the first six days, the procession passes every street and alley, but only the larger streets are included on the final day. There are also no roadside sacrifices; people simply offer incense. The Loyal and Defending King switches to a smaller palanquin, and a Marshal Wu is added to his honor guard, borne in a palanquin of his own. The goal of this inspection is to check one last time that all plague deities and plague demons have departed. The palanquin-bearers proceed at a much faster pace, enabling the tour of the city to conclude before midnight.

At this point, the procession enters the city through the southern gate (probably the Jui-an Men 瑞安門 (#4)), where all the criminals and sinners except the children have gathered on the street. All carry blazing torches, which turn the entire city a bright red. The men wave their torches wildly as the palanquin enters, obstructing its passage. This continues until the palanquin reaches Marshal Wen's temple at Hua-kai Shan, the palanquin advancing in fits and starts. The route is not long, but it takes until daylight for Wen to reach his temple. It is said that things are done in this way because the people want Wen to stay outside the city and expel epidemics. Others claim that it is a display of power to aid Wen, with fire cleansing all evil. If one examines what people of former times had to say about this, one cannot find a definitive answer.

(Two notes follow, the first describing the overlap of Wen's cult with that of the Emperor of the Eastern Peak, and the second explaining similarities between the Wenchow festival and the ancient Lustration Festival.)

The procession is staged by each of Wen's three temples in turn, with the route, starting point, and destination varying by each temple. For the procession to be able to pass through every single street and alley without missing one is no simple feat. The route placard (*lu-ching p'ai* 路徑牌) of the Pa-hsien Lou temple is still extant, and has been copied below.[18]

pp. 55-58 — Sending Off the Plague Spirits

Sending off the plague spirits is a ritual for expelling epidemics, and is performed by Taoists. Lay Taoists (*men-ko tao-shih* 門閣道士)[19] and lay Buddhists (*ching-yu* 經友) can only assist in these rites.

When an epidemic is in progress, the local elders gather in the Temple of the King of Eastern Ou (#2) to plan the rituals of exorcism (*chieh-jang* 解禳). Contributions are collected throughout the city, and with everybody afraid of death, few refuse to open their money bags. A Taoist altar is erected at the Temple of the King of Eastern Ou, and a huge Taoist offering is performed. This is called "The Great Offering Under the Heavens" (Lo-t'ien ta-chiao).

The festival starts with the King of Eastern Ou sending formal notices of consultation bearing his name to the Great Emperor Hua-kuang, the Mysterious Altar of Orthodox Unity (Cheng-yi hsüan-t'an 正一玄壇),[20] the Loyal and Defending King, the King of Martial Majesty (Wu-mu Wang 武穆王),[21] the King of Broad Nobility (Po-hou Wang 博侯王),[22] the King of Blessings and Protection (Fu-yu

---

[18] The contents of this placard may be found in Yeh, "Wen Yüan-shuai hsin-yang," pp. 127–128.

[19] I have not encountered this term previously. However, its usage in this passage seems to indicate a contrast between Taoists who live in monasteries and those who live in lay society. In this sense, the term seems similar to "fire dwellers" (*huo-chü shih* 火居師), also used to describe Taoist priests who marry and live outside of monasteries. See for example T'ien, *Liu-ch'ing jih-cha*, 27:5a–b.

[20] This may be a temple to Chao Kung-ming, who is often referred to by his title Marshal of the Mysterious Altar (*Hsüan-t'an yüan-shuai* 玄壇元帥). For temple data, see *WCFC* (1756), 9:7a and *YCHC* (1882), 4:47b.

[21] The Sung hero Yüeh Fei 岳飛 (1103–1141). For more on his cult, see *CKMCCS*, pp. 614–616. For information on his temple in Wenchow, see *WCFC* (1756), 9:8a.

[22] I have not found any information on this deity's cult in Wenchow. This could be because: 1) This deity's cult spread to Wenchow after the last Ch'ing gazetteer was

Wang 福祐王),[23] the Dignified and Succoring King (Chuang-chi Wang 莊濟王),[24] the Courageous King of the South (Yung-nan Wang 勇南王),[25] the Mighty and Numinous Duke (Wei-ling Kung 威靈王; the Prefectural City God),[26] and the Mighty and Numinous Count (Wei-ling Po 威靈伯; the County City God (#5)).[27]

Why is the King of Eastern Ou responsible for the expulsion rites? This is because he is considered the (spiritual) master of Wenchow. It is his responsibility to supervise any response to calamities afflicting his domain.

When all the temple managers have received these notices, they proceed to raise money throughout their respective neighborhoods in order to pay for the procession. Those in charge of the Taoist altar (set up at the Temple of Eastern Ou) appoint someone to carry charms and cleanse the streets, and all the residents of Wenchow engage in a massive clean-up (similar to that undertaken before Wen's third month festival).

A large boat is placed at the altar, in front of the Temple of the King of Eastern Ou. Its frame is made of strips of bamboo, and it is covered with paper. It is over ten feet long, and seven to eight feet wide. Three masts rise from its decks, and in its cabins are placed all manner of utensils for use in everyday life, albeit made of paper. It resembles those sampans that ply the oceans.

At six o'clock in the morning, on the first day of rituals held at the Taoist altar, the City God of Yung-chia County is the first deity to arrive. This because he is a (spiritual) local official, and therefore bears the greatest responsibility (for stopping calamities?), and also because he is the lowest-ranking deity (of the ten summoned). Next comes the City God of Wenchow Prefecture, who is also a local official but is allowed to be a little late because his rank is higher. (A brief note follows about the origins of City Gods). Following the City Gods come the Courageous King of the South, the Dignified and Succoring King, the King of Broad Nobility, and the King of Blessings and Protection. These gods were people from the working class (*lao-tung jen-min ch'u-shen* 勞動人民出身) (before deification) but are now seen as local gentry (*ti-fang shen-shih* 地方紳士). Then comes Yüeh Fei, who served

---

compiled (1882); 2) This deity was worshipped as a subsidiary deity (*p'ei-shen*) in the temple of another deity (most gazetteers rarely list subsidiary deities); or 3) His cult and temple did exist but were overlooked by the editors of Wenchow's local gazetteers.

[23] For data on his cult in Wenchow, see *YCHC* (1882), 4:32a–33a.

[24] *Ibid.*, 4:47a-b. See also *Yüeh-ch'ing hsien-chih* (1901), 3:23b.

[25] Same problem as in the case of the King of Broad Nobility.

[26] See *CCTC* (1736), 225:1b; *WCFC* (1756), 9:2a; and *YCHC* (1882), 4:8b.

[27] *CCTC* (1736), 225:1b; *WCFC* (1756), 9:2b; *YCHC* (1882), 4:9a–b.

his country with unreserved loyalty (*ching-chung pao-kuo* 精忠報國), and the Loyal and Defending King, who controls epidemics (*chu-kuan wen-yi* 主管瘟疫). These are all very important deities, so they follow (the other deities who seem like) the local gentry. The Mysterious Altar of Orthodox Unity has high rank but few responsibilities, so he comes even later. All these deities ride in open palanquins, with honor guards marching before them. They all take their places in the forward hall of the Temple of the King of Eastern Ou.

At this point, the King of Eastern Ou sends a runner to carry a document to the Temple of the Emperor Hua-kuang stating that all the other deities are at the temple reverently awaiting his arrival. After the managers of the Temple of the Emperor Hua-kuang have been notified, they immediately take the Emperor's statue and place it in a palanquin. The temple's managers and yamen runners all line up in formation, firecrackers are set off, and the palanquin proceeds to the Temple of the King of Eastern Ou through the main streets and past a branch temple (*hsing-kung* 行宮) for the King of Eastern Ou. By the time the Emperor arrives, the other nine deities and the King of Eastern Ou have proceeded to the front of the temple's main gate and are awaiting his arrival. He enters through the main gate, and all the deities follow him to take their seats the forward hall of the temple in order of rank. Tea is then served.

After all the deities have arrived, the Taoist in charge of rituals leads those in charge of the Taoist altar to the Supreme Jade Cave-Heaven (*T'ai-yü tung-t'ien* 太玉洞天)[28] (#6) to receive the spirit-tablets of the Three Pure Ones. (There follows an explanation of the identities of these three deities, and their possible links to the Three Treasures (*san-pao* 三寶) of Buddhism). These tablets are then brought into the forward hall of the Temple of the King of Eastern Ou through the main gate, with all the deities going out to welcome the Three Pure Ones. Next, the Three Pure Ones' tablets are then carried into the center of the main hall (a sign of their higher rank), with all the other deities lining up by rank along the eastern steps in audience.

When the audience ritual is complete, one Taoist (here referred to as "feathered official" [*yü-shih* 羽士]) reads an imperial edict from the Three Pure Ones, and chants in a high-pitched voice: "Loyal and Defending King Ling Ch'iung, ascend to the palace and

---

[28] This is a Taoist temple also known as the Jung-ch'eng Taoist Monastery (Jung-ch'eng Tao-yüan 容城道院), being named after the legendary Taoist Jung Ch'eng-tzu 容成子. It was built at Hua-kai Shan during the fourteenth century. Marshall Wen's temple at Hua-kai Shan was also constructed at this time. See *WCFC* (1756), 25:5b and *YCHC* (1882), 36:55a. The Supreme Jade Cave Heaven is the eighteenth of the thirty-six Taoist cave-heavens.

hear your orders!" The Loyal and Defending King quickly enters the courtyard, at which point the Taoist takes an arrow of command and presents it to him. (A note follows comparing this "arrow" to various jade tablets of ancient times. A longer note is on pp. 57–58 of the *WCFSC*.) The Loyal and Defending King receives his orders and leaves, followed by all the other deities who escort him out through the main gate where the procession starts from. The other deities then silently return to their places in the temple. For the next six days, Taoist priests will chant scriptures and perform rituals there.

After the Taoist rituals begin, all the city officials must reverently offer incense at the Temple of the King of Eastern Ou. The heaviest responsibility falls on the shoulders of the Yung-chia county magistrate, as he must also offer a memorial to the Heavenly Emperor (the Jade Emperor). The contents of this memorial involve this officials blaming himself for being of mean virtue and useless to the people he governs. His failings have sparked Heaven's anger, and resulted in all the people suffering for crimes he has committed. He states his willingness to bear the blame himself and pleads with the Jade Emperor to pardon the rest of the people. As for the rituals performed by the Taoists over this six-day period, these consist of Taoist scriptures, incantations, penances, and documents (*ching, chou, ch'an, wen* 經、咒、懺、文) with many styles that are too numerous to recount. The most amazing of these rites is "Raising the Nine-level Platform" (*ta chiu-t'ai* 打九臺), in which a nine-level platform is made using one-hundred tables.[29] The Taoists ascend, and blow their (snail) horns (*fa-lo* 法螺), pacing the Steps of Yü and performing rituals. A magical gourd is opened, out of which spurts yellow smoke. The county magistrate's memorial is burned in this smoke, and is said to have been thereby transmitted to Heaven.

At the same time these rites are being performed, every family in the city will come to the Temple of the King of Eastern Ou to burn incense and light candles. The paper ingots and spirit money they offer pile up like mountains. Most of these are burned in the temple furnace, but the finest ones, as well as more valuable offerings such as Buddhist or Taoist scriptures and documents, are placed on the plague boat.

The Loyal and Defending King conducts a tour of inspection which must be completed by the end of the sixth day and proceeds rain or shine. Those participating are excited and full of energy, never flagging. The route is similar to that [of the third month festival], the

---

[29] This rite may be similar to Shaohsing rituals studied by Hsü Hung-t'u. See his "Jih fan chiu-lou, yeh yen Meng-chiang".

honor guard is identical, and the indictment ritual (here called "issuing an indictment" [*fa-kao* 發告]) is also held. (What is different) is that the roadside sacrifices only include vegetarian offerings, and the yamen issues a proclamation forbidding butchers to slaughter animals.

After the procession has concluded, all the deities return to the Temple of the King of Eastern Ou and take their assigned seats in the forward hall. (To those who are watching), it seems as if these deities are talking to the plague gods (*wen-shen*), asking them to leave the Wenchow area. By nighttime, at high tide, lamps aboard the plague boat are lit, and it is carried through the main gate of the Temple of the King of Eastern Ou. This procession starts northwards, proceeding through the main street of the city. Finally, the boat is rapidly led through the Gate Overlooking the River (Wang-chiang Men) (#7) by a large crowd of people carrying torches and yelling in loud voices. Lamps are extinguished in all the houses and stores along the route, and no one dares make a sound or peek through the door. If anybody encounters the procession, he or she must join in and holler with the others. The eleven deities press forward behind the boat in order of rank, so that it may quickly be sent away.

When the procession reaches the (Ou) River, the boat is placed on a raft covered with dry grass and other flammable objects, and towed away eastwards by sampans. The Loyal and Defending King orders a marshal to take another boat and force the plague boat out to sea. The marshal is played by a beggar. The plague boat and the raft it sits on are set afire as they float away, after which the sampans and the marshal's boat return.

After the boat has been towed away from the river bank, all the lamps on all the palanquins are doused, and the procession reenters the city along the west bank through the Gate of Eternal Purity (Yung-ch'ing Men 永淸門) (#8), at which point the lamps are rekindled. The last deity to enter the city is the Courageous King of the South, who is said to have been a shipmaster before becoming a deity and is therefore in charge of all boat-related events. All the other deities wait until the lamps on his palanquin have been lit, and then they all process together through the Ward of Tranquillity and Peace (An-p'ing Fang 安平坊) (#9), over the Bridge of Supreme Peace (T'ai-p'ing Ch'iao 太平橋), and back to the Temple of the King of Eastern Ou. The Loyal and Defending King returns his arrow of command to the Three Pure Ones, who are then reverently borne back to the Cave Heaven of Supreme Jade. After this, all the deities return to their respective temples. Sometimes the managers of other temples will organize additional processions in the areas under their jurisdiction (*hsia-ching* 轄境) for one or two days (presumably to deal with any remaining plague spirits).

(Two notes follow this passage. The first is about the "arrow" of command, and the second discusses possible antecedents of the expulsion rites, including the Great Exorcism. Mao Tse-tung's poem entitled "Sending off the Plague Spirits" [see chapter 2] is also cited).

APPENDIX B

The Festival in Hangchow

The following is a translation of Fan Tsu-shu's description of Marshal Wen's Hangchow festival in *The Lost Customs of Hangchow* (*Hang-su yi-feng*).

The Festival and Market Fair of Marshal (Wen)

The Earth Spirit Marshal (Ti-ch'i yüan-shuai 地祇元帥) enfeoffed as the Loyal and Defending King of Eastern Wenchow has the surname Wen. According to legend, he was a government student of the previous (Ming) dynasty who came to the provincial capital (Hangchow) for the examinations. One night he overheard demons putting plague poison in a well, and threw himself into the waters in hopes of saving the people. When they fished out his body the next day, it had turned black all over. People knew he had been poisoned (and therefore didn't dare drink from the well). He was enfeoffed as a deity at that time.

Wen's birthday is celebrated on the eighteenth day of the fifth lunar month, although the festival and procession begin on the sixteenth. This festival is called "Capturing Epidemics" (*shou-wen*), and is of ancient origin indeed.

The well (Wen jumped into) lies on Sheep Market Road (Yang-shih chieh 羊市街)[1] at a temple named the Temple of Manifest Virtue. The deity of this temple is called the "old marshal" (*lao yüan-shuai* 老元帥).[2]

There are a number of (Marshal Wen) temples inside the city, but only the Temple of Manifest Virtue is said to have both wealth and influence (*yu ts'ai yu shih* 有財有勢). Other temples include: 1) The Loyal and Defending (King's) Taoist Monastery (Chung-ching Kuan

---

[1] This street is in the Ward of Preserving Tranquility (Pao-an Fang), the site to which the temple at West Lake was moved following its destruction during the Yüan. See *WLFHC*, vol. 3, pp. 590–594; vol. 4, pp. 270–278.

[2] Probably because this temple and its image of Wen were the oldest of those participating in the festival.

忠靖觀), which is near Upper Granary Bridge (Shang-ts'ang Ch'iao 上倉橋) and serves as the Censor-in-Chief's (*tu-hsien* 督憲) private temple (*hsiang-huo yüan* 香火院).[3] It has influence but no wealth (*yu shih wu ts'ai* 有勢無財), and its deity is called Marshal Ts'ang (Ts'ang Yüan-shuai 倉元帥);[4] 2) The T'ung-sheng Monastery (T'ung-sheng Ssu 童乘寺), located in the Pure River Ward (Ch'ing-ho Fang 清河坊). It has wealth but no influence (*yu ts'ai wu shih* 有財無勢), and its deity is called Marshal T'ung (T'ung Yüan-shuai 童元帥);[5] 3) The Sweet Springs Monastery (Kan-ch'üan Ssu 甘泉寺), located in front of the prefectural yamen. The deity of this monastery is extremely violent and wicked, and is called Marshal Kan (Kan Yüan-shuai 甘元帥);[6] and 4) The temple of Marshal P'i (P'i Yüan-shuai 皮元帥), named after its location in the leather market (*p'i-shih* 皮市). The Marshal Wen of this temple has a repulsive and loathsome face.[7] Only the Temple of Manifest Virtue organizes Wen's procession and festival.[8]

Each official's yamen, from that of the Provincial Governor (*fu-yüan* 撫院) on down, sends some of its head yamen runners (*ta-pan* 大班) to take part in the procession. The city yamen also sends four policemen who dress as barechested executioners. The Temple of Manifest Virtue's honor guard (here referred to as *yi-ts'ung* 儀從) would not be complete without them. In addition, each temple fields a large group of men who help organize the festival, their number reaching between four and five hundred.

Among the various troupes are stilt-walkers, children bearing incense burners, and people carrying dragon-lanterns, banners, and poles. There are also troupes of people bearing huge and elaborate floats, as well as those dressed as immortal lads (*hsien-t'ung* 仙童),[9]

---

[3] See *HCFC* (1922), 7:17b and 18a.

[4] There is a Sage Ts'ang Temple (Ts'ang Sheng Miao 倉聖廟) in Hangchow (*Ibid.*, 9:5b), but this should not be confused with the Chung-ching Kuan.

[5] *Ibid.*, 34:15a.

[6] *Ibid.*, 34:15a. A statue of Marshal Wen was enshrined in this temple in 1680.

[7] This is probably the Abbey of Eternal Tranquility (Yung-ning Yüan 永寧院); *Ibid.*, 35:42a. This temple should not be confused with that of the Leather Market King (P'i-ch'ang Wang 皮場王), a deity whose cult was popular in Hangchow and other areas of Chekiang. See *CKMCCS*, pp. 218–221; *HCFC* (1922), 9:29b–30b and 34:18b; and, *Hsi-hu chih* (1734), 15:33b–34a.

[8] The Republican edition of the Hangchow gazetteer contains a similar description of these temples, but adds a reference to a temple named the Taoist Monastery of Welcoming Immortals (Ying-hsien Kuan 迎仙觀), as well as a fifth temple at Hu-yeh, outside the city (see chapter 4); see *HCFC* (1922), 9:20b–21a. I have been unable to find any data concerning the Ying-hsien Kuan. For data on Wen's Hu-yeh temple, see *Hang-chou shih hsin-chih kao* (1948), *chüan mo*, 2a.

[9] These may be similar to immortal lad troupes which perform in processions on Taiwan. These troupes usually consist of a pair of young men dressed in robes

hunters, grooms, sweepers (*sao-tao* 掃道),[10] guards, and child stilt-walkers. Others carry portable floats (*chien-ko* 肩閣), as well as lanterns shaped like boats (*ch'uan-teng* 船燈).[11] There are also people (usually children) dressed as figures from fiction, as well as pilgrims and those who have made a vow to dress as condemned criminals. How could the total number of participants be less than ten thousand?

The extravagance and exquisiteness of these performers are truly impressive; otherwise, how could their performances create such a sensation, and cause people who live so far away to come and watch the festival? It is no lie to state that people from a thousand miles away will come.

On the fifteenth day of the fifth lunar month, all the temple assistants proceed to Wen's temple. Members of Hangchow's major lineages will rent out spaces in front of their homes to people who wish to watch the procession, with a space about six feet wide generally going for over ten foreign dollars. The most popular site is the space in front of the Provincial Governor's offices. Whole buildings are also rented out in this manner. Other miscellaneous expenses (for Marshal Wen's festival) are covered in a number of ways, some being as small as the few cash raised from each jasmine flower sold.

Each association hires its own porters, and the order in which they march must not be mixed up. Sedan chair bearers representing the seventy-two bearers' organizations inside the city all help carry Wen's palanquin, Each group numbers at least forty or fifty, and all wear the same style of clothing and hats. When the bearers change hands, it is called "hoisting the palanquin" (*sheng-chia* 陞駕). Each group of bearers has its own area through which it carries the palanquin, and they cannot exceed this by even one step.

When the temple assistants arrive at Wen's temple, they march inside through its main gate (*t'ien-men* 天門). They are accompanied by men bearing a pair of placards reading "The Carefree Man of the Empyrean," as well as a group of musicians playing various wind instruments.

Among those who always march with the assistants are the eight generals and the civil and martial justices, their faces covered with ashes. These are always played by bannermen (*ch'i-hsia-jen* 旗下人).[12] An additional troupe of martial dancers includes a pair of

---

wearing huge masks of smiling young immortals.

[10] These may be similar to certain individuals one sees in plague festivals in Taiwan, who sweep the streets the Lords pass through as they march in the festival's procession.

[11] See *Ch'ung-hsiu Che-chiang t'ung-chih kao* (1948), vol. 16:7b.

[12] No explanation is given as to why only bannermen could perform such roles.

men, one of whom wields a Wolf-tooth's Pole (*Lang-ya pang* 狼牙棒), and the other the Heaven and Earth Rings (*Ch'ien-k'un ch'üan* 乾坤圈). These weapons are over ten feet long, and have a circumference of seven to eight inches; both are made of tin. The two men carrying these weapons first square off, then turn their backs on each other and charge sideways.[13] In addition to these troupes, there are also tens of pairs of people dressed as members of the imperial guards (*chin-yi* 禁役), as well as people clad in court robes and wearing court hats. Their clothes and shoes are complete (replicas of the real items).

People fall silent when Wen's palanquin passes, the reason being that he is endowed with an awesome majesty which naturally inspires respect.

Wen is accompanied by an adjutant having the surname Yang, who is also known as the Cloud Immortal Commissioner (*Yün-hsien shih-che* 雲仙使者). He rides in an extremely small palanquin. His face is white and beardless, and he wears a general's armor and helmet. His awe-inspiring banners and civil and martial robes are also white. This temple's honor guard is also complete (as a real imperial honor guard would be). His assistants also carry some weapons like the Heaven-painted Spear (*T'ien-hua chi* 天畫戟; a two-pronged weapon), as well as a large throne. Yang's palanquin proceeds in front of Wen's. His temple is called the Samadhi Cloister (San-mei An 三昧庵), which is located at Board Alley (Pan-erh Hsiang 板兒巷) inside Blacksmith Lane (Ta-t'ieh Hung 打鐵街).[14]

The procession commences at the Hour of the Dragon (7:00–9:00 a.m.), and does not return to the temple until the fifth drum (3:00–5:00 a.m.). For this reason, many come to the city in the evening to watch the lantern displays.

Three days before the festival begins, a horse placard (*ma-p'ai* 馬牌)[15] is carried along the route, and sheets describing the procession's route are handed out. This is so that people who wish to watch the procession will not miss anything.

During the festival, the foodstuffs consumed are the finest and most expensive. In addition, the city's brokers and peddlers all make a

---

[13] There are many martial performances like this at festivals in Taiwan, the troupes usually being known as Sung Chiang Armies (Sung Chiang Chen 宋江陣). The men in these troupes occasionally dress as the bandit-heroes from the novel *The Water Margin* (*Shui-hu chuan*). These troupes are said to have developed out of local militias, as opposed to the Hangchow practice of drafting bannermen to march in the procession.

[14] See *HCFC* (1579), 97:10b–11a. There is also a temple to a General Yang located there, but he does not appear to be the deity mentioned above; see *HCFC* (1922), 11:9a–b.

[15] This is probably similar to the route placard of the Wenchow festival.

profit which never fails to triple that made during ordinary market-fairs.

BIBLIOGRAPHY

I. Primary Sources and Reference Works

A-t'o-p'o-chü kuei-shen ta-chiang shang-fo t'o-lo-ni ching 阿吒婆拘鬼神大將上佛陀羅尼經. *T* 1238.

A-t'o-p'o-chü kuei-shen ta-chiang shang-fo t'o-lo-ni shen-chou ching 阿吒婆拘鬼神大將上佛陀羅尼神咒經. *T* 1237.

A-t'o-p'o-chü yüan-shuai ta-chiang shang-fo t'o-lo-ni ching hsiu-hsing yi-kuei 阿吒薄具元帥大將上佛陀羅尼經修行儀軌. *T* 1239.

Ch'ang-Chao ho chih 常昭合志. Wang Chin 王錦 and Yang Chi-hsiung 楊繼熊, eds. 1904 edition.

Chang Huang-yen 張煌言 (1620–1664). *Chang Shui-ts'ang chi* 張水倉集. Peking: Chung-hua shu-chü, 1959.

Chang Tai 張岱 (1597–ca.1676). *T'ao-an meng-yi* 陶庵夢憶. *Ts'ung-shu chi-ch'eng* 叢書集成 edition. Shanghai: Shang-wu yin-shu-kuan, 1925.

Chang Yen 張炎. *Chung-tou hsin-shu* 種豆新書 (1760).

Chao Hsüeh-min 趙學民 (1719–1805). *Ch'uan-ya nei-wai-pien* 串雅內外編. Hong Kong: Chiu-lung shih-yung shu-chü, 1957.

Chao Tao-yi 趙道一 (fl.1294–1307). *Li-shih chen-hsien t'i-tao t'ung-chien* 歷世眞仙體道通鑑. *TT* 139–148; *CT* 296.

CCFSCC. Hangchow: Che-chiang jen-min ch'u-pan-she, 1986.

Che-chiang sheng ti-t'u ts'e 浙江省地圖冊. Shanghai: Hsin-hua shu-tien, 1988.

Che-chiang ti-li chien-chih 浙江地理簡志. Hangchow: Che-chiang jen-min ch'u-pan-she, 1985.

CCTC. Hu Tsung-hsien 胡宗憲, ed. 1561 edition.

CCTC. Li Wei 李衛, Chi Tseng-chün 稽曾筠, et. al., eds. 1736 edition.

(Ch'ung-hsiu) Che-chiang t'ung-chih kao 重修浙江通志稿. Che-chiang sheng t'ung-chih kuan, 1948.

Chen-hai hsien-chih 鎮海縣志. Tung Tsu-hsi 董祖義, ed. 1931 edition.

Ch'en Lin, 陳林 (d. 217 C.E.). *Ch'en K'ung-chang chi* 陳孔璋集. In *Chien-an ch'i-tzu chi* 建安七子集, Yang Te-chou 楊德周 (Ming), et. al., comp. Taipei: Chung-hua shu-chü, 1971.

Cheng-yi wen-ssu pi-tu shen-teng yi 正一瘟司辟毒神燈儀. *TT* 84; *CT* 209.

Ch'i Piao-chia 祁彪佳 (1602–1645). *Ch'i Chung-min Kung jih-chi* 祁忠敏公日記. Hangchow: Hang-chou ku-chiu shu-tien, 1982.

Chi-shuo ch'üan-shen hsü-pien 集說詮神續編 (1880). Huang Po-lu 黃伯錄. In *Chung-kuo min-chien hsin-yang tzu-liao hui-pien*.

Chia-hsing fu ch'eng-chen ching-chi shih tzu-liao tsuan 嘉興府城鎮經濟史資料纂. Chia-hsing: Chia-hsing t'u-shu-kuan, 1985.

CHFC. Liu Ying-k'o 劉應鈳, ed. 1600 edition.

CHFC. Yüan Kuo-tzu 袁國梓, et. al., eds. 1682 edition.

CHFC. Hsü Yao-kuang 許瑤光, ed. 1878 edition.

Chiang Chün 姜準 (late Ming). *Ch'i-hai so-t'an chi* 岐海鎖談集. Wenchow: Che-chiang sheng Yung-chia ch'ü cheng-chi hsiang-hsien che-yi-chu wei-yüan-hui, 1936.

Chiang-hsi t'ung-chih 江西通志. Liu K'un-yi 劉坤一, et. al., eds. 1881 edition.

Chiang-hsiang chieh-wu shih 江鄉節物詩. Wu Ts'un-k'ai 吳存楷 (Ch'ing). In *WLCKTP*, volume 4.

Chiang-nan t'ung-chih 江南通志. Yü Ch'eng-lung 于成龍, et. al., eds. 1684 edition.

Chiao Hung 焦宏 (1541–1620). *Kuo-ch'ao hsien-cheng lu* 國朝獻微錄. Taipei: Hsüeh-sheng shu-chü, 1965.

CTHC. Nieh Hsin-t'ang 聶心湯, ed. 1609 edition.

Ch'ien-t'ang hsien-hsien chuan-tsan 錢塘先賢傳贊. Yüan Chao 袁昭 (fl.1187–1227). In *WLCKTP*, volume 1.

Ch'ien Yung 錢泳 (1759–1844). *Lü-yüan ts'ung-hua* 履園叢化. Peking: Chung-hua shu-chü, 1983.

Chin-men chih 金門志. Chou K'ai 周凱 ed. 1836 edition.

Chin-yün hsien-chih 縉雲縣志. Ho Nai-jung 何乃容 and Ko Hua 葛華, eds. 1767 edition.

Ching-ch'u sui-shih chi yi-chu 荊楚歲時記譯注. Tsung Lin 宗懍 (fl. 501–565). T'an Lin 潭麟, ed. Hu-pei jen-min ch'u-pan she, 1985.

Chiu-huang huo-min pu-yi shu 救荒活民補遺書 (1443). Chu Hsiung 朱熊.

Chou Hsing-chi 周行己 (Sung). *Fu-chih chi* 浮沚集. *Ts'ung-shu chi-ch'eng* edition.

(Hsü-tsuan) Chü-jung hsien-chih 續纂句容縣志. Chang Chao-t'ang 張昭堂, ed. 1904 edition.

Chu-ting yü-wen 鑄鼎餘閒 (1899). Yao Fu-chün 姚福均, comp. In *Chung-kuo min-chien hsin-yang tzu-liao hui-pien*.

Chu-tzu nien-p'u 朱子年譜. Wang Mao-hung 王懋竑 (1668–1741), ed. Taipei: Shih-chieh shu-chü, 1968.

Ch'üan-chou fu-chih 泉州府志. Huai Yin-pu 懷陰布, ed. 1763 edition.

Ch'üan-chou chiu feng-su tzu-liao hui-pien 泉州舊風俗資料彙編. Ch'üan-chou: Ch'üan-chou min-cheng chü, 1985.

Ch'üan T'ang wen 全唐文 (1814). Tung Kao 董誥 (1740–1818), et. al., eds. Taipei: Ching-wei shu-chü, 1965.

Chuang Ch'o 莊綽. *Chi-lei pien* 雞肋編 (1133). Peking: Chung-hua shu-chü, 1988.

Chuang-tzu 莊子. Trans. Burton Watson. New York: Columbia University Press, 1968.

Chung-kuo hsi-ch'ü ch'ü-yi tz'u-tien 中國戲曲曲藝辭典. Shanghai: Shang-hai tz'u-shu ch'u-pan-she, 1983.

Chung-kuo li-shih ti-t'u chi 中國歷史地圖集. T'an Ch'i-hsiang 譚其驤, et. al., eds. 8 Volumes. Shanghai: Ti-t'u ch'u-pan-she, 1987.

CKMCCS. Hopeh: Ho-pei jen-min ch'u-pan'she, 1986.

Chung-kuo min-chien hsin-yang tzu-liao hui-pien 中國民間信仰資料彙編. Wang Ch'iu-kuei 王秋桂, Li Feng-mao 李豐懋, et. al., eds. Taipei: Hsüeh-sheng shu-chü, 1989.

Chung-kuo min-su chih: Che-chiang 中國民俗志：浙江. Lou Tzu-k'uang 婁子匡, ed. Taipei: Tung-fang wen-hua kung-ying she, 1970.

DMB. L. Carrington Goodrich and Fang Chao-ying, eds. New York: Columbia University Press, 1976.

ECCP. Arthur H. Hummel, ed. Washington, DC: U.S. Government Printing Office, 1944.

Encyclopedia of Religion. Mircea Eliade, et. al., eds. New York: Macmillan Publishing Company, 1987.

Fa-hai yi-chu 法海遺珠 (Ming). *TT* 825–833; *CT* 1166.

Fan Chih-ming 范致明 (Sung). *Yüeh-yang feng-t'u chi* 岳陽風土記. In *Yü-yüan ts'ung-shu* 芋園叢書, vol. 109. Nan-hai, 1935.

Fan Tsu-shu 范祖述 (late Ch'ing). *Hang-su yi-feng* 杭俗遺風 (1864). Shanghai: Wen-yi ch'u-pan-she, 1989.

Fang Shao 方勺 (1066–?). *Po-chai pien* 泊宅編. Peking: Chung-hua shu-chü, 1983.

Fu-chien t'ung-chih 福建通志. Li Hou-chi 李厚基, et. al., eds. 1938 edition.

Han-chou chih 漢州志. Liu Ch'ang-keng 劉長庚, ed. 1817 edition.

Han shu 漢書. Pan Ku 班固 (32–92) ed. Peking: Chung-hua shu-chü, 1962.

Han T'ien-shih chia-shih 漢天師家世. *TT* 1066; *CT* 1463.

HCFC. Ma Ju-lung 馬如龍, ed. 1686 edition.

HCFC. Cheng Yün 鄭雲, ed. 1784 ed.

HCFC. Ch'en Chü 陳橘, et. al., eds. 1922 edition.

Hang-chou shih hsin-chih kao 杭州市新志稿. Ting Jen-chün 丁人俊, ed. 1948 edition. In *Hang-chou shih-ti ts'ung-shu*, volumes 1–8.

Hang-chou shih-ti ts'ung-shu 杭州史地叢書. Hangchow: Che-chiang jen-min ch'u-pan-she, 1983.

Hang-chou ti-fang chih tzu-liao, ti yi, erh chi 杭州地方志資料，第一、二輯. Hangchow: Che-chiang jen-min ch'u-pan-she, 1987.

Hang-chün hsiang-te Piao-chung Kuan pei-chi-shih 杭郡庠德表忠觀碑記事 (1753). In *WLCKTP*, volume 1.

Hang-su yi-ch'ing ts'ui-chin 杭俗怡情翠錦 (1903). Anon. In *Chung-kuo shih-hsüeh ts'ung-shu* 中國史學叢書. Volume 32. Taipei: Hsüeh-sheng shu-chü, 1987.

Ho-wen cheng-ch'ao chi 和瘟正朝集 (1886). In *Kuang-ch'eng yi-chih. Tsang-wai tao-shu.* Volume 14, pp. 94–99.

Ho-wen ch'ien-chou ch'üan-chi 和瘟遣舟全集. In *Kuang-ch'eng yi-chih. Tsang-wai tao-shu.* Volume 15, pp. 355–358.

Hou Han shu 後漢書. Fan Yeh 范曄 (398–446). Peking: Chung-hua shu-chü, 1963.

Hsi-hu chih 西湖志 (1734). Li Wei, et. al., eds.

Hsi-hu lao-jen fan-sheng lu 西湖老人繁勝錄 . In *Tung-ching meng-hua lu, wai ssu-chung.*

Hsi-hu yu-lan chih 西湖遊覽志 (1547). T'ien Ju-ch'eng. In *WLCKTP*, volume 10.

Hsi-tzu-hu shih-ts'ui yü-t'an 西子湖十架餘談. Wang K'o-yü 汪砢玉 (1587–1643). In *WLCKTP*, volume 8.

HCLAC. Ch'ien Yüeh-yu 潛說友, ed. 1830 recarving of 1268 edition.

Hsin Chin-men chih 新金門志. Hsü Ju-chung 許如中, ed. 1959 edition.

Hsin-k'o ch'u-hsiang tseng-pu sou-shen chi ta-ch'üan 新刻出像增補搜神記大全. Ming dynasty. In *Chung-kuo min-chien hsin-yang tzu-liao hui-pien.*

Hsin-pien lien-hsiang sou-shen kuang-chi 新編連相搜神廣記. Yüan dynasty. In *Chung-kuo min-chien hsin-yang tzu-liao hui-pien.*

Hu-chou fu-chih 湖州府志. Tsung Yüan-han 宗源瀚 and Kuo Shih-ch'ang 郭式昌, eds. 1870 edition.

Hu-chou fu-chih ch'ien-pien 湖州府志前編. Ch'eng Liang 程量, ed. 1649 edition.

Hu-shan pien-lan 湖山便覽 (1875). Chai Hao (1735–1788) 翟灝, et. al., eds.

Huang Chen 黃震 (1213–1280). *Huang-shih jih-ch'ao* 黃氏日抄. In *Wen-yüan Ko Ssu-k'u ch'üan-shu* 文淵閣四庫全書. Taipei: Shang-wu yin-shu-kuan, 1983. Volumes 707–708.

Huang-cheng yao-lan 荒政要覽 (1589). Yü Ju-wei 俞汝爲.

Huang chu lüeh 荒箸略 (1608). Liu Shih-ao 劉世敖. In *Huang-cheng ts'ung-shu* 荒政叢書. 10 volumes. Yü Sen 俞森 (Ch'ing), ed. In *Shou-shan Ko ts'ung-shu* 守山閣叢書, volumes 67–70. *Pai-pu ts'ung-shu chi-ch'eng* 百部叢書集成 edition. Taipei: Yi-wen yin-shu-kuan, 1968.

Hucker, Charles O. *A Dictionary of Official Titles in Imperial China.* Stanford: Stanford University Press, 1985.

Huang Kung-chin 黃公瑾. *Ti-ch'i shang-chiang Wen T'ai-pao chuan* 地祇上將溫太保傳 (1274). *TT* 557; *CT* 780.

Hung-lou meng 紅樓夢 (*The Story of the Stone*). Trans. David Hawkes. 5 volumes. Harmondsworth: Penguin Books, 1973–1986.

Hung Mai 洪邁 (1123–1201). *ICC.* 4 volumes. Peking: Chung-hua shu-chü, 1981.

Jang-wen sheng-teng k'o 禳瘟聖燈科. In *Shang-ch'ing ling-pao chi-tu ta-ch'eng chin-shu, chüan* 14, *ting-chi* 丁集, *hsia* 下, 36b–39b. *Tsang-wai tao-shu*. Volume 16, pp. 520–522.

JHHC. Shen Ch'ao-hsüan 沈朝宣, ed. 1594 edition.

JHHC. Chao Shih-an 趙世安, ed. 1687 edition.

Ju-kao hsien-chih 如皋縣志. Liu Shou-t'ing 劉受廷 and Tso Yüan-chen 左元鎮, eds. 1808 edition.

Juan Yüan 阮元 (1764–1849), et. al. *Ku-ching ching-she hsü-chi* 詁經精舍續集. Lo Wen-chün 羅文俊 ed. 1842 edition.

———. *Liang-che chin-shih chih* 兩浙金石志. In *Shih-k'o shih-liao ts'ung-shu* 石刻史料叢書. Volumes 40–41. Yen Yi-p'ing 嚴一萍, ed. Taipei: Yi-wen yin-shu-kuan, 1966.

Kao Lien 高濂 (fl. 1587). *Tsun-sheng pa-chien* 遵生八牋 . Taipei: Shang-wu yin-shu-kuan, 1979.

Kao-shang shen-hsiao tsung-shih shou-ching shih 高上神霄宗師受經式. *TT* 1005; *CT* 1272.

(Ch'in-ting) Ku-chin t'u-shu chi-ch'eng 欽定古今圖書集成 (1725). Ch'en Meng-lei 陳夢雷, et. al., ed. and comp. 100 volumes. Taipei: Wen-hsing ch'u-pan-she, 1964.

Ku Yen-wu 顧炎武 (1613–1682). *Jih-chih lu chi-shih* 日知錄集釋. Ed. and comp. by Huang Ju-ch'eng 黃汝成. Taipei: Shih-chieh shu-chü, 1968.

Kuang-ch'eng yi-chih 廣成儀制. In *Tsang-wai tao-shu*. Volumes 13–15.

Kuo-hsüeh pei-tsuan 國學備纂. Wu Ying-yen 吳穎炎, ed. Taipei: Kuang-hsüeh-she yin-shu-kuan, 1978.

Kung Wei 龔煒 (1704–1769). *Ch'ao-lin pi-t'an* 巢林筆談. Peking: Chung-hua shu-chü, 1981.

Lang Ying 朗瑛 (fl. 1566). *Ch'i-hsiu lei-kao* 七修類稿. Peking: Chung-hua shu-chü, 1961.

Li-chi 禮記 (*The Book of Rites*). Trans. James Legge (1815–1897). New York: University Books 1967 reprint of 1885 edition.

Li Hsü 李詡 (late Ming). *Chieh-an lao-jen man-pi* 戒菴老人漫筆 . Peking: Chung-hua shu-chü, 1982.

LSHC. Chang Hsien 張銑, ed. 1846 edition.

LSHC. Li Chung-yüeh 李鍾嶽 and Li Yü-fen 李郁芬, eds. 1926 edition.

Li T'i-chai 厲惕齋 (1794–1867). *Chen-chou chu-chih tz'u* 振州竹枝詞. Taipei: Chung-hua ts'ung-shu wei-yüan-hui, 1958.

Liang Yü-sheng 梁玉繩 (1745–1819). *Ch'ing-pai shih-chi* 清白詩集 (1800).

Lin Chih-han 林之翰 (fl. 1662–1723). *Wen-yi ts'ui-yen* 瘟疫萃言. Shanghai: K'o-hsüeh chi-shu ch'u-pan-she, 1989.

Lin-hai hsien-chih 臨海縣志. Hung Jo-kao 洪若臯, ed. 1683 edition.

Lin-hai hsien-chih. Sun Hsi-ting 孫熙鼎 and Chang Yin 張寅, eds. 1935 edition.

Ling-pao wu-liang tu-jen shang-p'in miao-ching 靈寶無量度人上品妙經. *TT* 1–13; *CT* 1.

Liu-ho hsien-chih 六合縣志. Liu Ch'ing-yün 劉慶雲, ed. 1646 edition.

Liu-pu ch'eng-yü 六部成語. Hangchow: Ku-chi ch'u-pan-she, 1987.

Liu-shih chia-ts'ang 劉氏家藏. Liu Ch'un-yi 劉春沂. Taipei: Wu-ling ch'u-pan-she, 1982.

Lu Yu 陸游 (1125–1210). *Chien-nan shih-chi* 劍南詩集. In *Lu Yu chi* 陸游集. 5 volumes. Peking: Chung-hua shu-chü, 1976.

Lun yü 論語 (*Analects*). Confucius. Trans. James Legge. In *The Chinese Classics*. Volume 1. Oxford: Clarendon Press, 1865–1895.

Mao Tse-tung 毛澤東. *Mao Tse-tung shih-chi* 毛澤東詩集 (*The Poems of Mao Tse-tung*). Trans. Willis Barnstone and Ko Ching-po. New York: Harper and Row, 1972.

MLL. Wu Tzu-mu 吳自牧 (fl.1275). In *Tung-ching meng-hua lu, wai ssu-chung*.

Min-Hou hsien-chih 閩侯縣志. Ou-yang Ying 歐陽英, ed. 1933 edition.

Mochizuki Shinkō 望月信亨. *Bukkyō dai jiten* 佛教大辭典. Third Edition. 10 volumes. Kyoto: Sekai seiten kanko kyōkai, 1954–1971.

Nakamura Hajime 中村元. *Bukkyōgō Dai Jiten* 佛教大辭典. 3 volumes. Tokyo: Tokyo Shōseki, 1978.

Nieh Shang-heng 聶尚恒 (b.1572). *Ch'i-hsiao yi-shu* 奇效醫書. Peking: Chung-yi ku-chi ch'u-pan-she, 1984.

Ning-po fu-chih 寧波府志. Ts'ao Ping-jen 曹秉仁, et. al., eds. 1733 edition.

Nü-ch'ing kuei-lu 女青鬼律. *TT* 563; *CT* 790.

Pai Yü-ch'an 白玉蟾 (fl.1209–1224). *Hai-ch'iung Pai chen-jen yü-lu* 海瓊白眞人語錄. *TT* 1016; *CT* 1307.

Pao-ning Ssu Ming-tai shui-lu hua 保寧寺明代水陸畫. Peking: Wen-wu ch'u-pan-she, 1985.

Pei-fang chen-wu tsu-shih hsüan-t'ien shang-ti ch'u-shen chih-chuan 北方眞武祖師玄天上帝出深志傳 (also known as *Pei-yu chi* 北遊記). In *Ku-pen hsiao-shuo ts'ung-k'an* 古本小說叢刊, series 9, volume 1. Peking: Chung-hua shu-chü, 1990. *Journey to the North*. Trans. Gary Seaman. Stanford: Stanford University Press, 1988.

PYHC. Chu Tung-kuang 朱東光, ed. 1571 edition.

PYHC. Chin Yi-chün 金以竣, ed. 1694 edition.

PYHC. Hsü Shu 徐恕, ed. 1760 edition.

PYHC. Wang Li-fu 王理孚, ed. 1915 edition.

Po-wu chih chiao-chʿng 博物志校證. Chang Hua 張華 (232–300). Ed. Fan Ning 范寧. Taipei: Ming-wen shu-chü, 1981.

San-chiao yüan-liu sheng-ti fo-tsu sou-shen ta-ch'üan 三教源流聖帝佛祖大全. Ming dynasty. In *Chung-kuo min-chien hsin-yang tzu-liao hui-pien*.

San-chiao yüan-liu sou-shen ta-ch'üan 三教源流搜神大全. Taipei: Lien-ching ch'u-pan shih-yeh kung-ssu 1980 reprint of Yeh Te-hui 葉德輝 (1864–1927) 1909 edition.

Shang-ch'ing ling-pao chi-tu ta-ch'eng chin-shu 上清靈寶濟度大成金書 (1432). In *Tsang-wai tao-shu*. Volumes 16–17.

SHFC. Hsiao Liang-kan 簫良幹, ed. 1587 edition.

SHFC. Yü Ch'ing 俞卿, ed. 1719 edition.

SHFC. Li Heng-t'e 李亨特, ed. 1792 edition.

Shao-hsing hsien-chih tzu-liao, ti yi chi 紹興縣志資料，第一集. Shao-hsing hsien hsiu-chih wei-yüan-hui, 1939.

Shen-hsiao ch'ien-wen sung-ch'uan yi 神宵遣瘟送船儀. In *TFHY, chüan* 220.

SHC. Chang Feng-huan 張逢歡, ed. 1671 edition.

SHC. Niu Yin-mo 牛蔭磨 and Lo Yi 羅毅, eds. 1934 edition.

SHC. Hangchow: Che-chiang jen-min ch'u-pan-she, 1989.

Shih-chi 史記. Ssu-ma Ch'ien 司馬遷 (ca.135–93 B.C.E.). Trans. Burton Watson. *Records of the Grand Historian of China.* New York: Columbia University Press, 1961.

Shih shen 釋神 (1812). Yao Tung-sheng 姚東升. In *Chung-kuo min-chien hsin-yang tzu-liao hui-pien.*

Sou-shen chi 搜神記. Kan Pao 干寶 (fl. 317–350). Peking: Chung-hua shu-chü, 1979.

Su-chou fu-chih 蘇州府志. Ning Yün-p'eng 寧雲鵬, Lu T'eng-lung 盧騰龍, et. al., eds. 1691 edition.

Su Shih 蘇軾 (Su Tung-p'o) (1036–1101). *Su Tung-p'o chi* 蘇東坡集. 6 volumes Taipei: Shang-wu yin-shu-kuan, 1965.

Sui-shih hsi-su tzu-liao hui-pien 歲時習俗資料彙編. Taipei: Yi-wen yin-shu-kuan, 1970.

Sung-chiang fu-chih 松江府志. Po Jun 薄潤, ed. 1884 edition.

Sung hui-yao chi-kao 宋會要輯搞. Hsü Sung 徐松 (1781–1848), ed. Taipei: Hsin-wen-feng ch'u-pan-she, 1962.

Sung Lien 宋濂 (1310–1381). *Sung hsüeh-shih wen-chi* 宋學士文集. *Ts'ung-shu chi-ch'eng* edition.

———. *Sung Wen-hsien-kung ch'üan-chi* 宋文憲公全集. *Ssu-pu pei-yao* 四部備要 edition. Taipei: Chung-hua shu-chü, 1965.

Sung shih 宋史. T'o T'o 脫脫 (1313–1355), et. al., eds. Peking: Chung-hua shu-chü, 1977.

Sung ta chao-ling chi 宋大詔令集. Peking: Chung-hua shu-chü, 1962.

Ta-Ming hui-tien 大明會典 (1587). Taipei: Tung-nan shu-pao-she, 1964.

Ta-Ming yi-t'ung chih 大明一統志. Li Hsien 李賢 (1408–1467), et. al., ed. and comp. In *Wen-yüan Ko Ssu-k'u ch'üan-shu,* volumes 472–473.

Ta-ting fu-chih 大定府志. Huang Chai-chung 黃宅中, ed. 1849 edition.

T'ai-chou fu-chih 台州府志. Yü Ch'ang-lin 喻長霖, K'o Hua-wei 柯華威, et. al., eds. 1926 edition.

T'ai-p'ing kuang-chi 太平廣記. 5 volumes. Li Fang 李昉 (925–996), et. al., eds. Peking: Jen-min wen-hsüeh ch'u-pan-she, 1959.

T'ai-shang chu-kuo chiu-min tsung-chen pi-yao 太上助國救民總眞祕要. Yüan Miao-tsung 元妙宗 (fl. 1086–1116). *TT* 986–987; *CT* 1227.

T'ai-shang san-wu pang chiu chiao Wu-ti tuan-wen yi 太上三五榜救醮五帝斷瘟儀. *TT* 566; *CT* 809.

T'ai-shang shuo hsüan-t'ien ta-sheng Chen-wu pen-chuan shen-chou miao-ching 太上說玄天大聖真武本傳神咒妙經. *TT* 530–531; *CT* 754.

T'ai-shang tung-yüan Pei-ti T'ien-p'eng hu-ming hsiao-tsai shen-chou ching 太上洞淵北帝天蓬護命消災神咒經. *TT* 29; *CT* 53.

Taishō shinshū daizōkyō 大正新修大藏經. Takakusu Junjirō 高南順次郎 and Watanabe Kaikyoku 渡邊海旭, eds. 85 volumes. Tokyo: Taishō issaikyō kankokai, 1922–1935.

T'ai-wan hsien-chih 台灣縣志. Wang Li 王禮, ed. 1720 edition.

Tai Yü-sheng 戴玉生. *Ou-chiang chu-chih tz'u* 甌江竹枝詞.

T'ang-ch'i chih-lüeh 唐棲志略 (1769). Ho Ch'i 何琪. In *WLCKTP*, volume 1.

TFHY. 268 *chüan*. *TT* 884–941; *CT* 1220.

(Cheng-t'ung) Tao-tsang 正統道藏 (1444–1445). Including the *Wan-li Hsü Tao-tsang* 萬曆續正統道藏 (1607). 1120 threadbare volumes. Shanghai: Shang-wu yin-shu-kuan, 1923-1926.

        Reprinted in 60 hardbound volumes with *Cheng-t'ung Tao-tsang mu-lu so-yin* 正統道藏目錄索引. Taipei: Yi-wen yin-shu-kuan, 1977.

        Reprinted in 60 hardbound volumes. Taipei: Hsin-wen-feng ch'u-pan-she, 1977.

Tao-yao ling-ch'i shen-kuei p'in-ching 道要靈祇神鬼品經. *TT* 875; *CT* 1201.

TCHC. Hou Yüan-fei 侯元棐, ed. 1673 editon.

Te-ch'ing hsien hsin-chih 德清縣新志. Wu Hao-kao 吳鶚皋 and Wang Jen-hua 王任化, eds. 1923 edition.

Te-ch'ing hsien hsü-chih 德清縣續志. Chou Shao-lien 周紹濂, ed. 1808 edition.

Teng Chih-mo 鄧志謨 (fl. 1566–1618). *Wu-tai Sa chen-jen te-tao chou-tsao chi* 五代薩真人得道咒棄記 (1603). In *Ku-pen hsiao-shuo ts'ung-k'an*, series 10, volume 5.

Ti-ch'i fa 地祇法. In *TFHY*, *chüan* 253.

Ti-ch'i Wen Yüan-shuai ta-fa 地祇溫元帥大法. In *TFHY*, *chüan* 256.

Tien-shih chai hua-pao 點石齋畫報. Shanghai: Shen-pao kuan, 1884.

T'ien Yi-heng 田藝蘅 (1524–1574). *Liu-ch'ing jih-cha* 留青日札. Shanghai: Ku-chi ch'u-pan-she, 1985.

Ting Ping 丁丙 (1832–1899). *Hsü Tung-ho chao-ko* 續東河櫂歌 (1894). In *WLCKTP*, volume 4.

———. *Pei-kuo shih-chang* 北郭詩帳. In *WLCKTP*, volume 12.

Tsang-wai tao-shu 藏外道書. Cheng-tu: Pa-shu shu-she, 1992.

Tso chuan 左傳. Trans. James Legge. In *The Chinese Classics*. Volume 5.

Tz'u yüan 辭源. Shanghai: Shang-wu yin-shu-kuan, 1947.

Tu-ch'eng chi-sheng 都城記盛. Nai Te-weng 耐德翁. In *Tung-ching meng-hua lu, wai ssu-chung*.

T'ung-an hsien-chih 同安縣志. Lin Tseng-hsüeh 林增學, ed. 1929 edition.

Tung-ching meng-hua lu, wai ssu-chung 東京夢華錄, 外四種. Shanghai: Ku-tien wen-hsüeh ch'u-pan-she, 1956.

THHC. Yen Ch'en 嚴辰, comp. 1887 edition.

Tung-yüan cheng-ch'ao ch'üan-chi 洞淵正朝全集. In *Kuang-ch'eng yi-chih. Tsang-wai tao-shu*. Volume 15, pp. 309–314.

Tung-yüeh Wen T'ai-pao k'ao-chao pi-fa 東嶽溫太保考召祕法. In *TFHY, chüan* 254.

(Tseng-pu) Wan-pao ch'üan-shu 增補萬寶全書 (1823).

Wang Ch'ung 王充 (29–109). *Lun Heng* 論衡. Trans. Albert Forke. New York: Paragon Book Gallery, 1962.

Wang Po 王柏 (1197–1274). *Lu-chai chi* 魯齋集. *Ts'ung-shu chi-ch'eng* edition.

Wen-chou ching-chi chih 溫州經籍志. Sun Yi-jang 孫詒讓, ed. Hangchow: Che-chiang sheng-li t'u-shu-kuan, 1921.

WCFSC. Wu Chao-tsu 吳昭祖, Chang Ming-ch'e 張明車, and Yeh Chih-p'ing 葉志平, eds. Unpublished manuscript. No date.

WCFC. Chang Fu-ching 張孚敬, ed. 1537 edition.

WCFC. T'ang Jih-chao 湯日昭, ed. 1605 edition.

WCFC. Li Wan 李琬, ed. 1756 edition.

Wen Chung-ching Wang chuan-lüeh 溫忠鏡王傳略 (1879). Huang T'i-fang 黃體方, ed. and comp.

Wu-ch'ing chen-chih 烏青鎮志. Tung Shih-ning 董世寧, ed. 1760 edition.

Wu Lai 吳萊 (1297–1340). *Yüan-ying chi* 淵穎集. *Ts'ung-shu chi-ch'eng* edition.

WLCKTP (1877–1900). 12 volumes. Ting Ping, ed. and comp. Taipei: T'ai-lien kuo-feng ch'u-pan-she and Hua-wen shu-chü, 1967.

Wu-lin chiu-shih 武林舊事 (ca. 1280–1290). In *Tung-ching meng-hua lu, wai ssu-chung*.

(Tseng-pu) Wu-lin chiu-shih 增補武林舊事. Chu Yen-huan 朱延煥 (Ming). In *Wen-yüan Ko Ssu-k'u ch'üan-shu*, volume 590.

WLFHC. 6 volumes. Hangchow: Che-chiang jen-min ch'u-pan-she, 1987.

WLFSC (1863). Wang T'ung 王同. In *Hang-chou shih-ti ts'ung-shu*. Volumes 14–15.

Wu-lin hsin-nien tsa-yung 武林新年雜詠 (1775). Shu Shao-yen 舒紹言, et. al., comp. In *WLCKTP*, volume 4.

Wu-lin tsa-shih shih 武林雜事詩 (1879). Ting Li-ch'eng 丁立誠. In *WLCKTP*, volume 12.

Wu-lin ts'ao 武林草. Chao Shih-lin 趙士麟 (1629–1699). In *WLCKTP*, volume 4.

Wu Yu-ju hua-pao 吳友如畫寶. Shanghai: Pi-yüan hui-she, 1909.

Yang Ssu-ch'ang 楊嗣昌 (1588–1641). *Wu-ling ching-tu lüeh* 武陵競渡略 ("The Dragon Boat Race in Wu-ling, Hunan"). Trans. Chao Wei-pang. *Folklore Studies* 2 (1943): 1–18.

Yeh Sheng 葉盛 (1420–1474). *Shui-tung jih-chi* 水東日記. Peking: Chung-hua shu-chü, 1980.

Yeh Shih 葉適 (1150–1223). *Shui-hsin chi* 水心集. In *Yeh Shih chi* 葉適集. Peking: Chung-hua shu-chü, 1961.

Yü-hsia chi 玉匣記 (1684). Shanghai: Chin-chang t'u-shu-chü, n.d.

Yü-yao hsien-chih 餘姚縣志. Chou Ping-lin 周丙麟, ed. 1899 edition.

Yü Yen 俞炎 (1258–1314). *Shu-chai yeh-hua* 書齋夜話. In *Hsü-chü chen-pen ts'ung-shu* 續聚珍本叢書. Yen Yi-p'ing, ed. Volume 37. Taipei: Yi-wen yin-shu-kuan, 1967.

Yü Yüeh 俞樾 (1821–1906). *Yu-t'ai hsien-kuan pi-chi* 右臺仙館筆記 (1888). Taipei: Kuang-wen shu-chü, 1967.

Yüan Ming Ch'ing san-tai chin-hui hsiao-shuo hsi-chü shih-liao 元明清三代禁毀小說戲劇史料. Wang Li-ch'i 王利器, comp. Peking: Tso-chia ch'u-pan-she, 1958.

Yüeh-ch'ing hsien-chih 樂清縣志. Hsü Hua-min 徐化民, ed. 1685 edition.

Yüeh-ch'ing hsien-chih. Li Teng-yün 李登雲 and Ch'ien Pao-jung 錢寶鎔, eds. 1901 edition.

YCHC. Ch'eng Wen-chu 程文箸, ed. 1566 edition.

YCHC. Wang Kuo-t'ai 王國泰 and Cheng T'ing-chün 鄭廷俊, eds. 1682 edition.

YCHC. Ts'ui Hsi 崔錫, ed. 1761 edition.

YCHC. Chang Pao-lin 張寶林, ed. 1882 edition.

YCWCL (1833). Sun T'ung-yüan 孫同元. Hangchow: Ku-chi shu-tien, 1963.

II. Secondary Scholarship

Ahern, Emily Martin. *Chinese Ritual and Politics*. Cambridge: Cambridge University Press, 1981.

Aijmer, Goran. *The Dragon Boat Festival in the Hunan and Hupeh Plains: A Study in the Ceremonialism of Transplantation of Rice*. Stockholm: Ethnographical Museum of Sweden, 1964.

Akizuki Kanei 秋月觀嘆. *Dōkyō to shūkyō bunka* 道教と宗教文化 . Tokyo: Hirakawa, 1987.

Amano Genosuke 天野元之肋. *Chūgoku nōgyō keizairon* 中國農業經濟論. Tokyo: Ryūkai shosha, 1978.

Anderson, Poul. "The Practice of *Bugang*: Historical Introduction." *CEA* 5 (1989–1990): 15–54.

Atwell, William S. "Some Observations of the '17th Century Crisis' in Japan and China." *JAS* 45 (1986): 223–244.

———. "Ming Observers of Ming Decline: Some Chinese Views of the 'Seventeenth-century Crisis' in Comparative Perspective." *Journal of the Royal Asiatic Society* (1988): 316–348.

Bakhtin, Mikhail. *Rabelais and his World*. Trans. Hélène Iswolsky. Bloomington: Inidana University Press, 1984 (1965).

Baldrian-Hussein, Farzeen. "Lü Tung-pin in Northern Sung Literature." *CEA* 2 (1986): 133–169.

Baptandier-Berthier, Brigitte. *La Dame du Bord de l'Eau*. Nanterre, Paris: Société d'Ethnologie, 1988.

———. "The Kaiguan 開關 Ritual and the Construction of the Child's Identity." In *Proceedings of the International Conference on Popular Beliefs and Chinese Culture*. Volume II, pp. 523–586.

Bauman, Richard and Charles L. Briggs. "Poetics and Performance as Critical Perspectives on Language and Social Life." *American Review of Anthropology* 19 (1990): 59–88.

Bell, Catherine. "Religion and Chinese Culture: Toward an Assessment of 'Popular Religion'." *HR* 29 (1989): 35–57.

Benedict, Carol. "Bubonic Plague in Nineteenth Century China." *Modern China* 14.2 (April 1988): 107–155.

———. "Policing the Sick: Plague and the Origins of State Medicine in Late Imperial China." *Late Imperial China* 14.2 (Dec. 1993): 60–77.

Berling, Judith. *The Syncretic Religion of Lin Chao-en*. New York: Columbia University Press, 1980.

———. "Religion and Popular Culture: The Management of Moral Capital in *The Romance of the Three Teachings*." In Johnson, et. al., eds., *Popular Culture in Late Imperial China*, pp. 188–218.

———. "Channels of Connection in Southern Sung Religion: The Case of Pai Yü-ch'an 白玉蟾." In Ebrey and Gregory, eds., *Religion and Society in T'ang and Sung China*, pp. 307–333.

Bernhardt, Kathryn. *Rents, Taxes and Peasant Resistance. The Lower Yangtze Region, 1840–1950*. Stanford: Stanford University Press, 1992.

Bernhardt, Kathryn & Philip C. C. Huang, eds., *Civil Law in Qing and Republican China*. Stanford: Stanford University Press, 1994.

Bielenstein, Hans. "An Interpretation of Portents in the Ts'ien-Han-shu." *Bulletin of the Museum of Far Eastern Antiquities* 22 (1950): 127–143.

Birnbaum, Raoul. *Studies on the Mysteries of Manjusri: A Group of East Asian Mandalas and their Traditional Symbolism*. Society for the Study of Chinese Religions Monograph 2, 1983.

———. *Buddhism and Healing*. Boston and Shaftesbury: Shambhala Publications, Inc., 1990.

Bodde, Derk. *Festivals in Classical China*. Princeton: Princeton University Press, 1975.

Boltz, Judith. *A Survey of Taoist Literature: Tenth to Seventeenth Centuries*. Institute of East Asian Studies, Center for Chinese Studies, Chinese Research Monograph 32. Berkeley: University of California Press, 1987.

———. "Not by the Seal of Office Alone: New Weapons in the Battle with the Supernatural." In Ebrey and Gregory, eds., *Religion and Society in T'ang and Sung China*, pp. 241–305.

Bourdieu, Pierre. *Outline of a Theory in Practice*. Trans. R. Nice. Cambridge: Cambridge University Press, 1977.

Bredon, Juliet and Igor Mitrophanow. *The Moon Year*. Shanghai: Kelly and Walsh, Ltd., 1927.

Brokaw, Cynthia. *The Ledgers of Merit and Demerit*. Princeton: Princeton University Press, 1991.

Brook, Timothy. "Guides for Vexed Travellers: Route Books in the Ming and Ch'ing." *CSWT* 4.5 (June 1981): 32–77.

———. "Guides for Vexed Travellers: A Supplement." *CSWT* 4.6 (Dec. 1981): 130–140.

———. "Guides for Vexed Travellers: Second Supplement." *CSWT* 4.8 (Dec. 1982): 96–109.

———. "Family Continuity and Cultural Hegemony: The Gentry of Ningpo, 1368–1911." In Esherick and Rankin, eds., *Chinese Local Elites*, pp. 27–50.

———. *Praying for Power: Buddhism and the Formation of Gentry Society in Late-Ming China*. Cambridge, Mass: Harvard University Press, 1993.

Brown, Peter. *The Cult of the Saints. Its Rise and Function in Latin Christianity*. Chicago: University of Chicago Press, 1981.

Burke, Peter. *Popular Culture in Early Modern Europe*. Aldershot: Wildwood House, Ltd., 1988.

Burkhardt, Valentine R. *Chinese Creeds and Customs*. 3 volumes. Hong Kong: South China Morning Post, Ltd., 1958.

Cedzich, Ursula-Angelika. "Wu-t'ung: Zur bewegten Beschichte eines Kultes." In Gert Naundorf, et al., eds, *Religion und Philosophie in Ostasien. Festschrift für Hans Steininger zum 65. Geburtstag*. Würzburg: Königshausen and Neumann, 1985, pp. 33–60.

Chan, Leo Hak-Tung. "Narrative as Argument: The *Yuewei caotang biji* 閱微草堂筆記 and the Late Eighteenth-Century Elite Discourse on the Supernatural." *HJAS* 53.1 (June 1993): 25–62.

Chang Chi-yü 張繼禹. *T'ien-shih Tao shih-lüeh* 天師道史略. Peking: Hua-wen ch'u-pan-she, 1990.

Chang Ch'i-yün 張其昀. "Lun Ning-po chien-she sheng-hui chih hsi-wang" 論寧波建設省會之希望.. *Shih-ti hsüeh-pao* 史地學報 3.7 (May 1925): 1–17.

Chang Chia-chu 張家駒. *Liang-Sung ching-chi chung-hsin chih nan-yi* 兩宋經濟重心之南移 . Taipei: Po-shu ch'u-pan-she, 1985.

Chang Hsiang-hua 張翔華. "Pai-Yüeh min-tsu yü tuan-wu hsi-su" 百越民族與端午習俗. *Tung-nan wen-hua* 東南文化 5 (1991): 93–94.

Chang Hsün 張珣. *Chi-ping yü wen-hua* 疾病與文化 Taipei: Tao-hsiang ch'u-pan-she, 1989.

Chang Kuang-yü 張光宇. "Wu-Min fang-yen kuan-hsi shih-lun" 吳閩方言關係試論 . *Chung-kuo yü-wen* 中國語文 3 (1993): 161–170.

Chang, K.C. (Chang Kwang-chih). "Chinese Prehistory in Pacific Perspective." *Harvard Journal of Oriental Studies* 22 (1959): 100–149.

———. *The Archaeology of Ancient China*. 4th edition. New Haven and London: Yale University Press, 1983.

Chang Lun-tu 張論篤 and Huang Ching-chung 黃靖中. "Ching-tu, lung-chou yü lung-chou ching-tu chih yen-chiu" 競渡、龍舟與龍舟競渡. In *Chung-kuo min-chien wen-hua* 中國民間文化. Shanghai: Hsüeh-lin ch'u-pan-she, 1991. Volume 2, pp. 125–142.

Chang Tzu-ch'en 張紫晨. *Chung-kuo wu-shu* 中國巫術. Shanghai: San-lien shu-chü, 1990.

Chang Yung-yao 張永堯, et al., "Chia-hsing mi-shih hsi-su tiao-ch'a 嘉興米市習俗調查." In *Chung-kuo min-chien wen-hua*. Shanghai: Hsüeh-lin ch'u-pan-she, 1994. Volume 14, pp. 48–65.

Chao Yüan-jen 趙元任. *Hsien-tai Wu-yü yen-chiu* 現代吳與研究. Peking: K'o-hsüeh ch'u-pan-she. 1956.

Chavannes, Edouard. *Le T'ai Chan: Essaie de Monographie d'un Culte Chinois*. Paris: Ernest Leroux, 1910.

Chavannes, Edouard and Paul Pelliot. "Un Traité Manichéen Retrouvé en Chine." *Journal Asiatique*, Series 11, Volume 1 (March-April 1913): 99–391.

Che-chiang min-su yen-chiu 浙江民俗研究. Hangchow: Che-chiang jen-min ch'u-pan-she, 1992.

Che-chiang wen-hua shih 浙江文化史. Hangchow: Che-chiang jen-min ch'u-pan-she, 1992.

Ch'en Cheng-hsiang 陳正祥. *Chung-kuo wen-hua ti-li* 中國文化地理. Taipei: Mu-to ch'u-pan-she, 1984.

Ch'en Chien-ts'ai 陳建才, ed. *Pa-min chang-ku ta-ch'üan* 八閩掌故大全. Foochow: Fu-chien chiao-yü ch'u-pan-she, 1994.

Ch'en Ch'in-chien 陳勤建. "Pai-she hsing-hsiang chung-hsin chieh-kou te min-su yüan-yüan chi ch'i ch'ien-tsai tung-li" 白蛇形象中心結構的民俗淵源及其潛在動力. In *Pai-she chuan lun-wen chi* 白蛇傳論文集. Hangchow: Ku-chi ch'u-pan-she, 1986.

Ch'en Hsiang-ch'un. "Examples of Charms Against Epidemics With Short Explanations." *Folklore Studies* 1 (1942): 37–54.

Ch'en Hsüeh-wen 陳學文. *Ming-Ch'ing she-hui ching-chi shih yen-chiu* 明清社會經濟史研究. Taipei: Tao-ho ch'u-pan-she 1991.

Ch'en Keng 陳耕 and Wu An-hui 吳安輝, eds. *Hsia-men min-su* 廈門民俗. Hsia-men: Lu-chiang ch'u-pan-she, 1993.

Ch'en Ping 陳兵. "Yüan-tai Chiang-nan Tao-chiao" 元代江南道教. *Shih-chieh tsung-chiao yen-chiu* 世界宗教研究 2 (1986): 65–80.

Ch'en Sheng-k'un 陳勝崑. *Chung-kuo chi-ping shih* 中國疾病史. Taipei: Tzu-jan k'o-hsüeh ch'u-pan-she, 1981.

———. *Ch'ih-pi chih chan yü ch'uan-jan-ping: Lun Chung-kuo li-shih shang te chi-ping* 赤壁之戰與傳染病:論中國歷史上的疾病. Taipei Ming-wen shu-chü, 1983.

Ch'en Yao-hung 陳躍紅. et al. *Chung-kuo No wen-hua* 中國儺文化. Peking: Hsin-hua ch'u-pan-she, 1991.

Ch'en Yüan 陳垣 (1880–1971). *Nan-Sung ch'u Ho-peh hsin Tao-chiao k'ao* 南宋初河北新道教考. Peking: Chung-hua shu-chu, 1941.

Cheng Chih-ming 鄭志明. "Wang-yeh ch'uan-shuo" (shang) 王爺傳說(上). *Min-su ch'ü-yi* 民俗曲藝 52 (March 1988): 17–37.

———. "Wang-yeh ch'uan-shuo" (hsia) 王爺傳說(下). *Min-su ch'ü-yi* 53 (June 1988): 101–118.

Cheu Hock Tong. *The Nine Emperor Gods. A Study of Chinese Spirit-Medium Cults.* Singapore: Times Books International, 1988.

Chiang Chao-ch'eng 蔣兆成. "Ming-Ch'ing shih-ch'i Hang-Chia-Hu ti-ch'ü hsiang-chen ching-chi shih-t'an" 明清時期杭嘉湖地區鄉鎮經濟試探 In *Chung-kuo she-hui ching-chi shih yen-chiu* 中國社會經濟史研究 16 (Jan. 1986): 62–73.

———. "Lun Ming-Ch'ing Hang-Chia-Hu ti-ch'ü ts'an-sang ssu-chih-yeh te chung-yao ti-wei" 論明清杭嘉湖地區蠶桑絲絲業的重要地位. *HCTHHP* 18.4 (Dec. 1988): 11–25.

Chiang Hsiao-ch'in 將嘯琴. *Ta No k'ao* 大儺考. Taipei: Lan-t'ing shu-tien, 1988.

Chiang Pin 姜彬. "Chiang-nan ti-ch'ü she ch'uan-shuo chung ku-tai t'u-t'eng ch'ung-pai te nei-han" 江南地區蛇傳說中古代圖騰崇拜的內涵. In *Chung-kuo min-chien wen-hua.* Shanghai: Hsüeh-lin ch'u-pan-she, 1992. Volume 7, pp. 145–160.

———, *Wu-Yüeh min-chien hsin-yang min-su* 吳越民間信仰民俗. Shanghai: Shang-hai wen-yi ch'u-pan-she, 1992.

Chiang Yi-min 江一民. "Kuan-yü shen-wu 'T'iao Wu-ch'ang' ch'u-k'ao" 關於神舞跳五猖初考. *Wu-tao yi-shu* 舞蹈藝術 13 (1985): 142–146.

Ch'ien Mu 錢穆. *Kuo-shih ta-kang* 國史大綱. Taipei: Kuo-li pien-yi-kuan, 1953.

Ch'iu Te-tsai 仇德哉. *T'ai-wen miao-shen chuan* 台灣廟神傳. Tou-nan: Tsung-ching hsiao-hsin-t'ung shu-chü, 1979.

Chou Chen-ch'üeh 周振鶴 and Yu Ju-chieh 游汝杰. *Fang-yen yü Chung-kuo wen-hua* 方言與中國文化. Shanghai: Shang-hai jen-min ch'u-pan-she, 1986.

Chou Hou-ts'ai 周厚才. *Wen-chou kang-shih* 溫州港史. Peking: Jen-min chiao-t'ung ch'u-pan-she, 1990.

Chou Yi-liang. "Tantrism in China." *HJAS* 8 (1945): 241–332.

Chu Chien-ming 朱建民. "Tung-yüeh miao 'Fa-fu' k'o-yi ch'eng-shih yü kao-kung fa-shih tsai pien-shen fa-fu chung te kung-neng" 東嶽廟法符科儀程式與高功法師在變神法符中的功能. *Min-su ch'ü-yi* 91 (Sept. 1994): 465–502.

Chu Te-lan 朱德蘭. Ch'ing k'ai hai-ling hou te Chung-Jih Ch'ang-ch'i mao-yi-shang yü kuo-nei yen-hai mao-yi" 清開海令後的中日長期貿易商與國內沿海貿易. In Chang Yen-hsien 張炎憲, ed. *Chung-kuo hai-yang fa-chan shih lun-wen-chi* 中國海洋發展史論文集. Nankang: Sun Yat-sen Institute of Social Science, 1988. Volume 3, pp. 369–416.

Ch'ü T'ung-tsu. *Law and Society in Traditional China*. Paris: Moulon, 1961.

———. *Local Government in China Under the Ch'ing*. Cambridge, Mass.: Harvard University Press, 1962.

Ch'u Yen-pin 曲顏斌. *Chung-kuo ch'i-kai shih* 中國乞丐史. Shanghai: Wen-yi ch'u-pan-she, 1990.

Ch'üan Han-sheng 全漢昇. *Chung-kuo hang-hui chih-tu shih* 中國行會制度史. Shanghai: Hsin sheng-ming ch'u-pan-she, 1934.

Chüng Hung-yi 莊宏誼. *Ming-tai Tao-chiao Cheng-yi p'ai* 明代道教正一派. Taipei: Hsüeh-sheng shu-chü 1986.

Chuang Ying-chang 莊英章 and P'an Ying-hai 潘英海, eds. *T'ai-wan yü Fu-chien she-hui wen-hua yen-chiu lun-wen-chi* 台灣與福建社會文化研究論文集. Nankang: Institute of Ethnology, 1994.

Chung Hua-ts'ao 鍾華操. *T'ai-wan ti-ch'ü shen-ming te yu-lai* 臺灣地區神明的由來. Taichung: T'ai-wen sheng wen-hsien wei-yüan-hui, 1987.

Chung-kuo lung-chou wen-hua 中國龍舟文化. Hunan: San-huan ch'u-pan-she, 1991.

Chung Yü-lung 鍾毓龍 (1880–1970). *Shuo Hang-chou* 說杭州. Hangchow: Che-chiang jen-min ch'u-pan-she, 1983.

Cloud, Frederick D. *Hangchow: The "City of Heaven"*. Shanghai: Presbyterian Mission Press, 1906.

Cohen, Alvin P. "Fiscal Remarks on Some Folk Religion Temples in Taiwan." *Monumenta Serica* 32 (1976): 85–158.

———. "Coercing the Rain Deities in Ancient China." *HR* 17.3-4 (Feb.–May 1978): 244–265.

Connor, W.R. "Tribes, Festivals and Processions: Civic Ceremonial and Political Manipulation in Archaic Greece." *Journal of Hellenic Studies* CVII (1987): 40–50.

Coser, Lewis A. *The Functions of Social Conflict*. Glencoe, Ill.: The Free Press, 1956.

Day, Clarence. *Chinese Peasant Cults: Being a Study of Chinese Paper Gods*. Shanghai: Kelly and Walsh, Ltd., 1940.

Dean, Kenneth. "Field Notes on Two Taoist *Jiao* Observed in Zhang zhou in December, 1985." *CEA* 2 (1986): 191–209.

———. "Funerals in Fujian." *CEA* 4 (1988): 19–78.

——. "Manuscripts from Fujian." *CEA* 4 (1988): 217–226.

——. *Taoist Ritual and Popular Cults of Southeast China*. Princeton: Princeton University Press, 1993.

deBary, Wm. Theodore, ed. *Self and Society in Ming Thought*. New York: Columbia University Press, 1970.

Demieville, Paul. "La Situation Religieus en Chine au Temps de Marco Polo." *Oriente Poliana* (1957): 193–234.

——. *Buddhism and Healing*. Trans. Mark Tatz. Lanham, Md.: University Press of America, 1985.

Deschamps, Christian. "Deux Fêtes de Village en Corée." *CEA* 2 (1986): 172–181.

Dewoskin, Kenneth J. *Doctors, Diviners and Magicians of Ancient China: Biographies of "Fang-shih"*. New York: Columbia University Press, 1983.

Diamond, Norma. *K'un Shen: A Taiwan Village*. New York: Holt, Rinehart and Winston, 1969.

Dodds, E.R. *The Greeks and the Irrational*. Berkeley: University of California Press, 1955.

Doolittle, The Rev. Justus. *Social Life of the Chinese*. 2 volumes. Singapore: Graham Brash (Pte.) Ltd. reprint of 1865-1876 edition, 1986.

Doré, Henri. *Researches into Chinese Superstitions*. 10 volumes. Trans. M. Kennelly. Shanghai: T'usewei Printing Press, 1914–1931.

Douglas, Mary. *Purity and Danger*. London: Routledge and Kegan Paul, 1966.

Duara, Prasenjit. "Superscibing Symbols: The Myth of Guandi, Chinese God of War." *JAS* 47.4 (Nov. 1988): 778–795.

——. *Culture, Power, and the State: Rural North China, 1900–1942*. Stanford: Stanford University Press, 1988.

——. "Knowledge and Power in the Discourse of Modernity: The Campaigns against Popular Religion in Early Twentieth-Century China." *JAS* 50.1 (Feb. 1991): 67–83.

DuBose, The Rev. Hampden C. *The Dragon, Image, and Demon*. New York: A.C. Armstrong and Son, 1887.

Dubs, Homer. "An Ancient Chinese Mystery Cult." *Harvard Theological Review* 35 (Oct. 1942): 221–239.

Dudbridge, Glen. *The Legend of Miao-shan*. Oxford Oriental Monographs, Number 1. London: Ithaca Press, 1978.

——. "Yü-ch'ih Chiung 尉遲迥 at An-yang: An Eighth-Century Cult and Its Myths." *Asia Major*, Third Series, Volume III, Part 1 (1990): 27–49.

Duke, Michael S. *Lu You*. Boston: G.K. Hall and Company, 1977.

Duncan, Marion H. *Customs and Superstitions of Tibetans*. London: The Mitre Press, 1964.

Dunstan, Helen. "The Late Ming Epidemics: A Preliminary Survey." *CSWT*, 3.3 (Nov., 1975), 1–59.

Eberhard, Wolfram. "Temple-Building Activities in Medieval and Modern China: An Experimental Study." *Monumenta Serica* 23 (1964): 264–318.

———. *Erzählungsgut aus Südost-China*. Berlin: Walter de Gruyter, 1966.

———. *Guilt and Sin in Traditional China*. Berkeley: University of California Press, 1967.

———. *The Local Cultures of South and East China*. Leiden: E.J. Brill, 1968.

Ebrey, Patricia Buckley and Peter N. Gregory. "The Religious and Historical Landscape." In Ebrey and Gregory, eds., *Religion and Society in T'ang and Sung China*. Honolulu: University of Hawaii Press, 1993, pp. 1–44.

Eco, Umberto. "The Frames of Cosmic 'Freedom'." In Thomas A. Sebeok, ed., *Carnival!* In *Approaches to Semiotics*, number 64 (Berlin: Mouton Publishers, 1964), pp. 1–9.

Eliott, A.J.A. *Chinese Spirit Medium Cults in Singapore*. London: Royal Anthropological Institute, 1955.

Elvin, Mark. *The Pattern of the Chinese Past*. Stanford: Stanford University Press, 1973.

———. "Market Towns and Waterways: The County of Shanghai from 1840 to 1910." In Skinner, ed., *The City in Late Imperial China*, pp. 441–473.

Esherick, Joseph W. and Mary Backus Rankin. "Introduction." In Esherick and Rankin, *Chinese Local Elites and Patterns of Dominance*. Berkeley: University of California Press, 1990.

Fan Hsing-chün 范行准. *Chung-kuo yi-hsüeh shih-lüeh* 中國醫學史略. Peking: Chung-yi ku-chi ch'u-pan-she, 1986.

———. *Chung-kuo ping-shih hsin-yi* 中國病史新義. Peking: Chung-yi ku-chi ch'u-pan-she, 1987.

Fan Shu-chih 樊樹志. *Ming-Ch'ing Chiang-nan shih-chen t'an-wei* 明清江南市鎮探微. Shanghai: Fu-tan ta-hsüeh ch'u-pan-she, 1990.

Fei Hsiao-t'ung. *Peasant Life in China: A Field Study of Country Life in the Yangtze Valley*. London: Kegan Paul, 1939.

Feng Han-yi and John K. Shryock. "The Black Magic in China Known as *Ku*." *Journal of the American Oriental Society* 55 (1935): 1–30.

Feuchtwang, Stephan. "City Temples in Taipei Under Three Regimes." In Mark Elvin and G. William Skinner, eds., *The Chinese City Between Two Worlds*. Stanford: Stanford University Press, 1974, pp. 263–303.

———. "School Temple and City God." In Skinner, ed., *The City in Late Imperial China*, pp. 581–608.

———. *The Imperial Metaphor. Popular Religion in China*. London and New York: Routledge, 1992.

Flint, Valerie I.J. *The Rise of Magic in Early Medieval Europe*. Princeton: Princeton University Press, 1991.

Fortune, Robert (1813-1880). *A Residence Among the Chinese*. London: J. Murray, 1857.

Frazer, James G. *The Golden Bough: The Roots of Religion and Folklore*. New York: Avenal Books, 1980 reprint of 1890 edition.

Freedman, Maurice. *Chinese Lineage and Society: Fukien and Kwangtung*. London: Athlone, 1966.

———. *The Study of Chinese Society: Essays by Maurice Freedman*. G. William Skinner, ed. Stanford: Stanford University Press, 1979.

Fu Hsi-hua 傅希華. *Pai-she chuan chi* 白蛇傳集. Shanghai: Shang-hai ch'u-pan kung-ssu, 1955.

Fukui Kōjun 福井康順, Sakai Tadao 酒井忠夫 et. al., eds. *Dōkyō* 道教. 3 volumes Tokyo: Heika Shuppansha, 1983.

Gamble, Sidney. *Ting Hsien: A North China Rural Community*. Stanford: Stanford University Press, 1968.

Geertz, Clifford. *Negara: The Theatre State in Nineteenth Century Bali*. Princeton: Princeton University Press, 1980.

Gernet, Jacques. *Les Aspects Economiques du Bouddhisme dans la Société Chinoise du Ve au Xe Siècle*. Paris: École Française d'Extrême Orient, 1956.

———. *Daily Life in China on the Eve of the Mongol Invasion, 1250–1276*. Stanford: Stanford University Press, 1962.

———. *A History of Chinese Civilization*. Cambridge: Cambridge University Press, 1983.

Girard, Rene. *Violence and the Sacred*. Trans. Patrick Gregory. Baltimore and London: The Johns Hopkins University Press, 1979 (1972).

Goodrich, Anne S. *The Peking Temple of the Eastern Peak: The Tung-yüeh Miao in Peking and its Lore*. Nagoya: Monumenta Serica, 1964.

Gould-Martin, Katherine. "Medical Systems in a Taiwanese Village: Ong-ia-kong (Wang-yeh-kung 王爺公), the Plague God as Modern Physician." In Arthur Kleinman, et al., eds., *Medicine in Chinese Cultures: Comparative Studies of Health Care in Chinese and Other Societies*. Washington, DC: U.S. Dept. of HEW, 1975, pp. 115–141.

Granet, Marcel. *Danses et Légendes de la Chine Ancienne*. Paris: Presses Universitaries de France, 1926.

———. *Festivals and Songs of Ancient China*. Trans. E.D. Edwards. London: Routledge, 1932.

Grimes, Ronald L. "Ritual Studies: Two Models." *Religious Studies Review* 2 (1976): 13–25.

———. "Victor Turner's Social Drama and T.S. Eliot's Ritual Drama." *Anthropologica*, N.S. 27.1–2 (1985): 79–100.

Groot, Jan J. M. de. *The Religious System of China*. 6 volumes. Leiden: E.J. Brill, 1892–1910.

Grootaers, Willem A. "The Hagiography of the Chinese God Chen-wu." *Folklore Studies* 11 (1952): 139–181.

Habermas, Jürgen. *The Structural Transformation of the Public Sphere.* Trans. Thomas Burger with the assistance of Frederick Lawrence. Cambridge, Mass: Harvard University Press, 1989.

Handlin-Smith, Joanna F. "Benevolent Societies: The Reshaping of Charity During the Late Ming and Early Ch'ing." *JAS* 46.2 (June 1987): 309–338.

Hanks, W.F. "Text and Textuality." *American Review of Anthropology* 18 (1989): 95–127.

Hansen, Valerie. *Changing Gods in Medieval China, 1127–1276.* Princeton: Princeton University Press, 1990.

———. "Gods on Walls: A Case of Indian Influence on Chinese Lay Religion?" In Ebrey and Gregory, eds., *Religion and Society in T'ang and Sung China,* pp. 75–113.

Harrell, C. Stevan. "When a Ghost Becomes a God." In Wolf, ed., *Religion and Ritual,* pp. 193–206.

Harrison, Simon. "Ritual as Intellectual Property." *Man* N.S. (1992): 225–243.

Hartwell, Robert. "Demographic, Politcal, and Social Transformations of China." *HJAS* 42 (1982): 365–442.

Hayes, James. *The Rural Communities of Hong Kong: Studies and Themes.* New York: Oxford University Press, 1983.

Hertz, Robert. "St. Besse: a Study of an Alpine Cult." Trans. by Stephen Wilson. In Wilson, ed., *Saints and their Cults.* Cambridge: Cambridge University Press, 1983, pp. 55–100.

Ho Ping-ti. "The Geographic Distribution of *hui-kuan* (Landsmannschaften) in the Central and Upper Yangtze Provinces — with Special Reference to Interregional Migrations." *Tsing Hua Journal of Chinese Studies,* New Series V, Number 2 (Dec., 1966): 120–152.

———. *Chung-kuo hui-kuan shih-lun* 中國會館史論. Taipei: Hsüeh-sheng shu-chü, 1966.

Hodous, Lewis. *Folkways in China.* London: A. Probsthain, 1929.

Hopkins, Donald. R. *Princes and Peasants. Smallpox in History.* Chicago and London: University of Chicago Press, 1983.

Hsia Chih-ch'ien 夏之乾. *Shen-p'an* 神判. Shanghai: San-lien shu-tien, 1990.

Hsia T'ing-yü 夏廷棫. "Kuan-yü Hang-chou Tung-yüeh Miao" 關於杭州東嶽廟. *Chung-shan ta-hsüeh min-su chou-k'an* 中山大學民俗週刊 41 and 42 (1929): 77–78.

Hsiao Fan 蕭璠. *Ch'un-ch'iu chih Liang-han shih-ch'i Chung-kuo hsiang nan-fang te fa-chan* 春秋至兩漢時期中國向南方的發展 . Taipei: Kuo-li T'ai-wan ta-hsüeh wen-hsüeh yüan, 1973.

Hsiao Kung-ch'üan. *Rural China: Imperial Control in the Nineteenth Century.* Seattle: Unversity of Washington Press, 1960.

Hsiao Ping 蕭兵. *No Cha chih feng. Ch'ang-chiang liu-yü tsung-chiao hsi-chü wen-hua* 儺蜡之風:長江流域宗教戲劇文化. Nanking: Chiang-su jen-min ch'u-pan-she, 1992.

Hsiao Teng-fu 蕭登福. *Tao-chiao yü mi-tsung* 道教與密宗: Taipei: Hsin-wen-feng ch'u-pan-she, 1993.

Hsü Ch'ing-hsiang 徐清祥. *Hang-chou wang-shih t'an.* 杭州往事談. Peking: Hsin-hua ch'u-pan-she, 1993.

Hsü Ch'un-lei 徐春雷. "T'ung-hsiang shen-ko kai-shu" 桐鄉神歌概述. In *Chung-kuo min-chien shen-hua.* Volume 14, pp. 189–208.

Hsü, Francis L.K. *Exorcising the Trouble-makers: Magic, Science, and Culture.* Westport, Conn.: Greenwood Press, 1983.

Hsü Hsiao-wang 徐曉望. *Fu-chien min-chien hsin-yang yüan-liu* 福建民間信仰源流. Foochow: Fu-chien chiao-yü ch'u-pan-she, 1993.

Hsü Hung-t'u 徐宏圖. "Che-chiang sheng Tung-yang shih Han-jen sang-tsang yi-shih chi yi-shih chü tiao-ch'a" 浙江省東陽市漢人喪葬儀式劇調查. *Min-su ch'ü-yi* 84 (July 1993), 197–224.

———. "Jih fan chiu-lou, yeh yen Meng-chiang — Shao-hsing Meng-hiang hsi ch'u-t'an" 日翻九樓，夜演孟姜 — 紹興孟姜戲初探. *Min-su ch'ü-yi* 92 (Nov. 1994): 781-818.

———. "No-hsi te ch'i-yüan, liu-hsiang chi ch'i tsai Che-chiang te yi-tsung" 儺戲的起源、流向及其在浙江的遺蹤" In *Chung-kuo min-chien wen-hua.* Shanghai: Hsüeh-lin ch'u-pan-she, 1994. Volume 13, pp. 165-166.

Hsü Ying-p'u 徐瑛璞. *Liang-che shih-shih ts'ung-k'ao* 兩浙史事叢考. Hangchow: Che-chiang ku-chi ch'u-pan-she, 1988.

Hu P'u-an 胡樸安, ed. *Chung-hua ch'üan-kuo feng-su chih* 中華全國風俗志. Cheng-chou: Chung-chou ku-chi ch'u-pan-she reprint of 1923 edition, 1990.

Huang Chan-yüeh 黃展岳. *Chung-kuo ku-tai te jen-sheng yü jen-hsün* 中國古代的人牲與人殉. Peking: Wen-wu ch'u-pan-she, 1990.

Huang, Philip C.C. *The Peasant Economy and Social Change in North China.* Stanford: Stanford University Press, 1985.

———. "The Paradigmatic Crisis in Chinese Studies: Paradoxes in Social and Economic History." *Modern China* 17.3 (July 1991): 299–341.

———. "'Public Sphere'/'Civil Society' in China? The Third Realm Between State and Society." *Modern China* 19.2 (April 1993): 216–240.

Huang Shih 黃石. *Tuan-wu li-su shih* 端午禮俗史. Taipei: Ting-wen shu-chü, 1979.

Huang Wen-po 黃文博. *T'ai-wan min-chien hsin-yang chien-wen lu* 台灣民間信仰見聞錄. Hsin-ying: T'ai-nan hsien-li wen-hua chung-hsin, 1988.

Huang Yu-hsing 黃有興. *P'eng-hu te min-chien hsin-yang* 澎湖的民間信仰. Taipei: T'ai-yüan ch'u-pan-she, 1992.

Hubert, Henri and Marcel Mauss. *Sacrifice*. Trans. H.D. Walls. Chicago: University of Chicago Press, 1964 (1899).

Hymes, Robert. *Statesmen and Gentlemen: The Elite of Fu-chou, Chiang-hsi, in Northern and Southern Sung*. Cambridge: Cambridge University Press, 1986.

———. "Not Quite Gentlemen? Doctors in Sung and Yüan." *Chinese Science* 8 (1987): 9–76.

Hymes, Robert and Conrad Schirokauer. "Introduction." In Hymes and Schirokauer, eds., *Ordering the World. Approaches to State and Society in Sung Dynasty China*. Berkeley: University of California Press, 1993, pp. 1–58.

Imura Kozen 井村哮村. "Chihōshi ni kisaisaretaru Shina ekirei ryakko" 地方志に記載されたろ支那疫癘略考. 8 Parts. *Chūgai iji shimpō* 中外醫治新報 (1936–1937).

Jen Chi-yü 任繼愈. *Chung-kuo tao-chiao shih* 中國道教. Shanghai: Shang-hai jen-min ch'u-pan-she, 1990.

Jen Chien 任建 and Lei Fang 雷方. *Chung-kuo kai-pang* 中國丐幫. Nanking: Chiang-su ku-chi ch'u-pan-she, 1993.

Johnson, David. "The Wu Tzu-hsü *Pien-wen* and its Sources." *HJAS* 40 (1980): 93–156, 465–505.

———. "The City God Cults of T'ang and Sung China." *HJAS* 45 (1985): 363–457.

———. "Communication, Class, and Consciousness in Late Imperial China." In Johnson, et. al., eds., *Popular Culture in Late Imperial China*, pp. 34–74.

———. "Actions Speak Louder than Words: The Cultural Significance of Chinese Ritual Opera." In Johnson, ed., *Ritual Opera, Operatic Ritual*, pp. 1–45.

———. "Scripted Performances in Chinese Culture: An Approach to the Analysis of Popular Literature." *Han-hsüeh yen-chiu* 漢學研究 8.1 (June, 1990): 37–55.

Johnson, David, Andrew J. Nathan and Evelyn S. Rawski, eds. *Popular Culture in Late Imperial China*. Berkeley: University of California Press, 1985.

Johnson, David, ed., *Ritual Opera, Operatic Ritual*. Berkeley: University of California Press, 1989.

Jordan, David K. *Gods, Ghosts and Ancestors. Folk Religion in a Taiwanese Village*. Stanford: Stanford University Press, 1972.

———. "The *Jiaw* (Chiao) of Shigaang (Hsi-kang): An Essay in Folk Interpretation." *Asian Folklore Studies* 35 (1976): 81–107.

———. "Changes in Postwar Taiwan and Their Impact on the Popular Practice of Religion." In C. Stevan Harrell and Huang Chün-chieh, eds. *Cultural Changes in Postwar Taiwan*. Boulder, Col.: Westview Press, 1994, pp. 137–160.

Jordan, David K. and Daniel L. Overmyer. *The Flying Phoenix*. Princeton: Princeton University Press, 1986.

Kaltenmark, Max. "The Ideology of the T'ai-p'ing ching." In Welch and Seidel, eds., *Facets of Taoism*, pp. 19–45.

Kanai Noriyuki 金井德幸. "Nansō saishi shakai no hatten" 南宋祭祀社會の發展. In *Shūkyō shakaishi kenkyū* 宗教社會史研究. Tokyo: Yuzankoku chuppan kaisha, 1977. pp. 591–610.

———. "Sōdai no sonsha to shashin" 宋代の村社と社神. *Tōyōshi kenkyū* 東洋史研究 38 (1979): 61–87.

———. "Sōdai Seisai no sonsha to dōshin" 宋代浙西の村社と土神. In *Sōdai no shakai to shūkyō* 宋代の社會と宗教. *Sōdai kenkyūkai kenkyū hokōku* 宋代研究會研究報告 2 (1985): 81–108.

Kao Chan-hsiang 高占祥, ed. *Lun miao-hui wen-hua* 論廟會文化. Peking: Wen-hua i-shu ch'u-pan-she, 1992.

Kao Yu-kung. "A Study of the Fang La Rebellion." *HJAS* 24 (1962): 17–61.

Katz, Paul R. "Demons or Deities? — The *Wangye* of Taiwan." *Asian Folklore Studies* 46.2 (Spring, 1987): 197–215.

———. "Wen Ch'iung — The God of Many Faces." *Han-hsüeh yen-chiu* 8.1 (June, 1990): 183–219.

———. "P'ing-tung Hsien Tung-kang Chen te sung-wang yi-shih: Ho-wen" 屏東縣東港鎮遞送王儀式:和瘟. *Bulletin of the Institut of Ethnology, Academia Sinica: Field Materials*, Occasional Series 2 (March 1990): 93–106.

———. "P'ing-tung Hsien Tung-kang Chen te ying-wang chi-tien: T'ai-wan wen-shen yü wang-yeh hsin-yang chih fen-hsi" 屏東縣東港鎮的迎王祭典:台灣瘟神與王爺信仰之分析. *Bulletin of the Institute of Ethnology, Academia Sinica* 70 (March 1991): 95–211.

———. "The Function of Temple Murals in Imperial China: The Case of the Yung-lo Kung." *Journal of Chinese Religions* 21 (Fall 1993): 45–68.

———. "Welcoming the Lords and the Pacification of Plagues: The Relationship between Taoism and Local Cults." Presented at the Association of Asian Studies Annual Meeting, Boston, March 24–27, 1994.

———. "Commerce, Marriage and Ritual: Elite Strategies in Tung-kang During the Twentieth Century." In Chuang and P'an, eds., *T'ai-wan yü Fu-chien she-hui wen-hua yen-chiu lun-wen-chi*, pp. 127–165.

———. "Rite of Passage or Rite of Affliction? A Preliminary Analysis of the Pacification of Plagues." *Min-su ch'ü-yi* 92 (Nov. 1994): 1013–1092.

———. "The Pacification of Plagues: A Chinese Rite of Affliction." *Journal of Ritual Studies* (forthcoming).

Kleeman, Terry. "Wenchang and the Viper: The Creation of a Chinese National God." Ph.D. dissertation, University of California at Berkeley, 1988.

————. "The Expansion of the Wen-ch'ang Cult." In Ebrey and Gregory, eds, *Religion and Society in T'ang and Sung China*, pp. 45–73.

————. *A God's Own Tale. The Book of Transformations of Wenchang, the Divine Lord of Zitong*. Albany: SUNY Press, 1994.

Kleinman, Arthur. *Patients and Healers in the Context of Culture*. Berkeley: University of California Press, 1980.

Kuhn, Philip A. *Rebellion and Its Enemies in Late Imperial China*. Cambridge, Mass.: Harvard University Press, 1970.

————. *Soulstealers. The Chinese Sorcery Scare of 1768*. Cambridge, Mass.: Harvard University Press, 1991.

Kuo Li-ch'eng 郭立誠. *Hang-shen yen-chiu* 行神研究. Taipei: Kuo-li pien-yi-kuan Chung-hua ts'ung-shu wei-yüan-hui, 1967.

Lagerwey, John. *Taoist Ritual in Chinese Society and History*. New York: Macmillan Publishing Company, 1987.

————. "Les Têtes des Demons Tombent par Milliers." *L'Homme* 101 (Jan.-March, 1987): 101–109.

————. "The Pilgrimage to Wu-tang Shan." In Naquin and Yü, eds., *Pilgrims and Sacred Sites*, pp. 293–332.

Lang, Graeme and Lars Regvald. *The Rise of a Refugee God. Hong Kong's Wong Tai Sin*. Hong Kong: Oxford University Press, 1993.

Le Roy Ladurie, Emmanuel. *Carnival in Romans*. Trans. Mary Feeney. New York: George Braziller, Inc., 1980.

Leung, Angela Ki Che. "Organized Medicine in Ming-Qing China: State and Private Medical Institutions in the Lower Yangzi Region." *Late Imperial China* 8.1 (June 1987): 134–166.

Li Chi. *The Formation of the Chinese People*. Cambridge: Cambridge University Press, 1928.

Li Ch'iao 李喬. *Chung-kuo hang-yeh-shen ch'ung-pai* 中國行業神崇拜. Peking: Chung-kuo hua-ch'iao ch'u-pan-she, 1990.

Li Ch'in-te 李勤德. "No-li, No-wu, No-hsi" 儺禮、儺舞、儺戲. *Wen-shih chih-shih* 文史知識 6 (1987): 55–59.

Li Ching-han 李景漢. *Ting-hsien kai-k'uang tiao-ch'a* 定縣概況調查. Peking: Chung-hua p'ing-min chiao-yü ts'u-chin-hui, 1934.

Li Feng-mao 李豐楙. "Chung K'uei yü No-li chi ch'i hsi-chü" 鍾馗與儺禮及其戲劇. *Min-su ch'ü-yi* 39 (1986): 69–99.

————. "*Tao-tsang* so shou tsao-ch'i tao-shu te wen-yi kuan" 道藏所收早期道書的瘟疫觀. *Bulletin of the Institute of Literature and Philosophy, Academia Sinica* 3 (March 1993): 1–38.

————. "Tung-kang wang-ch'uan, Ho-wen, yü sung-wang hsi-su chih yen-chiu" 東港王船,和瘟,與送王習俗之研究. *Tung-fang tsung-chiao* 東方宗教 3 (1993): 229–265.

————. "Hsing-wen yü sung-wen — Tao-chiao yü min-chung wen-yi kuan te chiao-liu ho fen-ch'i" 行瘟與送瘟—道教與民眾瘟疫觀的交流和

分歧. In *Proceedings of the International Conference on Popular Beliefs and Chinese Culture.* Volume I, pp. 373–422.

Li Kuo-ch'i 李國祁. *Chung-kuo hsien-tai-hua te ch'ü-yü yen-chiu.* 中國現代化的區域研究. Nankang: Institute of Modern History, Academia Sinica, 1982.

Lieu, Samuel N.C. *Manichaeism in the Later Roman Empire and Medieval China.* Dover, NH: Manchester University Press, 1985.

Lin Cheng-chiu 林正秋. *Nan-Sung tu-ch'eng Lin-an* 南宋都城臨安. Shanghai: Hsi-ling yin-she, 1986.

———. *Che-chiang ching-chi wen-hua shih yen-chiu* 浙江經濟文化史研究. Hangchow: Che-chiang ku-chi ch'u-pan-she, 1989.

Lin Cheng-ch'iu and Chin Min 金敏. *Nan-Sung ku-tu Hang-chou* 南宋古都杭州. Honan: Chung-chou shu-hua she, 1984.

Lin Fu-shih 林富士. "Shih-shih Shui-hu-ti Ch'in-chien chung te 'li' yü 'ting-sha'" 試釋睡虎地秦簡中的厲與定殺. *Shih-yüan* 史原 15 (1986): 2–38.

———. "Shih-lun Han-tai te wu-shu yi-liao-fa chi ch'i kuan-nien chi-ch'u" 試論漢代的巫術醫療法及其觀念基礎. *Shih-yüan* 史苑 16 (Nov. 1987): 29–53.

———. *Han-tai te wu-che* 漢代的巫者. Taipei: Tao-hsiang ch'u-pan-she, 1988.

———. "Shih-lun T'ai-p'ing ching te chi-ping kuan-nien" 試論太平經的疾病觀念. *Bulletin of the Institute of History and Philology, Academia Sinica* 62 (April, 1993): 225–263.

Lin Ho 林河. *Chiu-ko yü Yüan-Hsiang wen-hua* 九歌與沅湘文化. Shanghai: San-lien shu-tien, 1990.

Lin Yung-chung 林用中 and Chang Sung-shou 張松壽. *Lao Tung-yüeh. Miao-hui tiao-ch'a pao-kao* 老東嶽. 廟會調查報告. Hangchow: Che-chiang yin-shua-chü, 1936.

Ling Ch'un-sheng 凌純生. "Chung-kuo ku-tai she chih yüan-liu" 中國古代社之源流. *Bulletin of the Institute of Ethnology, Academia Sinica* 17 (1964): 1–44.

Lipman, Jonathan N. and C. Stevan Harrell, eds. *Violence in China.* Albany: SUNY Press, 1990.

Liu Chih-wan 劉枝萬. *T'ai-wan min-chien hsin-yang lun-chi* 臺灣民間信仰論集. Taipei: Lien-ching ch'u-pan shih-yeh kung-ssu, 1983.

Liu Hui 劉慧. *T'ai-shan tsung-chiao yen-chiu* 泰山宗教研究. Peking: Wen-wu ch'u-pan-she, 1994.

Liu, James T.C. "Liu Tsai (1165–1238): His Philanthropy and Neo-Confucian Limitations." *Oriens Extremis* 25 (1978): 1–29.

———. *China Turning Inward: Intellectual-Political Changes in the Early Twelfth Century.* Cambridge, Mass.: Harvard University Press, 1988.

Liu, James T.C. and Peter J. Golas, eds. *Change in Sung China. Innovation or Renovation?* Lexington, Mass.: D.C. Heath and Company, 1969.

Liu Nien-tz'u 劉念慈. *Nan-hsi hsin-cheng* 南戲新證. Peking: Chung-hua shu-chü, 1986.

Liu Shu-fen 劉淑芬. "San chih liu shih-chi Che-tung ti-ch'ü te ching-chi fa-chan" 三至六世紀浙東地區的經濟發展. *Bulletin of the Institute of History and Philology, Academia Sinica* 58 (1987): 485–523.

Lo P'ing 羅萍. "Che-tung min-chien ya-chü — Ya Mu-lien" 浙東民間啞劇 — 啞目連. *Hsi-ch'ü yen-chiu* 戲曲研究 16 (1985): 241–261.

Lo, Winston. *The Life and Thought of Yeh Shih*. Gainesville: University Presses of Florida, 1974.

van der Loon, Piet. "Les Origines Rituelles du Théâtre Chinois."*Journal Asiatique* 165 (1977): 141–168.

———. "A Taoist Collection of the Fourteenth Century." In *Studia Sino-Mongolica: Festschrift für Herbert Franke*. Wiesbaden: Franz Steiner Verlag, GMBH, 1979, pp. 401–405.

Lu Chia-mei 陸嘉美. "Wen-chou P'ing-yang Min-nan-yü yen-chiu" 溫州平陽閩南語研究. M.A. thesis, National Taiwan University, 1983.

Ma Shu-t'ien 馬書田. *Hua-hsia chu-shen* 華夏諸神. Peking: Yen-shan ch'u-pan-she, 1990.

Ma, Y.W. and Joseph Lau, ed. and trans. *Traditional Chinese Stories*. New York: Columbia University Press, 1981.

MacGowan, The Rev. J. *Chinese Folklore Tales*. London: Macmillan & Company, 1910.

Mackerras, Colin. *Chinese Theatre: From Its Origins to Present Day*. Honolulu: University of Hawaii Press, 1983.

Maejime Shinji 前島信次. "Taiwan no onyakugami, ōya, to sōō no fushū ni tsuite" 臺灣の瘟疫神，王爺，と送王の風習に就いて. *Minzokugaku kenkyū* 民族學研究 4.4 (Oct. 1937): 25–66.

Makita Tairyo 牧田啼亮. "Surikue shōkō" 水陸小考. *Tōhō shūkyū* 東方宗教 12 (July 1957): 14–33.

Mao Keng-ju 茆耕茹. "Wan-tung Nan-hsü-ho nan-an te 'T'iao Wu-ch'ang'" 皖東南胥河南岸的跳五猖. *Min-su ch'ü-yi* 92 (Nov. 1994): 1093-1123.

Maspero, Henri. *Taoism and Chinese Religion*. Trans. Frank Kierman. Amherst: The University of Massachusetts Press, 1981.

Matsumoto Koichi 松本告一. "Chō Tenshi to NanSō no Dōkyō" 張天師と南宋の道教. In *Rekishi ni okeru minshū to bunka* 歷史における民眾と文化 (Tadao Sakai Festschrift). Tokyo: Kokusho kankokai, 1982, pp. 337–350.

McKnight, Brian E. *Village and Bureaucracy in Southern Sung China*. Chicago: University of Chicago Press, 1971.

McNeill, William H. *Plagues and Peoples*. New York: Anchor Books, 1976.

Mitsuo Moriya 美部雄守部. *Chūgoku ko saijiki no kenkyū* 中國古歲時記の研究. Tokyo: Teikaku shōin, 1963

Miyakawa   Hisayuki   宮川尚志.   "Dōkyōshi   jōyori   mitaru   Godai"
道教史上見たろ五代. *Tōhō shūkyō*, 42 (1973): 13–34.

———. "Local Cults Around Mount Lu at the Time of Sun En's Rebellion." In
Welch and Seidel, eds., *Facets of Taoism*, pp. 83–102.

Mollier, Christine. *Une Apocalypse du Ve siècle —Étude du Dongyuan shenzhou
jing*. Paris: Institut des Hautes Études Chinoises, College de France,
1991.

Muir, Edward. *Civic Ritual in Renaissance Venice*. Princeton: Princeton
University Press, 1981.

Nakamura Jihei 中村治兵偉. "Sōdai no fū no tokuchō" 宋代の巫の特徵. *Chuō
daigaku bengakubu kiyō, shigaku ko* 中央大學文學部紀要，史學科 104
(March 1982): 51–75.

Nan Pei ch'ao ch'ien-ku Hang-chou 南北朝前古杭州. Hangchow: Che-chiang
jen-min ch'u-pan-she, 1992.

Naquin, Susan and Evelyn Rawski. *Chinese Society in the Eighteenth Century*.
New Haven and London: Yale University Press, 1987.

Naquin, Susan and Yü Chün-fang, eds. *Pilgrims and Sacred Sites in China*.
Berkeley: University of California Press, 1992.

Ni Shih-yi 倪士毅 and Fang Ju-chin 方如金. "Nan-Sung Liang-che she-hui
ching-chi te fa-chan" 南宋兩浙社會經濟的發展. *HCTHHP* 13.2 (June
1983): 110–119, 125.

Ning Chu-ch'en 佟柱臣. "Chung-kuo hsin-shih-ch'i shih-tai wen-hua te
to-chung-hsin fa-chan ho fa-chan pu-p'ing-heng lun" 中國新石器
時代文化的多中心發展和發展不平衡論. *Wen-wu* 357 (Feb. 1986):
16–30.

Nishijima Sadao. "The Foundation of the Early Cotton Industry." In Linda
Grove and Christian Daniels, eds. *State and Society in China: Japanese
Perspectives on Ming-Qing Social and Economic History*. Tokyo:
University of Tokyo Press, 1984, pp. 17–78.

Ofuchi Ninji 大淵忍爾. *Chūgokujin no shūkyō girei* 中國人の宗敎儀禮. Tokyo:
Fukutake Shoten, 1983.

Omura Seigai 大村西崖. *Mikkyō hattatsushi* 密敎發達志 (1918). Chinese
translation published in *Shih-chieh fo-chiao ming-chu i-ts'ung*
世界佛敎名著譯叢, volumes 72–74. Taipei: Hua-yü ch'u-pan-she,
1986.

Ono Shihei 小野四平. "Taisan kara Hoto ē" 泰山から酆都へ. *Bunka* 文化 27
(1963): 80–111.

Overmyer, Daniel. "Attitudes Towards Popular Religion in Ritual Texts of the
Chinese State: *The Collected Statutes of the Great Ming*." *CEA* 5
(1989–1990): 191–211.

Pang, Duane. "The *P'u-tu* Ritual." In Michael Saso and David W. Chappell,
eds., *Buddhist and Taoist Studies I*. Asian Studies at Hawaii, number
18. Honolulu: University of Hawaii Press, 1977, pp. 95–122.

Parker, Robert. *Miasma: Pollution and Purification in Early Greek Religion*. Oxford: Oxford University Press, 1983.

Pas, Julian F. ed. *The Turning of the Tide. Religion in China Today*. Hong Kong: Oxford University Press, 1989.

Po Sung-nien 薄松年. *Chung-kuo nien-hua shih* 中國年畫史. Liaoning: Liao-ning mei-shu ch'u-pan-she, 1986.

Po Sung-nien and David Johnson. *Domesticated Deities and Auspicious Emblems*. Berkeley: University of California Press, 1992.

Proceedings of the International Conference on Popular Beliefs and Chinese Culture. Taipei: Center for Chinese Studies, 1994. 2 volumes.

Radcliffe-Brown, A.R. "Religion and Society." In *Structure and Function in Primitive Society*. New York: The Free Press, 1965, pp. 153-177.

Ramsey, S. Robert. *The Languages of China*. Princeton: Princeton University Press, 1987.

Ranger Terence & Paul Slack, eds. *Epidemics and Ideas. Essays on the Historical Perception of Pestilence.* Cambidge: Cambridge University Press, 1992.

Rankin, Mary B. *Elite Activism and Political Transformation in China, Zhejiang Province, 1865–1911*. Stanford: Stanford University Press, 1986.

Rawski, Evelyn S. *Education and Popular Literacy in Ch'ing China.* Ann Arbor: Michigan University Press, 1979.

———. "Economic and Social Foundations of Late Imperial China." In Johnson, et al., eds., *Popular Culture in Late Imperial China*, pp. 3–33.

Rowe, William T. *Hankow: Commerce and Society in a Chinese City, 1796–1889*. Stanford: Stanford University Press, 1984.

———. *Hankow: Conflict and Community in a Chinese City, 1796–1895*. Stanford: Stanford University Press, 1989.

———. "The Public Sphere in Modern China." *Modern China* 16.3 (July 1990): 309–329.

———. "The Problem of 'Civil Society' in Late Imperial China." *Modern China* 19.2 (April 1993): 139–157.

Sakai Tadao. "Taisan shinkō no kenkyū" 泰山信仰の研究. *Shichō* 史潮 7 (1937): 70–118.

———. "Confucianism and Popular Educational Works." In deBary, ed., *Self and Society*, pp. 331–362.

Sangren, P. Steven. *History and Magical Power in a Chinese Community*. Stanford: Stanford University Press, 1987.

Schafer, Edward H. "Ritual Exposure in Ancient China." *HJAS* 14 (1951): 130–184.

———. *The Vermillion Bird: T'ang Images of the South*. Berkeley: University of California Press, 1967.

———. *The Divine Woman*. San Francisco: North Point Press, 1980.

Schak, David. "Images of Beggars in Chinese Culture." In Sarah Allan and Alvin P. Cohen, eds., *Legend, Lore, and Religion in China: Essays in Honor of Wolfram Eberhard on his 70th Birthday.* San Francisco: Chinese Materials Center, 1979, pp. 109–133.

———. *A Chinese Beggars Den: Poverty and Mobility in an Underclass Community.* Pittsburgh: University of Pittsburgh Press, 1988.

Schipper, Kristofer M. "The Divine Jester: Some Remarks on the Gods of the Chinese Marionette Theatre." *Bulletin of the Institute of Ethnology, Academia Sinica* 21 (Spring 1966): 81–95.

———. "The Written Memorial in Taoist Ceremonies." In Wolf, ed., *Religion and Ritual*, pp. 309–324.

———. "Neighborhood Cult Associations in Traditional Tainan." In Skinner, *The City in Late Imperial China*, pp. 651–676.

———. "Vernacular and Classical Ritual in Taoism." *JAS* 45.1 (Jan. 1985): 21–57.

———. "Taoist Ritual and Local Cults of the T'ang Dynasty." In *Mélanges Chinois et Bouddhiques* 22. *Tantric and Taoist Studies in Honor of Rolf Stein.* Michel Strickmann, ed. Bruxelles: Institut Belge des Hautes Études Chinoises, 1985. Volume 3, pp. 812–834.

———. "Seigneurs Royaux, Dieux des Epidemies." *Archives Sciences Sociales des Religions* 59 (1985): 31–40.

———. *The Taoist Body.* Trans. Karen C. Duval. Berkeley: University of California Press, 1993 (1982).

Schoppa, R. Keith. *Chinese Elites and Political Change: Zhejiang Province in the Early Twentieth Century.* Cambridge, Mass.: Harvard University Press, 1982.

Scogin, Hugh. "Poor Relief in Northern Sung China." *Oriens Extremis* 25 (1978): 30–46.

Seaman, Gary. "The Divine Authorship of the *Pei-yu chi.*" *JAS* 45.3 (May 1985): 483–497.

Seidel, Anna. "The Image of the Perfect Ruler in Early Taoist Messianism: Lao-tzu and Li Hung." *HR* 9.2/3 (Nov.– Feb., 1969–1970): 216–247.

———. "A Taoist Immortal of the Ming Dynasty: Chang San-feng." In deBary, ed., *Self and Society*, pp. 483–531.

———. "Traces of Han Religion in Funerary Texts Found in Tombs." In Akizuki Kanei, *Dōkyō to shūkyō bunka*, pp. 21–57.

Shang Tu 商都 (Yin Teng-kuo 殷登國). "Ch'ing-ch'ao Chiang-nan-jen shu-t'ien chu-yi te su-hsin" 清朝江南人暑天逐疫的俗信. *Li-shih yüeh-k'an* 歷史月刊 19 (Aug. 1989): 52–61.

Shiba Yoshinobu. *Commerce and Society in Sung China.* Trans. Mark Elvin. Michigan Abstracts, number 2. Ann Arbor: University of Michigan Press, 1970.

———. "Ningpo and its Hinterland." In Skinner, ed., *The City in Late Imperial China*, pp. 391–439.

———. *Sōdai Kōnan keizaishi kenkyū* 宋代江南經濟史研究. Tokyo: Tōyō bunka kenkyūjō, 1988.

Shih   Nien-hai 史念海. *Chung-kuo shih-ti lun-kao, ho-shan chi* 中國史的論稿, 河山集. Taipei: Hung-wen kuan ch'u-pan-she, 1986.

Shih Wan-shou 石萬壽. "Chia-chiang t'uan — T'ien jen ho yi te hsün-pu tsu-chih" 家將團 — 天人合一的巡捕組織. *T'ai-nan wen-hua* 臺南文化 22 (1986): 48–65.

Shih Yi-lung 石亦龍, "T'ung-an Lü-ts'u-ts'un te wang-yeh hsin-yang" 同安呂厝村的王爺信仰. In Chuang and P'an, *T'ai-wan yü Fu-chien she-hui wen-hua yen-chiu lun-wen-chi*, pp. 183–212.

Shryock, John K. *The Temples of Anking*. Paris: J.K. Shryock, 1931.

———. *The Origin and Development of the State Cult of Confucius*. New York and London: The Century Co., 1932.

Simmons, Richard Van Ness. "Northern and Southern Forms in Hangchow Grammar." In *Chinese Languages and Linguistics*, volume 1, *Chinese Dialects*. Nankang: Institute of History and Philology, 1992, pp. 539–561.

Sivin, Nathan. "Social Relations of Curing in Traditional China: Preliminary Considerations." *Nihon Ishigaku Zasshi* 日本醫學雜誌 23 (1977): 505–532.

———. "On the Word 'Taoist' as a Source of Perplexity. With Special Reference to the Relations of Science and Religion in Traditional China." *HR* 17.3–4 (Feb.– May 1978): 303–330.

Skinner, G. William, ed. *The City in Late Imperial China*. Stanford: Stanford University Press, 1977.

Smith, Arthur H. (1845–1932). *Village Life in China*. New York: F. H. Revell Co., 1899.

Smith, Richard J. *Fortune-Tellers and Philosophers. Divination in Traditional Chinese Society*. Boulder, Col.: Westview Press, 1991.

———. *Chinese Almanacs*. Hong Kong: Oxford University Press, 1992.

Stein, Rolf A. "Religious Taoism and Popular Religion from the Second to Seventh Centuries." In Welch and Seidel, eds., *Facets of Taoism*, pp. 53–82.

Strand, David. *Rickshaw Beijing: City People and Politics in 1920s China*. Berkeley: University of California Press, 1989.

Strickmann, Michel. "Sōdai no raigi: Shinsō undō to Dōka nanshū ni tsuite no ryakusetsu" 宋代の雷儀: 神霄運動と道家南宗に就いての略說. *Tōhō shūkyō*, 46 (1975), 15–28.

———. "The Longest Taoist Scripture." *HR* 17.3/4 (Feb.– May, 1978): 331–354.

———. "On the Alchemy of T'ao Hung-ching." In Welch and Seidel, eds., *Facets of Taoism*, pp. 123–192.

———. "The Taoist Renaissance of the Twelfth Century." Paper presented at the Third International Conference on Taoist Studies. Unterageri, Switzerland. Sept. 3–9 1979.

———. *Magical Medicine*. Draft manuscript, 1989.

———. "The *Consecration Sutra*: A Buddhist Book of Spells." In Robert E. Buswell, Jr., ed., *Chinese Buddhist Apocrypha*. Honolulu: University of Hawaii Press, 1990, pp. 75–118.

Sun Ching-ch'en 孫景琛. "Sung-tai Ta-No t'u k'ao" 宋代大儺圖考. *Wu-tao lun-ts'ung* 舞蹈論叢 2 (1982): 62–71.

———. "Ta-No t'u ming-shih pien" 大儺圖名實辨. *Wen-wu* 210 (March 1982): 70–74.

Sun K'o-k'uan 孫克寬. *Sung-Yüan tao-chiao chih fa-chan* 宋元道教之發展. Taichung: Tung-hai University, 1965.

———. *Yüan-tai Han wen-hua chih huo-tung* 元代漢文化之活動. Taipei: Chung-hua shu-chü, 1968.

———. *Yüan-tai Tao-chiao chih fa-chan* 元代道教之發展. Taichung: Tung-hai University, 1968.

Sung Chao-lin 宋兆麟. *Wu yü min-chien hsin-yang* 巫與民間信仰. Peking: Chung-kuo hua-ch'iao ch'u-pan-she, 1990.

Sung Kuang-yü 宋光宇. "T'ai-wan jih-chü ch'u-ch'i te wen-yi yü ying-shen" 臺灣日據初期的瘟疫與迎神. In Li Yih-yüan 李亦園, et al., eds., *K'ao-ku yü li-shih wen-hua* 考古與歷史文化. Taipei: Cheng-chung ch'u-pan-she, 1991, pp. 305–330.

———. "Shih-lun ssu-shih nien lai T'ai-wan tsung-chiao te fa-chan" 試論四十年來臺灣宗教的發展. In Sung Kuang-yü, ed., *T'ai-wan ching-yen (2) — She-hui wen-hua p'ien* 臺灣經驗 (2) — 社會文化篇. Taipei: Tung-ta t'u-shu ku-fen yu-hsien kung-ssu, 1994, pp. 175–224.

Sung, Margaret M.Y. "Chinese Dialects and Sino-Japanese." In *Chinese Languages and Linguistics*. Volume 1, pp. 563–585.

Sutton, Donald. "A Case of Literati Piety: The Ma Yüan 馬援 Cult from High-T'ang to High-Ch'ing." *Chinese Literature: Essays, Articles, Reviews* 11 (1989): 79–114.

———. "Ritual Drama and Moral Order: Interpreting the Gods' Festival Troupes of Southern Taiwan." *JAS* 49.3 (Aug. 1990): 535–554.

Tan Chee-Beng. "Chinese Religion and Local Communities in Malaysia." In Tan Chee-Beng, ed., *The Preservation and Adaptation of Tradition: Studies of Chinese Religious Expression in Southeast Asia. Contributions to Southeast Asian Ethnography* 9 (Dec. 1990): pp. 5–27.

Tanaka Issei 田中一成. *Shindai chihōgeki shiryō shū* 清代地方劇史料集. Tokyo: Tōyō bunka kenkyūjō, 1968.

———. "The Social and Historical Context of Ming-Ch'ing Local Drama." In Johnson, et al., eds. *Popular Culture in Late Imperial China*, pp. 143–160.

———. *Chūgoku gōson saishi* 中國鄉村祭祀. Tokyo: Tōyō bunka kenkyūjō, 1989.

———. *Chūgoku fūkei engeki kenkyū* 中國巫系演劇研究. Tokyo: Tōyō bunka kenkyūjō, 1993.

Taylor, Romeyn. "Ming T'ai-tsu and the Gods of Walls and Moats." *Ming Studies* 3 (1977): 31–49.

———. "Official and Popular Religion and the Political Organization of Chinese Society in the Ming." In Liu Kwang-ching, ed., *Orthodoxy in Late Imperial China*. Berkeley: University of California Press, 1990, pp. 126–157.

Teiser, Stephen. *The Ghost Festival in Medieval China*. Princeton: Princeton University Press, 1988.

———. "The Growth of Purgatory." In Ebrey and Gregory, eds., *Religion and Society in T'ang and Sung China*, pp. 115–145.

———. *The Scripture of the Ten Kings*. Honolulu: University of Hawaii Press, 1994.

Ter Haar, Barend. "The Genesis and Spread of Temple Cults in Fukien." In E.B. Vermeer, ed., *Development and Decline of Fukien Province in the 17th and 18th Centuries*. Leiden: E.J. Brill, 1990, pp. 349–396.

———. *The White Lotus Teachings in Chinese Religious History*. Leiden: E.J. Brill, 1992.

Thomas, Keith. *Religion and the Decline of Magic*. New York: Charles Scribner's Sons, 1971.

Tillman, Hoyt Cleveland. "Intellectuals and Officials in Action: Academies and Granaries in Sung China." *Asia Major*, Third Series, Volume IV, Part II (1991): 1–14.

Ting Pang-hsin 丁邦新. "Wu-yü chung te Min-yü ch'eng-fen" 吳語中的閩語成份. *Bulletin of the Institute of History and Philology, Academia Sinica* 59 (1988): 13–22.

Ts'ai Hsiang-hui 蔡相輝. *T'ai-wan te wang-yeh yü Ma-tsu* 臺灣的王爺與媽祖. Taipei: T'ai-yüan ch'u-pan-she, 1989.

Tseng Ch'in-liang 曾勤良. *T'ai-wan min-chien hsin-yang yü hsiao-shuo Feng-shen yen-yi chih pi-chiao yen-chiu* 臺灣民間信仰與小說封神演義之比較研究. Taipei: Hua-cheng ch'u-pan-she, 1987.

Tu Cheng-sheng 杜正勝. "Tao-lun — Chung-kuo shang-ku-shih yen-chiu te yi-hsieh kuan-chien wen-t'i" 導論 — 中國上古史研究的一些關鍵問題. In Tu, ed., *Chung-kuo shang-ku-shih lun-wen hsüan-chi* 中國上古史論文選集. Taipei: Hua-shih ch'u-pan-she, 1979, pp. 15–82.

Tung Ch'u-p'ing 董楚平. *Wu-Yüeh wen-hua hsin-t'an* 吳越文化新探. Hangchow: Che-chiang jen-min ch'u-pan-she, 1988.

Turner, Victor. *Schism and Continuity in an African Society: A Study of Ndembu Village Life*. Manchester: Manchester University Press, 1957.

———. *The Forest of Symbols*. Ithaca: Cornell University Press, 1967.

———. *The Drums of Affliction*. Oxford: Oxford Univesity Press, 1968.

———. *The Ritual Process. Structure and Anti-Structure*. Ithaca: Cornell University Press, 1969.

———. *Dramas, Fields, and Metaphors. Symbolic Action in Human Society*. Ithaca and London: Cornell University Press, 1974.

———. "Liminal to Liminoid, in Play, Flow, and Ritual: An Essay in Comparative Sociology." *Rice University Studies* (Special Issue on the Anthropological Study of Human Play) 60.3 (1974): 53–92.

———. *On the Edge of the Bush*. Tucson, Ariz.: University of Arizona Press, 1985.

———. *The Anthropology of Performance*. New York: PAJ Publications, 1986.

Turner, Victor and Edith Turner. *Image and Pilgrimage in Christian Culture*. New York: Columbia University Press, 1978.

Twitchett, Denis C. *Financial Administration Under the T'ang Dynasty*. Cambridge: Cambridge University Press, 1963.

———. "Population and Pestilence in T'ang China." In *Festschrift für Herbert Franke*, pp. 35-68.

Unschuld, Paul. *Medicine in China: A History of Ideas*. Berkeley: University of California Press, 1985.

Von Glahn, Richard. "The Enchantment of Wealth: The God Wutong in the Social History of Jiangnan." *HJAS* 51.2 (Dec., 1991): 651–714.

Wakeman, Frederic, Jr. "The Civil Society and Public Sphere Debate: Western Reflections on Chinese Political Culture." *Modern China* 19.2 (April, 1993): 108-138.

Walton, Linda. "Southern Sung Academies as Sacred Places." In Ebrey and Gregory, eds., *Religion and Society in T'ang and Sung China*, pp. 335–363.

Wang Nien-shuang 王年雙. *Nan-Sung wen-hsüeh chung chih min-chien hsin-yang* 南宋文學中之民間信仰. M.A. thesis, National Cheng-chih University, 1980.

Wang Shih-ch'ing. "Religious Organization in the History of a Chinese Town." In Wolf, ed., *Religion and Ritual*, pp. 71–92.

Wang Te-yi 王德毅. *Sung-tai tsai-huang te chiu-chi cheng-ts'e* 宋代災荒的救濟政策. Taipei: Chung-kuo hsüeh-shu chu-tso chiang-chu wei-yüan-hui, 1970.

Wang Yao 王躍. "Chiang-pei hsien Shu-chia hsiang Ta-t'ang ts'un Hu-chai te 'Ying-mao t'i-tai' chi-yi tiao-ch'a" 江北縣舒家鄉大塘村胡宅的迎茅替代祭儀調查. *Min-su ch'ü-yi* 90 (July 1994): 321–354.

Watson, Burton. *The Old Man who Does as He Pleases: Selections From the Poetry and Prose of Lu Yu.* New York and London: Columbia University Press, 1973.

Watson, James L. "Standardizing the Gods: The Promotion of T'ien Hou ('Empress of Heaven') Along the South China Coast, 960–1960." In Johnson, et. al. eds., *Popular Culture in Late   Imperial   China,* pp. 292–324.

Watt, John R. *The District Magistrate in Late Imperial China.* New York: Columbia Unversity Press, 1972.

Wechsler, Howard. *Offerings of Jade and Silk.* New Haven: Yale University Press, 1985.

Weinstein, Stanley. *Buddhism under the T'ang.* Cambridge: Cambridge University Press, 1987.

Welch, Holmes. *The Practice of Chinese Buddhism, 1900–1950.* Cambridge, Mass.: Harvard University Press, 1967.

Welch, Holmes and Anna Seidel, eds. *Facets of Taoism.* New Haven and London: Yale University Press, 1979.

Weller, Robert P. *Unities and Diversities in Chinese Religion.* Seattle,: University of Washington Press, 1987.

———. *Resistance, Chaos and Control in China.* Seattle,: University of Washington Press, 1994.

Wen Tuan-cheng 溫端政. *Ts'ang-nan fang-yen chih* 蒼南方言志. Peking: Yü-wen ch'u-pan-she 1991.

Wen Yi-to 聞一多 (1899–1946). *Wen Yi-to ch'üan-chi* 聞一多全集. Shanghai: K'ai-ming shu-tien, 1949.

Wiens, Herold J. *Han Chinese Expansion in South China.* Hamden, Conn.: Shoe String Press, 1967.

Wilkerson, James. "The 'Ritual Master' and his 'Temple Corporation' Rituals." In *Proceedings of the International Conference on Popular Beliefs and Chinese Culture.* Volume II, pp. 471–521.

———. "Self-referential Performances: Victor Turner and Theoretical Issues in Chinese Performative Genre." *Min-su ch'ü-yi* 90 (July 1994): 99–146.

———. "Rural Village Temples in the P'enghu Islands and their Late Imperial Coperate Organization." In *Proceedings of the Conference on Temples and Popular Culture.* Taipei: Center for Chinese Studies, 1995. Volume I, pp. 67-95.

Will, Pierre-Etienne. *Bureaucracy and Famine in Eighteenth-century China.* Trans. by Elborg Foster. Stanford: Stanford University Press, 1990.

Will, Pierre-Etienne, R. Bin Wong, et al. *Nourish the People. The State Granary System in China, 1650–1850.* Ann Arbor: University of Michigan Press, 1991.

Winslow, Charles-Edward Amory. *The Conquest of Epidemic Disease*. Madison: The University of Wisconsin Press, 1971.

Wolf, Arthur, ed. *Religion and Ritual in Chinese Society*. Stanford: Stanford University Press, 1974.

Wong, K. Chimin and Wu Lien-teh. *History of Chinese Medicine*. Tientsin: The Tientsin Press, Ltd., 1932.

Wu Cheng-han. "The Temple Fairs in Late Imperial China." Ph.D. dissertation, Princeton University, 1988.

Wu Yung-chang 吳永章. *Chung-kuo nan-fang min-tsu wen-hua* 中國南方民族文化. Nan-ning: Kuang-hsi chiao-yü ch'u-pan-she, 1991.

Yang, C.K. *Religion in Chinese Society*. Berkeley: University of California Press, 1961.

Yang, L.S. "The Concept of 'Pao' as a Basis for Social Relations in China." In John K. Faribank, ed., *Chinese Thought and Institutions*. Chicago: University of Chicago Press, 1957, pp. 291–309.

Yang, Martin. "Between State and Society: the Construction of Corporateness in a Chinese Socialist Factory." *Australian Journal of Chinese Affairs* 22 (1989): 31–60.

Yeh Ta-ping 葉大兵. *Wen-chou shih-hua* 溫州史話. Hangchow: Che-chiang jen-min ch'u-pan-she, 1982.

———. "Wen Yüan-shuai hsin-yang yü Tung-yüeh miao-hui" 溫元帥信仰與東嶽廟會. *Min-su ch'ü-yi* 72/73 (1991): 102–128.

———. "Wen-chou Tung-yüeh miao-hui p'o-hsi" 溫州東嶽廟會剖析. In *Chung-kuo min-chien wen-hua*. Shanghai: Hsüeh-lin ch'u-pan-she, 1992. Volume 5, pp. 235–251.

Yen Fang-tzu 顏芳姿. "Lu-kang te wang-yeh yü an-fang chu-t'an" 鹿港的王爺與暗訪初探. In Yü Kuang-hung, ed., *Lu-kang shu-ch'i jen-lei-hsüeh t'ien-yeh kung-tso chiao-shih lun-wen-chi* 鹿港暑期人類學田野工作教室論文集 Nankang: Institute of Ethnology, 1993, pp. 75–108.

———. "Lu-kang wang-ye hsin-yang te fa-chan hsing-t'ai 鹿港王爺信仰的發展形態." M.A. thesis. National Tsing-hua University, 1994.

Yen Hsing-chen 顏杏眞. "Ming-tai tsai-huang chiu-chi cheng-ts'e chih yen-chiu" 明代災荒的救濟政策之研究. *Hua-hsüeh yüeh-k'an* 華學月刊 142 (Oct. 1983): 14–24; 144 (Dec. 1983): 23–34; 147 (March 1987): 40–48.

Yen Wen-ming 嚴文明. "Chung-kuo shih-ch'ien wen-hua te t'ung-yi-hsing yü to-yang-hsing" 中國史前文化的同一性與多樣性. *Wen-wu* 370 (March 1987): 38–50.

Yi Hsi-chia 頤希佳, et. al. "T'ai-pao yü tso-she" 太保與做社. In *Chung-kuo min-chien wen-hua*. Volume 7, pp. 199–214.

Yin Teng-kuo 殷登國. *Chung-kuo shen te ku-shih* 中國神的故事. Taipei: Shih-chieh wen-wu ch'u-pan-she, 1984.

Yin Ya-chao 殷亞昭. *Chung-kuo ku-wu yü min-wu yen-chiu* 中國古舞與民舞研究. Taipei: Kuan-ya wen-hua shih-yeh yu-hsien kung-ssu, 1991.

Yoshioka Yoshitoyo. "Taoist Monastic Life." In Welch and Seidel, eds., *Facets of Taoism*, pp. 229–252.

Yü Chün-fang. *The Renewal of Buddhism in China: Chu-hung and the Late Ming Synthesis*. New York: Columbia University Press, 1981.

Yüan Ai-kuo 袁愛國. *T'ai-shan shen wen-hua* 泰山神文化. T'ai-an: Shan-tung ta-hsüeh ch'u-pan-she, 1991.

Yüan Ming Ch'ing ming-ch'eng Hang-chou 元明清名城杭州. Hangchow: Che-chiang jen-min ch'u-pan-she, 1990.

Yung Sai-shing (Jung Shih-ch'eng 容世誠). "Kuan Kung hsi te ch'ü-hsieh yi-yi" 關公戲的驅邪義意. *Han-hsüeh yen-chiu* 8.1 (June 1990): 609–626.

Ziegler, Philip. *The Black Death*. New York: Harper and Row, 1969.

Zürcher, Erik. *The Buddhist Conquest of China*. 2 volumes. Leiden: E.J. Brill, 1959.

———. "Prince Moonlight: Messianism and Eschatology in Early Medieval Chinese Buddhism." *T'oung Pao* 68 (1982): 1–58.

INDEX

Note: Page numbers followed by an *f* indicate figures; those followed by a *t* indicate tables; those followed by an *n* indicate footnotes.

251